Horror Stars
on Radio

ALSO BY RONALD L. SMITH

Comedy Stars at 78 RPM: Biographies and Discographies of 89 American and British Recording Artists, 1896–1946 (McFarland, 1998)

Horror Stars on Radio

*The Broadcast Histories of
29 Chilling Hollywood Voices*

RONALD L. SMITH

McFarland & Company, Inc., Publishers
Jefferson, North Carolina, and London

LIBRARY OF CONGRESS CATALOGUING-IN-PUBLICATION DATA

Smith, Ronald L.
Horror stars on radio : the broadcast histories of 29 chilling
Hollywood voices / Ronald L. Smith.
p.   cm.
Includes bibliographical references and index.

ISBN 978-0-7864-4525-7
softcover : 50# alkaline paper ∞

1. Horror radio programs—United States—History.
2. Radio actors and actresses—United States—Biography.
I. Title.
PN1991.8.H66S55   2010   791.44'616409730904—dc22   2009047853

British Library cataloguing data are available

©2010 Ronald L. Smith. All rights reserved

*No part of this book may be reproduced or transmitted in any form
or by any means, electronic or mechanical, including photocopying
or recording, or by any information storage and retrieval system,
without permission in writing from the publisher.*

Front cover: John Carradine in *House of Dracula*, 1945;
background and microphone ©2010 Shutterstock

Manufactured in the United States of America

*McFarland & Company, Inc., Publishers
Box 611, Jefferson, North Carolina 28640
www.mcfarlandpub.com*

Table of Contents

Introduction   1

1. Boris Karloff   7
2. The Wolfmen: Henry Hull and Lon Chaney, Jr.   29
3. Bela Lugosi   46
4. Vincent Price   64
5. The Horror Hams: Laird Cregar, John Carradine and Basil Rathbone   87
6. Professors of Pain: Lionel Atwill, George Zucco and Henry Daniell   127
7. Peter Lorre   144
8. Two-Shot Wonders: Claude Rains and Charles Laughton   171
9. Strange Ladies: Elsa Lanchester, Una O'Connor and Maria Ouspenskaya   196
10. Sinister Women: Gale Sondergaard and Agnes Moorehead   206
11. Scream Queens: Helen Chandler, Julie Bishop, Ann Doran, Louise Allbritton, Hillary Brooke, Evelyn Ankers, Jane Adams, Gloria Stuart, Elena Verdugo and Fay Wray   224
12. Radio's Own Horror Stars   241

Bibliography   249

Index   253

Introduction

The heyday of horror stars and horror films coincided exactly with the golden era of radio: the 1930s and '40s. The '20s had been silent. The '50s proved a lean decade for Karloff, Chaney Jr., Lorre, Lugosi and the rest, and radio gave way to television. In the '60s, radio was dead and, after the brief "monster mania" revival between 1963 and 1966, so were most of the horror film legends. As special effects gore replaced personality, there was less prime work in the '70s for the remaining horror veterans Vincent Price and John Carradine.

But "classic horror" lives! The old black and white movies of the '30s and '40s are revered, and there's been a revival in the appreciation for the simultaneous sinister doings the horror stars performed on radio.

On radio, these great stars thrilled listeners with voices that were completely original. A key aspect of horror film and radio success was a voice that was both unique and mysterious ... a stranger's voice, someone who couldn't easily be identified by location. Boris Karloff's timbre and accent could place him in England, Egypt, or beyond the grave. Peter Lorre's voice echoed his years in Hungary, Germany, England and America. Vincent Price's voice had elements of England and the American South; while the educated, gritty resonance of Henry Hull and Claude Rains also defied easy placement. Even the accent of Bela Lugosi was mysterious, as he could even be cast in Asian roles, his exaggerated diction both different from yet reflective of Hungarian, Russian and Rumanian.

When Karloff, Lorre or Price stepped before a microphone, the listener couldn't readily place where this creature had come from, adding an instant sense of fear and alarm—which only increased as these masters used their stage-trained acting skills. Their voices had soothing elements of softness, yet a sharp undercurrent of evil.

For the horror stars who gained attention with their film roles, radio work helped strengthen audience interest in their personalities—the same way actors in the 1960s would turn up on variety shows or series TV in order to put themselves in front of the public more than just the one or two times a year they were seen on the big screen.

This tome is about tombs, graveyards, ghosts and all the monsters and mayhem that come under the heading of "classic horror." It's the world of vampires and werewolves, the supernatural and paranormal, the homicidal and the criminal—classic struggles involving life, death and the afterlife performed by some of the world's most beloved actors and actresses.

The radio work done by classic horror's finest stars was often as talked about as their films. The best radio horror could never have been presented effectively in movies, and nobody even tried. In the golden age of film no director had the audacity to attempt the transformation of Karloff's "Cat Wife," or the ability to stage the rat attack that confronted Vincent Price in "Three Skeleton Key." And today? Today's animation techniques could finally make some of radio's most outrageous inventions visual—but could they match what a Karloff or Price put into the minds of listeners?

The classic example of radio over film is the failure of Barbara Stanwyck's movie *Sorry, Wrong Number*—compared to the original version on radio's *Suspense* series, starring Agnes Moorehead.

It's no surprise that in the '30s and '40s a notorious production on radio such as "Cat Wife" was talked about just as vividly as the movie *Cat People*, and favorite episodes of *Suspense* or *Lights Out* were requested and re-broadcast over and over.

While most readers know the stars in this book from their film work, the aim is to regenerate appreciation and interest in their classic radio work. That's why the biographical information generally doesn't stray too far into coverage of their film or stage work. The aim here is to illuminate some of the dark corridors cast in shadow by the passage of time and guide listeners to previously buried treasures. Those who enjoy Boris Karloff's *The Black Cat* or *Bride of Frankenstein* should dig up his "Wailing Wall" or "Cat Wife" and relish every rotten minute!

Boris Karloff believed horror "means something revolting"—the sight of a monster coming through the door. He was more interested in "terror," which is what is lurking unseen *behind* that door. This is why he, and his contemporaries, had such a respect and fondness for radio.

With radio, "terror" was the territory, and the very names of such shows as *Lights Out* and *Inner Sanctum* indicated that what could be triggered by words and sound effects, and an imaginative mind, was far more powerful than the "horror" one might view on a big silver screen.

Today, those who point to the artistry of silent films tend to be apologists: "Sorry there's no color, no 3D, no wide screen, but if you'll bear with these flaws—if you concentrate—you may be rewarded and educated."

The same is true of those who champion old radio: "Sorry there's no picture, and no stereo surround-sound—but if you'll bear with the flaws of these old mono recordings—if you concentrate..."

There's no reason for this kind of begging and wheedling. The best silent films and radio dramas are still gripping and accessible. In reality, the media of sight alone, or sound alone, should not be considered exercises in sensory deprivation. This is not handicapped art. When Charles Chaplin had a choice of using dialogue on films such as *The Circus* and *City Lights*, he chose to keep silent. And when Boris Karloff had a busy schedule of films, he still found time for *Inner Sanctum*.

He and Vincent Price were lifelong fans of the spoken word, and in their later years made recordings that added to the legacy of their radio years. This book lists all the audio work of the horror stars—both radio and 78s, vinyl, and CD re-issues.

There were dozens of classic horror shows on radio, but most of the enduring episodes seemed to star one of the big-name performers. Generations seem to key in on Karloff's version of "Cat Wife," and to have elevated even mediocre scripts like "The Doctor Prescribed Death" because Lugosi made the show so vivid. That's "star power."

These stars had voices so distinctive they were often imitated in their lifetime (Bobby "Boris" Pickett's Karloff, Paul Frees' Lorre, most everybody's Lugosi). Immortals, even after death they live on in "mimic tribute" (from Bill Hader's *Saturday Night Live* impression of Vincent Price to "Booberry," the Peter Lorre-styled voice in cereal commercials). It's no accident that oft-performed scripts such as "Cat Wife," "Three Skeleton Key," "Pit and the Pendulum" and "Sorry, Wrong Number" are best known in the versions performed by the stars who also flourished on stage and screen.

Robert Bloch, author of *Psycho* and many classic short stories, reflected that the "gore" movies that began to take over in the '70s and '80s were the antithesis of what the macabre and the thriller was all about:

> Anybody can provide something that is nauseating and disgusting. But this is not real terror. Real terror consists of acquainting the audience with a character that will be cared about, and then putting that character in jeopardy. The suspense comes from whether or not that character will escape or be done in. This requires plots and characterization. Not just a series of violent incidents in which the entire emphasis is on special effects.

That was the formula for *Lights Out*, *Suspense* and *Inner Sanctum*, and it required great actors. Bloch, who in 1974 crept behind a microphone to record "Gravely, Robert Bloch," reading two of his short stories (Alternate World AWR 3210), added:

> You know, it's strange, isn't it? In horror films, the great films of the past made stars out of Lon Chaney, Sr., out of Bela Lugosi, out of Boris Karloff, out of Peter Lorre and several others, until the fifties, Christopher Lee and Peter Cushing. But, there are no stars today! You have the multi-billion dollar budgets for those films, but there are no known stars. The stars are the special effects.

The stars in this book are the acknowledged kings and queens of classic film horror, not film mystery or science-fiction. That should explain the absence of nefarious, hoarse-voiced Sydney Greenstreet (on radio best known as being on the side of good, playing armchair detective Nero Wolf) or the distinctively sneering Edward G. Robinson, whose gangster roles were often more realistic—and in some ways more repugnant—than the "fun" monsters in full make-up.

A few well-known horror stars are not included in this book only because they were too early or too late for the "golden age of radio." Lon Chaney, Sr., only made one film "talkie" and died before the great radio horror and suspense shows hit the air. While Christopher Lee recorded some narration work (notably a set on Edgar A. Poe), his career began long after the golden age of radio.

The "golden age" of radio dates roughly from 1935 to 1952. That's when the great programs thrived. Few of them existed in the toddling years before the radio networks were established, and fewer were around during the tottering days when television took over. Author and *Boston Globe* critic Robert Taylor notes, "The official birth of network radio had occurred November 15, 1926, with the inaugural broadcast of the National Broadcasting Company over a hookup of twenty-four stations; the effective demise lay ahead, September 30, 1962, when the Columbia Broadcasting System canceled the last two dramatic shows."

Just as the "golden age" eluded top horror stars such as Lon Chaney and Christopher Lee, it often eluded eccentric supporting players ... fan favorites such as Dwight Frye and Ernest Thesiger. Fans of a beloved supporting player such as Una O'Connor will find all that there is to find, in radio credits, which isn't that much, but at least the entries include fresh biographical material and research not seen before. Their lack of representation here is probably due to one of three factors. First, many actors made the conscious decision to move to Hollywood for film roles—and most radio shows were broadcast from New York. Second, a lot of character actors had secondary jobs outside the business and simply couldn't chase low-paying radio assignments at the expense of film auditions. Third, if a supporting player like Dwight Frye was often too minor to receive billing in the average horror film, he was also not likely to win a major role in a radio drama.

Radio was a high-paying profession mostly for star singers and comedians—an Al Jolson, Jack Benny or Eddie Cantor. For a guest star such as Boris Karloff, the money may have been fairly decent, but more important was the publicity it generated and the "exercise" it provided. Between Broadway shows, or even during them, Karloff, Price or Hull would enjoy keeping sharp with radio scripts.

Unlike the comedians, who usually were identified by name in the radio listings (*Amos and Andy*, *Burns and Allen*, *The Fred Allen Show*), most horror and drama series lacked a star's name in the title. On a show such as *The Weird Circle*, the host wasn't even identified. There was no shortage of actors ready to play the Lone Ranger or the Shadow. The low pay and the competition for good roles meant that the bulk of radio acting was left to specially-trained artists who could only make a living if they were flexible enough to perform dozens of voices and juggle several assignments at the same time.

Tony Randall, in his memoir *Which Reminds Me*, offered some perspective on what it was like from the actor's point of view. He was just starting his career when radio was thriving:

> There were a lot of shows originating in New York then.... [They] didn't pay well, but if you did enough shows you made a living. A fifteen-minute sponsored show paid thirty-three dollars. An unsponsored fifteen-minute show paid, I believe, twenty-four dollars. The big evening shows, the half hours and hours, paid much better. And, in those days before tape, you did them twice. Once, let's say, at nine in the evening, and then again at midnight for the West Coast.

For Randall and the rest, a decision eventually had to be made: either work full-time doing dozens of anonymous voices, or spend more time auditioning for theater, TV and film work. The odds of graduating from minor roles to radio stardom in a drama were slim—with few examples such as William Conrad, who eventually got to play Matt Dillon on *Gunsmoke*, or John Dehner, who played Paladin on *Have Gun, Will Travel*. Randall obviously opted for television (launching his career on the *Mr. Peepers* sitcom).

Vincent Price recalled:

> There was a kind of perfection about the radio actor that was extraordinary. It was a very small group of people, and I always felt myself enormously privileged that I was able to join that group, because they didn't take everybody in—not by a long shot! If you liked radio as much as I did, you depended on these people. People like Lurene Tuttle and Hans Conried, who could do anything! [Tony Randall would have added Gary Merrill, Everett Sloane, Paul Stewart, Joe DiSantis and Ken Roberts to that list.]

> Radio acting had its own deceptive rules. Many famous film actors couldn't adapt to it ... they couldn't stand in front of a microphone ... they had to emote and move around, going out of range of the microphone. Or, the reverse, hugging the microphone and talking into it, popping p's and turning s's into a sibilant slush. Film actors accustomed to many takes and not trained in either stage or radio often lacked the energy needed to impress a listener, and some simply read flatly.

Radio could be a nerve-wracking job because in addition to being asked to perform live and flawlessly, many veteran radio actors enjoyed upping the ante by making the working environment even more challenging. Tony Randall admitted:

> Sorry to tell you this, [but] I didn't enjoy the gags actors played on one another. The object was always to break someone up while on the air live.... One standard prank was to stand in front of the table the announcer was seated at and take your cock out.... One day, a guy with his cock out wasn't getting the announcer's attention, and so he put it on the table. Without looking up the announcer slammed it with his fist as hard as he could. It hurts to get your cock slammed like that.

Another prank was to set fire to an actor's script as he stood at the mike reading it. That, I'm sorry to say, was typical of the level of the jokes. That, and lower.

While much has been made of television killing radio, the '30s and '40s were a time when movie and stage writers and performers adapted to radio, found what worked best, and mined all the gold the golden age could offer. Fred Allen wrote:

> Radio was the first free entertainment ever given to the public. Since it was piped into homes it was a service similar to running water. When the novelty of the shows wore off many people had more respect for running water than they did for radio. A house owner who would never think of speaking disrespectfully of the water in his house would rant around his radio set, sounding off about the dubious merits of some program he had just heard.

Allen believed that, aside from a lack of new concepts (and how many variations of "Cat Wife" or "Sorry, Wrong Number" could there be?), radio's demise in the 50's was "a by-product of advertising. Ability, merit and talent were not requirements of writers and actors working in the industry. Audiences had to be attracted, for advertising purposes, at any cost and by any artifice. Standards were gradually lowered."

In Fred Allen's personal case, he witnessed the destruction of his radio comedy series by the oncoming rush of quiz shows—a cheaper, easier form of entertainment for the sponsor's dollar. If he was around today, he'd point to the way sitcoms and dramas were replaced on television by quiz shows (Regis Philbin's *Millionaire* show once aired three nights a week, and Howie Mandel's *Deal or No Deal* became a sensation shortly after) and the increasingly outrageous "reality" shows.

Fortunately, much of the "golden age of radio" has been preserved, and it has stood the test of time. Many programs are still as exciting as ever, and even formulaic radio appearances have been elevated into grand entertainment, if not high art, simply by the artistry of the actors and actresses voicing the parts.

And in this book, you can read all about it.

But there's a final question: can you, personally, hear it?

Yes and no.

Most radio shows were not automatically preserved for archiving or re-runs, any more than early live TV shows were. Many shows were broadcast live, and nobody thought to make a transcription copy. The same "oh, it's only free entertainment, who'll want to hear it again" non-thinking that led NBC to "wipe" the first years of *The Tonight Show* and re-use the video tape was behind the decision not to make "transcription discs" of broadcasts.

Fortunately, some programs were indeed recorded onto 16-inch transcription discs for rebroadcast to the West Coast or overseas (during World War II many shows survived thanks to versions saved by Armed Forces Radio). A few enterprising producers chose transcription over live broadcast so they could syndicate the shows to local stations, or better time the programs to never exceed the half-hour or hour limit.

Vincent Price recalled that the actors on radio shows were not automatically given copies of their work:

> At the time it cost a lot of money to put them on acetate records, and you didn't get paid very much in radio. So unless it was a very special show, you didn't order it taken off the air.... [I]f I wanted a show like *The Saint* taken off the air, it would cost about $60! That was a lot of money in those days, and you weren't paid that much.

Since home-recording wasn't common, few '30s and '40s radio programs exist via copies made from a fan's radio wired to a recorder. Entire months of *Inner Sanctum* and *Lights Out* are missing, and countless others. Throughout this book, "lost" episodes are generally noted. Since some of these programs do turn up via a discovered transcription disc, there's always a chance that a forgotten rarity will one day be found.

In the 1970s, with copyrights lapsing or residing in a "gray area" fog in terms of ownership of reproduction rights, Radiola, Nostalgia Lane and a few other record labels issued radio programs on vinyl. Into the 21st century the old shows have appeared in compact disc sets from companies such as Radio Spirits, and even on Internet download sites like eMusic.com, archive.org, amazon.com, iTunes.com and others.

Additionally, many individuals sell radio shows via inexpensive mp3 (and similar) formats, which allow a hundred hours of radio programming to be placed on one disc. Some hobbyists "trade" shows on Internet forums, stream audio on Internet websites, or offer free downloading on blogs.

The author has made use of several of these sources, including www.otrcat.com, www.theradiolady.com, www.radio-showcase.com, www.otrsite.com, and www.otrnow.com. Internet websites come and go, but these have been around for a long time. There are also organizations for fan-to-fan trading or for borrowing classic shows for a monthly or yearly fee.

While some programs mentioned in this book have come from archive sources, including my collection, other private collections and libraries, most radio shows can be found on the ever-increasing pages of blogs, and in the catalogs of the major dealers in old radio programs. Thanks to public domain and a lot of competition, it's fairly inexpensive to build a library of great radio shows, so the good news is that a very healthy portion of the titles listed in this book can be easily acquired.

While most of the "golden age" stars were long gone before this book was even in the idea stage, I gratefully acknowledge some of the artists who, over the years, graciously sent letters or autographed a photo (including Gloria Stuart, Paul Frees, Hillary Brooke, Elena Verdugo, Fay Wray and Julie Bishop). Special thanks to the late great Vincent Price, who once sent a note of praise about a previous volume of forgotten lore, my comic food poetry tome *Let Peas Be with You*. Vinnie's quick note read: "Love the book!" Hopefully he would've liked this one, too.

The dead past has come back to life. Karloff and Lugosi are still rivals for our shivers and affection. The creaking door that seemed to have closed years ago has opened once again. Through radio magic, any room can once again become an inner sanctum, and while anyone can watch an old monster movie on a home video screen, it's still a fearsome challenge to put on a radio show and listen to it with ... lights out.

1

Boris Karloff

"Boris Karloff was perhaps the best of all," Vincent Price declared. In his 1978 children's book *Vincent Price: His Movies, His Plays, His Life,* Price noted the strange truth that the most horrifying star in movies was also beloved by children:

> He had the ability to appear to be both sinister and frightening. At the same time he had a sweetness about him—a kind of gentleness. He had a little lisp and a strange voice. He sounded so innocent that you never suspected him to be an evil person in films. You had sympathy for him, which is much scarier than if you know right off the bat that he is a villain. You see, you must be able to get sympathy from the audience as well as be able to frighten them. Otherwise you become inhuman.

Both Vincent and Boris recorded many successful spoken-word albums. There was a big difference in the material they narrated. Vincent Price was given witchcraft tales and Poe stories. But Boris? He read Mother Goose, Aesop's fables and children's stories by Kipling.

"Forget Frankenstein," Karloff once said of his narration work. "Take 'A Frog He Would a-Wooing Go.' By golly, a cat kills a mouse and a rat, and a frog is eaten by a duck. Awfully cruel and savage. As for *Grimm's Fairy Tales* ... well, for heaven's sake! We were all brought up on fairy tales and none of us turned out to be monsters—except maybe me."

Kids growing up in the '70s and '80s, when the old black and white horror films were not screened on TV as often as the later color gorefests, might indeed have first encountered Karloff as a children's story narrator, via the Dr. Seuss classic TV special *How the Grinch Stole Christmas.* Dr. Seuss himself, Theodore Geisel, recalled Boris' work on the project: "It was an exhausting day—everything went wrong—at the end of the day we were all wilted—except Boris. As we dragged ourselves off, he left whistling."

The transformation from obscure William Henry Pratt (November 23, 1887–February 2, 1969) to famous Boris Karloff had taken much longer than the time Dr. Frankenstein spent collecting body parts and finally bringing life to his monster. Before Boris could walk away from a microphone whistling, he'd put in time ditch digging and working in tiny obscure theaters. He was facing middle age and failure before he had even the promise of steady acting work, much less fame and fortune.

Karloff was born in Dulwich, England. He wrote his own biographical sketch of his early days, which was quoted in various bios of him, including a chapter in Calvin Beck's book *Heroes of the Horrors.* Karloff wrote:

> [As] the youngest of a fairly large family of eight sons and one daughter ... I knew very little of my father, James Pratt, who had spent his life in the Indian Civil Service. As I was the youngest ... I began to see less and less of my brothers. They seemed always to be abroad, either in India or China.... An elder brother had been on the stage under the name of George

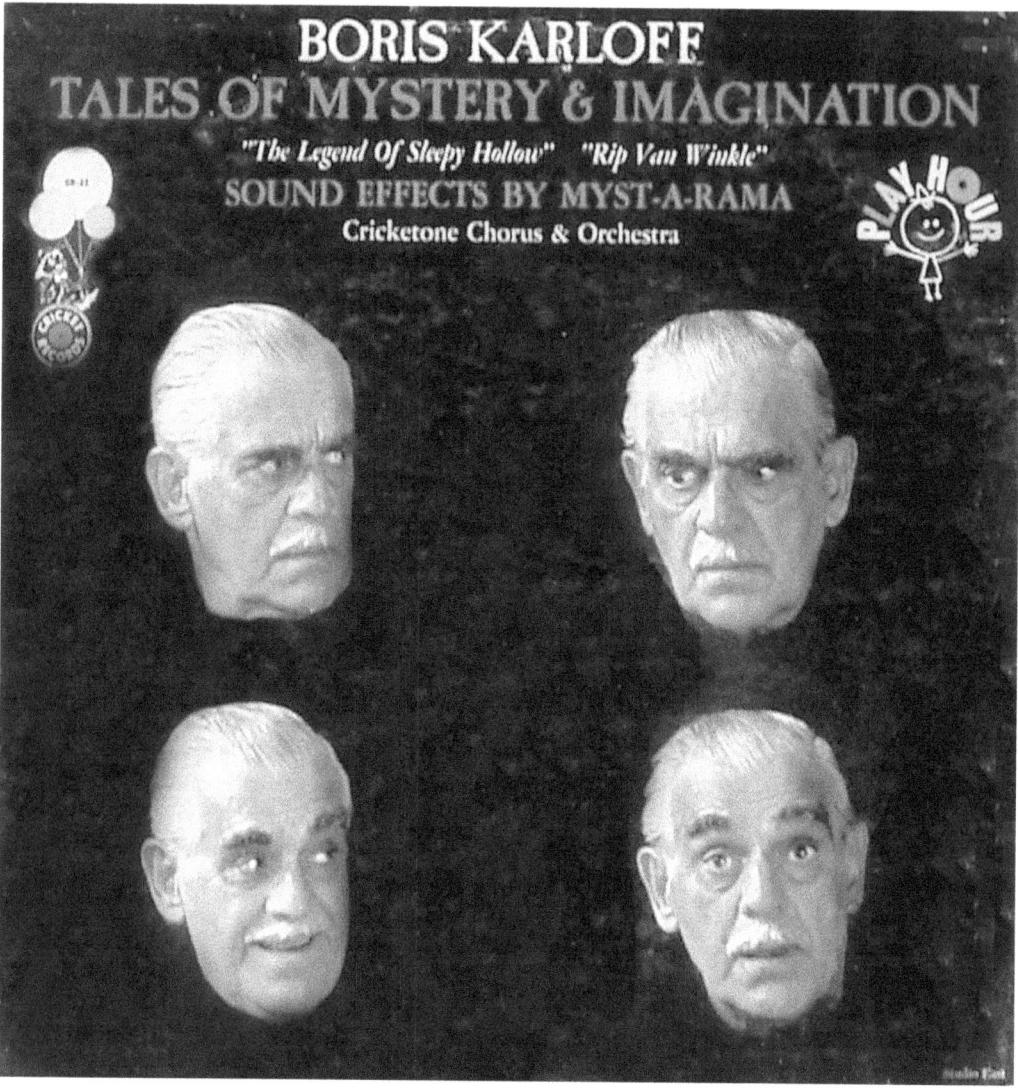

Karloff's straight narratives of "Rip Van Winkle" and "Legend of Sleepy Hollow" were periodically interrupted by kiddie songs when released as *Tales of Mystery and Imagination*.

Marlowe, when I was about eight years old. He was the one I knew best when the others were abroad. He played with Fanny Ward at the old Strand Theatre in *The Royal Divorce* ... and each year put on a show at the Enfield Cricket Club.

He never went very far on the stage, which was the reason he gave it up for a city job. But I tried to emulate him.... My brother's experience was held up to me by the elders of my family as the horrible example of what happens when you try to get on the stage. Forming a tribunal they pronounced: That I could not possibly succeed because I did not have George's looks or his talents. That it would be complete folly for me to try it.

Karloff left home in 1909. "I chose Canada because just about that time the Canadian government was sending out an appeal for immigrants. I had no idea what Canada was like." It was cold. There were few jobs beyond manual labor, such as the time he had to help dig a racetrack. "I reported for work without having had any breakfast, as I didn't have the money to buy it. The first day was a long, dreary ten hours of pick-and-shovel work. My hands were blistered at the end of that day. By the end of the week, they were merely calloused."

In 1910 he

Boris Karloff gives himself a knuckle sandwich in a somber publicity shot.

> glanced at a newspaper and saw an advertisement for a character actor for the Ray Brandon Players of Kamloops, British Columbia. I applied for the job using the name of Boris Karloff, which happened to be my mother's family name.... My first part was an old man of sixty—Hoffman, the banker husband, in *The Devil* by Molnar. At the end of the performance, as I was slinking away to some dark corner, the manager came toward me with a malevolent gleam in his eye. "Karloff, you know darn well you've never acted before. Still, we like you and you'll stay with us at four pounds a week."

He toured for a year with the company until they were stranded in Regina, Saskatchewan. This was a pattern to be repeated for years and years—gaining experience with minor touring companies, and having to perform manual labor when these stage troupes ran out of money or were run out of town. Hollywood was just another town that didn't have enough work for him:

> Spring of 1923. I was flat broke. The future very doubtful, I was told I could get a job driving a truck for a concrete and cement firm in Los Angeles. The first thing to do was to learn to drive. I spent Sunday with a friend learning to drive his car. Monday morning I applied for the job and got it ... I could take an occasional day to work in pictures.

One of the few stars who was sympathetic to the struggling actor's plight was Lon Chaney. After a long day at the studio,

> Chaney gave me a ride home. We talked for over an hour about the picture business and my own chances of getting somewhere. He said to me, "The secret of success in Hollywood lies in being different from anyone else.... Find something no one else can or will do—and they'll begin to take notice of you."

Karloff's break came playing a villain in *The Criminal Code*. It led to the monster role in *Frankenstein*. It was as simple as that, although many apocryphal stories described how Karloff was either the protégé of Chaney or that Bela Lugosi recommended him, or that Boris was somehow discovered lumbering around the studio and cited as the perfect guy for the new James Whale monster movie.

Slowly, billed either as "Karloff" or "Karloff the Uncanny," the middle-aged actor emerged from mute and near-mute roles to take his place as the sound era's great horror star. His unique voice (hollowly weathered by the many stage years), the British accent (blunted by so many years in Canada and America), and the pronunciation eerily marred by his appearing and disappearing lisp, became familiar to audiences when he found a welcome on radio's top horror shows: *Lights Out* and then *Inner Sanctum*.

According to early Karloff biographer Peter Underwood, in 1938

> He so scared America, in a radio adaptation of "The Evil Eye" on an Edgar Bergen–Charlie McCarthy show, that demands for an investigation were heard on the floor of the Senate! He continued broadcasting throughout most of 1938 when he took a vacation from films to play the lead in the successful NBC *Lights Out* dramas.

Another biographer, Karloff's friend Cynthia Lindsay, says that as memorable as the *Lights Out* shows were (and "Cat Wife" is easily among the Top Ten greatest radio shows of all time), Boris had a different favorite:

> *Information Please* was one of the professional activities from which Boris derived the most enjoyment. It was the forerunner of all quiz shows, and it was literate, tasteful, and funny. The regular panel consisted of John Kieran, Franklin P. Adams, and Oscar Levant; the quiz master was Clifton Fadiman. These brilliant gentlemen provided a show with never a dull moment. The program, for Boris, represented the first public demonstration of his intellectuality. This was no Monster—this was an erudite gentleman with a sophisticated sense of humor.

Karloff didn't mind spoofing the clichés of the horror genre when he made radio appearances. In an early appearance with Ozzie and Harriet Nelson, Karloff joined Bela Lugosi in singing "We're Horrible, Horrible Men." During his solo moment he cheerfully warbled about how though the movies made him seem terrible, "when my makeup is off, I'm really quite cute."

Karloff's film roles generally played off his dark, brooding appearance, and, aside from some growling as the Frankenstein Monster, it was mostly on radio that he was able to let himself go and test all the notes on the melodramatic scale. He was way over the top when he thought his dead wife was haunting him from inside "The Wailing Wall," and his most famous radio appearance of all was portraying the increasingly demented husband driven batty by "The Cat Wife."

"Cat Wife" first aired in 1936, and was re-broadcast in 1937. Only the 1938 version survives: "Tonight at the urgent request of hundreds of listeners, we bring you a repeat broadcast of the strange play which you have chosen as a highlight of all the *Lights Out* series."

Through most of the tense episode, Karloff's woeful voice serves as counterpoint to the evil meows and hisses of his strange bride. Karloff's classic role elicits sympathy from the listener, as he tries vainly to protect his wife and his sanity; but his secret is bound to be discovered. When an off-duty policeman drops by and becomes suspicious, Karloff is no longer the English gentleman but a hound from hell:

"Get out!"

"Now wait a second ... I'm not sayin' you're lyin', but maybe the animal's caught in the cellar without your knowing it."

"Get out ... I tell you there's no cat here! Get out! Get out of here! You heard me! Get out of my house! What are you standing there for? Get out! Get out!" [Cat yowl]

"No cat, eh? Well, what was that?"

"Nothing at all! You've got no right ... get out ... get out of here ... this is my house! Get out of here."

It was only a very brave veteran of the Grand Guignol who'd even attempt a script with that many "Get Out"s in it—while playing second fiddle to cat gut sound effects.

Vocally he became even more unhinged in "Wailing Wall" and other *Inner Sanctum* stories, that required shouting and screaming to abet the campy horror. His first *Inner Sanctum* episode was broadcast in January 1941, and he appeared in several programs over the next two years (lean years for Universal horror movies—his *Frankenstein* series having ended with *Son of Frankenstein* in 1939).

Now well over 50, Karloff's days as a violent, menacing screen monster were over, and as the radio era ripened and began to rot, he was being tapped and typed as either an evil scientist or misunderstood madman. One of the keys to these scripts was the gradual boil from cold, somber, sepulchral mutterings to fully heated rage. However, many writers, fearing the cliché of the melodramatic, seemed to favor keeping the undercurrent of malice and, like a lit fuse on dynamite, the suspense of the sizzle. In many of his later radio shows, Karloff stayed a shadowy, creepy creature before stepping out into the daylight to reveal his guilt or, in an occasional twist, innocence.

The prime minister of sinister: Boris Karloff in a publicity pose.

Karloff played variations on the human zombie, a man detached from morality, or so emotionally destroyed, that only a calm plan of revenge kept him moving. Typical of these is "The Final Reckoning" from his radio series *Creeps by Night*. In this show he plays a man numbed by years in prison but ready to get even with those who put him there.

Some of Karloff's most effective comedy work came from playing it straight, with just a twist of lunacy. Typical of this is his portrayal on *The Jack Benny Program* of a mournful stranger deadpanning the bizarre lines performed by Peter Lorre the year before:

KARLOFF: Pardon me please, but may I trouble you for a match?
BENNY: A match? I'm sorry, I don't have one. But I'll let you use my cigarette lighter.
KARLOFF: Thank you, you're very kind.
BENNY: Hey you! Come back with that lighter! Gimme that ... I thought you just wanted to light a cigarette.
KARLOFF: I do, but my cigarette is home.
BENNY: Wait a minute. You look so much like Boris Karloff.
KARLOFF: Thanks. You're looking well yourself. However, my resemblance to Mr. Karloff is purely physical. For instance, I would never think of going to a cemetery in the black of night, opening graves and stealing the gold teeth out of dead bodies. That's dishonest, you know.
BENNY: Yes. Wait a minute! You were trying to steal my cigarette lighter, weren't you?
KARLOFF: No, I'd like to buy it. I'll give you twenty thousand dollars for it.
BENNY: Twenty thousand dollars! I wouldn't want to take advantage of you. Tell you what ... I'll throw in an extra flint.

Spending huge sums for worthless items is only part of Karloff's solemn eccentricity. He also wants to spend his time at Jack's house.

BENNY: Don't you have any children?
KARLOFF: No. I married a smudge pot.
BENNY: You married a smudge pot? You haven't any children?
KARLOFF: No, but we're lousy with oranges.

On Eddie Cantor's show, Karloff not only endures the quivering host, but the wisecracks of Bert Gordon, "The Mad Russian." Karloff was promoting his Broadway role in *Arsenic and Old Lace* at the time.

CANTOR: Russian, I want you to know that standing before you is the famous creation of Frankenstein, the cruelest creature on the face of the earth, the monster without a brain.
RUSSIAN: Eddie Cantor, this is Adolph?
CANTOR: Of course not. Don't you recognize Boris Karloff, the screen's most fiendish villain? The grotesque looking boogie man?
RUSSIAN: Oh yes. Hello handsome.
KARLOFF: You think I'm handsome?
RUSSIAN: In a repulsive sort of way.
KARLOFF: Listen you Mongolian Mickey, one more insult from you and I'll strangle you. How would you like to be a corpse?
RUSSIAN: Is there any future in it?

For most of Karloff's radio variety appearances, he was a good-natured target for the comedian hosts. They could bounce plenty of gags off his bones. From a 1945 Fred Allen show:

BORIS: It's dark. Take my hand.
FRED: Gad, your hand is clammy, Boris. It feels like five eels with hangnails.

A few days before Halloween 1945, Karloff dropped in on Edgar Bergen and his dummy Charlie McCarthy; and, as usual, he had to employ his engaging haunted voice to help out a lifeless script. Charlie wants to hire Boris for some spooky Halloween fun:

KARLOFF: I'm here in answer to a call for a horror man.
CHARLIE: Well, pull up a slab and lie down! Just how horrible can you be?
KARLOFF: Well, have you had any bad dreams?
CHARLIE: Sure. Sure.
KARLOFF: Then you must remember me. I'm responsible for some very weird things.
CHARLIE: Did you change the name of 6th Avenue? [This was a local reference to Mayor Fiorella LaGuardia's recent re-naming of the thoroughfare to "Avenue of the Americas."]
KARLOFF: When do I start? You know I do my best work on a very dark night.
CHARLIE: So do I!
KARLOFF: This Halloween I have a blue-faced special ... with assorted shivers and a cold sweat for only $7.85.
CHARLIE: The only thing about you that scares me about you is your prices.
KARLOFF: Now, now, give me a chance. I'll work my skeletons to the bone ... don't be afraid ... this is the face I wore when I posed for the picture on a bottle of arsenic!
CHARLIE: That's pretty hard to swallow.
KARLOFF: Don't be afraid. Remember, you haven't lived until you've died.
CHARLIE: Now there's a hunk of logic.... Why are you looking at me like that?
KARLOFF: I like you ... you'd love it here among the skeletons. Wait a minute, friend. You know, you have a very interesting head. There's an experiment I'm dying to try ... I'd really scare people if I had two heads!
CHARLIE: Boris, you kill me! What am I saying? ... Bergen, Bergen ... help!

Boris's 5-minute *Reader's Digest* shows were sent to radio stations on transcription discs like this, a week's worth at a time.

One reason Karloff was so often on the radio in the 1940s, especially compared to his colleagues Lugosi and Lorre, was that he was frequently working on Broadway. New York City was the capital of the radio broadcasting industry, and when Boris had a night off—from everything from *Arsenic and Old Lace* (1941-4) to *The Linden Tree* to *The Shop at Sly Corner* (1948, 1949)—he could be found behind the microphone in a radio studio. His golden age of stage work matched up nicely with radio's thriving years in New York.

His friend Cynthia Lindsay, in her book *Dear Boris*, wrote: "Once a week he recorded at his home *Readers Digest* for American radio. He did this particular radio work all over the world and the programmes were broadcast from some four hundred American radio stations for twelve years."

In the early days of television, New York was also the place where many of the top dramas were produced. Live TV needed to draw from stage-trained actors who could learn lines quickly and adapt to any last-minute problems. Karloff was involved in a brief experiment with a simultaneous radio-television show. Between September 22 and December 15 of 1949, *Starring Boris Karloff* was heard on radio Wednesday night and performed for television the following evening.

Author Peter Underwood remembers the lost programs, and in his biography of Karloff reported:

> A quick day sufficed for his radio rehearsal, while video took up virtually the remaining six days of each week. The results were good radio shows and exceptionally good television programmes. On his initial show Karloff played a hangman, with Mildred Natwick as his horrified wife, and into this portrayal he put all his often recognized acting ability, coupled with enthusiasm for a challenging medium. Essentially a humble man, despite the fact that his fee from ABC also provided for the cast and story cost, he preferred to leave the selection of both to others.

If the selection tended toward the macabre, well, "'After all,' he would reply with a twinkling grin, 'I can't play Little Lord Fauntleroy, can I?'"

It was a noble experiment; and any bruises from it were instantly salved when Karloff found himself a successful "kiddie villain" as Captain Hook in the hit Broadway musical *Peter Pan* (1950–51). He was also the star of his own children's radio show, *Boris Karloff's Treasure Chest*, which aired from September 17 to December 17, 1950, and helped promote the stage production. Surviving episodes show him to be a bit too humble; he tends to become a disc jockey playing kiddie tunes and educational folk music, and doesn't often step up to sing or perform.

The ex-movie monster found that kids loved him more than they were frightened by him ("Just what I wanted," he would say), and he began to record fairy tales for the small New York–based Caedmon Records label, which sold their spoken word recordings to schools.

He was proud of his kiddie radio show and told an interviewer:

> I never talk down to children. I just put things over to them in simple language. I read from the classics, play really good recordings and then, perhaps, throw in some sneaky sound effects such as creaky hinges or a ship's bell tolling. But I always end my programme with some gay and happy music, and good is always victorious over evil.

New York was also home to most of the era's TV quiz shows. In December 1956, while he was playing Bishop Cauchon in the acclaimed Broadway show *The Lark*, Boris appeared on *The $64,000 Question* and ran up his winnings to $16,000 in the category of children's stories. He said that he stopped at that level after comparing both the odds and the taxes involved in going all the way.

Karloff's reputation still remained with horror, and any deviation from it seemed to require some kind of joke remark. When he played a "guardian angel" in a forgettable radio musical called "Yolanda and the Thief," the curtain call had to make reference to his venerable career in terror:

> BORIS: I want to thank Lisa Kirk and John Conte for the privilege of appearing with them.
> LISA KIRK: Oh just a moment Boris, when you thank us, that's putting the cart before the horse.
> JOHN CONTE: Correction, Lisa, in Boris Karloff's case, it's putting the cart before the hearse!
> LISA KIRK: Seriously, Boris, you're so used to playing frightful old meanies, how did it feel to play a good character like a guardian angel?
> BORIS: Frightful! Every time I did a good deed it made my flesh creep.

Karloff always liked to go back home to England (eventually moving there permanently). He sometimes appeared on British radio. In December 1953 he played Sir Francis

Kindly Karloff: Boris starred in a kiddie radio show for WNEW around the same time he hooked up with *Peter Pan* on Broadway.

Brittain in "Hanging Judge," which was part of a series called *The Play of His Choice*, produced by Cleland Finn. In an unusual twist, the script (based on a Bruce Hamilton novel) was written by Raymond Massey, the actor who had taken Karloff's role in the film version of *Arsenic and Old Lace* (which had dampened the stage joke about the character being a dead ringer for Boris Karloff).

As radio disappeared, the market for audio recordings emerged, and Karloff not only continued his children's fables, but added Kipling poems and even turned up on a major label release for Vanguard narrating "Peter and the Wolf." Children instantly accepted radio's scariest voice as a genial gentle voice of comfort and fantasy.

In yet another odd twist, Karloff's voice of calm, with its simultaneous undercurrent of menace, was used for public service announcement radio spots during the Cold War:

> Civil Defense is common sense. This is Boris Karloff. No one can guarantee the survival of every home during a nuclear war. But a strong Civil Defense can save millions of lives. Make sure yours is one of them. Learn how to protect your home. Call Civil Defense today.

In 1963 Karloff recorded a set of atmospheric short stories for Mercury, intended to be in every record store in time for Halloween. In radio style, the narration of Michael

Avallone's stories includes both sound effects and some jagged orchestration to underscore the story's punch line. These were supplied courtesy of an electronic music album in the Mercury vaults, Tom Dissevelt's *Song of the Second Moon*.

Released in two volumes, the first album offers seven tales: "The Man in the Raincoat," "The Deadly Dress," "The Hand of Fate," "Don't Lose Your Head," "Call at Midnight," "Just Inside the Cemetery" and "The Fortune Teller." The second album's six tales are: "The Vampire Sleeps," "Mirror of Death," "Never Kick a Black Cat," "The Ladder," "Nightmare" and "Voice from the Grave."

"Nightmare" opens (complete with groaning noises in the background):

> Did you ever feel as if you couldn't breathe? Your tongue's thick in your mouth, your throat is hoarse, your lungs are bursting for air, it seems as if the walls of your room are closing in on you, crushing you, crowding you, sealing you off from the rest of the world? And then you awake; it's only been a ghastly dream, a terribly vivid nightmare?

And the ending:

> If you ever imagine that fingers are at your throat, throttling you, don't twist and turn! Wake up! Open your eyes. Maybe it's a just a dream, but, someone could be killing you.

Karloff usually addresses the listener at the beginning and end of the tale. This can sometimes render a story somewhat ludicrous. The listener is most likely seated at home, listening in comfort, but the narrator implies otherwise. In one story about superstition and the gruesome fate of someone who walked under a ladder, Karloff concludes: "Please be careful. You never can tell, can you. Well, upon my soul. Here comes the sign painter to get his ladder and ... do you know, my friend ... you've been standing under it for the longest time!"

On television "the real Boris Karloff," sans make-up, hosted *The Veil* and then *Thriller*, and was welcomed back to the big screen in generally campy, full color horror-comedies such as *The Raven* (1963) and *Comedy of Terrors* (1964). The latter reunited him with Vincent Price and Basil Rathbone — all co-stars of the 1939 film *Tower of London*. In a letter to Cynthia Lindsay, quoted in her book *Dear Boris*, Price wrote about his special relationship with Boris which began with that early film:

> He and Basil Rathbone introduced me to a kind of joyousness of picture-making I too seldom encountered in the hundred films that came later. I identified with him immediately, as somehow I knew the villain was to be my role in movies, too.... Boris was a formidable star at that time ... but he went out of his way to make me feel welcome in a business I knew I was going to like.
>
> Over the years we met at parties and always enjoyed each other, but as always with actors it was on the set where friendships were amalgamated. You know the films we did, but I think two stand out in my mind — *The Raven* and *Comedy of Terrors*.... We loved working together and inventing the things everyone thought were written for us. It was fast company and always fun.
>
> We all have a problem with these movies — the suspicion that we are the victims of typecasting. Boris and I discussed this at length, coming to the obvious conclusion that so are John Wayne, Paul Newman, etc., etc.

While it was an imitator (Bobby "Boris" Pickett) who helped bring Karloff extra fame via the hit single "Monster Mash," Karloff turned up on the teen TV show *Shindig*, performing a snippet of that hit song, and then rapping a version of "The Peppermint Twist," complete with his own unique version of rockin' nonsense words: "papa papa doo-bah!" He even turned up in drag as "Mother Muffin" for an episode of the hip *Girl from U.N.C.L.E.* series, and narrated *Mondo Balordo*, a documentary about peculiar native rituals and sexual taboos around the world.

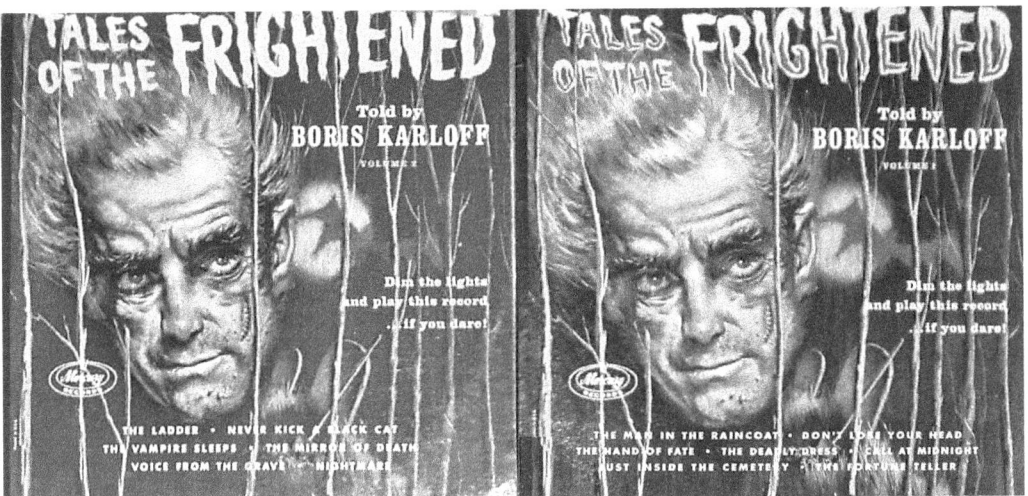

Short stories with music and sound effects: Mercury optimistically tossed two volumes of *Boris Karloff Tales of the Frightened* into record bins at the same time, one red the other blue.

Very spirited about matters that were making headlines, he sided with youth when it came to censorship.

In a 1957 issue of *Films and Filming* magazine, Karloff wrote:

"Censorship of any sort is a fearful thing," he told writer Herbert Kretzmer (in *The Daily Sketch*, 1958), "and the word DON'T is the most terrifying in the language."

I am opposed to censorship in any form. Censorship always seems to me to be a mistrust of people's intelligence. I believe that good taste takes care of license. It is also worth remembering that one does not have to go to see a film. Naturally, good taste plays a very important part in the telling of a horror story on film. Some have taste, others regrettably have not. As there are no rules laid down to give an indication of good taste; it is up to the film's makers. You are walking a very narrow tightrope when you make such a film. It is building the illusion of the impossible and giving it the semblance of reality that is of prime importance. The moment the film becomes stupid the audience will laugh and the illusion is lost ... never to be regained. The story must be intelligent and coherent as well as being unusual and bizarre ... in fact, just like a fairy tale or a good folk story.

The "horror" has to be for the sake of the story and not, as a few films have done, have a story outline just for the sake of injecting as many shocks as possible. The central character is most important in a horror picture because he is more complex. You must understand his point of view although you know he is mistaken. You must have sympathy for him although you know he is terribly wrong. Although you are pleased to see him destroyed you are sorry that it has happened. The special technique of horror film-acting is to stimulate the imagination. This is usually done by showing bits and pieces which gradually build up a picture in people's imagination.

Karloff was something of a workaholic, and despite his age and a formidable number of physical problems, he continued to appear in all kinds of movies. *Famous Monsters* editor Forrest J Ackerman, watching Boris on the set of a '60s production, was shocked at how bent and "crab like" he was when off-screen. Karloff literally needed oxygen on the set, and eventually took roles that allowed him to use a wheelchair. And still he worked.

He lived long enough to have become a legend. It wasn't just the editor of *Famous Monsters of Filmland* magazine writing articles that ended "Oh King, Live Forever." Thousands of critics and fans had the same feeling for him. There was so much adoration pour-

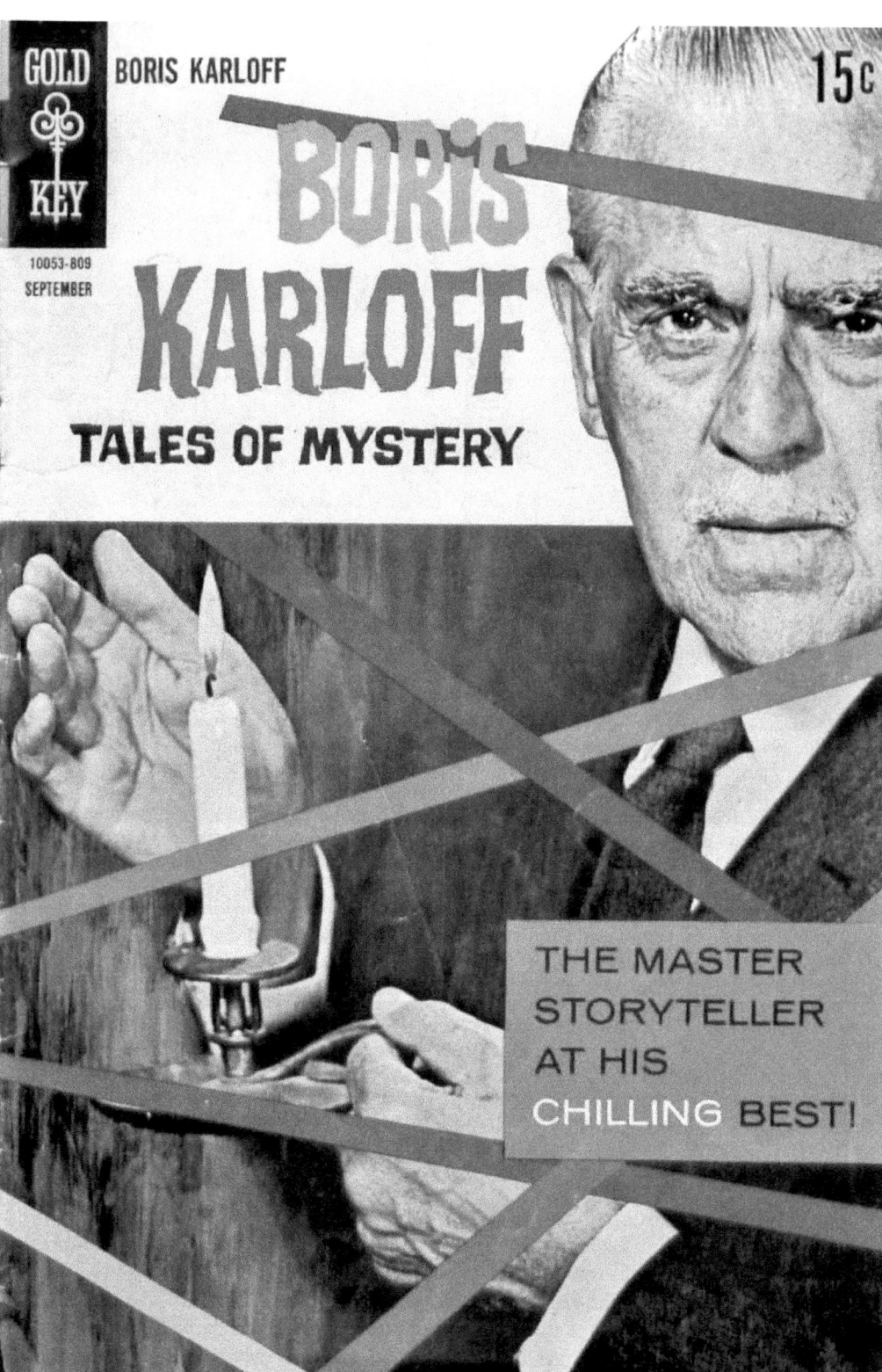

ing in that much of his mail had to be handled by the oddly Karloffian or Lovecraftian-named "Ardath Fan Mail Clinic," which dutifully sent out 5 × 7 pre-printed autographed photos of Boris, and a 4 × 5 snapshot of him as the Frankenstein Monster, to well-wishers writing to him.

With all of his supernatural roles involving ghosts and the undead, it was indeed something of a surprise when the news finally came of his passing. But in a cliché certainly in keeping with those in his wonderfully ripe radio shows, the man is still un-dead and immortal.

Radio

Hollywood on Parade (aka *Hollywood on the Air*). October 7, 1933, NBC, 15 min. Host Jimmy Fidler greets the stars of *The Lost Patrol*, and they perform a scene from the film. Boris Karloff, Victor McLaglen and Reginald Denny.

Hollywood on Parade. January 27, 1934, NBC, 15 min. Jimmy Fidler once again interviews Boris Karloff on his new film *The Lost Patrol*. Singer Maxine Doyle is also featured.

The Fleischmann's Yeast Hour (aka *The Rudy Vallee Program*). October 11, 1934, 60 min. Boris Karloff appears in the sketch version of *Death Takes a Holiday*. Rudy Vallee sings, and there's comedy from Lou Holz.

Hollywood on the Air. May 1935. Boris Karloff discusses *The Bride of Frankenstein*.

Shell Chateau. August 31, 1935, NBC, 60 min. Host Al Jolson greets guest Boris Karloff, who plays a rajah in the show's dramatic sketch, "The Green Goddess." Also on hand are George Jessel, Jack Stanton, Joyce Weathers, Maxine Lewis and Peggy Gardner.

The Fleischmann's Yeast Hour (aka *The Rudy Vallee Program*). February 6, 1936, 60 min. Boris Karloff performs some lines from "The Bells." No copies are known to exist.

The Royal Gelatin Hour (aka *The Rudy Vallee Program*). September 3, 1936, 60 min. Rudy Vallee is host to singers and comics, with Boris Karloff performing a dramatic scene from "Resurrection." No copies are known to exist.

Camel Caravan. December 8, 1936, 60 min. This variety show features Benny Goodman and his Orchestra, and Boris Karloff performs a scene from the classic *Death Takes a Holiday*.

The Royal Gelatin Hour (aka *The Rudy Vallee Program*). November 11, 1937. Boris Karloff performs a scene from "Danse Macabre."

The Chase and Sanborn Hour. January 30, 1938. Hosts Edgar Bergen and his dummy Charlie McCarthy welcome regular Don Ameche, singer Nelson Eddy and actress Dorothy Lamour. Amid the humor and songs, Boris Karloff sobers things up with his version of Poe's "Tell-Tale Heart," now titled "The Evil Eye." The transcription disc for this episode has apparently been lost.

Baker's Broadcast. March 13, 1938. Ozzie & Harriet are joined by the team of Karloff and Lugosi. Both horror stars get solo turns, with Karloff reading "The Supplication of the Black Aberdeen" by Rudyard Kipling. Later he and Bela sing "We're Horrible, Horrible Men."

Lights Out. March 23, 1938, NBC, 30 min. "The Dream." Boris Karloff has a nightmare. The show is also known as "Darrell Hall's Thoughts." Karloff made five appearances in a row on *Lights Out*, but only two survive—this episode and "Cat Wife."

Lights Out. March 30, 1938, NBC, 30 min. Boris Karloff in "Valse Triste." No copies survive; some radio catalogs, Internet-circulated downloads or mp3 files offer the version solemnly performed by Lou Merrill, Wally Maher and Gloria Blondell (December 29, 1942), and misidentified as Karloff's.

Opposite: **A rare honor: Boris Karloff's hosting of *Thriller* led to his own line of comic books in the '60s.**

Lights Out. April 6, 1938, NBC, 30 min. "Cat Wife." One of the first episodes of *Lights Out*, the show was a sensation when it aired June 17, 1936. The script was performed a second time on February 17, 1937. Neither survive. The third time was the charm: Boris Karloff stars, and the episode was preserved. He also performed "Cat Wife" for *Everyman's Theater* on October 18, 1940.

Local News Broadcast. April 11, 1938. Boris Karloff talks with a circus owner promoting the New York appearance of the Ringling Bros. and Barnum & Bailey Circus.

Lights Out. April 13, 1938, NBC, 30 min. "Three Matches." A lost episode.

Lights Out. April 20, 1938, NBC, 30 min. "Night on the Mountain." Lost episode.

Royal Gelatin Hour (aka *The Rudy Vallee Program*). May 5, 1938, 60 min. Rudy Vallee stars in this variety show which offers a dramatic highlight in Boris Karloff as Death in the one-act drama "Danse Macabre." He performed the same material on an earlier *Royal Gelatin Hour*.

The Eddie Cantor Show. January 16, 1939, 30 min. Eddie Cantor, Bert Gordon and Boris Karloff. This is a lost episode. Karloff's 1941 guest spot with Cantor exists.

Royal Gelatin Hour (aka *The Rudy Vallee Program*). April 6, 1939. Rudy Vallee offers songs and comedy, with guest star Boris Karloff in the featured dramatic short subject "Resurrection."

Kay Kyser's Kollege of Musical Knowledge. September 25, 1940, 60 min. Kyser's Koup was to get Karloff, Bela Lugosi and Peter Lorre to Ko-star in his film *You'll Find Out*. The three stars promote the movie on Kay's show.

Everyman's Theater. October 18, 1940, 30 min. Boris Karloff reprises the famous "Cat Wife" episode that he originally performed on *Lights Out*.

Inner Sanctum. January 7, 1941, Blue Network, 30 min. "Death for Sale." The classic horror show started its season on Tuesday nights, airing from 9:35 to 10:00 P.M. This, the first Karloff episode to be broadcast, still exists among collectors and fans. Unfortunately, most subsequent 1941–42 shows have been lost.

Information Please. January 24, 1941, Blue Network, 30 min. Clifton Fadiman presides over the panel of John Kieran, Franklin P. Adams, Lewis E. Lawes (warden of Sing Sing) and Boris Karloff.

Inner Sanctum. March 16, 1941, ABC, 30 min. "The Man of Steel." Boris Karloff starred in this lost episode.

Hollywood News Girl. March 22, 1941, NBC, 15 min. Boris Karloff discusses *Arsenic and Old Lace*.

Inner Sanctum. March 23, 1941, ABC, 30 min. Boris Karloff in "The Man Who Hated Death." Fans hate to hear that this is a lost episode.

Inner Sanctum. April 6, 1941, ABC, 30 min. Boris Karloff in "Death in the Zoo." Neither hide nor hair has been seen of this since it was broadcast; no transcription discs are available.

The Voice of Broadway. April 19, 1941, CBS, 15 min. Gossip columnist Dorothy Kilgallen talks with Boris Karloff, who promotes his hit play *Arsenic and Old Lace*.

Inner Sanctum. April 20, 1941, ABC, 30 min. Boris Karloff's "Fog" is lost.

Inner Sanctum. May 11, 1941, ABC, 30 min. Boris Karloff in "The Imperfect Crime," and not even an imperfect copy of it survives.

Inner Sanctum. June 1, 1941, ABC, 30 min. Boris Karloff in Edgar A. Poe's "The Fall of the House of Usher"; no copy has been unearthed.

Bundles for Britain. June 14, 1941, Mutual, 30 min. Boris Karloff and Constance Collier co-star.

Inner Sanctum. June 22, 1941, ABC, 30 min. Boris Karloff in the "Green Eyed Bat," another missing show that lowers the batting average of available Karloff-*Sanctum* titles.

Inner Sanctum. June 29, 1941, ABC, 30 min. Boris Karloff is "The Man Who Painted Death"; it's a wash, since this is another lost episode.

United Press Is on the Air. July 11, 1941, United Press syndication, 15 min. "Along Broadway with Joan Younger" is an interview show, with Boris Karloff promoting *Arsenic and Old Lace.* Also appearing are co-interviewer Russ Hughes and second guest Dorothy McGuire.

Inner Sanctum. July 13, 1941, ABC, 30 min. Boris Karloff stars in "Death Is a Murderer," another killer episode that hasn't been resurrected via transcription disc or tape.

Inner Sanctum. August 3, 1941, ABC, 30 min. "The Tell Tale Heart." Boris Karloff appears in one of the few episodes from the 1941 season that is still beating.

Inner Sanctum. October 26 1941, ABC, 30 min. "Terror on Bailey Street," starring Boris Karloff, is a lost episode.

The Eddie Cantor Show (aka *It's Time to Smile*). December 17, 1941, Red network, 30 min. Eddie Cantor and Boris Karloff. Sponsored by Ipana toothpaste, Cantor's *It's Time to Smile* Christmas show offers Eddie as a department store Santa Claus. Boris wants a "Didy-Doll," and when he plays with a yo-yo the fantasy is that it's "a Jap at the end of a string." Featuring Bert Gordon, Cookie Fairchild and Dinah Shore.

Information Please. February 20, 1942, Blue, 30 min. Clifton Fadiman hosts and welcomes two special guests to the panel, horror stars Boris Karloff and John Carradine.

Keep 'Em Rolling. February 8, 1942, Mutual, 30 min. In this wartime variety show, Boris Karloff performs in a drama called "In the Fog." Morton Gould and Clifton Fadiman are also on the show.

Inner Sanctum. April 4, 1942, ABC, 30 min. "Fall of the House of Usher." Boris Karloff returns to the Poe story a second time. No copy of the show exists.

Inner Sanctum. April 19, 1942, ABC, 30 min. "Blackstone," with Boris Karloff. Lost episode.

Inner Sanctum. May 3, 1942, ABC, 30 min. "Study for Murder." A psychologist studying murder becomes too deeply involved in his subject. Boris Karloff.

Inner Sanctum. May 24, 1942, ABC, 30 min. "The Cone," starring Boris Karloff. No copy exists.

Inner Sanctum. May 31, 1942, ABC, 30 min. "Death Wears My Face," with Boris Karloff. No copy exists.

Inner Sanctum. June 7, 1942, ABC, 30 min. "Strange Request," with Boris Karloff. No copy exists.

Inner Sanctum. June 21, 1942, ABC, 30 min. "The Grey Wolf," starring Boris Karloff. No copy exists.

Information Please. May 17, 1943, NBC, 30 min. Boris Karloff returns to the panel, along with regulars John Kieran and Franklin P. Adams.

Blue Ribbon Town. June 3 and/or July 24, 1943, CBS, 30 min. Groucho Marx is the star of the show, sponsored by Pabst Blue Ribbon Beer, with singer Virginia O'Brien and special guest Boris Karloff.

The Charlie McCarthy Show. January 30, 1944, NBC, 30 min. Edgar Bergen and Charlie McCarthy greet guest Boris Karloff on the subject of phrenology.

Creeps by Night. February 15–June 20, 1944, ABC, 30 min. Boris Karloff hosted this show, which was broadcast on Tuesday nights at 10:30 P.M. Episodes include: "The Voice of Death" (February 15, 1944), "The Man with the Devil's Hands" (February 22, 1944), "Untitled" (March 1, 1944), "Untitled" (March 7, 1944), "Dark Destiny" (March 14, 1944), "A String of Pearls" (March 28, 1944), "The Final Reckoning" (May 2, 1944), and "The Hunt" (May 9, 1944). Among the surviving classic episodes is "The Final Reckoning" (May 2, 1944), with Karloff as George Miller, finally paroled from prison and hardly seeming to be reformed; instead, it seems he's going to become another "Sweeney Todd," turning into a barber just to get close to a razor.

Duffy's Tavern. January 12, 1945, NBC, 30 min. Ed Gardner stars, with special guest Boris Karloff.

Suspense. January 25, 1945, CBS, 30 min. "Drury's Bones." The familiar topic of amnesia gets a workout in this familiar melodrama starring Boris Karloff as Terrance Drury, a man who can't quite remember the nefarious things he may have done.

The Fred Allen Show. October 14, 1945, NBC, 30 min. Fred's guest is Boris Karloff.

Inner Sanctum. October 23, 1945, CBS, 30 min. After a few years, Boris Karloff returns to *Inner Sanctum*, which is now on CBS at 9 P.M. Tuesday night. "Corridor of Doom" is the corridor of a mysterious hospital that dooms Boris Karloff. This is the first Karloff episode hosted by Paul McGrath, who replaced ghoulishly laughing Raymond Edward Johnson in May 1945.

The Raleigh Room (aka *Hildegarde's Radio Room*). October 23, 1945, NBC, 30 min. A variety show with an emphasis on music, ranging from tunes ("I've Got Gobs of Love for the Navy") to "Malaguena" (performed by Oscar Levant). Boris Karloff appears with make-up artist Perc Westmore. Boris recalls his Frankenstein make-up: "The best make-up comes from natural sources ... you remember how white my face was? Crushed chicken bones. And the dark eye shadow? Just a little dust off a tombstone." "How did you get your lips so red?" "[Evil laughter] Tomato juice."

The Charlie McCarthy Show. October 28, 1945, NBC, 30 min. Charlie risks becoming sawdust when he visits a haunted house with Boris Karloff. Starring Boris Karloff and Edgar Bergen.

Inner Sanctum. October 30, 1945, CBS, 30 min. "The Man Who Couldn't Die," starring Boris Karloff. Another lost episode.

Report to the Nation. November 3, 1945, CBS, 30 min. This Saturday afternoon variety show offers "Loch Lomond" sung by Maxine Sullivan, and Karloff in the dramatic sketch "Back for Christmas," by John Collier, while Alan Young stars in a comic sketch about a surgeon.

Inner Sanctum. November 6, 1945, CBS, 30 min. "The Wailing Wall." With a nod to Edgar Allan Poe's "The Black Cat," Boris Karloff decides to kill his wife and dispose of her body in a wall—only to be tormented by ghostly noises. Starring Boris Karloff and Jackson Beck.

Theater Guild on the Air (aka *U.S. Steel Hour*). November 11, 1945, ABC, 60 min. "The Emperor Jones" and "Where the Cross Is Made." The former is performed by Canada Lee and the latter by Boris Karloff and Everett Sloane.

The Fred Allen Show. November 18, 1945, NBC, 30 min. The post-war housing shortage leads a jittery Fred Allen to try renting space from Boris Karloff.

The Textron Theatre. December 8, 1945, CBS, 30 min. "Angel Street." Boris Karloff takes over the role originated by Vincent Price on Broadway, and then Charles Boyer in the film version (re-titled *Gaslight*). If anyone can drive a woman insane, it's Boris. Helen Hayes hosts, with Boris Karloff and Cedric Hardwicke.

Exploring the Unknown. December 23, 1945, Mutual, 30 min. "The Baffled Genie," with Boris Karloff and Charles Irving.

Information Please. December 24, 1945, NBC, 30 min. Clifton Fadiman once again welcomes Boris Karloff to the panel.

Show Stoppers. 1946, Textile Broadcasts syndication, 15 min. "Boris Karloff." In a program sponsored by Koret of California, Boris Karloff talks about his show-stopping performance in *Arsenic and Old Lace*, his early days performing in Canada, and his big break in *The Criminal Code*. He also reads from "The Beggarman," by Ivan Turgenev.

Request Performance. February 3, 1946, CBS, 9 P.M. A variety show featuring Roy Rogers, Frank Morgan, and Boris Karloff in "The Reconversion of Karloff."

That's Life. November 8, 1946, CBS, 30 min. Interview show featuring members of the audience and guest celebrities. Jay C. Flippen is a guest, and Boris Karloff reads a limerick and promotes his starring role in *On Borrowed Time*.

The Lady Esther Screen Guild Theatre. November 25, 1946, CBS, 30 min. "Arsenic and Old Lace." Boris Karloff gives radio audiences a taste of the original stage production. The hero role played by Cary Grant in the film version is taken by Eddie Albert. Boris Karloff, Eddie Albert, Verna Felton and Jane Morgan.

Unconquered. 1947, Paramount syndication, 15 min. Paramount's promotion for their new film was offered to any radio station who'd want to run it. Interviews are conducted with the film's headliners—Gary Cooper, Boris Karloff and Howard Da Silva.

The Jack Benny Program. January 19, 1947, NBC, 30 min. The second half of the show features Jack in one of the strangest sketches of all time, "I Stand Condemned." A man seems intent on giving money away—which sure seems like a dream come true to Jack. Starring Jack Benny, Phil Harris, Mary Livingstone, Rochester, Mel Blanc and guest Boris Karloff. The sketch was originally written for Peter Lorre, who performed it on a program the year before.

Lights Out. July 16, 1947, NBC, 30 min. "Death Robbery." It's a pretty mad scientist who brings his wife back from the dead. She's not crazy about it herself. Boris Karloff and Lurene Tuttle star. *Lights Out* had a strange history. It ran successfully on NBC from June 10, 1936, to July 16, 1939, for over 140 episodes. It returned to the air on October 6, 1942, and departed September 28, 1943, after another 52 episodes. NBC used it as a summer replacement series in 1945, 1946 and 1947. Less than half of these survive. Some sources indicate Karloff appeared in "The Undead" (July 23, 1947), but no copies exist to confirm it.

Lights Out. July 30, 1947, NBC, 30 min. "The Ring." A very mixed blessing here; evidently one side of a transcription disc survives, so listeners can hear the first half of the program and guess at the ending.

Philco Radio Time (aka *The Bing Crosby Show*). October 29, 1947, ABC, 30 min. In the show's highlight, Bing joins Victor Moore and Boris Karloff in a singing celebration of Halloween.

The Jimmy Durante Show. December 10, 1947, NBC, 30 min. Featuring Boris Karloff, along with Arthur Treacher, Candy Candido and Peggy Lee. In a change of character, Karloff plays disc jockey "Happy Sam the Record Man," shilling cucumber beauty cream to the ladies in the audience: "Do you have a winning smile but a losing face? When you walk into a room do mice jump on chairs? Then there's only one solution for your face. Pickle It cucumber cream."

Suspense. December 19, 1947, CBS, 30 min. "Wet Saturday." The John Collier story as performed by Boris Karloff, Hans Conried, Cathy Lewis and Wally Maher. One of the very few *Suspense* episodes that has been lost.

The Kraft Music Hall. December 25, 1947, NBC, 30 min. Al Jolson is the star, with Oscar Levant and announcer Ken Carpenter. Jolson has a flashback about Christmas—with Boris Karloff as Santa Claus.

Guest Star. September 12, 1948, Treasury Department syndication, 15 min. "The Babysitter." In this one-act drama, Boris Karloff plays an escaped felon who seems to be all alone with a young boy, who could be his next victim. The menace in babysitter Karloff's voice and the innuendo of his lines would make anyone—except this unsuspecting kid—very worried.

The NBC University Theatre. October 17, 1948, NBC, 60 min. "The History of Mr. Polly." Based on the H.G. Wells satire, this episode stars Boris Karloff, Ramsay Hill, Constance Cavendish, Naomi Stevens, Terry Kilburn, Arthur Q. Bryan and Ben Wright.

Sealtest Variety Theatre. October 28, 1948, NBC, 30 min. Guest Boris Karloff gets a few laughs before he gives way to second guest Jack Carson, who performs in a sketch with Dorothy Lamour.

Great Scenes from Great Plays. October 29, 1948, Mutual, 30 min. "On Borrowed Time," by Paul Osborn, features Boris Karloff as "Gramps," and veteran star of "elderly" roles Parker Fennelly.

Truth or Consequences. October 30, 1948, NBC, 30 min. Giddy host Ralph Edwards turns special guest Boris Karloff into a bearded swami to fool a contestant: "Boris Karloff, aren't we the Howl-oween devil?" The audience's roaring screams and howls as Karloff unmasks himself are pretty frustrating in audio format.

Theater USA. February 3, 1949, ABC, 30 min. Boris Karloff's episode, co-starring Carol Bruce, Hank Ladd and Joseph Szigeti, is lost. Apparently the entire season of approximately 33 episodes no longer exists.

Spike Jones Spotlight Review. April 9, 1949, CBS, 30 min. Spike Jones hosts special guest Boris Karloff.

Theater Guild on the Air (The U.S. Steel Hour). May 29, 1949, ABC, 30 min. "The Perfect Alibi," starring Boris Karloff and Joan Lorring, is a lost episode.

Sealtest Variety Theatre. June 23, 1949, NBC, 30 min. Boris Karloff offers both menace and comedy in his second appearance on Dorothy Lamour's show. Co-starring Eddie Bracken.

Starring Boris Karloff. September 21–December 14, 1949, ABC, 30 min. In an unusual move, ABC broadcast a radio version of each script on Wednesday nights at 9 p.m., and a television version was broadcast Thursday nights. No episodes survive of these evocative titles: "Five Golden Guineas" (September 21),"The Mask" (September 28), "Mungahara" (October 5), "Mad Illusion" (October 12), "Perchance to Dream," (October 19), "The Devil Takes a Wife" (October 26), "The Moving Finger" (November 2), "The Twisted Path" (November 9), "False Face" (November 16), "Cranky Bill" (November 23), "Three O'Clock" (November 30), "The Shop at Sly Corner" (December 7) and "The Night Reveals" (December 14).

The Bill Stern Colgate Sports Newsreel. January 13, 1950, NBC, 15 min. Karloff has a few minutes to joke about superstition. After an evil laugh, he begins, "Friday the 13th is my day ... I am Boris Karloff [another fiendish laugh]. Maybe you've seen me in the movies. Generally near midnight, and my ghostly hand is clutching a dagger, about to strike!" Then he debunks the myth: "One of the greatest writers of all time was buried on Friday the 13th. And his name was Edgar Allan Poe. Certainly his life wasn't jinxed, for he wrote the greatest murder mystery of all time, 'The Murders in the Rue Morgue' [laughs fiendishly]. That's my kind of story!"

The Bill Stern Colgate Sports Newsreel. July 21, 1950, NBC, 15. Boris Karloff is a guest-host for vacationing Bill Stern, and manages to find classic sports stories that involve crime.

Boris Karloff's Treasure Chest. September 17–December 17, 1950, WNEW, New York, 30 min. Karloff hosts a children's program for a local radio station, aired Sunday nights at 7 P.M. He reads classic story poems such as "Casey at the Bat" (October 1), and plays Burl Ives' version of "Blue Tailed Fly" and other folk tunes (November 26). The series was produced by Richard Pack and directed by John Grogan, with organ music by Kay Reed.

Theater Guild on the Air (The U.S. Steel Hour). December 24, 1950, 60 min. "David Copperfield." A stellar version of the Charles Dickens story featuring Boris Karloff as Uriah Heep, along with Flora Robeson and Cyril Ritchard.

Stars on Parade. May 4, 1951, Army and Air Force Syndication, 15 min. A production of the Armed Forces Radio Service." The Big Man." Boris Karloff is Big Al, a man needing an operation who comes up with a plan: "What an idea ... what an alibi; a guy in a hospital bed, sick and in pain from a major operation. It was the chance I've been trying to find for months. With practically no risk I could get rid of the one person who was blocking me from becoming a really big man. I could kill Rose, my wife."

Duffy's Tavern. October 5, 1951, NBC, 30 min. Archie the bartender discovers that the tavern owner is planning on selling the place—so he asks Boris Karlof to help scare away any potential buyer.

Phillip Morris Playhouse on Broadway. February 10, 1952, CBS, 30 min. "Journey into Nowhere," starring Boris Karloff and Charles Martin.

Theater Guild on the Air (The U.S. Steel Hour). February 24, 1952, NBC, 60 min. "Oliver Twist," starring Boris Karloff and Basil Rathbone. A lost episode.

Theater Guild on the Air (The U.S. Steel Hour). April 27, 1952, NBC, 60 min. "The Sea Wolf," starring Boris Karloff and Burgess Meredith. A lost episode.

Phillip Morris Playhouse on Broadway. June 1, 1952, CBS, 30 min. "Outward Bound." Boris Karloff and Charles Martin.

Inner Sanctum. June 22, 1952, CBS, 30 min. "Birdsong for a Murderer." Boris Karloff stars in the first episode that returns the program to Sunday nights at 9:30 P.M. The program no longer produced new scripts, but reprised fan favorites. "Birdsong for a Murderer" was originally aired on February 14, 1949, with Ted Osborne starring.

Inner Sanctum. July 13, 1952, CBS, 30 min. In "Death for Sale," Boris Karloff stars in a story about murder and insurance. The script was originally broadcast in January 1941.

Best Plays. July 6, 1952, NBC, 60 min. "Arsenic and Old Lace." Boris Karloff stars with Donald Cook, Evelyn Varden, Jean Adair, Ted Osborne and Joan Tompkins.

The MGM Musical Comedy Theatre. November 26, 1952, Mutual, 60 min. "Yolanda and the Thief." Starring Boris Karloff as the Guardian Angel, with John Conte and Lisa Kirk. The program offers several songs, including "Blue Moon," "You Stepped Out of a Dream," and "Got a Date with an Angel." The program was apparently syndicated and had two major airing dates, the other listed as February 20, 1952.

Phillip Morris Playhouse on Broadway. December 10, 1952, CBS, 30 min. "Man Against Town," starring Boris Karloff and Charles Martin.

Theater Guild on the Air (The U.S. Steel Hour). (April 5, 1953, 60 min. "Great Expectations," by Charles Dickens. Boris Karloff takes the role of Magwich in this production featuring Estelle Winwood and Rex Thompson.

Phillip Morris Playhouse on Broadway. April 15, 1953, CBS, 30 min. "Dead Past," starring Boris Karloff and Charles Martin.

Heritage. April 23, 1953, ABC, 30 min. "Plagues," with guest star Boris Karloff. A drama series on various historical topics, produced and directed by Sherman H. Dryer, with Charles Irving hosting.

Phillip Morris Playhouse on Broadway. June 17, 1953, CBS, 30 min. "The Shop at Sly Corner," by Edward Percy. Boris Karloff co-stars with Charles Martin.

The Play of His Choice. December 1, 1953, British radio syndication. "The Hanging Judge," by Bruce Hamilton, with Boris Karloff as Sir Francis Brittain.

Tales from the Reader's Digest. December 16, 1953. Boris Karloff pays a visit—and a few years later becomes the show's enduring host (1956–1968).

Tales from the Reader's Digest. 1956–69, Syndicated, 5 min. Boris Karloff. Karloff's program for *Reader's Digest* was, like the magazine, a potpourri of facts and anecdotes. A week of shows would be sent to radio stations on a long-play album, with the notation "For broadcast the week of…" However, station managers could choose to run the shows in sequence several times over the course of one day, or in any other manner. So the typical record label would say, "For broadcast the week of April 1, 1957," and then simply list the contents as Programs 56, 57, 58 (and, on the flip side, 59 and 60).

Through a typical year (1963), topics varied from "The Family Cat" (week of January 7) to "Comfort in Clothing" (January 21) to "Points to Ponder" (February 18) to "Mrs. John F. Kennedy" (March 4) to "Stan Musial" (April 1) to "Memory" (October 7) to "Minneapolis" (November 18).

Recollections at Thirty. September 26, 1956, NBC, 30 min. A variety show collecting old radio performances and records. Boris Karloff is heard in the 1938 version of "Cat Wife," as well as comedy from Colonel Stoopnagle and music from Vincent Lopez and Buddy Clark.

Easy as ABC. April 27, 1958, CBS, 30 min. "0 Is for Old Wives Tales." Sponsored by UNESCO (United Nations Educational Scientific Cultural Organization), this obscure, evidently lost program featured Boris Karloff, Peter Lorre and Alfred Hitchcock.

Flair. ABC Syndicated, 1960. *Flair*, hosted by Dick Van Dyke, was a daytime variety show intended to attract the same audience as NBC's *Monitor*. It premiered October 3, 1960. It featured a chorus singing jingles, musicians, comic talent from Charley Weaver to Phyllis Diller, and audio essays from everyone from tennis star Don Budge to Boris Karloff on a handful of episodes. On show #609, the chorus, to the tune of the Russian ballad "Dark Eyes," sings about Karloff telling you how to deal with your baby or children who are a puzzle to you. Karloff discusses the suburban problem of an unwanted little visitor:

Baby is napping, and you're stretched out with a new magazine, enjoying a short siesta before scrubbing the kitchen floor. Three-year-old Jackie from next door picks this moment for a social call. He knocks the way all little children do—as though they were performing a loud and lengthy drum solo. The dog starts barking, and the baby starts crying! End of siesta. Well, one mother we know devised a very effective way of dealing with these disturbers of the peace. On a large piece of construction paper she pasted a picture of a baby sleeping, and underneath she wrote, "Baby is asleep. Please do not knock." Tots who couldn't read the words could read the picture, and soon learned to refrain from knocking when the sign was on the door.

As with his *Reader's Digest* work, Karloff was used for general information pieces, not comedy or horror. Other mini-essays included "Naughty Words," "New Year's Eve" and "A Child's Privacy." From the latter: "To parents, the baby picture of Junior in his birthday suit may be 'utterly adorable.' To Junior—now aged five—it may be a source of inexpressible anguish when exhibited to visiting friends and relations." A set of seven of his scripts, which showed his annotations for line and word emphasis, were put up for Internet sale via Heritage Auctions, with the consent of the Karloff estate and his daughter, Sara Karloff Sparkman.

The Barry Gray Show. January 26, 1963, WOR, 120 min. A legendary lost program. Gray was a well known local radio personality in New York, able to secure both Peter Lorre and Boris Karloff as interview guests.

Audio

Boris Karloff recorded many albums for children, beginning circa 1958 with *The Ugly Duckling* and *Kipling's Jungle Books*. He also recorded spoken word material for adults, often on topics in keeping with his horror image, as well as the usual radio and soundtrack work. The following discography is divided into those three categories.

- KARLOFF'S NARRATION ALBUMS FOR CHILDREN

Kipling's Jungle Book: How Fear Came (Caedmon Records TC 1100).

Kipling's Jungle Book: Toomai of the Elephants (Caedmon Records TC 1176).

How the Alphabet Was Made (Caedmon TC 1361).

Just So Stories and Mowgli's Brothers (Caedmon 1038). The *Just So Stories* collection includes "How the Camel Got His Hump," "How the Whale Got His Throat," "How the Rhinoceros Got His Skin" and "Mowgli's Brothers."

More Just So Stories (Caedmon 1088). *More Just So Stories* offers "The Elephant's Child," "The Sing Song of Old Man Kangaroo," "The Beginning of the Armadillos" and "How the Leopard Got His Spots." *Other Just So Stories* (Caedmon TC 1139, also released as *The Cat Who Walked by Herself and Other Just So Stories* [Caedmon TC 1139]. The "other" stories are "The Butterfly That Stamped" and "How the First Letter Was Written."

Mother Goose (Caedmon TC 1091). Stories are read by Boris Karloff, Cyril Ritchard and Celeste Holm.

The Ugly Duckling and Other Tales by Hans Christian Andersen (TC 1109). The stories include the title track, "The Princess and the Pea," "Clod-Poll," "The Collar and the Shepherdess" and "The Chimney-Sweep."

The Little Match Girl and Other Fairy Tales (Caedmon Records TC 1117).

Let's Listen (Caedmon TC 1183). Boris Karloff reads "Petunia Beware" and "The Pony Engine," and Julie Harris reads "Six Foolish Fishermen" and "The Red Carpet."

The Legend of Sleepy Hollow and Rip Van Winkle (Pickwick CR-32, re-issued by Mr. Pickwick Records SPC-5156).

Tales of Mystery and Imagination: "The Legend of Sleepy Hollow" and "Rip Van Winkle" (Cricket 32).

Just So Stories (Musical Heritage Society, 1984).

How the Alphabet Was Made and Other Just So Stories (Caedmon Audio Cassette; ISBN: 9997744810).

Aesop's Fables (Caedmon Records TC 1221).

The Three Little Pigs and Other Fairy Tales (Caedmon TC 1129). Boris Karloff reads "The Three Bears," "The Three Little Pigs," "Jack and the Beanstalk," "The Old Woman and Her Pig," "Henny Penny," "Hereafterthis," "The Three Sillies" and "King of the Cats."

The Pied Piper of Hamelin and The Hunting of the Snark (Caedmon TC 1075). Karloff reads the classics by Robert Browning and Lewis Carroll.

Pony Engine and Other Stories (Caedmon 1355).

The Reluctant Dragon (Caedmon 1074).

The Ugly Duckling and Other Tales (Caedmon 1210).

The Pied Piper/The Hunting of the Snark (Caedmon TC 1075). Karloff reads Browning and Carroll.

Best Loved Fairy Tales (Childcraft 1206).

The Pony Engine and Other Stories for Children (Caedmon Records TC 1355). Boris shares narration chores with Julie Harris, and offers the Aesop stories "The Old Woman and Her Pig" and "The Country Mouse and the Town Mouse."

The Reluctant Dragon by Kenneth Grahame (Caedmon Records TC 1074).

The Little Match Girl (Caedmon 1117). The album includes that Hans Christian Andersen tale and four more: "The Swineherd," "The Top and the Ball," "The Red Shoes," and "Thumbelina."

Peter and the Wolf (Childcraft CMG-13, CLP-1201, Vanguard VSD2010 and Vanguard SRV 174 SD, SILVERLINE DVD AUDIO 288230-9). Karloff's "Peter and the Wolf" first appeared as a 78 rpm single from Mercury's kiddie label Childcraft. It also appeared on the full-length album compilation *A Child's Introduction to the Classics*. Karloff's narration, backed by the Vienna State Opera Orchestra and Mario Rossi, was first issued by Vanguard in May 1957, and has been in print in both vinyl, CD, and even an audio-DVD version (from Silverline). Most critics reviewing the multitude of narrators covering this piece (from Michael Flanders and Bea Lillie to Rob Reiner and David Bowie) generally place "Uncle Boris" at the top of their list of favorites.

Usually the Karloff children's recordings consist of his narration and perhaps a sprig of sprightly music at the end of a selection (notably *Aesop's Fables*). In *Tales of Mystery and Imagination* he periodically stops so that vocalists (the Cricketone Chorus and Orchestra) can offer kiddie songs. For example, when Karloff announces the disappearance of Ichabod Crane, this leads to a jovial tune about Crane's fate and who scared him away.

- KARLOFF'S GENERAL SPOKEN WORD ALBUMS AND HORROR RECORDINGS

The Pickwick Papers (Caedmon TC 1121).

Boris Karloff reads "The Story of the Goblins Who Stole a Sexton," and on the other side Sir Lewis Casson reads "Mr. Pickwick's Christmas."

Cymbeline (Caedmon SRS 236). Karloff co-stars as the King of Britain, with Claire Bloom and Pamela Brown.

Classics of English Poetry (Caedmon TC1301). Karloff is part of an ensemble cast who take turns reading poems.

Gunga Din and Other Poems (Caedmon TC 1193). Karloff is part of an ensemble cast who take turns reading poems.

Tales of the Frightened, Vol. 1 (Mercury mono MG 20816, stereo SR 60815). Volume one: "The Man in the Raincoat," "The Deadly Dress," "The Hand of Fate," "Don't Lose Your Head," "Call at Midnight," "Just Inside the Cemetery" and "The Fortune Teller."

Tales of the Frightened, Vol. 2 (Mercury mono MG 20817, stereo SR 60816). Volume two: "The Vampire Sleeps," "Mirror of Death," "Never Kick a Black Cat," "The Ladder," "Nightmare" and "Voice from the Grave."

- KARLOFF'S RADIO, STAGE AND FILM SOUNDTRACK MATERIAL

Many of Karloff's radio appearances were issued on disc in the '60s and '70s. These include: *Arsenic and Old Lace* (Command Performance 5), *Great Radio Horror Shows* (Murray Hill 933977), *Inner Sanctum: Birdsong for a Murderer* (Pelican 112), *Inner Sanctum: The Wailing Wall* (Radio Records RG 102), *Boris Karloff in the Inner Sanctum* (Radiola 125), and his brief "Guest Star" appearance in "The Baby Sitter" sketch (on Radiola 1027). Various transcription discs of old radio shows survive, and there's always a chance that a "lost" episode may miraculously turn up. Certainly there's hope for the vast number of *Reader's Digest* shows that were put on vinyl and shipped to radio stations. One of the labels that pressed this material was Gotham Recording Corporation in New York.

Original cast and soundtrack items include: *Dr. Seuss: How the Grinch Stole Christmas* (Leo the Lion 901), *The Daydreamer* (Columbia OL 6540 OS 29401966), *Mad Monster Party!* (RCA) and *Peter Pan 1950 Original Cast album* (Columbia OL 4312, CD: Columbia CK 4312).

An Evening with Boris Karloff and His Friends was released by Decca (DL 4833 and DL 74833 stereo). The nostalgia boom in the late '60s led to "voicetrack" albums, most notably a set of Decca discs that compiled, with a narration track, classic snippets from Marx Brothers, W.C. Fields and Mae West movies. Slightly more ambitious was this 1967 effort, with music and sound effects, which had Karloff read scripted recollections (by *Famous Monsters* magazine editor Forrest J Ackerman). There were audio clips from his movies, as well as memorable ones from Maria Ouspenskaya (her elegy for the wolfman) and Bela Lugosi ("I never drink wine"), among others. He even relishes the jagged cries of mad terror as Bramwell Fletcher sees a mummy come to life. Karloff begins his narration by saying, "I hope that some of these excerpts you're about to hear will serve to conjure up visions for you once again of the magic moments of terror in these classic tales."

The most interesting promotional item on Karloff is the American International Pictures 33⅓ record sent to radio stations in support of *The Raven*. Titled *Listen to the Voice of Edgar Allan Poe's "The Raven,"* the disc has Karloff reading the opening stanza of the poem, which then gives way to announcer Paul Frees describing the film, backed by radio-style sound effects of a thunderstorm: "The shriek of mutilated victims, music for my ears! Prepare yourself for, yes, a duel to the death!" Karloff concludes: "This is a sample of I, Boris Karloff, have the privilege of starring with Vincent Price and Peter Lorre ... I guarantee your blood will run cold ... it may be the last picture you'll ever see. What? Have I disturbed you? I didn't mean to..."

Atomic Platters (Bear Family 5 CD Set) is a German compilation of nuclear scare radio spots, obscure singles about the Cold War, parodies about Khrushchev, and yes, Karloff's 23-second "Civil Defense Spot: Protect Your Home."

Karloff appeared on one 45 rpm single: "Come My Laurie with Me/He Is There" (MOL 52).

2

The Wolfmen: Henry Hull and Lon Chaney, Jr.

Neither of the two classic werewolves of the silver screen wanted to achieve fame via a face full of fur. Yet today their enduring popularity rests mostly on hirsute horror film roles.

Lon Chaney, Jr., didn't even want to *be* Lon Chaney, Jr. After a lackluster career out of show biz, he began winning small film roles using his real name, Creighton Chaney. He got nowhere after several years, however, and ultimately gave in to studio pressure to change his name. Finally, his career had Lon-gevity. His memorable quote: "They starved me into it." Though critics point to his fine work in *Of Mice and Men*, most people know him by one word: Wolfman.

As for Henry Hull, critics praised him as an excellent Broadway character actor, and he was in one of the longest running plays in history, *Tobacco Road*. However, if the average person knows his name at all, it's most likely because he was the *Werewolf of London*.

On radio, Henry Hull's work is no different from most any other actor, as he was a busy performer in many character roles over the years. A vivid exception is his performance in "The Pit and the Pendulum," an episode in the venerable series *Suspense*.

Lon Chaney, Jr.'s only notable radio appearance was in support of his wolfman role in *Abbott & Costello Meet Frankenstein*, but in the '60s he made several recordings trading on his horror film fame.

Henry Hull

Getting the obvious pun out of the way quickly, Henry did a Hull of a job as the sound era's first werewolf. There wasn't much previous competition—it came from a forgotten silent version, *The Werewolf*, released in 1913; and most have seen neither hide nor hair of it.

When Hull got the assignment, he fought like a Nair salesman for the right to smooth away as much hair as possible. He made sure that the make-up allowed him to add facial expressions to the role.

Rather than a monster movie, Hull went into it believing his character was similar to Dr. Jekyll and Mr. Hyde or the Invisible Man, a tale rooted in a battle between a scientist and forces beyond his control. The literate script offered intellectual pretense, presenting a motive that paraphrased Oscar Wilde: "The werewolf instinctively seeks to kill the thing it loves the most." Another line in the film that smacks of Wilde wit is, "Marrying any man is risky; marrying a famous man is kissing catastrophe."

Hull plays Dr. Wilfred Glendon, a botanist looking for the "marifasa lumina lupina." He finds it blooming in Tibet during a full moon, and he also finds a werewolf, which quickly leads him down a hairy path to horror hell. Or, as one character warns him at the start of the movie, "There are some things it is better not to bother with"—a rather awkward variation on the more standard Universal Films sentiment (as spoken by the Invisible Man, for instance), "I meddled in things that man must leave alone."

After this film, Hull left monster movies alone, and was mildly surprised when, during the '60s horror film craze, he was suddenly the subject of a cult following. He told a reporter from *New Era*, a Connecticut newspaper (the 4/23/64 issue), that his grandchildren stayed up late one night to see it: "I understand they just laughed. Probably thought it was one of the funniest comedies they had ever seen."

Hull may have had a passing, cordial acquaintance with Boris Karloff, but he wasn't interested in competing with him—or Bela Lugosi. An anecdote published in the *American Cinematographer—The International Journal of Film & Digital Production Techniques* (January 1998) chronicled a brief encounter between Hull's wife and a horror legend. Both *Werewolf of London* and *Bride of Frankenstein* were being filmed at the studio at the same time, with a connecting corridor:

> Henry's wife came to visit him on the set, and she was directed to the *Bride* set by mistake. A technician told her, "You don't have to go around the buildings. There's a connecting corridor between the two stages." The corridor was dimly lit. As she proceeded toward the other end, she heard "thump! thump! thump!" Halfway through, she saw Boris Karloff coming down the

Henry Hull (right) has plans for Gary Cooper in *The Fountainhead* (1949).

corridor in full Frankenstein makeup, smoking a cigar. As they met, he said, "Good morning, Mrs. Hull." She shrieked, "*Aiee! Aiee! Aiee!*" She knew Boris, but in the dark corridor she didn't recognize him.

Hull's early years were far removed from Hollywood and monsters. He attended Columbia University in New York and later worked as a mineralogist. In a 1922 *Sunday News* article he recalled:

> I was working in the silver mines of Cobalt, Canada, for a number of years. The work brought me in contact with all the rougher elements of life—the kind of life which is described in melodramas, you know, although I must say it did not impress me as very melodramatic at that time. But I knew that wasn't what I wanted to do. I became connected with the Bell Telephone Company, and worked with them in the capacity of inspector of pole lines for several years. On one occasion I walked on foot during bitter weather from Ottawa to Detroit—a distance of about 550 miles—and at another time I traveled from Toronto to Buffalo, which was a still greater distance.

He won some respect on stage in *The Nigger* in 1911, playing both the slave and the sheriff trying to track him down. His acting career took off in the '20s, in both silent films (D.W. Griffith's murder mystery *One Exciting Night*) and on Broadway, where he co-starred as Paul Jones in the 1922 production of *The Cat and the Canary*. Critic Alexander Woollcott pronounced the show "a creepy thriller, nicely calculated to make every hair on your head rise and remain standing from 8:30 till nearly 11." Hull's stardom was still a decade away, as he toiled in various productions leading up to *Tobacco Road* (1933), the show that may be forgotten now, but lasted 3,182 performances and was one of Broadway's all-time greatest hits.

Prior to that show, Hull tended to play clean-cut fellows in dinner jackets. In a May 13, 1934, interview for the *New York Herald Tribune* he said of his *Tobacco Road* persona:

> One reason I've always wanted to play this type of part is that they are usually better written and developed than the leads. The leading part must carry the plot and is often a clothes horse. But authors give their character parts distinction and make them individuals instead of types. The actor has something to work with, and the result is more gratifying—provided, of course, that the actor is successful.
>
> If more young people would specialize in character roles at the outset of their careers—providing they can persuade producers of their ability to play them—we should have more successful players. Unless you are a star, the life of a leading man or leading woman is limited to about ten years, whereas if you play roles of any age you can go until you are ninety, earning your living in a profession that has more pitfalls than any other.

During World War II, Hull was often asked to host the *Treasury Star Parade* program, a 15-minute fund-raiser. Being a Broadway actor, and so close to the radio station, he was a natural for the assignment, and his guests sometimes included other stage stars, including Alfred Lunt and Lynn Fontanne (who appeared in separate shows, reading poetry, and together for "Miss Liberty Goes to Town"). Hull is gruff, precise and spirited as he introduces whatever opera singer, pianist or other performer is going to supply the entertainment, and in many shows he takes the spotlight himself, performing a dramatic monologue or taking part in a cautionary tale steeped in patriotic fervor and often laced with a touch of propaganda.

Listeners would be treated to a dramatization such as "Remember Pearl Harbor," "Chicago, Germany" (Arch Oboler's stern warning of what was at stake if America lost), "So Long, Son" (about a young man leaving college to fight for his country) or "For the Record," which was about a Nazi submarine attack and a woman about to give birth while in a lifeboat. "Scare" tactics included "A Challenge from the Youth of Germany" (featuring strident, German-accented boasts from a variety of youthful actors) matched up with the uplifting "Children of America Answer the Challenge." The intent was always to anger and fire up the listeners—to the point where they'd at least dig into their pockets and buy bonds. The show offered a good way for stars to donate their time and prestige to raise war bonds, and everyone from Bette Davis and Edward G. Robinson to Kay Kyser and Vaughn Monroe dropped by.

The show not only covered American participation in the war, but offered dramatic episodes about the Allies, including "I Saw the Lights Go Out in Europe," "The Pied Piper" (who rescued several children in France) and "Military Objective," about two dozen British children killed in German bombing raids. Other episodes have historic value for their premiere performances, including an episode that premiered Langston Hughes' "The Freedom Road."

Since the main point was to sell war bonds, Hull usually ended the show with a stirring speech. In an episode featuring Blake Clark, author of *Remember Pearl Harbor*, Hull ends the show with this fiery and feisty statement, delivered with tense, raspy urgency and ever-increasing rage:

> No one has ever doubted the courage or the fortitude of the American people under fire. No one has ever doubted their ability to get things done once they made up their minds. And the American people have made up their minds. We're going into this war to win! And we're all going to do our share. There's not even any room to argue about that! And we're going to buy United States war saving bonds and stamps to make sure we're going to win it! We're going to buy them regularly! We're to get the habit! And we're going to join the Treasury Payroll Savings Plan wherever we work! We're going to keep on working and we're gonna keep on saving and we're gonna keep on buying war stamps and bonds, because this is our country! And we're going to keep it ours!

Lines like that were well suited to Hull's resonant voice. Among the horror stars, he and Claude Rains probably had the most tension in their voices, and that makes his rallying cries urgent and difficult to ignore.

Hull's fondness for radio led him to his own series for a while, *True Story Theater*. Columnist John K. Hutchens praised it and found it habit-forming: "In some wistful mood this listening post has lately been occupying an ethereal seat every Wednesday, well, almost every Wednesday night at WOR-Mutual's *True Story Theatre*, whose honor and privilege it is weekly to present Mr. Henry Hull and a feminine co-star of, if possible, equal eminence."

At the time, *True Story* was a popular magazine. The radio stories, Hutchens explained,

> are tales fresh from the magazine whose name the program bears, and therefore hot with the breath of modern life.... The play begins at about 8:31 P.M. Eastern war time, following an introduction which consists of a filter mike voice proclaiming that truth is stranger than fiction, whereupon Mr. Hull introduces himself, the play and his co-star and gets the evening under way.
>
> *True Story Theatre* does capture a certain aroma of a bygone theatrical day ... it is the dialogue, chiefly, that does it. Many a gaffer who roamed Broadway in other times, and who now does his theatre-going in an armchair besides a radio, must listen to the conversation in the *True Story Theatre* plays and say, "Those were the days!"
>
> Consider the drama in which Mr. Hull recently portrayed a middle-aged man who had divorced his excellent wife in favor of a young jitterbug, and then realized, almost too late, what a mistake he had made.
>
> "What a fool I was to let you go," the man said aloud to himself, gazing at his first wife. Could Thornton Wilder write a line like that? For all his talent, he could not. Nor would a

sophisticated dramatist like Philip Barry, when he wanted to tell the audience something, feel that he could afford such an admirably simple exchange as: "Sit down. I'd like to talk." "At last. It's been so long."

True Story Theatre, like the stage of the past, is not above such forthright devices.... Are they clichés? No matter. They keep the story moving, and again, they pleasantly remind old playgoers of the days when a mystery play was a mystery play and not a study in psychology or something.

Mr. Hull is the type of actor who speaks with authority in this kind of fiction and the *True Story Theatre* clearly knew what it was doing when it hired him. Himself a veteran of the footlights, he knows how to let himself go. Give him a line such as "Her kisses are like fire on my lips"—in fact, one of the plays did give him that very line—and he can make the air waves sizzle with it. He can also be menacing by the astute use of pauses which, though they may have little to do with the sense of a line, lend it a momentous air. Finally, when the occasion demands, he can produce words in a torrent which might strike a fledgling playgoer as ranting, but to more experienced citizens is in the tradition of great acting.

Hull also appeared on variety shows and local programs. In his column "Listening In," radio reporter Sid Shalit reviewed "Listen to the People," a verse drama by Stephen Vincent Benét, narrated by Hull and featuring Howard Lindsay and Otto Preminger:

> The setting and material for Henry Hull's guest appearance on the Monday night concert hour were nothing short of perfect. In the shadow of Independence Day, Hull recited Walt Whitman's prophetic "I Hear America Singing." It sent goose pimples up and down the ear.

Hull kept vivid track of all his radio, film and Broadway credits. He was once asked to go over a list of his credits, either for an agent or a publicist. The surviving page is filled with his corrections and additions, most of them in pencil. The undated sheet probably was compiled circa 1939, since he proudly added the credits of a working actor ("Summer Stock 1938 ... Brooklyn, 1 week, Greenwich, 1 week, Ivoryton, Conn. 6 weeks, White Plains 2, Harmon 3, Westchester 3"). He drew a box in pencil and inside made an extra category for radio. He noted his *Treasury Star Parade* appearances as well as "34 air interviews," but didn't specify those—no doubt most were local, and promoting various Broadway shows he was appearing in.

On the back, in longhand, he wrote: "I might add that an understudy has never gone on for me. Also add two nervous breakdowns." And under this he printed:

2 other records
6 openings on Bway in one year
18 years—Never leaving Bway.

When he wasn't in a Broadway production, or persuaded to make a local New York radio appearance, Hull could be found at his Connecticut home, supervising the flora and fauna. He aged into something of a duplicate of his cantankerous character roles.

When newspaper interviewer Henry E. Josten caught up with the old *Tobacco Road* star for a profile in Connecticut's *New Era* newspaper, the actor was waxing about vegetation: "I love to work in my garden. I grow a pretty good head of lettuce, if I do say so myself. And I do practically all the maintenance needed on our property. We have about 40 acres here and taking proper care of that much land can be a fulltime job in itself."

As for catching *Werewolf of London* and other films he made via late movie re-runs, he said, "Sleep means more to me than any movie, even my own." He did admit that anyone staying up for it would get a nice shock:

> It was a pretty good get-up, wasn't it? A lot of the credit belongs to Jack Pierce, a master make-up man on the Universal lot in those days. Jack had a special talent for transforming men into freaks. The Frankenstein monster was also one of his creations.

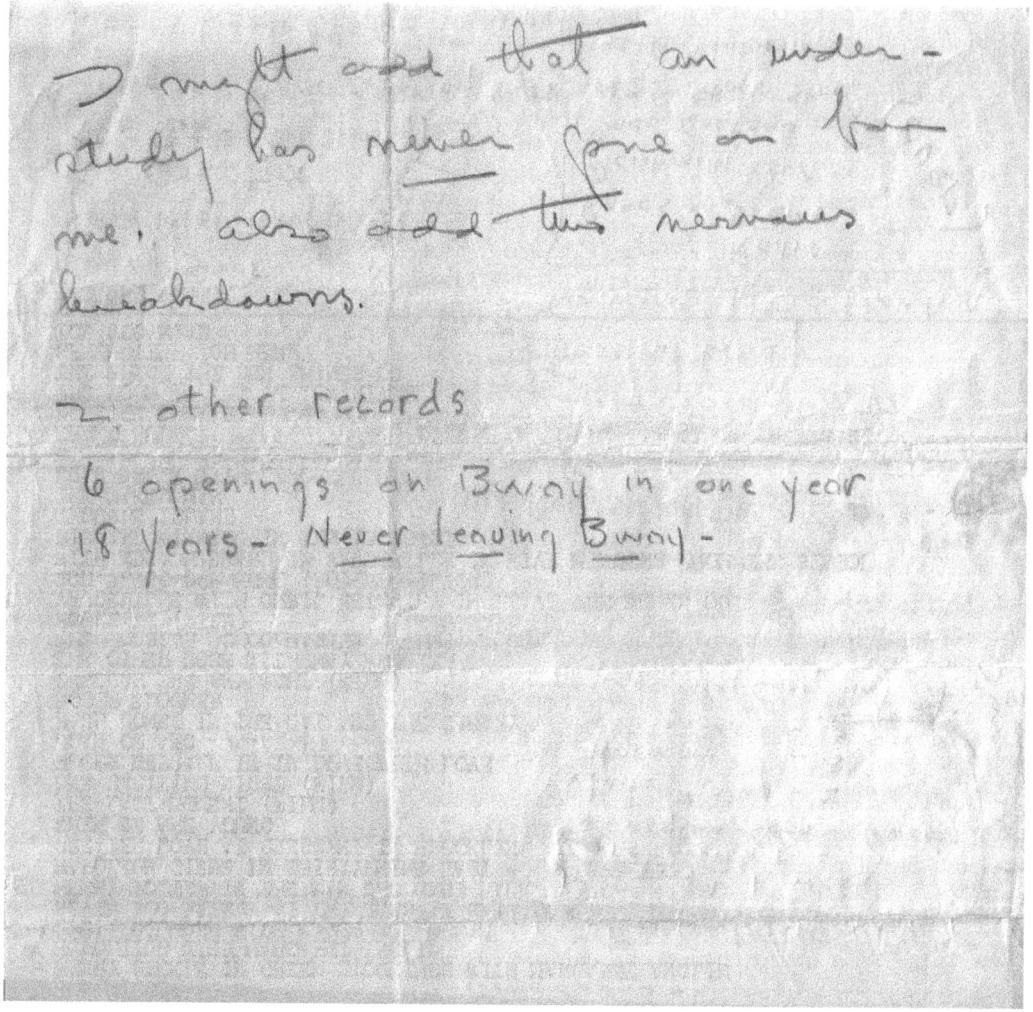

Henry Hull's pencil corrections on a vintage '40s resume include a note on the back telling his publicist, "I might add that an understudy has never gone on for me. Also add two nervous breakdowns."

I got out of the monster mold while the getting was good. The studio liked the job I had done as the *Werewolf of London* and they wanted to groom me for similar roles, but I declined because I didn't want to be limited to work in horror films. I'm glad I did, too, because it opened the door for me to a large variety of roles in many other films, including the very successful Jesse James series with Tyrone Power and Henry Fonda.

Fans are fond of noting that Hull's sister-in-law Josephine was memorable in a horror outing of her own; she played the dotty but murderous "Aunt Abby" in both the Broadway and 1944 film version of *Arsenic and Old Lace*. The former Josephine Sherwood, born in Newtonville, Massachusetts (1886–1957), was married to Henry's brother Shelley.

Hull's radio work, like his stage and film work, includes a lot of classic melodramas and adaptations culled from world literature. Most horror fans consider his audio high-

The poster for *Werewolf of London* (1935), showing Henry Hull with lycanthropy on his mind.

light to be "The Pit and the Pendulum," which he performed on an episode of *Suspense* on November 28, 1947.

Hull pioneered the role, which was subsequently played (using the same script) by Jose Ferrer, Vincent Price and Raymond Burr on various *Suspense* episodes over the years. The incidental music was composed by Bernard Hermann, who would create the soundtracks for several classic Hitchcock movies.

Each actor's interpretation varies in temperament. Price and Burr were more humble working actors than stars when they appeared on the show. They avoid affectation and read with sincerity. Ferrer, a rising Broadway star already basking in the glow of critical praise, is the only one who attempts the role with the robust bravado one would *not* expect from a tortured and starved prisoner.

As for Hull, he offers a balanced reading, tending to be a bit stage-florid on the more dramatic lines, but more film-intimate for the narration itself. Hull elicits sympathy from the start, as he wearily reads the opening words of John Dickson Carr's adaptation of Poe: "I was sick, sick unto death with that long agony, and when at length they unbound me, and I was permitted to sit, I felt my senses were leaving me."

Once he discovers that he is being held by the Inquisition, he tries to use reason against the shadowy figures who have captured him:

> "Gentlemen."
> "We hear you my son."
> "I, I'm very deeply infirmed. I've been confined for many months in a dungeon. I—I've been tormented by nightmares."
> "Conscience..."
> "God help me ... I am a French officer ... a prisoner of war. By what right do you try me in this court? By military law..."
> "Is military law above God's law?"
> "I—I don't know. I did my duty, that's all! Long live the Emperor!"

After the script's political and philosophical twists comes what horror fans crave—poor Henry forced into the pit, with the sound effects of the pendulum going back and forth, the chatter of rats, and, for an added twist that wasn't in the Poe original, the hallucinated voice of his wife. As the character's spirits and madness ebb and flow, the prisoner goes back and forth between exclamations of Shakespearean agony and more realistic mutterings of misery.

Hull had a knowledge of Poe going back many years before this radio production. In October 1936 he played the melancholy author in *Plumes in the Dust*, a Broadway show produced by Arthur Hopkins and written by Sophie Treadwell. When it previewed in Baltimore, the governor of Maryland proclaimed "Edgar Allan Poe Week." The show was performed at a theater that was only a block away from Poe's grave.

Hull preferred stage work to standing in front of a radio microphone or a studio camera. He told writer Elsie Rand,

> You can't hypnotize the camera. You *can* hypnotize an audience to the point where they forget your art and react to voice and gesture. In the theatre, there is a mob psychology in operation helping you to put over a scene. But the camera is completely indifferent to hypnotism. You must fall back on sheer technique, and pray to the gods that your scene is effective.

He elaborated on his craft, and its pitfalls, for *Cue* magazine, in their September 11, 1937, issue:

> It has been suggested that I vent a little spleen on the prevalence of the bad manners of "first nighters." Great day in the morning, did you ever participate in any mixed gathering, be the social barriers up or down where there wasn't some underbred, overfed or slightly soured guy whose sole purpose in being born wasn't simply to annoy his mother and whose pre-natal mission had been successfully carried out through life?
>
> Bad manners are as universal as rose bugs and there is no spray short of chlorine that is an effective germicide. I suppose there are some actors who profess to being annoyed, upset or made to feel snookish by the over-profuse applause—when it is for somebody else. I'm not. I love it. I love enthusiasm in an audience.... The lack of applause in making pictures is a serious dampener to the spirits of the actor and he never knows whether he has moved (or should I say *will* move) his audience.
>
> [Only the stage can] satisfy the acting ego ... there is that yearning, burning, deep down inside of every actor for applause.
>
> An actor is—must be—a case of arrested development. No sane adult-minded man or woman with a sense of true self-appreciation would learn a lot of words someone else had written and try to make them sound like his own. I know politicians do it but they aren't quite human

either. No well balanced grown-up, unless he's slightly pickled or a small town cut-up, likes to "dress up" in pap's hat and spats and tail coat, paint his face a sallow salmon color and cavort, disport or bestrew himself in front of an audience, take himself seriously and discuss his inner mature forces or unbroken line of communion.

In a 1950 interview with Vernon Scott, Hull admitted:

My best parts were always those of unreconstructed rebels. In movies it was my role as newspaper editor in *Jesse James*. In the theater it was Jeeter Lester in *Tobacco Road*, and the best TV thing I ever did was *Mr. Finchley versus the Bomb*. All people are subconscious nonconformists. But they're clubbed into being good little citizens and learn to follow orders. Well, not me. I'm still a rebel and I always will be.

This included taking a stance against anyone interfering with his bucolic lifestyle:

I remember 25 years ago some government inspectors from Hartford came to my farm to destroy my crop of currant bushes. They thought some kind of insect bred in the bushes causing an elm blight. I ran them right off the place with a shotgun and they never came back. But they ruined the currant crop in the state before they found out the bushes were not responsible for the blight.

Hull wasn't the type to stray from the farm on long vacations, but when he did, he discovered that his familiar face always earned him recognition. He told Kimmis Hendrick in *The Christian Science Monitor* (June 3, 1965), "Thanks to pictures, I can go anywhere in the world and people speak to me on the street. They know me."

He and his wife had a long marriage, which Hull typically acknowledged with a New Englander's logic: "My wife and I agreed early, that if you can't get along with one man or woman, you probably can't get along with another."

The opinionated star wrote a column called "Over 65" for a journal published by the Medical Society State of Pennsylvania, and in one column he described the lifestyle that was working for him well into old age:

I don't hate anybody or anything. All my hates are purely abstractions. All my loves are visible and concrete. I am never idle. I do not day-dream. I do not read modern clap-trap. I smoke too much and I talk too much. I know that human life is one gigantic joke and some day I'll see the point and laugh like anything and then I'll be perfectly willing to pass on to other and newer and possibly stranger conditions and circumstances. Meantime, I mean to go on working hard, playing hard, and thinking hard.

Henry Hull is looking a wreck in Alfred Hitchcock's *Lifeboat* (1944).

Radio

Roses and Drums. April 24, 1932–March 29, 1936. Henry Hull had the recurring role of Nathan Hale in this Sunday afternoon series.

Shell Chateau. July 20, 1935, NBC, 60 min. Al Jolson is the host, with special guests comedian Willie Howard and Henry Hull in a one-act play about Henry VIII.

The O'Neill Cycle. August 1937, Blue Network, 60 min. Hull was featured on "Where the Cross Is Made," one of the four Eugene O'Neill plays broadcast as a special summer series in August.

The Texaco Star Theatre. February 1940, CBS, 60 min. Ken Murray is the host and handles most of the comedy segments. Frances Langford, Kenny Baker and Irene Ryan are the regulars, with Henry Hull appearing in the show's dramatic highlight, "Juarez and Maximillian."

The Cavalcade of America. February 27, 1940, Blue Network, 30 min. A dramatization of "The Spy," by James Fenimore Cooper, showing how shoemaker Enoch Crosby proved invaluable to General George Washington. With Henry Hull, Ian MacAllaster, Frank Readick, Kenny Delmar, William Pringle, Alfred Shirley, Jeanette Nolan, John McIntire and Ray Collins.

Lincoln Highway. December 7, 1940, NBC, 30 min. "The Traveler." A beauty contest winner turns suicidal after being disfigured in a car crash. Starring Alice Frost and Henry Hull.

The Cavalcade of America. March 5, 1941, Red Network, 30 min. "Voice in the Wilderness." The story of William Penn and the Quakers. With Henry Hull, George Coulouris, Agnes Moorehead, Karl Swenson, Jeanette Nolan, Alfred Shirley, William Johnstone, Ray Collins, Elliott Reid and John McIntire.

Honest Abe. April 5, 1941–June 28, 1941, CBS, 30 min. Hull replaced Ray Middleton starting April 5, 1941. Middleton played Lincoln when the show first premiered on July 13, 1940.

Nightmare at Noon. May 18, 1941, Mutual, 15 min. A broadcast of "I Am an American Day" features Henry Hull's reading of the Stephen Vincent Benet war poem "Nightmare at Noon."

Listen to the People. July 4, 1941, NBC, 30 min. The Council for Democracy offers a drama by Stephen Vincent Benet. Hosted by Howard Lindsay and featuring Henry Hull.

True Story Theater of the Air. 9/23/42–12/30/42, Mutual, 30 min. Hull hosted the dramatic program on Wednesday nights at 8:30 P.M.

The Eyes and Ears of the Air Force. 1942, Ground Observer Corps syndication, 15 min. The importance of the "Grounds Observer" is covered. Henry Hull is the guest, discussing how he performs his duties in Old Lyme, Connecticut. Narrated by Westbrook Van Voorhis.

The Roll Call of the Nation. 1942, Treasury Department syndication, 30 min. "A Report on the State of the Nation." Featuring Henry Hull, William Hargrave, and Al Goodman and His Orchestra.

This Is War. March 28, 1942, Program #7, NBC, 30 min. Norman Corwin wrote and directed this program encouraging listeners to comply with restrictions and to increase productivity. Narrated by John Carradine and John Garfield, with Henry Hull, Katherine Locke and Frank Lovejoy.

Treasury Star Parade. 1942–1943. Henry Hull hosted dozens of programs in this series, which was syndicated by the Treasury Department. Some of the better efforts from the series were "Education for Death," "Bishop of Munster," "White Cliffs of Dover" (with Lynn Fontaine), "There's a Nation" (with Conrad Thibault) and "I Saw the Lights Go Out in Europe," co-starring Edward Kalenyi.

Suspense. January 12, 1943, CBS, 30 min. "The Pit and the Pendulum." Edgar A. Poe's tale of the Spanish Inquisition was adapted by John Dickson Carr.

The NBC University Theatre. September 24, 1948, NBC, 30 min. "Gulliver's Travels" starred Gale Gordon, Henry Hull, Jack Carroll and Jack Kruschen.

The NBC University Theatre. February 6, 1949, NBC, 60 min. This adaptation of "Gulliver's Travels" starred Henry Hull, Hugh Thomas, Eda Reiss Merin, Mark Van Doren and Parley Baer.

The NBC University Theatre. April 10, 1949, NBC, 60 min. "Moby Dick." Starring Henry Hull, Hy Averback, John Beal, John Dehner, Lester Schott, Ralph Moody and Steven Chase.

The NBC University Theatre. July 2, 1949, NBC, 60 min. "The Ides of March," a play based on the letters of Julius Caesar. Starring Georgia Backus, Henry Hull, Jan Arvan, Lawrence Dobkin, Lynn Allen, Maya Gregory and Parley Baer.

Family Theatre. July 13, 1949, Mutual, 30 min. "Moby Dick," a capsule version of the story, hosted by Celeste Holm and featuring Dane Clark, Henry Hull, William Conrad and Joseph Kearns.

Great Days We Honor. Syndicated, 15 min. Henry Hull starred in several broadcasts of this Jewish series which featured Sabbath services and the music of Eve Queller on organ, and the Chorus of the School of Sacred Music–Hebrew Union College. Episodes featuring Hull include "Shabbas," "Rosh Hashana," "Day of Atonement," "Chanukah," "Purim," "Pesach (Passover)," "Shevuos," and "Succoth."

Lon Chaney, Jr.

He lacked the striking, mobile features of Lon Chaney. He didn't have the magnetic personality of Bela Lugosi. He was not the sophisticated and polished actor Vincent Price was. His voice wasn't distinctively creepy like Boris Karloff's, and he lacked Karloff's unique posture and physical presence. So what in the world made Universal Studios turn away from Karloff, Lugosi and any number of other actors to give Lon Chaney, Jr., virtually every monster role they had, including the werewolf, the mummy, Frankenstein's monster and even Dracula?

Today we'd call it "demographics." Karloff and Lugosi, kings of horror in 1931, were skewing "old"—and old-fashioned in the 40's. They were either British or European. As a new decade approached, and young Americans were about to enter a world war, Lon Chaney, Jr., was a near-perfect symbol for them. He was an average man caught in a bewildering horror.

In *The Wolf Man* he played exactly what he was—a strong, decent-looking, good-natured American lug helplessly out of his element (here in the grip of a sinister European curse). He fought valiantly, despite an obviously limited intellect, and Chaney Jr.'s "Lawrence Talbot" won over the sympathy of movie audiences. The movie was in theaters on December 9, 1941, with world war and the bombing of Pearl Harbor on the minds of all American citizens.

Lon, at first unwilling even to become "Lon Chaney, Jr.," was now playing unwilling, unhappy monster roles, and was cast in a variety of "hard luck" suspense films. He took over Karloff's monsters in *Ghost of Frankenstein* (1942) and *The Mummy's Ghost* (1944), and he replaced the gaunt and elegant Lugosi as *Son of Dracula* (1943).

None of this was very satisfying for him. His co-workers noticed that he was drinking on the set, often blaming it on being alternately bored and, in many cases, tormented by the constricting and clumsy monster make-up he was required to wear as he stood around waiting for the moment he'd lumber over to some villager or heroine and "scare" them. He alluded to his father in his diary entry for January 13, 1942:

> Remember that he suffered agonies while making some of these pictures. Like to know how he felt about it himself. Finally they called him the man with a thousand faces. Can only remember one, the one with a smile. if he could take it like that, guess I can too. Hope so anyway.

In a broadcast of *Jack Linkletter's Hollywood* (though a TV show, it survives in audio version only, circulating among horror fans and radio show collectors), Lon mentioned his early life with his father and the bizarre circumstance of his birth:

> I'm kind of a strange guy. I was born dead. I weighed two and a quarter pounds. Well, my dad took me when I was born, and he went out to a lake. I was born right beside a lake. And he stomped on the ice, cut a hole in it, and dunked me. This brought me to life. Then he brought me inside and started to massage me, and he kept me alive. He built me one of the first incubators, I guess. It was made out of a shoebox. It was made out of a shoebox lined with cotton and holes on the top. And that was my beginning.

Lon Chaney was a vaudevillian and a touring actor, sometimes using his son as a comical prop in his act, balancing him in one hand. He also used his son for some petty larceny—wearing an oversized coat, he'd go into a bar where a free lunch buffet was served, and he'd pass his son enough sandwiches to hold the family for lunch and dinner. Meanwhile, Lon's mother also struggled to find work as an actress, and ultimately attempted suicide on stage via poison. The scandal ended the Chaney marriage, and the toxic fluid damaged Mrs. Chaney's throat, ending her career.

While Chaney's film successes finally brought him fame and fortune, he didn't want his son to go into show business, and young Creighton tried a succession of other professions. On Jack Linkletter's show, Lon described his entry into films:

> My poor old pappy died. I always had ham in my soul. I used to go to parties and make up songs. One night I made up a song. And it was to the liking of a producer who happened to be at the party. He said, "Why don't you come to the studio and sing it to the music department, and maybe we can sell it." So I did. I went to the studio. This particular studio, you had to go through the casting office in order to get to the music department, so on the way through I was introduced to the casting director, and he gave me the big handshake. He says "You ought to be in pictures ... $250 a week." He says "give me your phone number and just wait for my call." And I went down to my office, I resigned my job, I went home, and I sat by the phone. And do you know, that was 37 years ago. And that guy hasn't called me yet!

Fortunately, others did, and he began to get some film work as Creighton Chaney, but much more when he became Lon Chaney, Jr. Amateur psychologists believed Junior was having problems living up to his father's level of artistry and fame. His first wife divorced him, citing alcohol as the primary factor; and in 1936, he married his second wife. There were arguments and infidelities. Ultimately, on April 22, 1948, Lon argued with her, stormed out to his truck, and gulped down 40 sleeping pills. Fortunately, he was brought to a hospital in time. Analysts might say he continued his suicide attempts the old-fashioned way—by his constant drinking.

Chaney's role as the mentally challenged Lenny in *Of Mice and Men* was much-imitated ("Which way did he go George?" was a dumbly-spoken catch-phrase in several Warner Bros. cartoons), but, fortunately, he wasn't typed for more moron roles. The best he could do, sans make-up in the '40s, was his *Inner Sanctum* B-movie series in which he played a variety of bewildered men (usually tormented by self-doubt and bizarre curses).

Ironically, the radio series *Inner Sanctum* was home to Boris Karloff, who logged more guest roles on the show than any other Hollywood star.

By 1948 the classic monsters had worn out their welcome and were ripe for satire. In *Abbott and Costello Meet Frankenstein* Chaney not only played the Wolf Man, but did some stunt work in the Frankenstein Monster make-up, throwing a lab assistant through a window.

Chaney Jr.'s only noteworthy surviving radio appearance was on *The Abbott and Costello Show* (June 2, 1948), which promoted their film together. In the sitcom episode, Lon is going to date Lou's girlfriend. Lou challenges the burly film villain, who lives up to his image:

LON: Costello, don't you get fresh with me! Remember one thing, I am the Wolf Man.
BUD: Yes, Costello, when the sun goes down, he turns into a wolf.
LOU: Him and five million other guys!

That gag was lifted directly from the movie. Typical of the formula, further wisecracks follow:

LOU: Lon Chaney, see my fist? Waddya think of it?
LON: Dirty, ain't it.
LOU: Chaney, the last guy I had a fight with, he's in the hospital. And he'll be there for the next two years.
LON: Yeah? Who is he?
LOU: Young Dr. Malone. He don't graduate till 1950.
LON: Listen you little sawed-off runt, you know what I'm gonna do, I'm gonna bite your head off and chew it up and swallow it!
LOU: If you do, you'll have more brains in your stomach than you do in your skull.... You keep away from Honeysuckle Epstein. I'm warning you to withdraw.
LON: Yeah, and suppose I don't wanna withdraw?
LOU: Then I withdraw my warning....
Wattsamatta, Chaney, aren't there any other girls in your life?
LON: Yeah. But there ain't any life in my other girls! Ha ha! Ahhh ha...
LOU: There wasn't any life in that joke, either.

Luckless, lonely Lon Chaney, Jr., in a typically pitiful publicity picture.

The comedy team saved their other major co-star, Bela Lugosi, for a separate show. It's also possible that they knew better than to keep Lugosi and Chaney Jr. waiting in the same green room. The two did not get along. Lugosi was irked by Lon's down-home manners (which seemed disrespectful and too familiar to the Old World star). Lugosi, ever sensitive to rivalry, was still smoldering over having only a minor role in *The Wolf Man* and, worse, watching Lon turn into the *Son of Dracula*.

The reserved, formal Lugosi, and the gregarious, cheerful Chaney met up a few years later when both were on the skids and co-starring in *The Black Sleep*. Lugosi, frail and coming off an addiction to morphine, found himself again spending too much time with the hard-drinking Chaney Jr., who often advised film directors to get what they could early before his efficiency became impaired.

Reginald LeBorg, director of *The Black Sleep*, described the problems between Bela and Lon (on page 161 of the book *Lugosi, Master of the Macabre*), admitting:

> There was, I won't say hate, but a certain rivalry going on between Chaney and Lugosi from the Universal days when they both played Dracula. You see, Lugosi was the great Dracula, but then something happened at Universal and they gave the part to Chaney. There was a terrible rivalry between them before I even arrived at Universal. It came out on *The Black Sleep*. Chaney was sore at something Lugosi brought up and it nearly came to a fight. Chaney picked him up a little bit, but put him down. We stopped him. We kept them apart quite a bit.

This was not the first time Lon's joking and guileless demeanor had irked a "serious" actor. In *The Wolf Man* he played opposite Claude Rains, a Universal horror star himself (*The Invisible Man* and *Phantom of the Opera*), now handed a supporting role. Not only were Rains' lines skimpy, he was keenly aware of the height disparity between him and Chaney. What in the world had gone wrong when a well-schooled British actor was being literally overshadowed by an oversized amateur trading on the fame of his father?

Evelyn Ankers, in an interview with Arthur Lennig (quoted on page 229 in his book *The Count*), recalled a fight scene between Rains and Lon:

> Claude took a wild swing with the walking stick, which had a very heavy head—made from metal with the wolf's head—and it hit Lon in the face. Lon took pain very well, but poor Mr. Rains was almost overcome with the thought that he had actually done some violence to another person. Either that, or maybe he used his exceptional acting talents and was getting even with Lon for something that Lon might have pulled on him.

Co-workers mostly remember Lon fondly. Elena Verdugo, who played the wolf man's love interest in a subsequent film, recalled him as "a lovely, friendly man," and John Carradine, a co-star in the same movie, labeled him "a big, good-natured slob." Another actor, Robert Quarry, noticed that Lon was having an affair with a young woman who began sporting bruises. He questioned her about it, and she told him, "He's very sweet when he's sober."

Beverly Garland appeared with Lon in one of his many '50s B-movies, *The Alligator People*. Lon didn't play the half-man, half-lizard who walked around with a ludicrous fake alligator head. He played the far nastier role of a mean and alcoholic swamp denizen. She recalled to *Videoscope* writer Joe Kane:

> Oh, he was such a kick. He was the nicest man. I think that he really wished he could have worked way back when, like his father worked. He loved doing his own makeup. He just felt that his father got to do the things that he really wanted to do himself. And he really gets into his parts. He looked like the wrath of God in that movie, and he loved it.... In *The Alligator People* he really scared me. He's really good. And a lovable teddy bear on top of it.

Another *Videoscope* magazine writer, Tom Weaver, elicited some Chaney Jr. anecdotes from Robert L. Lippert, Jr., who worked with Lon on two early '50s cheapies, *The Black Pirates* and *Bandit Island*. Lippert recalled their life on location in El Salvador:

> Lon was a great guy. Don't laugh, but he said he was impotent at that time. He was drinking too much. Every goddamn night, we were into Casa de Puta—those are whorehouses. We'd all go to the cathouse, not to get laid, but to drink, and to get away from the local people. We wanted our privacy.... I don't think he wanted to lay these girls. He'd rather drink. Tell stories. He was a great storyteller, he could go on and on and on and on.

According to Lippert, Lon was "a good actor ... all the crews, the working guys, knew Lon, and they had nothing but good things to say about him. He was a regular guy." He was so good-natured that "he would never say, 'Oh, that guy's no good,' or something like that. He never did that. He never downed anybody."

Most of his co-workers felt that Lon was a simple, down-to-earth guy. In an interview for horror fan magazine *Scarlett Street*, Ann Doran (who co-starred with Lon in the Bob Hope comedy *My Favorite Brunette*) described Lon in one word: "dumbbell."

She felt his big success as the moronic Lennie in *Of Mice and Men* was typecasting:

> Lon Chaney was a lovely, lovely man—and yet he was as stupid as he could be. He was really a dumbbell, and that's what he always played—a dumbbell, a big, lumbering dumbbell. Pleasant enough, nice enough—but he was a dumbbell, that's all. If anyone told a joke, he wouldn't

know what the hell they were talking about. He never got it ... he was just not the smartest guy in the world, believe me.

Lugosi's biographer, Arthur Lennig, may have hit the coffin nail on the head when he characterized Bela's rival as: "An unexciting actor—a pall of dull sincerity hung over him. Chaney created characters that were more to be pitied than respected, more cringing than aggressive, more plebeian than aristocratic. If ever a star lacked charisma it was Chaney, Jr."

What Chaney did have—in abundance—was fan sympathy. Whether the victim of a curse (as in *The Wolf Man*) or the victim of B-movie scripts, Lon was clearly a man pure of heart, denied happiness by factors beyond his control. From his first decent film to his last decent film, he played a victim with a limited IQ. Even the best laid plans failed him in *Of Mice and Men*, and he was too dumb to know he was dead in *The Indestructible Man*.

Although alcoholic, suffering from a variety of illnesses, and not taken very seriously as an actor, Chaney Jr.'s last years were not nearly as desperate as those of his rival, Lugosi. The "Famous Monsters" boom of the mid–60s found him live, if not completely well, and able to guest on everything from *Route 66* (even doing a scene back in mummy makeup) to daytime quiz shows and nighttime talk shows. By this time, fans were very familiar with Lon's unique voice, with its sorrowful spookiness and slightly rural whine.

After the song "Monster Mash" became a hit, and Bobby "Boris" Pickett released the sequels "Monster Motion" and "Monster Holiday," Lon was asked to cover the latter. It's a recitation about the ghouls acting badly, planning to rob Santa, who will give them all they want. Lon even ad-libs some lines toward the end. The record's flip side was an instrumental.

Chaney's other notable rapping was a "cannibal orgy" fantasy, which can be heard over the opening credits of his cheapie film *Spider Baby*. It's available on a compilation album of Ronald Stein soundtrack music from Varese Sarabande and includes both the hard-driving single (with its thumping beat and ominous horns) and some rehearsal outtakes that give fans a glimpse into Lon's agreeable nature and sense of fun. He begins a take with: "Cannibal spiders creep and crawl. Boys and goils ... goils!" He laughs at his own mistake, and a technician quips, "You got a Brooklyn ghoul there."

Later, Lon reads another line and adds his own quip: "Take fresh rodents, toadstools and weeds.... Mix seven legs on an eight-inch beast. Eight inch? Jeez, what a beast!"

Few film bloopers from the '40s and '50s were kept, so these few minutes of audio outtakes are really the only proof of how easily Lon got along with people,

The Indestructible Man (1956), Lon Chaney, Jr., begins to show his age in the 1950s.

how down to earth he was, and that he possessed both a sense of humor and a dedication to getting it right.

Chaney Jr. was the subject of a *Star Close-Up* biography for the BBC in 1968 and was even a guest on *The Tonight Show* in October 1969. He suffered from throat cancer, but when asked about his raspy voice, he blamed it on the growling he said he had to do for eager Wolf Man fans.

Chaney's health problems worsened, and by the time he made *Dracula vs. Frankenstein* he had to lie down between takes. He told one cast member, "There's nothing left for me; I just want to die." An article in *Famous Monsters of Filmland* asked fans to write him and show him their support, and when the letters poured in, Lon told editor Forrest J Ackerman that the support "really makes me feel good."

The good-natured monster star was hoping to put together a spoken word album similar to Boris Karloff's *Tales of the Frightened* double album set, but only two stories were recorded. They appear on the posthumous album called *The Wolf Man Speaks*, filled out, ironically enough, with horror recitations performed by Bobby "Boris" Pickett.

The three-minute "shaggy dog" tales Lon performs are campfire horror anecdotes: "The Red Knife" and "The Yellow Ribbon." Both are set up like long jokes, and both have a "gotcha" punch line. That's *literally* the case in "The Red Knife."

Lon is effective in setting the scene: "Once a group of young boys were playing in a place they shouldn't. The graveyard!" A boy discovers a knife lying on a tombstone, and takes the red-handled prize home. The ghoulish owner of the knife wants it back, and slowly climbs the stairs as the boy lays in bed trembling.

Note: By way of "spoiler alert," in case you're hoping to find the album, avoid the next paragraph.

Lon reads the story well and is abetted by eerie sound effects ranging from a ticking clock to a clap of thunder:

> "Now I'm on the first step. Now I'm on the second step. Now I'm on the third step. Now I'm on the fourth step." Davy was petrified. "Now I'm on the fifth step. Now I'm on the sixth step. Now I'm on the seventh step. Now I'm on the eighth step." Davy was trembling all over. "Now I'm on the ninth step. Now I'm on the tenth step. [suspenseful pause] I've GOT YOU!"

As for "The Yellow Ribbon," this, too, features a trick ending, but doesn't rely on the narrator shouting it. A husband keeps wondering why his wife always wears a ribbon around her neck. After several minutes of set-up: "So John untied the yellow ribbon, ever, ever so gently..." and Lon reveals the secret.

Chaney's love of kids, and enthusiasm for "bedtime" stories, shows in these two brief examples, and it's sad that he was unable to complete the project, suffering as he was from a variety of ailments (the *New York Times* obituary even listed beri-beri among his illnesses).

Chaney, in a twist more in line with the Frankenstein Monster than the wolf man, ultimately willed his body to science for experimentation.

Radio

The Abbott and Costello Show. June 2, 1948, ABC, 30 min. Guest Lon Chaney fights with Lou Costello over the affections of one Honeysuckle Epstein. Vocals from Susan Miller. The supporting cast includes Elvia Allman, Veola Vonn, and Michael Roy.

Audio

In the pre–VHS era, the movie soundtrack to *Of Mice and Men* was issued as a two-lp set on the Mark 56 label.

Chaney reads two short (three minute) tales, "The Red Knife" and "The Yellow Ribbon," on *The Wolf Man Speaks: Lon Chaney's Last Recordings* (Garrison Records 14006). The album is fleshed out with music and some narrations by Bobby "Boris" Pickett. The same tales also appear on *Ticklish Tales of Terror*, by Bobby "Boris" Pickett and Lon Chaney (Label-Aire 14005). Perhaps due to some licensing problem, *Wolf Man Speaks* sports a photo of Oliver Reed in werewolf make-up on the cover, instead of Lon as *The Wolf Man*.

Chaney's cover version of "Monster Holiday" backed with the dance instrumental "Yuletide Jerk" (Tower 114) was released in 1965. It was re-issued on cassette via *Christmas Is for Kids* in 1989 (Cema Special Markets), and on the CD *Christmas Comedy Classics* (Priority Records), with singles by Stan Freberg, Mel Blanc and others. The cannibal orgy rap from *Spider Baby* is available via *Not of This Earth*, a collection of Ronald Stein's film scores and music on Varese Sarabande CD (VSD 5634).

3

Bela Lugosi

The first horror star to chill with his voice as much as his villainy was Bela Lugosi, star of *Dracula* in 1931.

Arthur Lennig, the longtime fan who ended up as Lugosi's first biographer, admitted in his book *The Count* that:

> What is most clearly memorable is Lugosi's accent—one that no impersonator has quite imitated correctly. Yes, it is Hungarian, but it is also Lugosian as well. In the inflections, the certain turn of the word, the odd way his lips and jaw muscles function, he seems to speak with great effort, as if he were forcing a mouth long dead to move again. His consonants are stressed, and the vowels are heavier and more drawn out.

Lennig offered a phonetic version of Lugosi saying "forcing a mouth long dead": "forse-ink a mau-tih longk deadt." The author added, "The overall effect is guttural, strong, masculine, somehow the very personification of evil, although someone once said that Lugosi's trouble was that his tongue was too big for his mouth!"

The accent was so big it became an obstacle to steady work. Some producers believed that the accent made him difficult to understand, while others felt he could not be used in any average role because the ethnicity would be hard to explain. Many thought that he couldn't even play a Hungarian doctor, restaurant owner or musician, since his face and voice were so identified with that of a vampire.

Lugosi was not alone. Most any Hollywood star with an accent shared his fate. Greta Garbo retired early, Marlene Dietrich rarely played anything but herself, and Warner Oland ended up in the Charlie Chan series until he suffered a nervous breakdown and died.

Boris Karloff believed another problem with Lugosi was that he didn't really understand the English language. In an interview with Robert C. Roman for *Films in Review* (August-September issue, 1964), he expressed his opinion:

> Poor old Bela. It was a strange thing. He was really a shy, sensitive, talented man who had a fine career on the classical stage in Europe. But he made one fatal mistake. He never took the trouble to learn our language. Consequently, he was very suspicious on the set, suspicious of tricks, fearful of what he regarded as scene stealing. Later, when he realized I didn't go in for such nonsense, we became friends. He had real problems with his speech, and difficulty interpreting lines. I remember he once asked a director what a line of dialogue meant. He spent a great deal of his time with the Hungarian colony in Los Angeles, and this isolated him.

Karloff seemed to have a bit of sympathy for Lugosi, while Lugosi has often been portrayed as being jealous of his rival. Bela Lugosi, Jr., reported that there was no rivalry that he could remember, but Lugosi's *Mark of the Vampire* co-star Carroll Borland recalled in her introduction to the book *The Films of Bela Lugosi* that "They hated each other!

Lugosi said that Karloff took his parts, and that was it." As portrayed by Martin Landau in the biopic *Ed Wood*, Lugosi flew into a curse-filled rage if someone was complimentary of Karloff, who had usurped his crown of "horror king" with initially mute and near-mute roles in *Frankenstein* and *The Old Dark House*.

As the horror craze of the '30s grew, the two men were often pitted against each other in classic films, but on radio they were together only once. For Ozzie and Harriet's program, Boris and Bela sang the brief but pungent bogey-man song "We're Horrible Horrible Men." To a jaunty beat, the two barely synchronize on the chorus (which doesn't make the lyrics any more intelligible), and each takes a turn on his own.

Lugosi may have appeared on local radio more than a few times in 1931 and 1932 to promote *Dracula*. No audio has survived, but dialogue exists on paper from his guest spot at Los Angeles station KFI. Whether it's a script that Lugosi delivered as he made the rounds promoting the movie, or a transcript of that broadcast is hard to determine. Lugosi tells the audience:

> I read the book *Dracula*, written by Bram Stoker, 18 years ago, and I have always dreamed of creating and playing this part of Dracula. Finally the opportunity came. I have played Dracula over one thousand times on the stage, and people often ask me if I still retain my interest in the character. I do—intensely.
>
> Because many people regard the story of Dracula as a glorified superstition, the actor who plays the role is constantly engaged in a battle with the audience, in a sense, since he is constantly striving to make the character so real that the audience will believe in it.
>
> Now that I have appeared in the screen version of the story, which Universal has just completed, I am, of course, not under the daily strain in the depiction of the character. My work in this direction was finished with the completion of the picture, but while it was being made, I was working more intensely to this point than I ever did on the stage.
>
> Although *Dracula* is a fanciful tale of a fictional character, it is actually a story which has many essential elements of truth. I was born and reared almost in the exact location of the story, and I came to know that what is looked upon as a superstition of ignorant people is really based on facts which are literally hell-raising in their strangeness—but which are true.
>
> Many people will leave the theater with a sniff at the fantastic character of the story, but many others who think just as deeply will gain insight into one of the most remarkable facts of human existence. *Dracula* is a story which has always had a powerful effect on the emotion of an audience, and I think that the picture will be no less effective than the stage play.
>
> In fact, the motion picture should prove even more remarkable in this direction since things which could be talked on the stage can be shown on the screen in all their uncanny details.

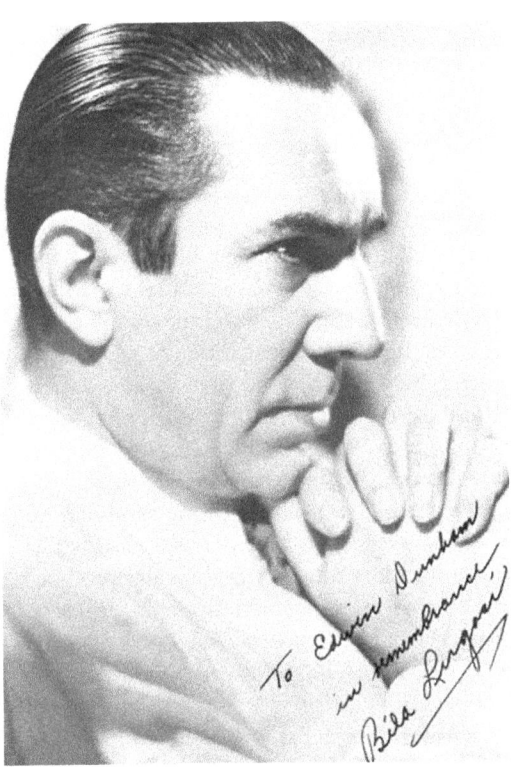

The greater profile: did John Barrymore make a film as well-known as *Dracula* (1931)?

The basic details of Lugosi's life reveal a man with a passionate interest in

Bela Lugosi, ravin' at Boris Karloff in a scene from *The Raven* (1935).

both stage and screen. Born Béla Blasko on October 20, 1882, in Lugos, Hungary, he was a banker's son with a flair for the dramatic. He attended the Budapest Academy of Theatrical Arts, learning the weighty, histrionic style so necessary for reaching audiences in the far rows of a theater that might not have the best lighting or acoustics. For silent films he used the name Arisztid Olt. A union organizer, he was successful with theater owners but less so with the increasingly powerful Communist regime. In 1919 he escaped to Germany, made some films there, and arrived in America in 1921. The 1927 stage production of *Dracula* was a Broadway sensation, and after touring with it, he was able to win the coveted title role for the film. Legend has it that Lugosi was also a prime candidate to play the monster in Universal's production of *Frankenstein*. He tested for the role, but as make-up man Jack Pierce put it, "Lugosi thought his ideas were better than everybody's."

Whether it was ultimately a quarrel over the make-up that would distort his features, or the lack of dialogue, Lugosi was unhappy, and Universal wasn't thrilled with either the screenplay or proposed director, Robert Florey. The *Frankenstein* project was eventually re-worked, with Karloff as star and James Whale as director.

Evidently as a form of concession, the following year the studio assigned Florey to an adaptation of Poe's "Murders in the Rue Morgue," with Lugosi, sans elaborate make-up, as the star. From there, Universal teamed Bela and Boris in a pair of classics very loosely based on Poe's works.

He can Count on trouble: Dwight Frye, as Renfield, is going to rabidly lose his mind to Bela Lugosi's *Dracula* (1931).

In *The Black Cat*, Bela offers a masterfully delivered sound-byte. When he hears a derisive put-down of "supernatural baloney," he takes massive umbrage and slowly declares: "Supernatural ... perhaps. Bah-low-ney, perhaps *not!*"

David Manners, who worked with Bela and Boris in *The Black Cat*, still had vivid images of the rivals when interviewed by Rick McKay for *Scarlet Street* magazine (January 1999) at the age of 97: "Karloff. Very grand, but so withdrawn. But he was always polite. A gentleman." As for Lugosi: "Oh, I never did get to know him—not really. He was not someone I cared to know. Not really."

Universal didn't care much for Lugosi either. The studio returned Karloff to starring roles and relegated Lugosi to a patchwork of B-movies. Lugosi's work for the remainder of the decade offered very few standouts: some vampire films for MGM, an A-film credit in *Ninotchka*, and the bizarre role of Ygor in *Son of Frankenstein* (1939).

Since actors were often booked on radio shows only when they had important films to promote, Lugosi rarely received an invitation. It was probably in an attempt to promote *Son of Frankenstein* that co-stars Boris Karloff and Bela Lugosi dropped by *Baker's Broadcast*, a show featuring Ozzie and Harriet Nelson. During the show, Bela insisted he wasn't like his strong, vicious image:

HARRIET: You have a weak heart?
BELA: Oh, but definitely, my dear. I get scared like anything.

Bela wanted Nintendo, Boris wanted Wii, so they settled on chess: Lugosi and Karloff try to check each other in *The Black Cat* (1934).

> HARRIET: Oh! I don't believe it.
> BELA: If someone says boo to me, I'm liable to faint.
> OZZIE: Boo!
> BELA: That's why I was never able to look at my pictures. Once I saw myself in Dracula and I was home in bed for a week!

Physically unrecognizable as the snaggletoothed, shaggy-haired Ygor in *Son of Frankenstein*, Lugosi remained "Dracula" to the general public. In 1939 he appeared as "Mr. Dracula" on *Texaco Star Theater*, and was obligingly bloodthirsty in an odd sketch called "Dracula at Sunnybrook Farm." The rubes on the farm offer up deadpan gags:

> PAW: Lookie there, Maw, a dead body just come rollin' down the stairs.
> MAW: Anyone we know?
> PAW: Yep, yep, I reckon it's our eldest son Herman.
> MAW: How can ya tell, Paw, he ain't got no face left.
> PAW: Well, I know them suspenders anywhere. Somebody probably killed him, Maw. I don't see how the boy could bite himself in the neck that way.
> MAW: Well now, I don't know, Paw, Herman was mighty clever. How many killin's we had this week?
> PAW: Five of our kids and the hired man. Makes me mad; we got plenty of kids but help is scarce!

They hope the weird doings don't cause "star border Mr. Dracula" to leave. Lugosi enters with an appropriately ghoulish and elongated greeting, complete with low, stagey laugh:

"Good *morning* ... heh heh heh..." He claims to have had a rough night: "I didn't sleep at all. Last night I was out on a bat!" With many a sinister chuckle during the small-talk, he invites the remaining members of the family up to his room. Systematically they exit with a scream and go thumping down the stairs. Finally the (still-attached) head of the household puts her foot down:

> MAW: I just want you to know, I's anemic! When you first came here, eight of us used to sit around the kitchen range. Now you and I gotta have a talk before you become the lone ranger.
> LUGOSI: I murdered them all!
> MAW: Aw gee, why did you do that? Murder's an awful bad habit to get into. It's worse than chewing tobacco. Now aren't you ashamed killing all those innocent people? Everywhere you look, bodies!
> LUGOSI: All right. So I ain't neat!

The uncharacteristic slang gives that last line some added laughs. It was a favorite ploy of radio comedy writers to try and get a well-known star to play against type.

This was further evidenced on his *Mail Call* guest spot. Lugosi acknowledges the problem of being a horror star as he plays off fussy character actor Edward Everett Horton:

> LUGOSI: This is Bayla Loogosi.... Everybody here in the United States thinks of me only as a character in horror pictures.... I wouldn't mind being a monster for the rest of my life, honest I wouldn't, if only one picture, one teensy weensy little picture, I could play a nice guy! It would be so wonderful!
> HORTON: There, there, Mr. Lugosi, I know exactly how you feel — in every movie I've ever made, I cringe. Like this: oh, oh dear..."

Guest Gregory Ratoff toys with the idea of casting Horton as a werewolf, and Lugosi as a typical college student, but the script coasts on easy wordplay:

> "Bela, Bela, pull in your fangs!"
> "What?"
> "Fangs!"
> "Oh you're welcome!"

Despite the plentiful horror programs on the air, ones that so regularly featured Boris Karloff or Vincent Price, Bela's dramatic output consists of only three surviving shows. It's possible that part of the problem was that Karloff and Price were often in Broadway productions, with access to New York's radio studios, and Lugosi was at a disadvantage living on the West coast.

Lugosi's dramatic roles in "The Doctor Prescribed Death" and "Thirsty Death" date from 1943 and 1944, at a time when his film career was in serious B-movie decline, and he was prone to touring in stage productions and one-man shows. Apparently he was in New York at the right time to star in "The Doctor Prescribed Death" during the first season of *Suspense*.

Always able to wrench the best out of far-fetched coincidences and overdramatic dialogue, Lugosi's ripe and over-the-top personality makes this a memorable show. As Dr. Antonio Basile, he tells his publisher about a crackpot notion (or "thee-o-ree," as he calls it) that he's convinced can work: "As a psychologist I have worked out a theory, a theory I know to be sound. I contend that a person who has decided to kill himself can very easily be turned from *this* desire to taking the life of another! I can prove my theory, and, if necessary, that is exactly what I will do!"

"Suppose it will? What good have you accomplished if you can prove it will work?"

This naturally prompts a paranoid reply: "You've never liked me!" Then comes the

Front and back of the Mark 56 release of "The Doctor Prescribed Death" (episode from the series *Suspense*). Helping to make up for the chintzy 15 minutes per side, the label called on Bela Lugosi, Jr., to step to the microphone for a brief introduction.

inevitable threat: "I show you whether I'm insane!" Then he repeats himself: "I know you don't like me, but I'm going to prove that my theory's sound! Tonight!"

Bela goes to the aptly named Suicide Bridge, finds a woman about to jump, and convinces her that she's being foolish. The jilted girl is hypnotized by Lugosi logic: "Why shouldn't *he* be the one to suffer?" Lugosi repeats, "He should be made to suffer ... kill him instead. He double-crossed you. He deserved it.... You won't get caught if you follow my instructions. I know!"

When Lugosi returns to the publisher's house and explains that his theory is about to be proven true, he's ridiculed: "The whole idea is mad.... And for heaven's sake, stop laughing!"

Those that wish to discover and enjoy this old show should skip this paragraph. For those who want to know just how coincidental and ludicrous the plot is ... as it turns out, the woman Lugosi has saved from killing herself was jilted by his own book publisher! Even more coincidental, Lugosi had no knowledge of this until she happened to show him a picture of the cad carrying on with a new lover. And the new lover is ... Lugosi's own wife! When he discovers his wife's treachery, he amazingly controls himself enough to incorporate the problem into his plot. He has the suicidal woman shoot the publisher with his wife's gun. The wife is neatly incriminated and all is well—except that Lugosi's theory is *not* sound. The woman commits the homicide but then continues on with her suicide, leaving behind a note that explains all that happened. Facing jail, Lugosi does the only thing that makes sense (in this script). He jumps out a window. Thus, the show's narrator snarls, "His entire theory worked—in reverse!"

With Karloff a regular on *Inner Sanctum*, and Peter Lorre hosting a summer series of *Mystery in the Air*, it seemed inevitable that someone would tap Lugosi for a regular series. He had his chance with a pilot for a show to be titled *Mystery House*. The episode was titled "Thirsty Death."

The announcer, quite the optimist, erroneously notes, "Bela Lugosi is currently being starred in a series of *Mystery House* pictures at Universal Studios..." At the time, Lugosi was lucky to get even bit parts at Universal. Mostly he was mired at Monogram. Before this radio broadcast he had been in *The Corpse Vanishes*, *Bowery at Midnight*, and the Bowery Boys entry, *Spooks Run Wild*. After the broadcast, he would be back at Monogram in *The Ape Man* and yet another Bowery Boys effort, *Ghosts on the Loose*.

The Universal movie alluded to in the pilot episode of *Mystery House* was a production called *House of Mystery*, which was ultimately released under a new title, *Night Monster*. Typical for Lugosi (who was killed off after a very brief scene in Universal's *The Wolf Man*), this Universal film had only a small "red herring" role for him.

If Universal execs ever heard Bela's *Mystery House* show, it didn't inspire them to sponsor it as a radio series or turn it into a film project. Ironically, Universal instead began to adapt radio's *Inner Sanctum* for a low-rent series of "Inner Sanctum Mystery" movies starring Lon Chaney, Jr. (an actor who had never appeared in an *Inner Sanctum* radio show).

The "thirsty death" of Lugosi's *Mystery House* refers to a symptom of hydrophobia. The familiar jungle horror tale includes the requisite frightened natives, rabid howling dogs and a breathless heroine who is the source of all the trouble.

With husband Lugosi away, his wife (Lurene Tuttle) journeys through uncivilized terrain to the home of her ex-lover (John Carradine): "I couldn't bear to remain home. I was afraid." Husky-voiced Carradine is in a romantic mood: "You don't love him, you never have! Darling, come away with me. I'll make you happy, I swear I will."

Lugosi arrives soon after, and he seems to know his wife is nearby: "A comfortable place you have here—just the kind of place that would appeal to my wife. We're thinking of building next year, and if you don't mind, I'd like to take a look at the bedroom."

"No! I'd rather you didn't!"

"Oh? The bedroom is occupied, perhaps?"

"The bedroom is in a frightful mess.... I must remind you it must soon be dark."

"You think I should be on my way?"

Lugosi admits he has patients to care for—poor wretches in the throes of terminal rabies—so he makes a convenient exit ... only to return when they least expect it:

"Aren't you happy to see your devoted husband again?"

"What sort of comedy do you think you're playing?"

"A romantic one, but only as a supporting player. I am sure you'll be the first to admit that."

"We can explain everything if you'll only give us a chance, you blind, stupid jealous fool!"

Lugosi has a fiendish plan:

"I'm not mad, but unfortunately it will be impossible to say the same about one of you." Having killed a rabid dog, "I filled my

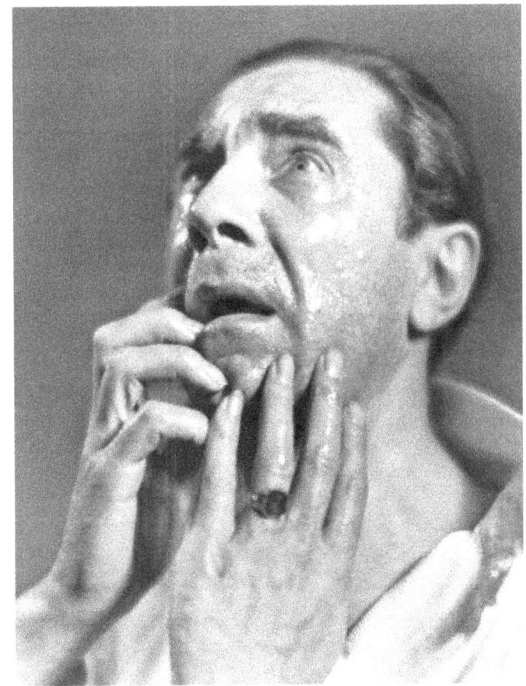

Bela Lugosi sweats it out in a moment that evokes his jungle radio episode *The Thirsty Death*.

hypodermic needle with its saliva. It's saliva brimming with hydrophobia. Then I came back here, came back all the way through the forest. I came back with my hypodermic needle!"

He claims to have injected "just one of you ... ha ha ha. Very soon you'll find out. Very soon the one who is infected will begin to feel the symptoms.... When the mad person attacks the healthy person, the knife will prove useful! Ha ha ha ... goodbye!"

As with so many twist-ending suspense tales, the balloon of ever-increasing tension yields a flatulent raspberry when there's no explosive pay-off.

In this case (for those who want to know the ending), mad doctor Lugosi has only pretended to have injected the wife or lover, but his wife imagines she has all the symptoms of hydrophobia. Her lover, seeking to put her out of her misery, uses the knife that the doctor left behind. The "joke" is on the doctor, who has discovered, too late, a note from his wife indicating she had no intention of agreeing to Carradine's hopes for rekindling their romance.

While Karloff's *Lights Out* and *Inner Sanctum* shows were crisp and histrionic, the moldiness of Lugosi's jungle melodrama could hardly have encouraged radio executives to pick up *Mystery House*. Complicated and tiresome plots were now all too standard in the burgeoning world of *Weird Circle*, *Creaking Door* and other imitative, contrived radio horror shows. Horror was no longer a draw at movie theaters, and was losing its sting on radio, too.

The idea of casting Lugosi as a jilted husband was also not in keeping with his image. In an interview for the January 1931 *Motion Picture Classic* (titled "The Feminine Love of Horror," and written by Gladys Hall) he declared:

> It is women who love horror.... Women wrote me letters. Ah, what letters women wrote me. Young girls. Women from seventeen to thirty. Letters of a horrible hunger. Asking me if I cared only for maiden's blood. Asking me if I had done the play because I was in reality that sort of Thing. And through these letters, couched in terms of shuddering, transparent fear, there ran the hideous note of—hope. They hoped that I was Dracula. They hoped that my love was the love of Dracula.... It was the embrace of Death their subconscious was yearning for. Death, the final triumphant lover.
>
> It made me know that the women of America are unsatisfied, famished, craving sensation, even though it be the sensation of death draining the red blood of life.

These vintage Lugosi lines prove him a better dramatist than the authors of most of his radio scripts. He also had a flare for creating unusual theories. He once said:

> It is women who love horror. Gloat over it. Feed on it. Are nourished by it. Shudder and cling and cry out—and come back for more. Women have a predestination to suffering. It is women who bear the race in bloody agony. Suffering is a kind of horror. Blood is a kind of horror. Therefore women are born with a predestination to horror in their very blood stream. It is a biological thing.

It seemed that women may have been losing their enthusiasm for the aging vampire—and his main audience now was people looking for a laugh. Familiarity seemed to help breed comic contempt, and after more than a decade as a legitimate spook, Lugosi's screen roles were getting a bit campy, as he played a foil in movies opposite the East Side Kids and then Abbott & Costello.

Lugosi seemed to be a good sport about it, perhaps hoping that by kidding his horror image he'd be accepted for some other type of work.

His 1943 spot with Fred Allen was primarily a publicity gimmick. Appeasing Universal's publicists, he makes sure to mention *Frankenstein Meets the Wolf Man*, a film having the unpleasant irony of Lugosi forced into the Frankenstein make-up and mute role of his rival Karloff.

Fred Allen, always fair and mindful that his own looks were the fodder for comedy, allowed Lugosi to fire a line at him: "You look like something that fell out of the closet the night I was on *Inner Sanctum*." (No, it didn't seem to make any difference to the writers that Karloff had starred on that show, but never Lugosi.)

After Fred cracks that Bela was caught "shoplifting in a blood bank," and promotes *Frankenstein Meets the Wolf Man*, Bela describes the monster business:

> BELA: Hissing to an actor who plays monsters is applause.
> FRED: They say that a radiator started hissing and Karloff got up and took four bows.
> BELA: Yes, yes, when people stop hissing Karloff and me, we'll be through.
> FRED: And when people start hissing me, I'll be through! And it could start tonight.
> BELA: With your face, Fred, you could go into the monster business.

Another reason Bela wasn't often on radio probably had to do with his sight-reading skill—or lack thereof. Often a script was constantly changing and being edited for time right up to broadcast. With English a second language, he was always wary of sounding foolish, and without a lot of time to study the nuances of a script, an embarrassing mistake could be broadcast to millions of people.

In a sketch in which Fred subleases Lugosi's haunted home, the script reads: "Drop up this afternoon. If I am not home, go in and look around." When Lugosi miscalculates the cadence and the comma, the sharp veteran Allen fires a quip that seems to momentarily shame and fluster the serious and sensitive Hungarian:

> FRED: May I see your house?
> BELA: Sure, here is the address. Drop up this afternoon.
> FRED (expecting Lugosi to continue): Fine. [long pause]
> BELA: Eh, if I'm not home.
> FRED (reacting to the awkward silence): I thought you'd left for home! [laughter from the audience, and a smattering of applause over Allen's quick remark]
> BELA (grimly): "Anyhow, if I am not home, go in and look around, Fred. Here's the key. I'll see you later.

Bela Lugosi raised smiles with some soggy bad jokes on radio, as this publicity still might indicate.

Lugosi doesn't get many lines in the show's big sketch; perhaps the writers anticipated disaster. When Fred finally visits Lugosi's haunted house, he encounters various female ghouls and even a disembodied head, with plenty of veteran radio performers handling the roles. Only in the last few minutes does Bela once again meet Fred Allen. Fred grabs hold of Bela and quips, "Gad, your hand is clammy, it's like holding five eels with hangnails." There's a sudden noise.

"What was that shriek?" asks Fred.

"It was nothing. It came from the furnace."

"The furnace?"

"Yes, I used to burn oil, but I converted to people."

Ultimately, as with a Karloff guest-spot (which had the same damn hand joke), Fred discovers that the Hollywood horror star is a real-life madman:

"You lured me here to kill me. You're mad, Lugosi, mad!"

"I'm making a monster greater than Frankenstein's. I'm building a radio monster! I will use the brain of Red Skelton. The body of Skinnay Ennis. And the singing voice of Georgie Jessel."

"What do you want from *me*?"

"I've heard your program. My monster needs a lot of nerve!"

At this point, 1943, it had been nearly a decade since Karloff and Lugosi had received equal billing in *The Black Cat* and *The Raven*. He was more likely to joke around with a radio comedian, and glower at the film antics of a Leo Gorcey or Lou Costello. Perhaps some of the joking inspired him to simply not take himself too seriously.

Carroll Borland recalled that Lugosi could show a wicked sense of humor. One night during a West Coast revival of *Dracula*, a dramatic and quiet moment was fractured by a woman in the audience. She could be heard holding a brainless conversation with her friend, saying, "I always fry mine in butter." Lugosi had to control himself ... from laughing:

> He was not offended; he was just delighted. Another night I was limp, over his arm, and as he leaned over he slipped an ice cube down my neck! This was Bela Lugosi! Very childlike; he was a childish man. I suppose I shouldn't say that, but he was very simple. But he was a charmer.... Lugosi had this marvelous sense of humor that nobody ever saw.

On Rudy Vallee's *Fleischman Hour*, he co-starred in a quickie opposite flighty, air-headed actress Billie Burke. The naïve Miss Burke wants to rent Bela's haunted house. Her silly, squeaky voice is a comic contrast to his deliberately slow and spooky cadence.

> BELA: Do come in, won't you?
> BILLIE: Do you always lock the door?
> BELA: Yes. One never knows who might try to get out.
> BILLIE: Out?
> BELA: Yes.
> BILLIE: Don't you mean "in"?
> BELA: No.
> BILLIE: My name is Billie Burke, and your name is?
> BELA (with elaborate mystery): I'm the Bat ... look into my eyes. [sudden scream] I take parts of people and put them together ... I'm building a human being.... All I need is a brain.
> BILLIE: Well, don't feel badly, we can't all be quiz kids.
> BELA: Look into my eyes, I am a vampire.
> BILLIE: I thought you said you were an old bat.
> BELA: I am a vampire bat. Have you ever heard of a vampire?
> BILLIE: Certainly, at baseball games they always say "Kill the Vampire!"
> BELA: I eat meat—raw meat—three times a day. Now do you know what I am?
> BILLIE: You're a capitalist.

Lugosi faithfully gave his lines the overdramatic enunciations expected of him—a comic contrast to the chirps of Billie Burke.

Similarly, he plays a grimly dangerous scientist opposite quipster Bob Hope and twittery, lemony-voiced character actor Sterling Holloway for a wartime *Command Performance* half-hour sitcom.

In this burlesque of Superman, Bob Hope takes the first half of the show to flirt with

Paulette Goddard (as Lois Lane). When mad scientist Lugosi (as Dr. Bikini) exclaims to a victim, "You will suffer! Suffer! SUFFER!" fluty Holloway (as Atoll, his assistant) hoots, "Gee, you scared me, too!"

Dr. Bikini magnanimously declares, "Atoll, you have been working hard, so I'm going to double your weekly allowance—this week you get two pints of blood. After all, you are smart. You have a head on your shoulders." Atoll whines desperately, "Oh! Get it off!!!"

Getting even with the "noisy King Sisters upstairs," Lugosi manages to get the singing group into his power: "Let us throw the King sisters into the soap machine. King Sisters, forward march!"

"Hey Alice, bring up the rear."

"I can't, I'm not built that way."

After this wartime double-entendre gets the biggest laugh of the night, Lugosi supervises the bizarre transformation of singing stars into soap. One assumes that this plot device was written with no knowledge of the soap-making and lampshade-creating techniques the Nazis had been performing in concentration camps.

> LUGOSI: Now they're in! Now start the machine! These girls will make wonderful bars of soap!
> HOLLOWAY: Think we can get 16 cakes out of each bar of soap?
> LUGOSI: No, they are still the King Sisters. No matter how you slice them, you will only get eight to the bar.

This surviving radio broadcast may have been the highlight of the mid–40s for Lugosi. His film career and personal life would soon skid to a new low. Around 1948, seeking treatment for "shooting pains" in his legs, most likely sciatica, he was prescribed morphine and was soon hopelessly addicted. He managed to get off morphine, but only to try methadone and Demerol. He also took barbiturates to be able to sleep. His career was also in a haze.

His obscurity is evidenced by his pathetic guest spot on *Candid Microphone*. How could someone not recognize Bela Lugosi—in face, or in voice? A woman browsing the antique shop where he has been planted is totally oblivious to his spooky talk and his outrageous accent:

"That's an original skull with the original hair on it. Do you like it?"

"That's certainly unusual. I don't know..."

"This was originally an arm bone of a young girl in Africa. When she was sacrificed by their gods, her lover saved her bone and made a pipe out of it. Isn't that lovely?"

"Mmm."

Lugosi doesn't seem to be making much of an impression, and without a script, he flails on, ad-libbing what he hopes will be horrific or funny material.

"You have a wonderful skull," he tells the woman, with grand insinuation. "In a civilized country like America I cannot get enough skulls. As far as the law is concerned I need a donation from the party who would like to leave me their skulls. Would you do that?"

"No."

"If I could manufacture something practical out of it?"

"I imagine you could," the customer shrugs.

"I could make of your skull a tobacco jar. So any time I stuffed my pipe I would have to think of you."

The woman hasn't shown much fear, shock, disgust or amusement. Lugosi brings it to a close, confiding, "That little chat we had now was recorded."

She's vaguely surprised, and still isn't sure she's in the presence of a movie star. Lugosi doesn't even mention his most famous role:

"May I introduce myself. My name is Bela Lugosi."
"Really?"
"King of the Zombies."
"I don't believe it!"

By the time the serious monster movies collapsed and it was time for *Abbott and Costello Meet Frankenstein*, in 1948, Dracula had been played by John Carradine in *House of Dracula* and *House of Frankenstein*. Carradine was not considered for the Dracula role in the Abbott and Costello picture—but neither was Lugosi. A studio memo dated September 9, 1947, had Ian Keith set for the part; but, fortunately, Bela had some lobbyists help in this last-ditch effort to rescue his career and his "Dracula" identity, even if it was in a comedy.

Lugosi's view on humor was quite serious. As quoted in Arthur Lennig's book *The Count* (page 199), "You can't make people believe in you if you play a horror part with your tongue in your cheek," Lugosi said. "The screen magnifies everything, even the way you are thinking. If you are not serious, people will sense it. No matter how hokum or highly melodramatic the horror part may be, you must believe in it while you are playing it."

Interviewed by the *New York Times* after coming aboard for the film, Lugosi insisted: "There is no burlesque for me. All I have to do is frighten the boys, a perfectly appropriate activity. My trademark will be unblemished."

Bela appeared on Abbott and Costello's radio show to promote the film and further menace the comedy team. Lon Chaney, Jr., appeared separately on a different episode. The two never got along, especially when the hulking, jovial Chaney would address the austere Hungarian as "Pops!"

Bud and Lou's radio visit to Lugosi is just an excuse for some bad puns, made memorable by the personalities involved:

LUGOSI: Come in. I make myself a sandwich.
LOU: What kind of a sandwich?
LUGOSI: It's a rattlesnake burger, covered with pickled toads and diced bat wings.
LOU: Do you put ketchup on it?
LUGOSI: What, to get heartburn? No! It's too bad you won't be here for breakfast. We are having Shrouded Wheat.
BUD: Hey Costello, look at that funny looking machine over there in the corner.
LUGOSI: That's my Sears machine. On that, I manufacture robots.
LOU: Get it, Abbott? Sears Robots!

A few years later only Chaney Jr. would receive an invitation to appear with Bud and Lou for a live TV show. This was probably for the best, since Lugosi was aging, and found it difficult to both memorize lines for live television and deal with ad-libbing comedians. He learned this the hard way after starring with Milton Berle in a 1949 *Texaco Star Theater*. The fast-paced comic's timing didn't match the old horror star's pace, and Berle was quick to let the audience know. He quipped to the audience that Lugosi "could kill jokes" even better than people.

In 1949 Lugosi was facing a crisis. Movie roles were sparse. Television was not an option. His drug addiction was worsening. The golden era of radio drama had long passed, along with *Inner Sanctum* and *Lights Out*. The old-fashioned monsters were out. With real-life crime drama still grinding away on radio, Lugosi played out his last important dramatic radio role on *Crime Doesn't Pay*.

He played a sociopath with twin desires for women and fire—and the convenient gambit of disposing of his women via his pyromania. *Crime Doesn't Pay* was a low-budget variation on *Dragnet* and *Gangbusters*, and Lugosi's lurid episode was titled "Gasoline Cocktail."

As fire engine sirens wail in the background, he floridly cries, "I'm going out! The fire is near here!"

His wife, also possessing a Hungarian accent, grumbles, "You and your fires. What are you, a little boy? Stop chasing fire engines. Grow up."

"That was my mistake. Growing up."

"Of all the silly things to say."

"Silly? What else is there to do for excitement?"

"I could mention a few things—like taking your wife out, for instance."

"I mean real excitement! Action! Like the ladders going up, the hoses dragged up the fire escapes. People jumping into nets. All the bells! The sirens!"

Later he waxes nostalgic: "In the old days in Budapest you ran after the engines with me."

"Now I wish I hadn't."

"There was excitement then. Now what? A job to go to, with men I would not care to look at. And back to this, this house, day after day, night after night."

The story slowly burns and sputters along a familiar melodramatic line. It turns out Lugosi has been cheating on his wife and taking other flames to the fires. Sometimes he's the firebug who started the blaze. When one woman demands marriage, and Lugosi can't oblige since he has a bored wife at home, the relationship comes to a fatal end.

"Is love nothing in this country without marriage?" Lugosi fumes. "Again, I'm rejected!" Always able to turn the pathological and illogical into logic, Lugosi makes the hokum believable, even as the story turns into a routine police procedural, the cops finding clues to track down the man who has left a trail of burnt buildings and burnt-out women.

Bela's little speech after the drama ends has some of the illogic of his radio character, Nick Segadin. He does a pretty decent job of reading a badly worded script overloaded with commas and pauses:

> Legally, Nick was sane, and he paid the penalty exacted by society. But society itself bears a large part of Nick's guilt. Nick never found proper training and education. Nick never found the opportunity to release his energies in the right direction. So you see, as always, it comes back to us, the responsible citizens of our community. If we see to it, that the roots of crime, the social conditions which bring gangsters and warped people like Nick, are removed, we have taken a long step on the way to a better world for ourselves as well as the criminals. Crime does not pay!

Lugosi was a "responsible citizen" of his community, and a rare extant copy of a local radio show (few of these were preserved back then) offers an example of Lugosi talking about topical issues rather than his acting career. At the time, Lugosi was starring in a stage production of *Arsenic and Old Lace*.

The dull 15-minute public affairs program, *Quarter Hour with William S. Gillmore* (sponsored by Stuhmer's Bakery), characterizes guest Lugosi as: "A Catholic, a Democrat, and a man who is interested in helping to bring real liberation to his native land, Hungary." The host pronounces Bela's name with an accent on the third syllable. He's "Mr. Lou-go SEE."

As president of the Hungarian Council for Democracy, Lugosi was promoting a speech on "The New Liberated Hungary" at the Manhattan Center: "Our position is that the liberation of the Hungarian people, as well as all people who have lived under Fascism, will be a logical outcome of the policies of Roosevelt." Lugosi notes that the Hungarian underground is the "common denominator of resistance which binds all the people who have felt the whiplash of Fascism. Like the heroic people of France, and Poland, and Greece and Yugoslavia, the people of Hungary, the real Hungary, are fighting!"

Lugosi fought his drug addiction, and in 1955 he had himself committed to the California State Hospital as a drug addict, a rare example of a celebrity admitting to using narcotics. It got him more publicity than he'd seen in decades ... but no film offers.

Fortunately, two *Dracula* fans came to his rescue. His fifth and final wife, Hope, had sent him encourage fan letters of "hope." He was glad to have the stability of a wife to come home to. Another fan, Edward D. Wood, Jr., buoyed him professionally by making him the star of a few notorious low-budget movies, with promises of more.

Lugosi was still reading scripts and hoping for a miracle when he quietly died. His wife, used to his habit of taking naps, wasn't particularly alarmed when she noticed him in the throes of a deep sleep one day. When she finally decided to take a better look, she discovered that he had died. He was buried in his Dracula cape, which gave one last thrill to friends and fans attending the funeral.

Lugosi's end, August 16, 1956, came well before the arrival of *Famous Monsters of Filmland* magazine, the "Monster Mash" hit single, *The Munsters* TV show and the rest of the "monster mania" pop culture explosion of the mid–60s. The fad that would replenish the interest in Boris Karloff and Vincent Price, both of whom made many recordings, only had fans wondering why there were no discs in the record store featuring Bela Lugosi.

Only one audio performance exists via a large "transcription disc." It's a reading of Poe's "The Tell-Tale Heart." It seems to date from around 1946. Bela may have recorded it for his agent, who would have been deputized to make copies and send them out to anyone interested in booking Bela's solo stage act (which included an enactment of the Poe tale). It may also have been recorded by a radio station to promote Lugosi's appearance at a local venue. There's a slight possibility Lugosi envisioned a release on 78 rpm—as Sidney Greenstreet once recorded a 2-disc set of "Cask of Amontillado."

Don't knock Wood; Ed gave Bela Lugosi hope for better days, as he poses in costume for what ended up as *Plan 9 from Outer Space* (1959).

Lugosi's rendition of "The Tell-Tale Heart" is certainly as valid (if a bit more florid) than the extant recordings from other narrators. The only unintentional laugh to be found is when Lugosi's buoyant tongue travels too quickly across one of the lines. He misses the "so" before the "no," declaring: "If you think me mad, you will think no longer."

Lugosi said in the cracked Universal classic *The Raven* in 1935, "Poe, you are avenged!" For those who, during his lifetime, praised a John Barrymore or a Paul Muni over Lugosi, the Hungarian horror star is "avenged," too—his films, his memorabilia, and his radio shows are more in demand than most any items from the more critically praised stars of his generation.

Radio

Baker's Broadcast. March 13, 1938. Boris Karloff and Bela Lugosi appear together and sing "We're Horrible, Horrible Men." Lugosi also gets to banter with comfy hubby-and-wife team Ozzie and Harriet.

The Tuesday Program. October 17, 1939, CBS, 30 min. Walter O'Keefe hosted an interview/variety show which featured Lugosi and special guest Mary Martin.

The Texaco Star Theatre. November 15, 1939, CBS, 60 min. A variety show offering both comic and dramatic sketches. From Hollywood, host Ken Murray presents Bela Lugosi in the silly satire "Dracula of Sunnybrook Farm," while New York host Burns Mantel presides over "The Criminal Code," a prison drama with Burgess Meredith. Other guests: Frances Langford, Kenny Baker, Irene Ryan, Jimmy Wallington, Helen Claire and Arthur Byron.

Kay Kyser's Kollege of Musical Knowledge. September 25, 1940, 60 min. Cornball Kyser managed to land the three major horror stars of the day for his surprisingly flat *You'll Find Out*. Boris Karloff, Bela Lugosi and Peter Lorre helped promote the film via this episode of Kay's radio show, which apparently has been long lost.

Play Broadcast. May 2, 1941, Mutual, 30 min. Bill Anson was the host of this quiz show. Lugosi happened to be in Chicago where the show originated, and dropped by for a brief promotional visit.

Three-Ring Time. March 6, 1942, Blue Network. Milton Berle is the host, with Peter Lorre and Bela Lugosi. No copies of this have survived.

Suspense. February 2, 1943, CBS, 30 min. "The Doctor Prescribed Death." Mad Doctor Lugosi has a theory that someone about to commit suicide could just as easily be re-directed into committing homicide instead. Starring Bela Lugosi, Geraldine Fitzgerald, Lou Merrill and host Joseph Kearns as "the Man in Black."

Texaco Star Theatre. April 25, 1943. Bela Lugosi guests on Fred Allen's program for some dry humor and vivid wordplay.

Revenge of the Vampire promo spot. October 1943. Around Halloween of 1943, some radio stations ran a two-minute speech from Lugosi which was produced by Columbia Studios. They were

Bela Lugosi recorded "The Raven" on disc, and is seen here as a Poe-obsessed doctor in the film of the same name.

releasing a new vampire film starring Lugosi, and he wanted to tell the listening audience, "Don't think that you are safe from vampires. Oh no! Supernatural beings are not chained to their graves. They are free to roam the entire world"—at a theater near you.

Mystery House. 1944, NBC, 30 min. "The Thirsty Death." Bela Lugosi, John Carradine and Lurene Tuttle star in a jungle melodrama involving hydrophobia and the evil games of a jealous husband. This was the "pilot" episode for a proposed series. It bears no relation to the radio series *Mystery House*, which was syndicated in 1946 and starred Nanette Sargent and Forrest Lewis as Barbara and Dan Glenn, book publishers (à la Random House) with an interest in crime.

Quarter Hour with William S. Gallmor. April 23, 1944. For a local broadcast, Lugosi discusses politics.

Mail Call. May 11, 1944. Bela Lugosi, Edward Everett Horton and Gregory Ratoff appear in a sketch on this wartime variety series.

Command Performance, Program #238. Fall, 1946, 30 min. Usually this variety series (circulated via transcript for broadcast to servicemen overseas) offered sketches and songs. Here, instead of variety acts, the half hour offers a compete parody of "Superman," with Bob Hope as Clark Kent, Paulette Goddard as Lois Lane, Bela Lugosi as the mad scientist "Bikini" and Sterling Holloway as his assistant "Atoll."

House Party. October 6, 1949. Art Linkletter was the host of the *House Party*, which was on radio before moving on to a long television run.

The Rudy Vallee Show. October 22, 1946. With guests Bela Lugosi and Billie Burke.

The Candid Microphone. October 24, 1947, 30 min. Allen Funt, host. Bela Lugosi hasn't much to do when he replaces a shopkeeper and tries to sell an unsuspecting woman a bunch of ghoulish items. Since she is too foggy to recognize Bela's voice or accent, she's equally oblivious to his attempts to shock her with talk about buying and selling skulls.

The Adventures of Ellery Queen. March 19, 1947, CBS, 30 min. "The Specialist in Cops." One of the special features in some episodes of the series was a guest appearance by a celebrity who, like the "armchair detective" home listener, would sit and puzzle over the solution. Unfortunately, as with the episodes that featured Orson Welles, Lucille Ball, Helen Hayes and Edward Everett Horton, the Lugosi program is presumed forever lost.

The Abbott and Costello Show. May 5, 1948, ABC, 30 min. The old reliable script: Jittery comic visits the home of a horror star. Starring Bud Abbott, Lou Costello, Elvia Allman, Sidney Fields, and Bela Lugosi.

Tales of Fatima. September 10, 1949, CBS, 30 min. "The Men in the Shadows." Bela Lugosi guests on the mystery program starring Basil Rathbone. Only one episode of Rathbone's show has survived, and this isn't it.

Crime Does Not Pay. December 12, 1949, MGM syndication, 30 min. "Gasoline Cocktail." Working from a script by Ira Marion, Bela Lugosi stars in a pyromaniac drama that could provide thrills or laughs, depending on the listener.

Audio

Lugosi's "Thirsty Death" radio episode of *Mystery Playhouse* was released as part of the box set *Great Radio Horror Shows* (Mystery Hill 933977), and "The Doctor Prescribed

The modest grave marker for the immortal count, Bela Lugosi.

Death" was issued by two different record companies—as *Command Performance* #5 (a half hour of Boris Karloff in "Arsenic and Old Lace" is on the flip side) and *Mark 56* #611 (with the broadcast divided into 15 minutes for each side).

Snippets from "Dracula" are on *An Evening with Boris Karloff and His Friends* (Decca DL 4833 and DL 74833 stereo), and the soundtrack to Lugosi's Bowery Boys film *Spooks Run Wild* is part of *The East Side Kids Come Out Fighting* (Murray Hill 57393).

The DVD *Lugosi: Hollywood's Dracula* features a bonus CD disc that includes the complete episodes of *Command Performance* and *Mystery House*, as well as snippets from *Texaco Star Theater*, *Baker's Broadcast* and his interview with William S. Gallmore. The soundtrack for *Lugosi: Hollywood's Dracula* was also issued via an indie mail order company on CD; but, being a soundtrack, it mainly features the background music, sans narration, from the documentary. It does include *Baker's Broadcast*, *Texaco Star Theater*, *Mail Call*, *The Rudy Vallee Show* and *Candid Microphone* radio appearances.

4
Vincent Price

All through his career, Vincent Price had a special appreciation for radio. In his 1978 autobiography he wrote, "I started to do radio work in 1936.... There were variety shows, dramatic shows, comedy shows, quiz shows, interview and talk shows, and series shows. I even tried my hand at soap opera." Indeed, he was in the cast of *John's Other Wife*, among others, and once estimated he'd performed over 2,000 radio roles, many of them uncredited bit parts in late '30s productions.

He felt radio audiences paid attention: "I think television audiences don't have to work—that's why they fall asleep half of the time." And he always mourned the loss of good radio. "In California, you drive enormous distances and I have the radio on all the time, and I'd like to hear something good."

It was probably this spirit that led him to take on the rather low-paying work for Caedmon Records, issuing so many albums of poetry, witch tales and Poe stories ... and to perform narration for Alice Cooper and Michael Jackson. It was all part of his fascination with the power and magic of a voice coming through a radio or through stereo speakers, sparking the imagination.

Price never believed radio was truly dead, and was willing to help out in any effort to revive the old media—including '70s efforts such as a syndicated Sears-sponsored radio show and his own *Price of Fear* British program, as well as some BBC horror broadcasts in the '80s.

For a paperback collection of stories based on his *Price of Fear* show, Vincent penned a salute to the gone but not forgotten art form:

> Radio is my favorite entertainment medium. I really mean this, though I've had a go at most of the others: stage, cinema, television, even musical comedy and the lecture platform.
>
> Radio is the neatest of all the show biz media. Neat seems a funny way to describe it, but it's, well, just neat! There doesn't seem to be that disturbing, unnerving waste of time which is so much a part of film work. It's always been well organized and, by the very nature of it, always on time. Oh how important that is to artists of any discipline! Also, it is concentrated and consecutive, it does not start in the middle and end at the beginning like so much television and film work ... and the fact of not having to memorize lines relieves the radio artist of that bugaboo of the stage.
>
> But what makes radio really exciting is the all-round creativity of it. The writer creates the original, then the director creates the ambiance for the actors, and the brilliant technicians who manipulate the tapes, dials, sounds and music create the atmosphere. But the most creative of all participants in the joys of radio are the listeners, the audience. While we in the broadcasting studio are giving our all to them, they in their turn are truly creating us. The listener is set designer, costume designer, make-up man, and even the casting department. They see the characters, they hear, then put them into the drama quite literally, in make-up, into the set, the wardrobe, even the mood and atmosphere.

4. Vincent Price

Vincent Price had a great range of vocal colors. Yes, he had the requisite voice of menace—the chilling, somber and resonant tone associated with the classic Poe tales that he recorded. But he also had a humorously fey side (exemplified by his radio role of Simon Templar on *The Saint*) and a comfortable brand of bogey-man ham that helped make "Thriller" a hit for Michael Jackson.

He was probably the most beloved and magnetic of all the horror stars because he had all their traits ... as well as his own. He was handsome in a more normal way than Lugosi, as capable of comic timing as Peter Lorre (or even Price's friend Red Skelton), as gentle and refined as Karloff, as tall and imposing as contemporary Christopher Lee, as much a roguish comic villain as Cyril Ritchard's Captain Hook, and as capable of Shakespearean excess and horrific woe as Basil Rathbone.

Vincent's voice floated indefinitely and indefinably in its own timbre and accent. Some assumed he was born in England, as Karloff was. He was actually born in St. Louis, Missouri, and in his 1978 book *Vincent Price on Vincent Price* he modestly states:

> My voice sounds just like everybody else who comes from Missouri.... I really don't think that I have an unusual voice. Of course, there are times that people recognize me over the phone, and this has happened even in Australia. But to me, it doesn't sound that way.

Vincent Leonard Price, Jr. (May 27, 1911–October 25, 1993), was the youngest of four children. He had a comfortable, affluent homelife (his father was an executive for the National Candy Company), and to complete his schooling he left the Midwest to attend Yale. After graduation, he moved on to the Courtauld Institute of the University of London, and it was in England in 1935 that he began to win serious acting assignments. When the British production of *Victoria Regina* came to Broadway, Price found himself back in America and winning glowing reviews.

As other enterprising stage stars discovered, the numbness of a Broadway run could be freshened by taking acting roles in New York's other thriving venue: radio. Vincent was keen to work with the major talents of the day, from Helen Hayes to Cornelia Otis Skinner, often appearing on local radio programs that offered scenes from current theatrical productions.

Price's daughter, in her biography of her famous father, acknowledges the importance of his radio work at the time:

> Alone in New York and ever eager to work and to learn, he quickly found a niche doing radio work. Some years later a character on the comedy radio series *Duffy's Tavern* would say of Vincent, "He's got that sweet soothing kind of a voice; you don't know whether to listen to it or pour it on a waffle." Indeed, his immediately recognizable voice and his aptitude for learning his lines fast made Vincent a natural for

Bold Evil: Vincent Price gets under the crew's skin in a guest spot on '60s TV's *Voyage to the Bottom of the Sea*.

radio, where actors were often asked to work with scant rehearsal time, disorganized or unfinished scripts, and cramped conditions. Actors who could master the medium often found they were in high demand.

She added that while he was scoring his early Broadway triumph in *Angel Street* (his first role as a murderous villain),

> He often appeared unbilled on one of the daytime radio soap operas such as *Valiant Lady* and *Helpmate*, claiming "they were such fun and you learned a whole area of acting you were never trained to do." As well as the soaps, he also participated in numerous weekly series. One of his favorite radio ventures was a serial called *Johnny Presents* with Tallulah Bankhead, who frequently asked Vincent to appear on the show.

Price had an affinity for strong, bawdy women like Bankhead. His third wife, Coral Browne, whom he'd met on the set of *Theater of Blood*, was known for her promiscuity with both sexes (prior to their marriage) and her use of profanity. Radio's outrageous Ms. Bankhead was a delight to him: "I had many a good time with Tallulah. She was a talker, full of ribald gossip, true and, better than true, made up." Backstage moments with Bankhead could literally become more like bathroom moments. Vincent recalled the time "she was sitting on my washbasin, and suddenly I realized that she was taking a leak. You know, if she hadn't been, I'd have been terribly disappointed. Because that was part of the Tallulah legend."

In an interview with Lawrence French, Vincent mentioned that even after his formative years on stage, he didn't want to give up his radio work:

> When I first went out to Hollywood as a movie actor, I had it written in my contract with 20th Century–Fox that I had the freedom to do radio. Of course there was no television at the time. But they were really very sticky about this. They were kind of angry that I should want this. I said, "I feel radio is my training ground, and that's where I want to work," so they let me do it. But of all the contract players, I was one of the few allowed to do radio, anytime I wanted to, as long as it didn't interfere with any filming. Then Fox finally put their own radio show on the air.... We did a lot of adaptations of Fox pictures: I did "Laura," "The Lodger" and "Hangover Square." Anyway there was one show where they had two little starlets. Two pretty girls who were very sweet who were up and coming stars. And ... none of them could do radio, because radio is not just getting up and reading, it is acting. Well, Lurene Tuttle was playing the Mother on the show, and after a day of rehearsal they told one of the little starlets she would have to go, so Lurene took over that part. Then the following day they got rid of the next starlet and Lurene took her part. It ended up with Lurene playing five or six different parts. Lurene was a great friend of mine, and had been a great leading lady on the stage, but it ended up with me being absolutely hysterical, because she was playing a woman 80, a woman 50, a woman 40, a child 13, any part that came up. So it was only Lurene and myself in a show that should have been seven people! I finally had to work on a separate mike because I couldn't look at her. She changed her whole characterization. She was brilliant.

Price's films in the 1940s included an odd mix of roles, as he played hero, villain, or weak fop (the pretty-boy boyfriend in *Laura*). Film studios weren't sure what to do with someone a bit too tall (six foot four), and in voice and demeanor quite different from the average leading man.

One early horror role had Vincent relying on his voice alone: *The Invisible Man Returns* (1940), a role he repeated for a brief gag in *Abbott and Costello Meet Frankenstein* (1948). His villainy in '40s films was more realistic than grand guignol; in *Shock* (1946) he played a murderous psychiatrist, and he was the sadistic husband in *Dragonwyck* (1946).

He first appeared on radio's *Suspense* in 1943, and by November 30, 1948, he was so well known for terrifying roles on radio and in movies that it was the main source of jokes for his guest appearance on *Command Performance*. He hosts the episode of the popular radio variety program, with announcer Hy Averback remarking on his evil persona:

"Seems to me that in every picture you've done lately you go around knifing beautiful women or strangling pretty girls."
"Yes, Hy, and I'm so tired of that ... I'd like to invite girls over for dinner—and poison the food.... In my next picture things will change. I do a love scene with gorgeous Rita Hayworth.... I hold her close, and her curves are as round as an Alka-Seltzer tablet.... We melt into a passionate kiss, a burning kiss..."
"And then?"
"The natural thing, I drop her in the water and listen to her fizz!"

During the war years Vincent was most often heard on the *Treasury Star Parade*, which helped boost morale. One episode featured "The Song of the United Nations," written by Shostakovich on the Russian battlefield.

Price's gripping ability to enact a stirring, vivid script is in evidence as he reads lines that in lesser hands would sound overbaked:

Over the guns and the planes and the weeping comes another sound, the rhythmic sound of marching feet, the arrogant cadence of the conquerors' boots on the soil of seventeen countries.... But listen again, what do you hear? Deep and powerful, rhythmic and strong, the sound of free men singing! Singing songs that guns and planes and the ruthless heel of the conqueror cannot still!

Later in the show Vincent talks about Mussolini and insane and oppressive laws. He raises the alarm against dictators

wiping out what is known as civil life ... leaving a world of warring nations, whose women slave perpetually in factories, whose children weep fatherless and motherless in state institutions for the rearing of children, where they will be taught the crafts of war, educated to slaughter ... with neither love nor mercy in their hearts? This is the utopia promised by the Fascists.
We cannot share their hatred and merciless brutality, but we can hate the things they stand for with a greater hatred than they have ever known.... Destroy this monster.

The "monster movie" actors have always been unfairly denigrated while "serious" performers walk away with awards, but who could imagine anyone but a Vincent Price reading those florid lines effectively?

Coming from the stage, working in a variety of movies, Price managed to avoid being typed as a horror star in the '40s, and that was proven when he was given the radio assignment of portraying *The Saint*, a role that had been played by many actors both on radio and in film. His show premiered in 1947 (the same year 20th Century–Fox failed to renew his film contract), and in a way it cemented Price's persona for the general public. The character Simon Templar, like Price, was a cultured, basically non-violent person with a keen, almost preening interest in crime and evil, and a droll sense of humor.

While the show was forgotten by most, Vincent recalled a bit of déjà vu:

Hardly anyone remembers radio as it was then, so there is no point in going on about what fun it used to be. But I would like to tell of one eerie experience I had.
We were shooting *The Masque of the Red Death* in England in 1964. Between takes I would wander around the studio. I soon found out that, on the soundstage right next door they were shooting a television series. It was *The Saint*, and Roger Moore was starring as Simon Templar. The strange thing about that was that I had played the very same role in the radio series from 1947 to 1951.

Leslie Charteris (born Leslie Yin in Singapore), the half–Asian, half–British author of the books about the sleuthing Simon Templar, once stated that "the Saint could have been superbly played, albeit in different styles, by such actors as Ronald Colman, Cary Grant, or Doug Fairbanks Jr.; and if this is my conception of the role, it should be obvious that such totally different types as Louis Hayward and George Sanders were hopelessly miscast." He didn't seem to have a comment for the radio versions, but Vincent loved playing the Saint, calling him "the suavest character" he ever portrayed.

The Saint first arrived on radio in October of 1940, with Terrance de Marney in the title role. It didn't last long. Another try, in 1945, with Edgar Barrier also failed, and in the summer of that year Brian Aherne took the role but only ran with it for a few months.

Two years later it clicked with Price in the lead, and it seemed like the writers tailored their scripts for Vincent's voice, creating a fun mix of mystery and humor. The Saint became the confident dandy who enjoyed the discomfort he caused to both rogues and the incompetent police detectives who were always irked by his intrusion into the case.

At some points during its run *The Saint* was a "sustaining" show, with no regular sponsor. While hoping to fill the space with paying spots, the producers ran "public service" announcements. Price usually ended the show with a passionate speech on behalf of a good cause.

For example, after "The Color-Blind Killer" (an ironic title, considering that art-connoisseur Price was color blind himself), Vincent announced:

> Ladies and gentlemen, in a prejudice-filled America, no one would be secure; in his job, his business, his church, or his home. Yet racial and religious antagonisms are exploited daily by quacks and adventurers, whose followers make up the lunatic fringe of American life. Refuse to listen to or spread rumors against any race or religion. Help to stamp out prejudice in our country. Let's judge our neighbors by the character of their lives alone, and not on the basis of their religion or origin.

Vincent felt *The Saint* was a positive and important step, since it was his first opportunity to sustain a character over many episodes, rather than, on the Broadway stage, play the same character doing the same lines night after night:

> It was a challenge that I wanted very much at that point in my career; to try and create somebody. I'm not really that interested in doing that kind of thing in television. *The Saint* had a lot more dimensions than you're allowed in television. You're visual and therefore you're limited. But in radio drama you can create anything you want, and it has more excitement, really.

Price left *The Saint* in 1951, ironically replaced by Tom Conway, brother of the best known film incarnation of the character, George Sanders. The series ended the same year.

Most episodes of the show still survive, and they still hold up, thanks to Price's genuine appreciation of his character's flippancy.

A typical introductory moment from "Contract for a Saint" (July 9, 1950) has Simon interrogating a suspect, and both exchanging lines of grim drollery:

"Are you Ronald Stanton?"
"Yes, and you?"
"Simon Templar."
"Simon Templar! As I live and breathe!"
"No, as I do."
"Put up your hands!"
"I thought gunplay was out of your line, Mr. Stanton."
"Sometimes one is forced to take matters into one's own hands. But I assure you I don't relish it, so please do as I say. Because if I'm forced to shoot you, I know I shall be quite ill."

Just as the stylish series was ending its run, Price guest starred in two of the best horror scripts radio ever produced. The last gasps of truly memorable radio horror came with "Three Skeleton Key" and "Blood Bath."

In an interview for the Chicago radio program *Those Were the Days* in 1971, Price happily recalled:

> I did *Escape* and *Suspense*, and the audience really had to build the sets, to create the make-up, to figure out what they thought the people were like, what the ambiance of the drama was like. It was terribly exciting and almost everybody that I've ever known who started in the theater who has made a success in the theater started in radio. Radio was the greatest training ground for actors that ever was.
>
> I did one called "Three Skeleton Key," about three men who were trapped in a lighthouse.... It's still one of the most exciting shows that I think I've ever done in my life. It was tremendously thrilling.

It was based on an *Esquire* magazine short story written by George Toudouze. James Poe's effective radio adaptation made it a classic. *Escape* broadcast their first version of it with Elliot Reid as the star. The show received such acclaim that four months later, March 17, 1950, it was broadcast again. This time it starred Vincent Price.

Vincent Price proudly shows off his baby daughter Victoria.

An inverted variation on "Leinengin vs. the Ants," and taking off from where Edgar A. Poe's "Pit and the Pendulum's" rats began. The simple tale is about a plague of rats invading an isolated lighthouse from a ghost ship run aground.

It's a lonely island lighthouse where a few humans have lived and worked in peace, but it's surrounded by

> churning water; gray-green, scum dappled, warm as soup, and swarming with gigantic, bat-like devil fish, great violet schools of Portuguese man-of-war, and yes, sharks, the big ones, the fifteen-footers. And as if this weren't enough, there was a hot, dank, rotten-smelling wind that came at us day and night off the jungle swamps of the mainland. A wind that smelled like death...

Price shares his lighthouse hell with two men, one a coward and the other demented (even more looney than the legendary fly-eater Renfield in *Dracula*). Price has almost as much trouble with his crazy friend as with the invading rats. Vincent plays Jean, who narrates the tale, which then dissolves into scenes of dialogue:

> JEAN: Auguste was the talkingest man I'd ever met. The talkingest and the ugliest. He was hunchbacked, stood four feet high, had red hair and big blue eyes. It seems he'd been an actor in Paris.
> AUGUSTE: Yes, yes, indeed! Played in over two hundred different productions, dear boy. At the Grand Guignol. Oh, but it was monstrous, horrible, the way we used to scare the audiences. I—I was hated. Yes, yes. They used to throw things and hiss and bare their teeth at me.... Yes, gave it up completely, I really did. Couldn't stand it any longer."

Price is soon distracted from his comrades by the swarming rats. It's a classic confrontation between brains and brutality, defense and offense, man-made barricade and nature's destructive fury. The first rat gets through:

> He was as big as a tomcat. Bigger. And his eyes were wild and red. His teeth, long and sharp and yellow. He went for us, starved and ravenous, and we fought him, fought that one rat all over the room. It was—oh, believe me, I do not exaggerate, it was like fighting a panther!

More of them get through:

> The air of the gallery was thick and fetid with the stink of them. The light was dim, brown, filtered through the crawling mass that swarmed over the glass all about us. We could not see the sky. Nothing. Nothing but them. Their red eyes. Their claws. Their wriggling, hairy snouts. Their teeth..."

Poe described rats. So did the mad Renfield in *Dracula*, shouting about the thousands, millions of them, "their eyes blazing red." But leave it to radio to thrill and repulse listeners with ripe descriptions abetted by sound effects—small chitters and squeaks that rise and become a fiendish stampede.

"Three Skeleton Key" would become, along with "Sorry, Wrong Number," one of the most oft-broadcast scripts in radio. Price took part in another version of it for *Suspense*. The script is basically the same, but some aspects were streamlined and others strengthened.

In addition to cutting most of Auguste's fanciful lines, the *Suspense* episode dispenses with those "talkingest, ugliest" lines designed to make Price's character earthy. In *Suspense*, the slang vernacular is dropped, and Price is even more the average man like the listeners at home.

For a contrast in editing, here's a portion of Price's *Escape* script, with bracketed segments indicating what was removed from the *Suspense* version:

> JEAN (describing the lighthouse): She was a beauty. [Big steel and bronze baby with the sun gleaming through the glass walls all about, bouncing blinding little beams off the big shining reflectors, glittering and refracting through her lenses. The whole gigantic bulk of her] balanced like a ballerina on the glistening steel axle of her rotary mechanism. [She was a sweetheart of a light.]

Removing phrases like "bronze baby" and "sweetheart of a light" took the Raymond Chandler–esque muscle and bravado from Price's character. It also strengthened the real meat of James Poe's script, his ability to create repulsive word pictures. When Price and his men first glimpse the rats festering on board the sinking ship, "The decks were swarming with a dark brown carpet that looked like a gigantic fungus...."

James Poe offered even more nauseating images for his script "Blood Bath," which aired on *Escape* on the warm evening of June 30, 1950. Like "Three Skeleton Key," the story takes place in humid surroundings, this time the jungles of the Amazon.

The rats of "Three Skeleton Key" "would scramble into a solid ball, biting each other, clustering like grapes. From time to time, a whole knot of them would slip and fall the hundred ten feet to the surf below...."

But in "Blood Bath" the rodents are flying:

> Vampire bats! Ever seen em? They're small, rather fragile looking little things. By day they hang, heads down from the trees, wings folded like—like clusters of rotten fruit. By night, they hunt. They have razor sharp teeth, bite like the finest steel scalpels. Their object is to break the skin very gently, start the blood to coming, then they simply hang on, and sip. Without mosquito netting we had a rough time, a sleepless time...

Price is victimized by both nature and his greedy and insane comrades, one of whom meets his end in the river:

> One moment we saw him, swimming weakly, his large, fever-ridden eyes turned imploring toward us. The next moment he was gone, leaving only a large, red patch on the water.... The piranhas are small ... with large, powerful jaws ... teeth like broken glass and an insatiable, maniacal appetite for flesh!

The program would be just another routine horror show without Vincent's vocals. As the embodiment of every civilized listener, his voice is perfect, registering squeamish repugnance and mortal dread. He's a gentleman in a savage land; listening, you can almost visualize the familiar grim twist to Price's lip and a vague squint as he tells the tale.

Price rarely presented a truly effeminate or effete character, aside, perhaps, from his

The front cover for Radiola Records starred Peter Lorre in an episode of *Suspense*, but the back cover was for Vincent Price and his much more chilling "Bloodbath."

one-man Oscar Wilde show in the 1980s, but throughout his career there was something markedly reserved, cultured and almost submissive in his personality. If his characters weren't perfumed, some were most definitely cologned. These two classic radio episodes have one thing in common: Price's civilized man battling and losing against small, beady-eyed creatures that should easily be crushed by fist or foot.

The vivid notoriety Price received from the *Escape* programs probably helped him move on to the "Poe series" of films in the 1960s, almost all of them keyed to his persona as a cultured and refined gentleman with morbid sensitivity (*Fall of the House of Usher*) and a distaste for becoming involved in gruesome tribulations (*The Raven*).

Price's first contact with Poe was via an episode of *Suspense*. The radio show's adaptation of "The Pit and the Pendulum" is somewhat more faithful to the Poe story than the more famous film version he would make years later. Here he is the helpless victim: "I was sick, sick unto death with that long agony, and when at length they unbound me and I was permitted to sit, I felt that my senses were leaving me. The sound of the inquisitorial voices seemed merged in one dreamy, indeterminate hum…"

In this tale of the Inquisition, the radio script veers into fantasy by having the captive imagine his wife Beatrice is guiding him:

"I can't, I can't endure any more…. Oh Beatrice, I have been much humbled, but I won't have you see me in tears. I order you to go!"
"Jean, in the name of heaven!"
"In the name of heaven, go!"

Speaking of going, this particular scene is broken up by a commercial for Ex-Lax.

Price appeared on many more episodes of *Suspense* and similar-styled shows, such as *Obsession*. On the latter, in an episode called "Paranoia" (also known as "Compartment B, Car 92"), he's in his clever and sneering villain mode. He plays a death row prisoner handcuffed on a train headed for prison. He naturally plans an escape, and is bold enough to tell it to the man guarding him:

I wouldn't confide this to anyone but you inspector…. For some time now I've been rather worried that I myself might be mentally afflicted…. You see, I've only recently become aware of a certain Machiavellian cleverness in my actions and plots. A cleverness that I must admit was not previously endowed in me…. Strangely enough, I'm going to rather enjoy killing you.

Radio had been a source of great artistic triumph in horror for Vincent Price. Following his replacement of Charles Laughton in a stage tour of *Don Juan in Hell* in 1952, Vincent scored a cinematic horror hit with *House of Wax*.

After this surprise success (and Price was quite dubious about the 3D movie being supervised by one-eyed director Andre De Toth), Price found the casting doors open more and more for him to become filmdom's new horror hero. Fortunately, waxy make-up was rarely called for. Unlike Karloff and Lugosi, it was rare that Price played an ugly monster, as he did rather late in his career for two somewhat campy *Dr. Phibes* movies.

In films such as *The Raven* and *Comedy of Terrors*, and on many TV programs, Vincent had fun with his bogeyman typecasting. Audiences were captivated by his self-deprecating humor, and could see that he was having as much of a good time as they were. A good time was important, because Price's '60s horror films were not always well-paying. The "Poe series" was done for a low-budget studio, and Price was glad that it was indeed a series and a dependable meal ticket for himself and the other surviving stars from the old days—Karloff, Lorre and Rathbone.

To Jay Maeder in a 1986 *Daily News* interview, Price recalled:

There were those of us who had voices. We had our heyday and then we were relegated to costume pictures. Boris Karloff and I read *The Raven* [script] and we said, well, lovely to be working together but what is the point of this picture?... In the end, of course, it was the voices. So! How can we scare the little bastards this morning?

Price's voice was central to his successful films—from a scene in *House on Haunted Hill*, where he uses it to breathe supernatural life into a skeleton, to the opening of *The Raven*, when he reads from the famous poem. With his Poe film successes, Price became the successor to Basil Rathbone for the Caedmon Records series of short story recordings. Price was a keen student of the author:

> Edgar Allan Poe may be the most popular writer this country has produced. At the basis of life is mystery. Probing that mystery is one of the foremost tasks of communication. People want to be scared. It's a catharsis.... It seems to me, all the best films, plays, novels, whatever, have this basic mystery at the core. They are in a sense, mystery stories. Even Hamlet was a ghost story.... Mystery, of course, is the basis for all religion. How did we get here? What are we doing? Where are we going?

With reliable offers always coming in for his horror work, Price had plenty of time for writing books (memoirs, cookbooks, books on painting) and indulging his passion for buying works of art for himself (and even for others; he had a lucrative deal with the Sears corporation to buy items they could re-sell).

Price would often stay in modest hotels when he was making films, so he could spend the saved money on buying local art work. Sometimes when film producers economized too much, Price was able to help. On the set of *The Conqueror Worm*, the hired caterer didn't show up. Vincent snapped into action, cooking food for the 60 members of the cast and crew.

While his contemporaries, including Karloff, Lorre and Rathbone, departed their mortal coils, Price continued on into an age when critics actually began to respect him as an actor, and horror as a genre. One of Price's favorite films was the well received *Theatre of Blood*, co-starring Diana Rigg. She admired his unique technique: "He chooses very carefully his moments to go just a bit over the top, and that's what makes him a discriminating actor." Price insisted that horror roles required this aspect: "I believed you can't just play them straight or they don't come to life. They have to be overplayed."

To his great relief, Price's high standing as an actor led him to a project he found greatly rewarding—a one-man show as Oscar Wilde. He performed it on Broadway, and then took it on the road. He also went on

Vincent Price displays artwork that probably never made it to his own stately home in this scene from *Reprieve*, aka "Convicts 4."

regular lecture tours, where he might give a talk on art, or read poetry and answer audience questions. There was only one drawback: "It is lonely. Oh, there are always people around. And they're always nice to you. An actor is seen by so many people so many times on the screen that he almost becomes family. But you know very well you can be surrounded by people and still remain lonely."

His daughter recalled:

> Vincent was frequently asked to perform with symphony orchestras all over the United States, among them those of Baltimore, St. Louis, Denver, Houston, Los Angeles, Philadelphia, and Seattle.... Then Leonard Slatkin set "The Raven" to music for Vincent, and this became one of his most-requested performance pieces. One reviewer wrote, "Price's voice is a treat to the ear. His delivery is conversational, his diction is impeccable, and his flair for drama is strong."

Young at heart, Price even embraced rock and pop music, and agreed to perform juicy horror narrations for albums by Alice Cooper and Michael Jackson.

Price was paid outright for his quick work on Jackson's "Thriller," and did not receive any royalty. When "Thriller" went multi-platinum, Price realized a lot of money could've come his way. In her biography of her father, Victoria Price noted that when Michael Jackson paid millions in a settlement "in respect of charges of his possible misconduct with a young boy, Vincent channeled his ill feelings about his own mistreatment into a joke: 'All I can say is that Michael Jackson fucked me—and I didn't get paid for it!'"

The '80s were placid years for Price, and included the steady job of hosting the PBS television series *Mystery*. He had performed in a few radio productions for the BBC in the '80s, but acknowledged, "People now are visually oriented," and radio was mostly "48 hours of news every 24." There were few venues like the BBC or PBS for any type of radio production. He doubted radio in the old sense could ever make a comeback:

> Too many commercials. I remember during the time that radio was drifting out and television was drifting in, we would do re-makes of the great shows that we had done in the great days of radio, and they would be cut so, and interfered so by the commercials that they lost their impact. Radio has a continuity that is just marvelous, as a play does. I miss it very much.

The charming Mr. Price ("Vinnie" to his friends and fans) was adored by his colleagues and always gracious to his fans. As he became more frail, one of his favorite "chores" had to be curtailed—answering his fan mail. He typed out a form letter, the signature jagged and showing the difficulties of writing in old age, and it was xeroxed and sent to his well-wishers:

> You are most kind to have requested a signature from me. I appreciate that, and I have tried all along to oblige with replies whenever possible.
> Sad to say that my particular trials involved with being 82 have made reading and writing just too exhausting for me, and I now have to conserve my strength to get me by.
> Have been holding off on this moment for as long as possible, so forgive me if you have had to wait for this particular response.
> My acting career has been a joy, and letters like yours have all been a part of it.
> Please accept my good wishes, even though, from this point, I have to forego anything further in the form of a reply.
> My very best,
> Vincent Price.

Always his horror persona was first and foremost in the minds of interviewers and the hearts of fans. Like Karloff before him, he viewed these parts as good fun, and their continued appeal based on sympathy and empathy:

I have never played a part in which I was really a monster. My specialty is playing men who have been hurt by life, men who have been betrayed. My major motivation in horror films is one of revenge.

My job as an actor was to try to make the unbelievable believable and the despicable delectable.

Radio

Fleischmann's Yeast Hour. June 18, 1936, NBC, 60 min. Price said he appeared on radio in England when he was first starring in a play there, but nothing from overseas has apparently survived. Likewise, it's been difficult to find any of his very early appearances on local soap opera shows when he first arrived on Broadway. His first major radio credit is this variety show, which focuses on the upcoming Joe Louis vs. Max Schmeling fight, with both fighters briefly speaking. Cornelia Otis Skinner stars in a scene from "There's Always Juliet," and Vincent Price is in the cast. Midge Williams sings "Dinah," and Joe Cook offers a comedy routine.

Great Plays. February 26, 1939, Blue Network, 60 min. "A Doll's House." An adaptation of the Ibsen drama featuring Ruth Gordon and Vincent Price.

Treasury Star Parade. 1942–43, Treasury Department, 15 min. Vincent Price was a frequent host of this patriotic program, and the classic episodes include #72, featuring Igor Gorin premiering Shostakovitch's "Song of the United Nations"; #79, "The Price of Free World Victory," a speech by Vice President Henry Wallace; #81, "Sacrifice for Victory," describing the heroic women of China in their battle against the Japanese enemy; #85, a war bond drive highlighted by Milton Douglas singing "Everybody, Every Payday"; #90, a memorable show with Carl Sandburg reading his poem "Lexington"; and #102, "It Isn't Peanuts," with guest star Edward G. Robinson.

Other memorable episodes include #110, "The Sound of an American," with Tallulah Bankhead; #112, with Roy Halee singing "Der Fuehrer's Face"; #113, with Carl Sandburg returning to read "The Man with the Broken Fingers"; #114, "The Ballad of Bataan," with Orson Welles; #115, "Prayer for Americans," with Helen Hayes and Orson Welles; #122, "Mein Kampf," with John Nesbitt; and #128, "The Book and the Beast," with special guest Margo.

Similar programs made during the same era include these two 15 minute shows: *The New National Guard Show*, Program #35, National Guard syndication, "7900 Empire State"; and an episode of the *Crusade for Freedom* fund appeal called "The Tank That Jan Built," co-starring Lurene Tuttle and Paul Frees.

The Columbia Workshop. May 10, 1942, CBS, 30 min. "Chapter One" features the openings to various famous books. Guest star Vincent Price.

Suspense. November 23, 1943, CBS, 30 min. "The Strange Death of Charles Umberstein." A spy tale co-starring Vincent Price and Hans Conried.

The Lux Radio Theatre. March 6, 1944, CBS, 60 min. "The Letter," starring Bette Davis, Herbert Marshall, Vincent Price and Bea Benaderet.

Screen Guild Theater. May 1, 1944, CBS, 30 min. "A Night to Remember." Lucille Ball and Brian Donlevy are the stars in this show, sponsored by Lady Esther, but Vincent Price makes a late appearance to promote next week's show, "Dark Angel," starring Merle Oberon and Ronald Colman.

Suspense. June 1, 1944, CBS, 30 min. "Fugue in C-Minor" is about a ghostly pipe organ, courtesy of writer Lucille Fletcher. Starring Vincent Price, Ida Lupino and Bea Benaderet.

The Cavalcade of America. January 29, 1945, Red Network, 30 min. In "A Race for Lennie," Frederick Grant Banting and Charles H. Best discover insulin. Hosted by Walter Huston and starring Vincent Price.

The Lux Radio Theatre. February 5, 1945, CBS, 60 min. "Laura." Several members of the film's cast perform in this radio adaptation: Dana Andrews, Gene Tierney and Vincent Price.

The Screen Guild Theatre. July 16, 1945, CBS, 30 min. "Flesh and Fantasy." A fortune teller predicts murder. Starring Edward G. Robinson, Vincent Price and Dame May Whitty.

Columbia Presents Corwin. July 17, 1945, CBS, 30 min. "The Undecided Molecule" features a gimmicky Norman Corwin script, told in verse, and starring Vincent Price, Groucho Marx, Robert Benchley, Keenan Wynn and Sylvia Sidney.

Theatre of Romance. October 9, 1945, CBS, 30 min. "Angel Street." Price starred in the original Broadway version of this tale, which is better remembered as the film *Gaslight*, with Charles Boyer. Here, Vincent Price is the star, and his victimized wife is played by Anne Baxter.

Hollywood Star Time. February 3, 1946, CBS, 30 min. In "Shock," a doctor has committed murder. This short version for radio listeners too cheap to go to the movies stars Vincent Price and Lynn Bari.

The Screen Guild Theatre. April 1, 1946, CBS, 30 min. In "On Borrowed Time," Death comes for an old man who wants to borrow a little more time. Starring Lionel Barrymore, Agnes Moorehead and Vincent Price.

Hollywood Star Time. April 7, 1946, CBS, 30 min. "Hangover Square" is a radio adaptation of the Laird Cregar film. This gothic story of obsession co-stars Vincent Price, Faye Marlowe, Joseph Kearns and Linda Darnell.

Suspense. April 11, 1946, CBS, 30 min. "The Name of the Beast" features Vincent Price in two familiar guises: painter and murderer. Co-starring Cathy Lewis.

Hollywood Star Time. May 19, 1946, CBS, 30 min. With "The Lodger," once again in 1946 Vincent takes a radio role based on a Laird Cregar film. Is he an ordinary tenant or Jack the Ripper? Co-starring Cathy Lewis.

Suspense. September 12, 1946, CBS, 30 min. "Hunting Trip." A simple hunting trip turns into an exercise in paranoia and murder. Co-starring Lloyd Nolan and Vincent Price.

The Lux Radio Theatre. October 7, 1946, CBS, 60 min. With "Dragonwyck," one of Price's favorite early film roles is re-told in a radio adaptation with Gene Tierney, Vincent Price, Gale Gordon, Jay Novello and Jeff Corey.

The Adventures of the Saint. July 9, 1947, CBS, 30 min. Vincent played Simon Templar on *The Saint* for CBS Radio (1947–1948), Mutual Radio (1948–1950) and NBC Radio (1950–1951).

The 1947 episodes: July 9, "Political Intrigue"; July 16, "Rare Painting Smugglers"; July 23, "Blackmail"; July 30, "The Doll with a Broken Head"; August 6, "Murder for Buried Treasure"; August 13, "The Steel-Ice Murders"; August 20, "Family Gun-Play"; August 27, "Baby Adoption Ring Blackmail"; September 3, "Baseball Team Shooting"; September 10, "The Man Who Ran Away"; September 17, "Blackmail in Phony Rare Books"; September 24, "Murder for Life Insurance"; October 1, "Murder on the High Seas"; October 8, "The Saint Gets the Bird"; October 15, "A Gangster District Attorney"; October 22, "A Schizophrenic Psychiatrist" (aka "The Color Blind Killer"); October 29, "Greed Causes Murder" (aka "Mr. Ritchie's Loss"); November 5, "The Diathermy Machine"; November 12, "The Case of the Hasty Hearse"; November 19, "A Political Frame-Up"; November 26, "The Case of the Five Hundred Lemons"; December 3, "Playing with Fire"; December 10, "The Case of the Confused Cadillacs"; December 17, "The Connolly Silver Mine"; December 24, "The Nineteen Santa Clauses"; December 31, "The Case of the Chilly Corpse."

Favorite Story. January 14, 1947, NBC, 30 min. "Mr. Shakespeare." What would Hollywood do if Shakespeare turned up? Most likely a script titled "Romeo Meets the Cat People." The writing team of Jerome Lawrence and Robert E. Lee concoct a confection for Vincent Price and William Conrad.

The Screen Guild Theatre. January 20, 1947, CBS, 30 min. "Dragonwyck." Price had performed a radio version three months previously. This show's sponsor, Lady Esther, takes half the time *Lux Radio Theatre* needed to go through the paces of this historical tale. Starring Teresa Wright and Vincent Price.

The Lux Radio Theatre. February 17, 1947, CBS, 60 min. In "Devotion," two women are in love with the same ... priest? Vincent Price co-stars with Jane Wyman, Virginia Bruce, June Whitley, Alan Reed and Janet Scott.

The Sealtest Village Store. March 20, 1947, NBC, 30 min. The merriment includes Jack Haley, Eve Arden, a little boy named Joey Preston who can play the drums, and, in a stretch-sketch, Vincent Price as "Vinnie the Hillbilly."

Family Theatre. June 12, 1947, Mutual, 30 min. "Laughing into Glory" is an uplifting story about the town preacher, starring Vincent Price, Ralph Moody and Gerald Mohr.

The Lux Radio Theatre. September 29, 1947, CBS, 60 min. "The Web." The boss orders a hit—and then double-crosses the man who did the dirty work. Co-starring Edmond O'Brien, Ella Raines and Vincent Price.

Hollywood Fights Back. October 26, 1947, ABC, 30 min. A special sponsored by the First Amendment Committee. As the Red Scare and Senator McCarthy become more and more ominous, top stars take a patriotic step forward to the microphone, including Lauren Bacall, Lucille Ball, Humphrey Bogart, Charles Boyer, Joseph Cotten, Richard Conte, Melvyn Douglas, June Havoc, John Huston, Paul Henreid, William Holden, Danny Kaye, Evelyn Keyes, Peter Lorre, Burt Lancaster, Myrna Loy, John Garfield, Vincent Price, Edward G. Robinson, Paulette Goddard, William Wyler and Robert Young.

The Adventures of the Saint. January 7, 1948, CBS, 30 min.

The 1948 episodes: January 7, "Open Season on Saints"; January 14, "The Second Case of the Chilly Corpse"; January 21, "Crime Wave"; January 28, "The Case of the Ardent Artichoke"; February 4, "The Disappearing Dentist"; February 11, "The Case of the Warmblooded Ghost"; February 18, "Retribution"; February 25, "The Case of the Cigar Store Indian"; March 3, "The Case of the Unhappy Homicide"; March 10, "The Death of a Fighter"; March 17, "The Saint Is Framed"; March 24, "The Case of the Unkindest Cut"; March 31, "The Jewels of Fang Ta"; April 7, "The Latest Style in Murder"; April 14, "The Case of the Lopsided Triangle"; April 21, "Hard Money"; April 28, "The Case of the Indiscreet Parakeet"; May 5, "Tiger by the Tail"; May 12, "Jail Break"; May 19, "With No Tomorrow"; May 26, "The Case of the Blonde Who Lost Her Head" (aka "The Fake Amnesia Killer"); June 2, "Pearls Before Swine"; June 9, "The Case of the Department Store Dummy"; June 16, "Night Club Story"; June 23, "The Fence."

The Lux Radio Theatre. September 13, 1948, CBS, 60 min. "Another Part of the Forest" is a Civil War drama from Lillian Hellman, co-starring Ann Blyth, Walter Huston and Vincent Price.

Command Performance. November 30, 1948, 45 min. Vincent Price hosts the program and offers some deliciously grisly jokes. Also in the cast are Joan Davis and June Foray, plus songs from Kay Starr.

Suspense. December 2, 1948, CBS, 30 min. "The Hands of Mr. Ottermole" features a nice combination of co-stars—severe-voiced Claude Rains and silky smooth Vincent Price. Who has the hands of a stranger?

The Adventures of the Saint. January 7, 1949, Mutual, 30 min.

The 1949 episodes, which included re-runs of previous shows: July 10, "Blackmail"; July 17, "Murder for Buried Treasure"; July 24, "Family Gun-Play"; July 31, "The Saint Goes Underground" (aka "The Connolly Silver Mine"); August 7, "Rare Painting Smugglers"; August 14, "Greed Causes Murder" (aka "The Old Man's Car"); August 21, "A Political Frame-Up"; August 28, "Baseball Team Shooting"; September 4, "Death of a Fighter"; September 11, "Retribution"; September 18, "A Schizophrenic Psychiatrist" (aka "The Color-Blind Killer"); September 25, "Political Intrigue"; October 2, "The Latest Style in Murder"; October 9, "Hard Money"; October 16, "The Case of the Warm Blooded Ghost"; October 23, "The Second Case of the Chilly Corpse"; October 30, "The Case of the Indiscreet Parakeet"; November 6, "The Case of the Unhappy Homicide"; November 13, "The Case of the Blonde Who Lost her Head" (aka "The Fake Amnesia Killer"); November 20, "The Disappearing Dentist"; November 28, "The

Case of the Lopsided Triangle"; December 4, "The Saint Is Framed"; December 11, "Bookstore"; December 18, "The Case of the Department Store Dummy"; December 25, "The Nineteen Santa Clauses."

The Lucky Strike Program Starring Jack Benny. February 6, 1949, CBS, 30 min. Jack gets overinvolved playing the butler Smedley as he rehearses a drama scene with cute Claudette Colbert and cad Vincent Price. Vincent: "I married you for your money ... blind little fool ... as soon as you divorce me the happier I'll be.... Smedley, pack my clothes." Jack: "I wouldn't touch your dirty clothes! You stinker!"

The Philip Morris Playhouse. February 25, 1949, CBS, 30 min. In "Leona's Room," a vaudevillian with a mind-reading act manages to get a theater critic to pay attention—via blackmail. Co-starring Vincent Price and Cathy Lewis.

The Thirteenth Juror. April 23, 1949, NBC, 30 min. "What Happened to John Wilkes Booth?" co-starred Vincent Price and Hans Conried. This seems to be the only show produced, and may have been the pilot episode for a proposed series starring Price.

The Croupier. September 21, 1949, ABC, 30 min. "The Roman" is the pilot episode starring Paul Frees, Dan O'Herlihy and Vincent Price. ABC took a gamble, but briefly: "I am the Croupier ... I spin the wheel of life." Some sources indicate the program was on the air until November 16, but this is the only surviving program.

Family Theatre. October 12, 1949, Mutual, 30 min. "The Happy Prince" stars Loretta Young with Vincent Price.

The Adventures of the Saint. January 1, 1949, Mutual, 30 min.

The 1949 episodes: January 1, "The Case of the Chilly Corpse"; January 8, "The Cake That Killed"; January 15, "Pearls Before Swine"; January 22, "The Case of the Lonesome Slab" (aka "Murder in the Theater"); January 29, "A Gangster District Attorney"; February 5, "The Murderous Music Box"; February 12, "The Fencem"; February 19, "The Stiff Swami"; February 26, "The Case of the Hasty Hearse"; March 5, "Jail Break"; March 12, "The Girl with the Canvasback Bag"; March 19, "For the Record"; March 26, "The Case of the Two-Headed Girl"; April 2, "Design for Murder"; April 9, "One Artichoke to Go"; April 16, "The Non-Visiting Visitor"; April 23, "Husband Without Future"; April 30, "Murder of a Champion; May 7, "Twin Killing"; May 14, "The Bilious Baron"; May 21, "The Mummy's Mummy"; May 28, "The Damp Dilemma."

The Adventures of the Saint. July 2, 1950, NBC, 30 min. Vincent's show moves to NBC. Guest stars include Richard Crenna (November 19, 1950, "No Hiding Place"), Edmond MacDonald and Herb Vigran (December 3, 1950, "Marvin Hickerson, Private Eye"), and Jerry Hausner doing the voices of a monkey and a baby for December 10 ("The Chiseling Chimpanzee") and December 17 ("Simon Minds the Baby").

The 1950 episodes: June 11, "The Sinister Sneeze" (aka "The Prize Fighter"); June 18, "A Sonata for Slayers" (aka "The Music Murder"); June 25, "The Dangerous Diaper"; July 2, "A Real Gone Guy" (aka "Music Can Be Murder"); July 9, "The Problem of the Peculiar Payoff" (aka "Contract on the Saint"); July 16, "Follow the Leader" (aka "Death of the Saint"); July 23, "The Frightened Author" (aka "The Fighter's Contract"); July 30, "The Case of the Previewed Crime" (aka "The Author of Murder"); August 6, "The Corpse Said Ouch" (aka "The Frances Blake Case"); August 13, "Reflection on Murder"; August 20, "Dossier on a Damsel in Distress"; August 22, "The Case of the Lonesome Slab" (aka "Murder in the Theater"); August 27, "Cupid and the Corpse" (aka "The Tony Cartega Case"); September 3, "The Baseball Murder"; September 10, "The Horrible Hamburger"; September 17, "The Ghost That Giggled" (aka "The Key," with Barry Sullivan substituting for Vincent Price); September 24, "Dossier on a Doggone Dog" (aka "It Shouldn't Happen to a Dog," with Barry Sullivan substituting for Vincent Price); show goes on hiatus for a month; October 29, "It's Snow Use" (aka "Wanted as a Husband"); November 5, "Miss Godby's School for Girls" (aka "The Kidnapped Daughter"); November 12, "The Dame on the Doorstep" (aka "The Return of Harry Morgan"); November 19, "No Hiding Place" (aka "Murder Plot in Prison"); November 26, "The Terrible Tintype" (aka "The Missing Picture"); December 3, "Martin Hickerson, Private Eye" (aka "The Young Detective"); December 10, "The Chiseling Chimpanzee"; December 17, "Simon Minds the Baby"; December 24, "The Christmas Eve Problems" (aka "The Saint Is No Saint); December 31, "The Grim Reaper."

Escape. January 31, 1950, CBS, 30 min. "Present Tense." Written by James Poe and starring Vincent Price, Charles McGraw, Joan Banks, Harry Bartell, Ben Wright, Tom Tully and Jeff Corey. Since *Escape* and *Suspense* were both produced by the same man, scripts were often reused. Price later reprised "Present Tense" on *Suspense* in 1957.

Escape. March 17, 1950, NBC, 30 min. "Three Skeleton Key." Following the premiere broadcast starring Elliot Reid (November 15, 1949), the episode received this encore, now with Vincent Price in the lead. He performed the script again for *Suspense* in 1956.

United Nations Radio Broadcast. April 17, 1950, 60 min. The program, a Peabody Award–winner for writer Norman Corwin, is about an international "Bill of Rights" (also known as "Document A/777"). Vincent Price was one of many guest stars making a brief appearance, along with: Charles Boyer, Ronald Colman, Joan Crawford, Lena Horne, Marsha Hunt, Charles Laughton, Laurence Olivier and Edward G. Robinson.

The Philip Morris Playhouse. May 6, 1950, CBS, 30 min. "Murder Needs an Artist." Vincent Price and William Conrad co-star.

Escape. June 30, 1950, CBS, 30 min. "Blood Bath." If the hideous Amazon jungle beasts don't feast on Vincent's red blood, his fellow travelers will. Vincent Price, Wally Maher, Ted de Corsia and Tony Barrett star.

The Screen Guild Theatre. October 5, 1950, ABC, 60 min. "Champagne for Caesar" is an adaptation of the hit comedy film about a TV quiz show's star contestant. Featuring Ronald Colman, Vincent Price, Audrey Totter, Barbara Britton and Art Linkletter.

Family Theatre. October 25, 1950, Mutual, 30 min. "Jane Eyre." The familiar Bronte tale is re-worked for star Donna Reed, with support from Vincent Price and Ben Wright.

Stars Over Hollywood. December 30, 1950, CBS, 30 min. "Continental Cowboy." Cowboy star Sagebrush Sam finds he has fans even on the continent. With Vincent Price, Hans Conried, and Ramsay Hill.

Hollywood Calling: George Fisher Interviews the Stars. 1951, 3 min. Fisher's program was syndicated to radio stations via a 15-minute disc, and was aired at different times and dates around the country. Vincent Price was briefly interviewed twice during the show's run.

The Adventures of the Saint. January 7, 1951, NBC, 30 min. Guest stars included Sheldon Leonard (February 4, "The Carnival Murder"; February 25, "The Big Swindle"; and April 22, "The Lady Who Leaned"), Edmond MacDonald (March 18, "The Birds and Bees of East Orange"), William Conrad (March 25, "Formula for Death"), and Ed Begley (April 1, "Simon Carries the Ivy").

The 1951 episodes: January 7, "Ladies Never Lie—Much"; January 14, "Simon Takes a Curtain Call" (aka "The Mercer Bennett Case"); January 21, "Tuba or Not Tuba, That Is the Question"; February 4, "The Carnival Murder"; February 11, "The Bride Who Lost Her Groom"; February 18, "Next of Kin" (aka "The Noon Deadline"); February 25, "The Big Swindle" (aka "The Amnesia Victim"); March 4, "The What-Not What Got Hot" (aka "The Stolen Furniture Move"); March 11, "Button, Button" (aka "The Shipboard Mystery"); March 18, "The Birds and Bees of East Orange" (aka "The Bookstore Murder"); March 25, "Formula for Death"; April 1, "Simon Carries the Ivy" (aka "The College Campus Threat"); April 8, "The Ghosts Who Came to Dinner"; April 15, "The Strange Bedfellows" (aka "The Mayor's Son"); April 22, "The Lady Who Leaned" (aka "The Missing Gun"); April 29, "Fishes Gotta Eat" (aka "The Missing Husband"); May 6, "Win and Lose"; May 13, "The Girl with the Built-In Spring"; May 20, "Pin No Roses on My Corpse."

Duffy's Tavern. January 26, 1951, NBC, 30 min. Archie decides his tavern could be an actors' club. Starring Ed Gardner and Vincent Price.

This Is Your FBI. May 18, 1951, ABC, 30 min. "The Straw Hat Shakedown" offers a tale of backstage blackmail. Vincent Price, Betty Blythe, Betty Lou Gerson and Harry Morgan star, along with J. Edgar Hoover giving a few cautionary words.

Hollywood Star Playhouse. February 5, 1951, ABC, 30 min. "Calculated Risk."

Hollywood Star Playhouse. September 20, 1951, ABC, 30 min. "Hour of Truth."

Guest Star. October 11, 1953, Treasury Department, 15 min. "Holiday from Crime" stars Vincent Price, Ted de Corsia and Virginia Gregg.

Stars Over Hollywood. March 20, 1954, CBS, 30 min. In "The Incredible Truth," a publisher rejects a manuscript because it's impossible to believe. Vincent Price, Jeanne Bates and Rosemary De Camp co-star.

Family Theatre. June 9, 1954, Mutual, 30 min. "Where's There's a Will" is the familiar story of people fighting over an inheritance. Rosalind Russell introduces the show, which stars Vincent Price, Ted de Corsia and Jack Kruschen.

Guest Star. September 18, 1955, Treasury Department, 15 min. Vincent Price in a mini-drama co-starring Barbara Eiler and Olan Soule.

Army of Stars. December 1955, 30 min. Sponsored by the Salvation Army, the program concentrates on Christmas music, with Vincent Price reading the classic ("Yes, Virginia...") newspaper piece "Is There a Santa Claus?"

NBC Radio Theatre. January 8, 1956, NBC, 30 min. "The Snake Pit" is inside the hell of an insane asylum. Vincent Price and Agnes Moorehead are featured.

The CBS Radio Workshop. April 6, 1956, CBS, 30 min. "Speaking of Cinderella, or: If the Shoe Fits" is a modern version of the fairy tale, with Vincent Price, Lurene Tuttle, Virginia Gregg, Harry Bartell, Jeanette Nolan and Vic Perrin.

Guest Star. April 15, 1956, Treasury Department, 15 min. "The Grey Hat" is a mini-drama involving a prosecutor who finds that the defendant is his fiancée's brother. Co-starring Vincent Price and Lawrence Dobkin.

Suspense. November 11, 1956, CBS, 30 min. "Three Skeleton Key." Vincent Price reprises the classic ratty lighthouse story that he originally performed on *Escape.* Co-starring John Dehner and Ben Wright.

Recollections at Thirty. February 20, 1957, NBC, 30 min. A variety show featuring sound clips, radio snippets and recordings from 20 years past. The '30s return with Jessica Dragonette and Al Jolson singing; Helen Hayes and Vincent Price are heard again in a scene from *Victoria Regina*; and there's comedy from Fibber McGee and Molly.

Suspense. March 3, 1957, CBS, 30 min. With "Present Tense," Vincent Price, star of the original episode presented on *Escape*, is back for the new version. Co-starring Daws Butler, Joe Di Santis and Jack Kruschen.

The CBS Radio Workshop. April 21, 1957, CBS, 30 min. "The Son of Man." Stars Raymond Burr, Herbert Marshall, Robert Young, Vincent Price and Victor Jory.

Suspense. June 9, 1957, CBS, 30 min. "The Green and Gold String" stars Vincent Price, Irene Tedrow, Lou Krugman, Ben Wright and Jeanette Nolan.

Suspense. November 10, 1957, CBS, 30 min. "The Pit and the Pendulum." The classic script, performed many times on *Suspense*, is now a star vehicle for Vincent Price as the delirious victim of Inquisition torture. Co-starring Ellen Morgan as the hallucinated voice of his wife, with Jay Novello, Ben Wright and John Hoyt.

Army of Stars Salutes the Salvation Army. December 1957. This special program syndicated by the Salvation Army features Christmas music and a recitation from Vincent Price. No copy is known to survive; it may be a re-run of their 1955 show, which also featured Price.

Yours Truly, Johnny Dollar. February 2, 1958, CBS, 30 min. "The Price of Fame Matter." Dollar tries to make sense of guest star Vincent Price (as himself) reporting a $100,000 theft. Perhaps it's the work of "the Gray Cat"? Co-starring Vincent Price, Virginia Gregg and Howard McNear.

Says Who? March 16, 1958, CBS, 30 min. Quiz show hosted by Henry Morgan, with guest panelist Vincent Price joining Dagmar, Orson Bean and Joey Adams.

Suspense. June 1, 1958, CBS, 30 min. "Rave Notice" is a classic story of an actor hoping to use his dramatic skills to get away with murder. Vincent Price takes the role that had been assigned in earlier productions to Milton Berle (October 12, 1950) and Hans Conried (October 21, 1954). An actor gets into an argument with his director: "You fat pig! What do you know about acting?" "I know actors, and you're no actor—you stink!" "I'll kill you for saying that! I'm going to kill you!" "You can't even deliver that line. You stink!" Price's co-stars are Lou Merrill, Peter Leeds and Jack Kruschen.

Suspense. October 19, 1958, CBS, 30 min. "Three Skeleton Key." Vincent Price again reprises the role he played on both a 1956 episode of *Suspense* and a 1949 broadcast of *Escape*. Co-starring Ben Wright and Lawrence Dobkin.

Easter Sunrise Service. March 29, 1959, CBS, 60 min. Vincent Price offers "Thoughts for Easter," and Dale Evans sings "Stranger of Galilee," highlighting a program of sacred music presided over by Pastor Richard Lee of the Little Church of Hollywood.

Suspense. July 19, 1959, CBS, 30 min. "An Occurrence at Owl Creek Bridge." The Ambrose Bierce story with the punishing twist ending as performed by Vincent Price, Barney Phillips, Cathy Lewis and Norman Alden.

The Salvation Army. December 1959, 30 min. This annual special syndicated by the Salvation Army features an "Army of Stars" led by Margaret Roggero, Dorothy Kirsten and Cesare Curzi, with a recitation from Vincent Price.

Studio One. October 12, 1967, 30 min. "A Conversation with Vincent Price" is an interview hosted by Sam Pierce focusing on Price's association with Sears as an art buyer, his love of cooking and his interest in Native American poetry.

Voice of America. February 23, 1968, 30 min. "The Wine of America." *Escape/Suspense* director William N. Robson gets Vincent Price to narrate this heady documentary.

The Price of Fear (BBC). Vincent Price starred in a series of programs for the BBC World Service in 1973–74, and the show was brought back briefly in 1983. British radio and TV shows often don't conform to the rigidity of American programming; a show could run 28 minutes or 34, and might be scheduled erratically as well. Various authors were involved in the project, notably Roald Dahl (the episode "William and Mary"). William Ingram wrote all six of the final episodes. A few premiered within the same week ("Remains to Be Seen" on December 17; "Meeting in Athens" on December 20, 1973), others arrived several months later, while several more didn't premiere until the summer of 1974. In 1983 another six more appeared. The 21 episodes in total:

1973–1974: "Remains to Be Seen," "Meeting in Athens," "Come as You Are," "The Speciality of the House," "Ninth Removal," "Cats Cradle," "William and Mary," "Blind Man's Bluff," "The Man Who Hated Scenes," "An Eye for an Eye," "Guy Fawkes Night," "Lot 132," "Waxwork," "Fish," "Soul Music."

1983: "Goody Two Shoes," "To My Dear, Dear Saladin," "Family Album," "Out of the Mouths," "Not Wanted on Voyage," "Is Anybody There."

The KIIS Hall of Horrors. October 31, 1973. Vincent Price hosted a Halloween special, reading eight 3-minute spook anecdotes: "Fraternity Initiation," "Father Weber's Rescue," "Wild Goose Tavern," "The Woman in Black," "The Fox Sisters," "Harry Tallow's Headaches," "Maria's Mind Possessed" and "A Package for Dr. Masters."

Aliens in the Mind. January 2, 1977, BBC. Vincent co-starred with Peter Cushing in this six-part serial which ran from January 2, 1977, to February 6, 1977. The show was broadcast on Sunday evenings, 7:02–7:30 P.M., and was produced by John Dyre, written by Rene Bijenico and co-starred Henry Stamfer, Sandra Clark, Shirley Dickson, Andrew Spear, Steve Titus, Joan Matheson and William Eagle.

Sears Radio Theatre. February 05, 1979–September 28, 1979, 60 min. Romance, adventure, westerns, comedy and mystery were the subjects, rotated each night. Monday was "Western Night," with Lorne Greene hosting, while Tuesday was Andy Griffith's "Comedy Night." Wednesday's "Mystery Night" was helmed by Vincent Price, and "Love and Hate Night" on Thursdays was given to Cicely Tyson. Friday's "Adventure Night" was first introduced by Richard Widmark, and later by Howard Duff.

The only consistent voice was announcer Art Gilmore. Many top stars appeared on these shows, including Henry Morgan, Marvin Kaplan, Pat Buttram and Jesse White in comedies, June Lockhart and Virginia Gregg in romance, Keith Andes in adventure, and John Dehner, Stephen Markle and Lloyd Bochner in westerns.

The original run lasted only till August of 1979, but re-runs continued through September. Re-titled *The Mutual Radio Theater*, and without the sponsorship of Sears, the programs were rerun one last time, starting in December of 1979 and continuing into the first months of 1980.

As Boris Karloff did with the old *Thriller* TV show, Vincent Price spends less than a minute setting the scene for the night's drama, usually sketching in the opening scene's locale or describing the people about to embark on their suspenseful journey. For "Carmilla," he begins with a bit of poetry:

This is Vincent Price.

> But first, on earth, as Vampire sent,
> Thy corpse shall from its tomb be rent;
> Then ghastly haunt thy native place,
> And suck the blood of all thy race.

That my friends, is a verse written by the poet Lord Byron. The vampire is a truly fabulous being that rises from the grave to prey upon sleeping persons who then become vampires themselves. Driving a stake through the heart of one of the undead while he lies slumbering in his coffin during daylight hours is said to put an end to his blood-seeking wanderlust. Fate brought Carmilla and Amy together in the city of Vienna in 1922, not long after an armistice had ended the first world war. They appeared to be equally young, beautiful, innocent. But one was an ageless vampire, the other an unsuspecting victim. And that's just the beginning of our story.

"Hostages" (February 7) was the third show in the series but the first hosted by Vincent Price. The episode starred Virginia Gregg, Vic Perrin and Olan Soule. The following week, February 14, Price hosted "The Thirteenth Governess," with Howard Duff, Lurene Tuttle and Marvin Miller. On February 21, 1979, it was "The Ouija Spells Murder," starring Louise Heath, Joan McCall and Sam Edwards; and on February 28, 1979, "Wanda," starring Byron Kane, Lucy Taylor and Peggy Webber.

On March 7, 1979, Vincent Price hosted "Carmilla," with Antoinette Bower, Anne Gibson, Olan Soule and Don Diamond; on March 14, 1979, "Going Home," starring Anne Gibbon, Jack Kruschen and Vic Perrin; March 21, 1979, "Mushrooms, Darling?" with Ben Wright, Betty Harford and Marvin Miller; and on March 28, 1979, "Cajun Death," with Barney Phillips, Don Diamond, Linda Kay Henning and Parley Baer.

On April 4 Vincent hosted "Improvisation," with William Schallert, Janet Waldo, Mary Jane Croft, Daws Butler, Parley Baer and Don Diamond; April 11, 1979, "The Ham That Cried Wolf," starring Parley Baer, Olan Soule, Lou Krugman and Vic Perrin; April 18, 1979, "The Old Boy" (script by Arch Oboler), starring Elliott Lewis, Mary Jane Croft, Virginia Gregg, Vic Perrin and Jerry Hausner; and on April 25, 1979, "The Sabbatical," with Jeff Corey, Paula Winslowe and Marvin Miller.

The month of May brought "Miniatures" (May 2); "Assassin" (May 9), with Ivor Barry and Antoinette Bower; "Nightmare" (May 16), with Joan McCall; "Test of Love" (May 23), with Antoinette Bower and Len Birman; and "Leading Case" (May 30), with Lurene Tuttle and Byron Kane.

In June, the shows were "Whisper in My Ear" (June 6), starring Vic Perrin and Antoinette Bower; "Perfect Hostess" (June 13), with Marvin Miller, Virginia Gregg and Hans Conried; "Anniversary" (June 20), with Joan McCall and Denise Galick; and "Game of Cat and Mouse" (June 27), with Tyler McVey.

In July the programs were "Melisa" (July 4), with Russi Taylor, Mary Jane Croft and True Boardman; "Girl on the Billboard" (July 11), with Rick Jason and Joan McCall; "The Joke's on Guess Who?" (July 18), with Barney Phillips; and "Ransom" (July 25), with Lurene Tuttle and Vic Perrin.

The last Price-hosted mystery show in the *Sears* series (their 128th broadcast) was "Voodoo Lady" (August 1), with Helen Martin and Kim Hamilton. The series went into reruns until it left the air in late September.

Night of the Wolf (BBC 1984). Vincent Price returned to the airwaves via a two-hour BBC special written by Victor Pemberton and co-starring Price's wife Coral Browne, along with Peter Whitman and Sheila Grant.

Audio

Vincent Price recorded many classic spoken word albums for the scholastic Caedmon Records label, and also an odd assortment of more commercial releases for mainstream companies. The discography is divided between the educational spoken arts material, radio work and ephemera.

- SPOKEN WORD

Vincent Price took over for Basil Rathbone in recording Poe for Caedmon. His first full-length album was the 1975 recording *The Gold Bug* (Caedmon TC1449), followed by *Imp of the Perverse, Berenice and Morella* (Caedmon TC1450) and *Ligeia* (Caedmon TC 1483). Price's *Gold Bug* and all of Basil Rathbone's recordings were issued as a 4-disc vinyl set, *The Edgar Allan Poe Soundbook* (Caedmon SBR 106), and eventually all of the Price and Rathbone material emerged on CD as *The Edgar Allan Poe Collection* (Harper Audio ISBN: 0694524190). "Berenice" and "The Gold Bug" also appear in the CD compilation *Tales of Terror* (Harper Audio ISBN: 0-06-051187-7), along with other old Caedmon titles, including "Ghost Ship," performed by Douglas Fairbanks, Jr., and a dramatized version of "Dracula" with David McCallum.

Price recorded four albums of witchcraft and horror stories for Caedmon (and one additional title that was released on the more commercial Capitol label): *A Coven of Witches Tales* (Caedmon 1973, CDL51338), *A Graveyard of Ghost Tales* (Caedmon 1973, CPN 1429), *Witches, Ghosts & Goblins* (Caedmon 1974, CDL32393, nominated for a Grammy Award), and *A Hornbook for Witches* (Caedmon 1976, CDL5 1497).

For *Witchcraft & Magic* (Capitol Records 1969) Vincent Price narrates (from a script by Terry D'Oberoff), with electronic score by Douglas Leedy. Album notes declare of Price: "His voice surrounds you, lifts your mind and transports it across the landscape of Hell. His articulation chews every word and savors every bite."

Price's Caedmon catalogue also includes a collection of John Collier—*Fancies and Goodnights*, featuring the stories "Evening Primrose" and "The Touch of Nutmeg Makes It," reissued by Harper Audio (ISBN: 0898452171).

Price joins Melvyn Douglas, Ed Begley and Carl Sandburg on the Caedmon album *Great American Speeches* (Caedmon TC 2016).

Always flattered to be approached for more serious projects, Vincent appreciated the chance to record an entire album of *The Poetry of Shelley* (Caedmon TC 1059), including "When Soft Voices Die," "Ozymandias," "Prometheus Unbound," "My Soul Is an Enchanted Boat," "To a Skylark," "Ode to the West Wind" and "Adonais."

Vincent Price Reads Two Odes of John Keats was released on the small Spa Records label. The poems were "To a Nightingale" and "On a Grecian Urn."

Price appears on *Classics of American Poetry* (Caedmon TC 2041) and *Great American Poetry* (Caedmon TC 2009), and these vinyl albums were re-issued via *Great American Poetry* (on cassette by Audio Editions, ISBN: 0945353774) in a double set. Along with Price, the readers include Julie Harris, Ed Begley and Eddie Albert. Price's contributions are "The Indian Burying Ground," by Philip Freneau; "The Skeleton in Armor," by Henry Wadsworth Longfellow; "Barbara Frietchie," by John Greenleaf Whittier; and "The Marshes of Glynn," by Sidney Lanier.

It's pronounced "Lie-jay-uh," according to Vincent Price. One of Vinnie's many Poe albums.

- RADIO RECORDINGS

Various commercial albums contain some of Price's radio work, most notably the BBC audio tapes for *Aliens of the Mind*, *Night of the Wolf* (BBC ZCF 502) and *The Price of Fear* (BBC ZBBC 1118).

Episodes from *The Saint* have turned up on a compilation from Radio Spirits, as well as Hodder Headline Audiobooks (HH335, HH336, HH337).

Price's excellent *Escape* episode "Blood Bath" is paired with a *Suspense* program, "Till Death Do Us Part" (with Peter Lorre) for Radiola Records (1041).

CBS distributed a transcript disc for their series *Dimension*, featuring the topic "The Most Influential Person in My Life." Each participating celebrity gets between one and two minutes; and, in addition to Price, the list includes among the 18 cuts: Phyllis Diller, Jack Carter, Celeste Holm, Margaret Mead, Stanley Kramer, Lester Lanin, Fannie Hurst, Peter Ustinov, Hugh Downs, Gogi Grant, John Scopes, Mischa Elman and Melvin Belli.

Another album issued for radio stations is *Odyssey* (Blanc Communications).

Price also narrated over a dozen episodes of *The Constant Invader*, syndicated to radio stations by the National Tuberculosis Association. The public service show, aimed at raising awareness and funds, ran 15 minutes. Some of the titles in the series: "The Family Doctor," "Youth Rehabilitation," "The Old Treatment vs. the New," and "Children and TB."

Ephemera

Price's material outside the horror and classic literature genres was quite eclectic.

His Son: The Life and Times of Jesus (CBS 2704) is a double album set with such chapters as "The Nativity," "Jesus Crosses Paths with Miriam," "The Crucifixion," "The Blessed Redemption" and "Virtue Hath Its Own Reward." The cover illustration is the two words "His Son," with a stained glass image of Christ in the "o." Price also issued the obscure 1971 recording *Vincent Price in "The Bible Answers."* Another unusual item is *You Don't Have to Be Very Big at All* (Word 703).

Co-Star: The Record Acting Game. You Act Scenes Opposite Vincent Price (Co-Star CS 110) came next. Roulette's short-lived Co-Star label issued 15 albums with such stars as Tallulah Bankhead, June Havoc, Fernando Lamas, Sir Cedrick Hardwicke and Paulette Goddard. Each record included a script of eight dialogue scenes. The main challenge, then and now, is to time the pauses left by the star so that "your" dialogue blends in. Price chose to perform eight scenes adapted from *The Importance of Being Earnest*.

Gallery: Vincent Price Presents Great Paintings (Dot Records DLP 3195) begs the question of how does one actually present Modigliani, Utrillo, Degas, Dali, Goya, van Gogh, Matisse, Gauguin, Chagall and other artists in an *audio* format? Why, "in musical impressions" composed by Ned Freeman and performed by Ochestra dei Concerti di Roma, with Paul Baron conducting. The cover offers a nice picture of bow-tied Vincent in an art gallery.

In *America the Beautiful* (Columbia Masterworks, 91A 02013 / ML 5668) Price narrates a flowing history of great poems, and performs "Paul Revere's Ride," "The Star Spangled Banner," "Trees," "A Visit from St. Nicholas," "Jesse James," "Casey at the Bat," "Casey Jones," "The New Colossus," "Chicago," and "America the Beautiful."

In 1977, Nelson Industries of Marina del Rey issued *Push-Button Cookery*, a set (records or a dozen cassettes in gift box) with Price offering his insights and recipes. Topics include: "Dining at Versailles," "Delights from the Sultan's Pantry," "Cusina Italiana," "Dinner at the Casbah," "The Bard's Board," "Classical Spanish Cuisine," "La Cocina Mejicana," "Bounty of Paradise," "The Wok," "Exotic Delights from the Far East," "Foods from the Austro-Hungarian Empire" and "Food of the Gods."

Continuing the food motif is *Mr. Vincent Price: Wine Is Elegance* (Nelson Industries, 1977), a bonus for buyers of *Push-Button Cookery* (aka *Vincent Price International Cooking Course*).

The Wilde idea: Vinnie leaves pauses so *you*, script in hand, can act opposite him in scenes from *The Importance of Being Earnest.*

A Musical Panorama for Symphony Orchestra and Male Choir (aka *Alexander Laszlo: The World of Century Twenty First*) was narrated by Vincent Price and sold at the Seattle World's Fair. And on blue vinyl, too (Capitol SGP 6258).

One of the more ambitious failures of 1960–61 was the set of *City Guide* and *Museum Guide* books published by Panorama/Columbia Record Club. Each package contained an awkward set of 32 color slides that were mounted on two boards and could only work with special projectors, a seven inch 33⅓ record, and a brittle 11 × 8 hardcover book with pictures. Price narrated four museum tour guides: "The Pitti Palace" in Florence, "The Louvre" in Paris, "The Prado Museum" in Madrid, and "The Museum of Impressionism" in Paris. He also narrated three guides to countries: Italy, Greece and Spain.

The usually apolitical Price turns up on the Stanley Myron Handelman comedy album *Spiro T. Agnew Is a Riot* (Cadet CCX 1). He plays one of the advisors trying to figure out ways to keep the vice president from wreaking havoc with his malaprop speeches, and is part of an ensemble cast that includes Jack DeLeon, Pat McCormick, Rich Little and Jo Ann Pflug. He's also briefly heard wisecracking on *Zingers from the Hollywood Squares*, a soundtrack from the TV series (Event EV 6903).

Price was greatly disappointed with the failure of his Broadway musical *Darling of the Day* (RCA LSO 1149), which survives in both vinyl and CD format, and includes several earnest songs, such as "To Get Out of This Life Alive," which isn't a ghoulish number but reflects the show's plot (an artist figuring his work might sell better if he was dead).

Price's voice was part of the fun in the animated "The 13 Ghosts of Scooby Doo" (*Scooby-Doo's Snack Tracks: Ultimate Collection*, Rhino 75505), and he sings on the soundtrack for *The Great Mouse Detective* (Varese 5359), and on *Sammy Sings Fain, Again*, which offers a lot of demo performances by Fain of his hit songs, such as "I Can Dream Can't I," "That Old Feeling" and "You Brought a New Kind of Love to Me" (Library of Congress). The composer gives way to Vincent, who narrates the track "If These Walls Could Speak." Vincent was host of a 1990 series by that title, in which visitors got a chance to visit a different place each episode: Kronberg Castle, Iolani Palace, Edinburgh Castle, Sutter's Mill, Virginia City Nevada, etc.

Price has narration moments in the songs "Welcome to My Nightmare" (Alice Cooper), "Number of the Beast" (Iron Maiden), and "Thriller" (Michael Jackson). Less well known is the British single (EMI 2659) he recorded of "Monster Mash," with a few typically mild and friendly asides ("Do the Monster Mash ... it won't hurt, I promise!") and the lyric change, "Tell them Vincent sent you..." It's backed with a disco version of Shakespeare's witch's brew from *Macbeth*. A female chorus ("What will it be! Bard's Own Recipe!") backs Vincent as he joyfully recites the familiar gruesome ingredients ("Eye of newt and toe of frog, wool of bat and tongue of dog..."), now titled "The Bard's Own Recipe." As Zacherley and Bobby "Boris" Pickett did in horror novelty tunes before him, Vinnie ad-libs some remarks during the song's musical fade-out: "Well, that may be the Bard's recipe, but he'll never learn to cook like mother. Waiter, would you chill this wine a little more, please?"

5

The Horror Hams: Laird Cregar, John Carradine and Basil Rathbone

Whether described as "gothic" or "grand guignol," the meaning is the same: horror can be hammy. Classic terror on radio often was abetted by histrionic music and an overload of sound effects: howling wind, strange noises and any combination of unnatural laughter and unholy screams. These traits would be satirized on *Inner Sanctum*, complete with musical organ stabs, maniacal laughter and the famous creaking door.

Yet, *Inner Sanctum* was seriously horrific despite its emphasis on embarrassing cliché, and performers had to "go over the top" in order to compete with all the sound effects and spook music. Horror stars had been doing it for years on screen, where they commanded an audience's attention despite raging thunderstorms, exploding scientific laboratories or booming scores for full orchestra.

In the world of gothic ham, the tortured hero is also the torturing villain (Dr. Jekyll, Dr. Frankenstein, the Phantom of the Opera, the Invisible Man, etc.), and his struggles of lust, creation, power or revenge are Shakespearean in their level of supreme tragedy.

It's been argued that ham acting came naturally enough from stage performers who had to loudly over-emote to reach the cheap seats. The recorded works of classic readers of soliloquy or poetry, from John Barrymore to Dylan Thomas, often seem designed to show off the voice rather than the writing.

Barrymore (memorable as Dr. Jekyll in the silent era and Svengali in talkies) was the master Shakespearean ham, expected to trill an "r" as he widened an eye, curled a lip and shook a fist. In his wake, well-schooled in Shakespeare and possessed of magnetic acting skills, were several stars who found themselves in histrionic horror films more often than *Hamlet*.

John Carradine was a friend of Barrymore's and a legend for actually wearing a cape and emoting Shakespeare as he strolled the streets. His deep and hollow voice made an impression in a variety of quality roles, including the ex-preacher in *The Grapes of Wrath*. He was quickly swallowed up into the horror and sci-fi genre, and among his prize recordings there is his treatment of Edgar Allan Poe's poems (with moody organ music in the background).

Affectionately dubbed a "hambone," Basil Rathbone turned Sherlock Holmes into a theatrical, larger-than-life hero in five times as many radio shows as films, and made a series of Edgar Allan Poe recordings that can still be relished for their pungency in punctuation.

As for Laird Cregar, he vaulted from a vanity production of Oscar Wilde on stage into a series of grand guignol performances, including a classic "Jack the Ripper" turn. Unlike Carradine or Rathbone, Cregar had an unrequited passion for romantic star status, and he longed to discard his black cape for the white-lace shirt and silk cravat of the gothic leading man. It would cost him his life.

Laird Cregar

Charles Laughton found ways of making his unusual face and hefty frame work for him, and he found some artistic satisfaction in playing outsiders. Young Laird Cregar did not see things the same way.

When he was increasingly typed into villain roles, he found it a fate worse than death. The radical measures he took to try and stop his slide into Hollywood horror roles proved fatal.

Born Samuel Laird Cregar in Philadelphia (July 28, 1914–December 9, 1944), he acquired some of his gothic flair during his school days in England. He performed with the Stratford on Avon Players, and had he stayed in England he felt he would've been a star in Shakespeare repertory.

Back Stateside after the death of his affluent father, Cregar attended Philadelphia Episcopal Academy and appeared in productions at the Germantown Hedgerow Theater. His impetuous move to New York City brought him a job at the Paramount Theater—as an usher. This was a step up from his position as a clerk at Macy's department store.

Laird Cregar shows true acting ability ... in striking a harmless, cuddlesome pose.

The aspiring thespian found better luck on the West Coast, earning a scholarship to the Pasadena Community Playhouse. At 6' 3" he was a standout in any crowd, and cultivated the friendships of men who shared his interests in the arts. One of them was affluent enough to back Cregar in a vanity production of *Oscar Wilde*. The "right people" saw him, and the aspiring theatrical giant received several offers from Hollywood studios.

As his *Herald Tribune* obit only a few years later would mention, "Samuel Laird Cregar was almost as much of a 'boy wonder' as Orson Welles, but unlike the latter he had come to be typed as a sinister villain. To this end he brought a silky voice under which lay the hint of violence." While Welles relished radio, a perfect vehicle to show off his voice, Cregar wanted to be *seen*.

In an interview with Dee Lowrance for *Movie Star Parade* (she told readers to "pronounce Cregar to rhyme with cigar") he admitted his obsession with being noticed:

> I've driven friends and relations crazy since I can remember. I used to spend hours making faces into the mirror then run out and say: "What's this face?" to anyone I could nab. My "trapped rat" face was something, also my man-into-beast. In Philadelphia, where I grew up, they thought I was mad.

His madman role in *The Lodger* won him instant notoriety as a promising new villain, most critics remarking with surprise that this young man barely out of his 20s could rival the old grim and gruesome characters like Karloff and Lugosi. Of *The Lodger*, Cregar grumbled, "It's the kind of plum part which keeps an actor in fear that what he does next will in no way live up to it."

Some of the fan magazines wondered why he wasn't married—as if there weren't already hints of his homosexuality in the Hollywood underground. Cregar offered a stock line to Dee Lowrance: "I've seen too much phony marriages around me. I'd hate to take a bride, split up after a year or so and find myself giving some unworthy person half of my very, very hard-earned worldly goods."

One of Cregar's first radio appearances was for *Treasury Star Parade*, the 15-minute patriotic program designed to help sell war bonds. Sometimes the program offered a dramatic sketch intended to arouse indignation and stir patriotic contributions. Cregar joins Fredric March for "Address Unknown," a chronicle of Germany's rise to power via a set of letters between Max and his friend Martin. Fredric March is Max and Cregar is Martin, living in Munich, where Max's sister also lives, unable to escape the rise of Nazism. The story begins around 1933, and Max writes: "Who is this Adolf Hitler who seems rising toward power in Germany? I do not like what I read of him."

Martin writes back:

> I think in many ways Hitler is good for Germany, but I am not sure. The man is like an electric shock, strong as only a great orator and zealot can be, but I ask myself, is he quite sane? His brown shirt troops are of the rabble, they pillage and have started a bad Jew-baiting. But these may be minor things, the little surface scum when a big movement boils up. For I tell you my friend there is a surge! A surge! The people everywhere have had a quickening. The old dispair has been thrown aside like a forgotten coat. A leader is found, yet cautiously to myself I ask, a leader ... to where?

The alarm for listeners keeps escalating as the nightmare grows, and the character Martin throws aside his friendship with Max for his allegience to Hitler: "This Jew trouble is only an incident. Something bigger is happening—the rebirth of this New Germany.... We hold our heads up before nations ... but no, you will be a Jew first and wail for your people. This is the Semitic character. I regret our correspondene must close this way, Max." And it gets worse when Max keeps on writing with more and more frantic concerns, especially when Max's letters to his sister come back "Address Unknown," and he looks to Martin for help. Is his sister dead or alive? Is Martin cruel enough not to care?

Early in February of 1943, *Lux Radio Theatre* presented "The Maltese Falcon," with Laird Cregar (the announcer pronouncing the last name "Cree-gar") given third billing, now considered a major star alongside Edward G. Robinson and Gail Patrick. Naturally enough, even though Cregar was not physically seen, he was cast as the bulky searcher for the treasure, Mr. Gutman. While Robinson isn't far from his Warner Bros. rival Bogart in his gangster grumbling as Sam Spade, and a fair Peter Lorre sound-alike takes the task of becoming Joel Cairo, Cregar doesn't choose to mimic the gruff voice of Sydney Greenstreet.

Cregar becomes suitably daunting simply by using his crisp diction and affecting an air of superiority and breeding:

> "Ah, Mr. Spade, delighted to see you, delighted. We'll have a little drink. Say when, Mr. Spade."
> "I'll leave it to you."
> "Ha ha ha ha, excellent, excellent. I distrust a man who says when. If he's got to be careful not to drink too much it's because he's not to be trusted when he does. You're a close-mouthed man, Mr. Spade?"
> "I like to talk. I enjoy it."
> "Better and better! I distrust a close-mouthed man. He generally picks the wrong time to talk and says the wrong thing. Well sir, we'll talk."

In a *New York Post* interview on the last day of 1943, Cregar analyzed his career this way:

> Maybe the quirk and the fact that villainy is my special forte—although I hate to be symbolized as such—comes from being a direct descendant of John Wilkes Booth. [Booth's mother was Cregar's great great grandmother.] He was a ham and so am I. It doesn't seem to run in the family, though. None of my five brothers ever had any interest in show business.

The year 1943 had been exhausting. Professionally, he had attained fame, but in a loathsome horror role. Physically, he was suffering a dieter's nightmare of deprivation as he struggled to carve away at his 300-pound frame. Emotionally, he was still recovering from the September murder of his friend, actor David Bacon, who had evidently been stabbed in the back at an all-male brothel and bled to death in a desperate attempt to drive away for help.

Cregar began 1944 by guest-starring in three episodes of *Inner Sanctum*, broadcast January 8 ("The Death Laugh"), January 22 ("The Song of Doom") and February 5 ("Dealer in Death"). None of them have survived. The percentage of surviving transcription discs or tapes from that series is quite small.

Starring on *Inner Sanctum* and promoting a horror image only intensified Cregar's determination to change his image at all costs. The "silky voice" he used on radio would have to be matched by a new, slim, romantic face and body for films.

Writer Joe Scadden, Jr., writing for *Hollywood Studio Magazine* (September 1982), chronicled how Laird's Jack the Ripper role in *The Lodger* led him to rip away at his own bulky flesh:

> On completion of *The Lodger*, Laird began his overpowering struggle to become a leading man. He dieted strenuously, and, in a dangerously short period of time, lost 85 pounds. Unfortunately for him, the powers at Fox (read Zanuck) would take no heed of his metamorphosis. After the success of *The Lodger* they acquired a contemporary novel, *Hangover Square*, the story of yet another tortured young man. Laird was stunned when Fox announced it as his next assignment, again under John Brahm's direction. When he balked at accepting the role, he was put on suspension. Finally, he relented and reluctantly agreed to star.

Centering on a pianist given to homicidal spells of dementia, *Hangover Square* was fully intended to play off the success of *The Lodger*, with a bit of a *Phantom of the Opera* twist—Cregar having to expertly mime the florid piano concerto concocted by Alfred Hitchcock's veteran soundtrack maestro, Bernard Herrmann.

Cregar told reporter Tyra Fuller in September 1944 that playing the piano in the film and matching it to the pre-recorded music was surprisingly tough: "It's awful, you can't imagine how difficult it is to try and get your hands and fingers in the right places at the right time so the camera and recording will click."

It takes a ham to make an audience suspend disbelief, and Cregar was able to chill as he moves from velvet-voiced pianist to wide-eyed madman. This contrast of softly pleasant voice with evil deeds would be a ticket to fame for Vincent Price, who co-starred with Cregar in the 1941 film *Hudson's Bay*; but *Hangover Square* would be the last movie for the troubled star.

His last radio appearance was on *Suspense*, a program that Price would visit again and again. Cregar stars in "Narrative About Clarence," a kind of mental ward twist on "The Man Who Came to Dinner."

He plays a character sounding part Vincent Price and part Monty Woolley. An officious, egotistic "mental scientist" banished from America for fifteen years, he turns up at his half-sister's home announcing that he intends to stay until he can set up a sanitarium:

> The mind, the human mind, with all its strange powers for good and evil; that is my province.... I penetrated deep into the mysteries of the human mind, and then I discovered a psychic power transcending the mere gray matter of the human brain.... I shall continue my investigations into ... the occult. Is that clear?

With his imposing ability to read minds and predict behavior, he is too formidable to be crossed—although his half-sister's husband (Hans Conried) shows an ever-increasing hostility. Conried begins to plot murder when "Uncle Clarence" starts performing "magic" tricks for their young daughter by using a hypnotic cat's eye ring.

Cregar is magnetic and spooky when putting the girl into a trance: "Look at the ring. Look, and see. Look right in the center of the cat's eye. That's it. First you feel terribly terribly sleepy. And then you see the most wonderful things..."

In typical *Suspense* fashion, the husband tries to get the madman out of his house, but the authorities think *he* is crazy and that Clarence is his doctor.

Cregar, joining that long line of chillingly intelligent villains, uses his mockingly sophisticated voice to chide and torment his victims. The unhinged husband finally begs to know Clarence's evil game:

> "Why do you say you want to kill my wife and child?"
>
> "Because my mother meant more to me than anything in the world. She died in giving birth to this silly, shallow person you call your wife. I have hated her since the day she was born. And I hate the child, because having no right to life, she commits the sacrilege of inheriting my mother's beauty. They must both be destroyed, the murderer and the imposter!"
>
> "You are mad..."
>
> "Am I? Did I *really* say what you think you just heard me say? Or is it only part of your insanity?"

The unpleasant tale unravels to ultimately chill and repulse the listener, and Cregar takes a brief curtain call while his movie *The Lodger* gets a plug.

The haunting line "I Am with You Always" is on the grave marker for Laird Cregar.

Ironically, nine months later, in December 1944, *Suspense* would adapt *The Lodger* for radio, followed the next week by another tale that would seem to have been perfect for Cregar, *The Brighton Strangler*. But by then, young Laird Cregar had met his untimely end.

In late November 1944 he underwent abdominal surgery at Good Samaritan Hospital in Los Angeles, the final step in his plan to present a new, permanently slim physique for film roles. His body was weak from both the operation and having already dieted away dozens of pounds, and the actor suffered a heart attack. He was placed in an oxygen tent, but a few days later he suffered a second heart attack and died, on December 9, 1944. At the funeral, his eulogy was delivered by Vincent Price.

Radio

Hello Americans. January 10, 1943, CBS, 30 min. Orson Welles created this mini-series that salutes people and events in South America. Featuring Orson Welles, Hans Conried, Laird Cregar, Agnes Moorehead and Ray Collins.

Lux Radio Theatre. January 25, 1943, CBS, 60 min. "This Gun for Hire," with Joan Blondell, Laird Cregar and Alan Ladd.

Soldiers with Wings. 1943, Mutual, 30 min. Only one transcription disc seems to have survived, so listeners will only get half the story of a soldier's return from duty. Starring Laird Cregar, Martha Tilton, Frances Dee and Edward Waters.

Lux Radio Theatre. February 8, 1943, CBS, 60 min. "The Maltese Falcon," with Edward G. Robinson and Gail Patrick.

Lux Radio Theatre. April 12, 1943, CBS, 60 min. "Once Upon a Honeymoon," with Claudette Colbert, and Brian Aherne.

Suspense. July 27, 1943, CBS, 30 min. "The Last Letter of Dr. Bronson," starring Laird Cregar.

The Kate Smith Show. December 3, 1943.

Inner Sanctum. January 8, 1944. "The Death Laugh" is the first of three lost episodes of the show starring Laird Cregar.

The Radio Hall of Fame. January 9, 1944. The dramatic sketch "Moonlight" stars Laird Cregar in this variety series. Garry Moore performs a monologue, and there are also laughs from Fanny Brice and Hanley Stafford.

Star for a Night. January 18, 1944, Blue Network, 30 min. Recorded at the Ritz Theatre in New York, Laird Cregar guest stars, along with host Paul Douglas, in a re-working of "Dr. Jekyll and Mr. Hyde." This is another one of those frustrating shows where a missing transcription disc leaves listeners with only half the program.

Treasury Star Parade. 1944, Treasury Department syndication, 15 min. "Address Unknown," starring Fredric March and Laird Cregar.

Inner Sanctum. January 8, 1944, CBS, 30 min. "The Death Laugh."

Inner Sanctum. January 22, 1944, CBS, 30 min. "The Song of Doom."

Inner Sanctum. February 5, 1944, CBS, 30 min. "Dealer in Death." All three episodes of *Inner Sanctum* are still on the lost list.

Suspense. March 16, 1944, CBS, 30 min. In "Narrative About Clarence," Laird Cregar is the commanding presence come to visit and frighten all his relatives.

John Carradine

Very Shakespearean, ergo very eccentric, John Carradine (February 5, 1906–November 27, 1988) was bombastic enough to impress the spectacle-oriented director Cecil B.

DeMille. The year was 1932, and the thin actor had managed some very minor roles, including a brief blink in *The Invisible Man*.

Carradine recalled: "DeMille saw an apparition—me—pass him by, reciting the gravedigger's lines from *Hamlet*, and he instructed me to report to him the following day. The director was so impressed with my rich, deep voice that he had me recite the Beatitudes, which, unfortunately, wound up on the soundtrack emanating from another actor's mouth."

The film, *Sign of the Cross*, was just one of many to feature Carradine in a minor role. He was a member of a Satanist cult in the Karloff and Lugosi starrer *The Black Cat* (1934), and gasped at the sight of Karloff in a blind hermit's shack in *Bride of Franken-*

The Grapes of Wrath (1940): a rare "A" picture for John Carradine (center), co-starring Dorris Bowden (left) and starring Henry Fonda (right).

stein (1935). In 1936 he played the sadistic guard keeping an eye on Dr. Mudd in *Prisoner of Shark Island.*

Despite a good co-starring opportunity in the classic Henry Fonda film *The Grapes of Wrath*, Carradine found himself a minor figure in big-budget films, but the star of low-budget horror fare. He became Universal's new Dracula in the 1940s—leading to 40 years of cheap horror film purgatory.

As genre expert Joe Kane (the *Daily News*' "Phantom of the Movies" and editor of *Videoscope*) eulogized at the star's passing:

> Carradine will be best remembered for his prolific contributions to the fright-film field. In a scare-screen career that spanned more than 45 years, from 1942's *Captive Wild Woman* to 1988's *Evil Spawn*, Carradine lent his flamboyant talents to literally scores of low-budget celluloid shockers, where he was frequently cast as vampires, ghouls, and mad scientists of every conceivable stripe. More often than not, especially in recent years, Carradine's wonderfully eccentric, generally crazed cameos supplied the only reason for seeing the films in which he appeared. Watching *Billy the Kid vs. Dracula* or a *Horror of the Blood Monsters* minus Long John's charismatic participation would be to risk an instant cerebral short-circuit.

Looking back on it all, Carradine said, "I never made big money in Hollywood. I was paid in hundreds, the stars got thousands. But I worked with some of the greatest directors in films and some of the greatest writers. They gave me freedom to do what I can do best, and that was gratifying."

Born Richmond Reed Carradine in New York City, his mother was a surgeon and his father switched from being a lawyer to being a writer: "My father had been a London correspondent for the Associated Press just before I was born. But he had contracted tuberculosis, and the London climate didn't do him any good. He died when I was quite small."

Young John started out as a painter, but by 1927 was in California working in a Shakespearean stock company. He loved the stage, but Hollywood was where the money was, and where he could indulge in a bohemian lifestyle, enjoying the company of like-minded thespians after hours. He even sought out John Barrymore, journeying to the esteemed actor's home unannounced. Barrymore instantly recognized Carradine as a kindred spirit, and invited him in to share a drink.

The *New York Times* obituary for Carradine duly noted:

> In private life he amusedly cultivated a reputation as an eccentric and a bit of a ham. Grandly bedecked in a red-lined satin cape and wearing a wide-brimmed hat, he liked to stroll the streets of Los Angeles and New York sonorously reciting Shakespearean dialogue. In Hollywood he was sometimes called the "Bard of the Boulevard."

New York Post writer Jerry Tallmer recalls, "Old ham, in fact, was what I think—just barely think—he would have owned up to most undisguisedly, if you caught him right." Carradine once dropped by Tallmer's apartment and

> reached for a bottle and settled in for a long night's journey into dawn. He talked about Shakespeare. He did Shakespeare. He talked about *La Boheme*, and all about opera. "What? You've never seen *La Boheme*? And you pretend to be educated?" There, sitting in a deep Knoll armchair, bottle in hand, he performed, sang, spoke, all of *La Boheme*.... I've never seen *La Boheme*. I don't have to. I've seen John Carradine.

In a 1986 piece published in the fanzine *Fangoria*, Carradine recalled the golden era when ham-voiced actors were respected and admired:

> That was the time when there was a big British colony in Hollywood. The best English actors came to Hollywood and did well. I knew all of them. Most were good friends of mine. David

Niven was a good friend, and Basil Rathbone was a close friend. There were others whom I admired a great deal.

Like another actor in love with his own voice, Bela Lugosi, Carradine would in later years claim that he turned down the non-speaking role of the Frankenstein monster in 1931. He told *Fangoria*, "I was interested in playing the monster. They made a life mask and everything, but then I found out all I had to do was grunt! I turned it down and they gave it to Boris."

Ironically, when Carradine took over for Bela Lugosi as Universal's Dracula, he was more concerned with visuals than voice:

> When they asked me to play Dracula I said yes, if you let me make him up and play him the way Bram Stoker described him—as an elderly, distinguished gentleman with a drooping mustache.... They didn't like a big mustache, so I had to trim it and make it a very clipped, British mustache. It wasn't really in character.... The English critics said I was the best Dracula, which was very nice considering that I had been preceded by Bela who did a hell of a job. After all, he had played that character for years.

Carradine co-starred in some low-budget movies with Lugosi and remembered him as "a charming man and a hell of an actor. He used to come on the set with a bottle of claret, which he sipped at a little bit all day long. He never got drunk, never lost a line, never lost his tempo or his accent, which was native to him."

At Monogram studios in the 1940s, Carradine starred in poorly scripted and directed films, and felt the problem began at the top, with owner "Frank Kane ... an ignorant man. It's reported that at a board of directors meeting, he said, 'Gentlemen, we are standing on the brink of an abcess.' He meant abyss."

Carradine's reputation as a skilled scholar and skull-faced scarer led him to radio's *Information Please*, joining the panel with Franklin P. Adams, John Kieran and Boris Karloff:

> CLIFTON FADIMAN: "In deference to our monstrous guests this evening, we start off with a question about victims of one sort or another. I want you to identify for us, a victim of treachery in fact or in fiction who was shot in the back of the head. Mr. Karloff?"
> BORIS: "I think that would be Jesse James?"
> CLIFTON: "It was Jesse James. Who shot him, Mr. Carradine?"
> JOHN: "I did."
> CLIFTON: "We never had it more pleasantly explained. What was your fictional name in the play, Mr. Carradine?"
> JOHN: "Bob Ford."
> CLIFTON: "Robert Ford. Yes."
> ADAMS: "Dirty little coward who shot Mr. Howard..."
> CLIFTON: "Now now, we want to have as much friendly badinage, Mr. Adams, as we can on this program. Also, Carradine's a darn sight bigger than you are..."

Later on there are some questions on Shakespeare, including specific scenes from *Hamlet, Macbeth, Othello*. For each question

Carradine cared: a stickler for detail, John Carradine went back to the description in Bram Stoker's book, and added a mustache when he vamped in *House of Dracula* (1945).

Carradine proceeds to illustrate the answer by reciting several complicated lines from memory. At one point the admiring Fadiman declares, "I'd like to explain to the audience that Mr. Carradine is not reading from the book!"

Carradine was one of the many busy character actors who chose films over radio work. One of his rare radio appearances was opposite Bela Lugosi in "The Thirsty Death," the pilot episode of a proposed radio series; but it was Lugosi who had the flashy madman's role.

Carradine used his lofty Shakespearean image to ham it up in a sketch on the *Dean Martin and Jerry Lewis Show*. John's son needs a babysitter—Jerry Lewis. Carradine and Dean Martin are waiting for Jerry in Carradine's apartment. John, the cliché of a ham actor, puts on grandiose airs, pronouncing "theater" as "thee-taw":

> JOHN: "I can't understand it, Dean. What could be keeping that partner of yours? He's been gone over an hour. It's nearly time for me to leave for the *thee-taw!*"
> DEAN: "Don't worry, I'm sure he'll be here in time."
> JOHN: "But we should leave in less than five minutes!"
> DEAN: "We will make it. You really love the theater, don't you John?"
> JOHN: "Love the *thee-taw?* The *thee-taw's* me whole life. I live for *thee-taw*, I eat the *thee-taw*, I *drrrink* the *thee-taw*, and when I stand back and look at myself..."
> DEAN: "Yes?"
> JOHN: "Sometimes I think I'd be better off with a good thick steak!"

Carradine returns late in the episode to discover that a few hours with Jerry Lewis has changed his intellectual son into a tap-dancing jive bopper who wants to belt out "Darktown Strutter's Ball." Again Carradine is called on to declaim in a pompous and florid manner, leading to a deliberately off-character punchline:

> JOHN: "You've *undermined* ten years of the most *extensive* cultural training. You've *contaminated* his mental faculties. You've taken a *beautiful* thing and *desecrated* it!"
> JERRY: "I what?"
> JOHN: "You've loused everything up!"

Radio was, of course, eclipsed in the '50s and died in the '60s, but another form of audio, the record album, became popular, and the audience that still hungered for listening excitement found it in several Carradine recordings.

Carradine was an inspired choice to join Ben Wright and Hoagy Carmichael on *Poetry and Jazz* (World Pacific WP 1409), a 1958 collection of poetry from William Carlos Williams, Dylan Thomas, Lawrence Ferlinghetti, Langston Hughes and others. The words were mated to hip jazz from the Ralph Pena Quartet, Bob Dorough Quintet and others.

Carradine's two contributions are "Poets to Come" (by Walt Whitman, performed with the Jazz Canto Ensemble, with music by *Little Shop of Horrors* soundtrack composer Fred Katz) and the more ambitious "Night Song for the Sleepless," by Lawrence Lipton, with music composed by Benny Collette and played by the Chico Hamilton Quintet.

With typical 1950s bongos and "Quiet Village" woodwinds from Chico Hamilton, Carradine fully bakes the imagery of death and drugs and tragic hipness:

> A dozen hands outstretch. Here, take and drink! Drug the pain with this, the poppy. Marijuana. Flay the flesh with passion ... sink into the dim half-underworld, the dream of death in life. And now walk tall upon the earth! Now, dance! In haze of music overheard. And all the while, in Amazon, the blue and orange Toucan preens, the boa glides, the poison arrows fly. Tibetan wizards sway from side to side...

And the era's beatniks were swaying, too.

Part of the charm of Carradine is that his acting is both hipster and ham-ster. The best ham horror stars know how to wink at the audience while delivering their all-too-serious declarations. Carradine's history of cheap horror films had to be a draw for both a record producer and the audience, so even the stuffiest corn could pop when he was behind the microphone, his almost too-deep-to-be-true hollow voice resonating each unreasonable line.

Some poems and literature, from Shakespeare to Poe, test an actor's skill in handling the lurid and the lucid, and quite often listeners enjoy a theatrical approach that puts things over the top. Ham actors have had a field day with works that deliberately cross and re-cross the lines of comedy and tragedy—for example, "Casey at the Bat" (which was recorded by Vincent Price).

"The Raven," which has been endlessly parodied, was given a dash of *Inner Sanctum* organ when Carradine performed it. His album *Poe with Pipes* is a delicious example of spiced ham, and was produced by Verne Langdon, a make-up artist who co-partnered in a company that made Halloween masks sold in the back of *Famous Monsters of Filmland* magazine.

"He had a magnificent voice," Langdon recalled in a VideoScope magazine interview conducted by Terry and Tiffany DuFoe:

> So John showed up at Whitney Studios, where the pipe organ was.... And I had typed all of the poetry in very large type so Mr. Carradine could read it easier. I hand the pages to him. "These are the things we're going to be doing." He looks through them and he says, "Very good." And he hands me back the whole stack. I say, "Well, you'll want to read from these." He says, "I don't need to." I said, "You mean you know them?" He smiled and answered wryly, "Rather well."

The scholarly actor rarely got a word wrong:

> He went right down the line, knowing every title in his mind that we were doing, in the order we wanted it done—every poem, word for word! He didn't miss a word. He didn't miss an intonation. He didn't miss a beat. It was perfect. No two takes. My jaw was on the floor by the time we were done. Then he went home and I put the music behind it.

Actually, Carradine did miss a word or two, and mumble a bit. On "Annabel Lee" he mutters that "her highborn kin-men came and bore-r away from me." The poem's last line changes from "in her tomb by the sounding sea" to "in her tomb by the side of the sea." And on "The Raven" the narrator beholds a "pallid bust" of Pallas, not a "placid bust."

It takes a ham to recite some of Poe's most wonderfully over-baked lines. In "Conqueror Worm," both listener and actor can relish "much of Madness, and more of Sin, and Horror, the soul of the plot!"

Other oddities and entities for Carradine hunters include a full-cast radio-style version of *White Cargo* (Audio Masterpiece LPA 1215), with Sonia Sorel as the infamous Tondeleyo and Carradine as Witzel; the Broadway original cast album to *A Funny Thing Happened on the Way to the Forum*, in which he sings on one cut, "Everybody Ought to Have a Maid" (Capitol SW 1717); and his appearance on the dais for the "Executive Reception and Dinner" held at the Hotel Pierre at Christmas 1952, issued as a red vinyl souvenir by the Arthur Tickle Engineering Works. They evidently brought their workers and families together for some festivities, and hired musicians, opera singer Hilde Gueden, and John Carradine to supply the entertainment.

One side of that album is instrumental music, the other features a reading from Carradine. "I always begin my programs with a passage from the Bible," he tells the crowd. This time it's the story of the baby Jesus, from the Gospel According to St. Luke. Actually, he ends the program with it, since the master of ceremonies thanks Carradine (the last name here pronounced to rhyme with whine) and goes on to introduce the performance by Madame Gueden.

Recordings hardly amounted to much money for Carradine, so he spent most of his last years working in B-movies and appearing on stage.

In 1975 he starred in a Chicago production of *Arsenic and Old Lace*, with the gimmick casting of Zsa Zsa and Eva Gabor as the play's murder-minded sisters. The Gabors got $10,000 a week, and he received $1500. Michael Sneed of the *Chicago Sun Times* recalled the star's backstage lifestyle:

> Scotch, no ice, was his drink and he never refused one. Having had a large quantity, he would go into his dressing room, put on his dressing gown, do the crossword to compose himself, and it was as if someone else had climbed into his body. He would go on and never slur a word of dialogue when he should have fallen on his nose.

After a performance he was quite amiable: "He loved the public and had untold patience with pictures and autographs for his fans."

Aging but ageless, when Carradine appeared in a film called *The Sentinel* in 1977, *Newsweek* counted it as his 466th movie. How they arrived at the figure is a mystery, since most sources can't find even half that number. Counting actual stage performances probably would've exceeded 466, and the actor kept adding to the count. He even returned to Broadway in 1981, playing the blind hermit in a doomed production of *Frankenstein*.

The show would only last one performance, but leading up to it, Carradine was proud to point to his huge list of credits. He told the *Daily News*:

> Only one actor, Donald Crisp, ever made more movies than me. And this *Frankenstein* is my 179th play! Most of them were in stock, of course. But I spent a lot of time on Broadway, too.... So here I am. One of the producers called my agent and I read the part and it seemed sympathetic. Besides, the money was right and the billing was right.

Carradine made a brief return to radio in the 1970s when he lent his sepulchral voice to the introductions for a handful of classic horror tales, including "The Monkey's Paw." The radio series never got beyond a few episodes, produced with anonymous cast and featuring an over-active Theremin-styled solo instrument adding music to the musty scripts. Each show was about 22 minutes, perhaps ambitiously hoping for 8 minutes of commercials. "The Monkey's Paw" episode has Carradine opening the show in grand style:

> Why don't you make yourself comfortable while I dim the lights, just a bit. Oh, by the way, you don't frighten easily, do you? I ask because the story we're about to present is one that has frightened people terribly for many years. Incidentally, I do hope you have someone listening with you, because I wouldn't want you to be alone. You know, there's something very ominous about the darkness when you're alone. Each noise you hear, the sound of footsteps, the hoot of an owl, the creaking of a door, can be terribly frightening when you're alone...

Carradine had supported the first generation of Universal monster stars in the 1930s and '40s, and worked with the new generation of Hammer stars (including Christopher Lee and Peter Cushing) in the '60s and '70s. Out-lasting most of his vintage friends was a bittersweet achievement. At age 76 he told the *Los Angeles Times*: "Lately I'm honored all over the country, yet the powers-that-be in Hollywood won't give me a job. I work all the time on stage, of course. But Lord knows how long it's been since I've had a major movie." A typical stage part on the "straw hat" trail was playing the irascible lead in productions of *On Golden Pond*.

Anecdotes about Carradine followed him everywhere. A reporter queried him about the time a fan asked him to autograph a copy of Shakespeare. Carradine was supposed to have refused, responding, "Would you ask a priest to autograph the Bible?" The actor listened to this retelling and said:

> I don't remember that. I don't remember that at all. But I wouldn't be surprised. That's exactly the sort of arrogant thing I would have said in those days. Not now. Oh no, never now. Now I'm much too humble for that.

Part of his humility included touring in a 1981 vaudeville review, the notorious *Roy Radin's Vaudeville Show*. Radin, ultimately a victim of foul play, had created a mini-career out of bringing '60s icons—from Frank Fontaine to Joanne Worley—on the road to small towns and college campuses. Carradine supplied the dramatic moments in the show by reciting Shakespeare, while Zippy the Chimp cavorted, the Harmonica Rascals offered music, and Tiny Tim sang. Tiny Tim said at the time that Carradine got "a very respectable reception. He told me that actors were special and when an actor goes onstage he only has himself. I often wonder what goes through his mind when we're on the bus."

Doing cheap horror films or obscure vaudeville tours couldn't have been more embarrassing than hearing rumors of his own death. Emphatically one of the undead, he once heard how "a talk show host referred to the late John Carradine. So I simply rung up the host and said, 'This is the late John Carradine ... I'm calling from the tomb.'"

By the time of his passing, the actor had already seen a new generation of Carradines reach stardom. Keith had some hits as a singer, and David had a long-running TV series. In all, he had five sons and four wives; his last marriage, at age 69, was to a bride of fifty. In 1979 he and a variety of his sons appeared in an episode of *The Fall Guy* TV series, and in 1984 *Carradines in Concert* was filmed but not released.

In the end, always described as thin, if not gaunt, Carradine was ravaged by arthritis and other ailments. He said, "I still have a brain and a voice," and vowed to use those tools to his dying day.

Befitting a star of the macabre and the unusual, some mystery surrounded Carradine's death. Early reports had the frail star stricken after climbing the steps of the Duomo, a famous Milan cathedral, and remarking, "Milan, what a beautiful place to die." In reality, his sons Keith and David found him languishing in a ward at Fatebenefratelli Hospital, weakened by heart and kidney failure.

Films featuring the late actor were still being released posthumously long after he died, less a tribute than a casualty of sometimes shooting a few days' work that a director could use for any number of future projects.

Not long before he died he looked back on the acting business:

> My first major movie was *Winterset*, I remember, and that was a long long time ago. There have been a lot of changes since then, most of them bad. Hollywood is dead. The major studios all abdicated, and those days will never come back, the days of the moguls. Louis B. Mayer, Darryl Zanuck. They were tyrants, every one of them, but they did a hell of a lot for actors, especially Mayer. He found them, trained them, developed them, publicized them and paid them well. Where is the training ground for young actors today? Television? Hah!

Carradine deserves the last word on his radio, television and film roles: "Good or bad, it was work."

Radio

Kay Parker in Hollywood. 1933, 5 min. Carradine appeared as an interview subject on Parker's syndicated program.

Good News of 1938. February 10, 1938, NBC, 60 min. A variety show featuring Fanny Brice as Baby Snooks, singer Alan Jones, and comedian-character actor Frank Morgan. John Carradine, Virginia Bruce, Jimmy Stewart and Gale Gordon appear in the centerpiece of the show, an adaptation of the W. Somerset Maugham drama *Of Human Bondage.*

Information Please. October 31, 1941; February 20, 1942; May 8, 1942, Blue Network, 30 min. Host Clifton Fadiman. The February 20 show finds the panel both erudite (John Kieran and Franklin P. Adams) and frightening (John Carradine and Boris Karloff).

This Is War, Program #7. March 28, 1942, NBC, 30 min. Typical wartime propaganda and patriotism from writer-director Norman Corwin. Listeners are cautioned that if they aren't working up to their capacity on the production line, they "have blood on their hands." Narration by John Carradine. Starring John Garfield, Henry Hull, Katherine Locke and Frank Lovejoy.

Mystery House. 1944, NBC, 30 min. "The Thirsty Death." This is the one and only episode of a proposed series for Bela Lugosi. John Carradine and Lurene Tuttle play ex-lovers who meet up in a jungle surrounded by rabid dogs, angry natives, and an even more diabolic Lugosi as the jealous husband.

Lest We Forget: These Great Americans, Program #11. 1946, Syndicated by the Institute for Democratic Education, 15 min. "The Story of Woodrow Wilson," starring John Carradine.

The Garden of Allah (1936) as only Hollywood could dream it: Marlene Dietrich, John Carradine and Basil Rathbone.

The Adventures of Ellery Queen. October 23, 1946, CBS, 30 min. "The Adventure of the Woman Who Died Several Times." A specialty of the show was to feature a "guest armchair detective" to try and solve the mystery along with the listeners at home. John Carradine is the woeful guest, wondering if he can get a supply of the sponsor's product (aspirin).

Broadway Talks Back. October 28, 1946, Mutual, 30 min. A current production of *The Duchess of Malfi* is discussed by critics Joseph Shipley and John Gardner, along with cast members John Carradine and Miss Jean Dalyrimple.

Marine Story, Program #16. 1948, syndicated by the Marine Corps, 15 min. John Carradine stars in this episode about a lieutenant in Texas during that state's early era of lawlessness, and the battle of the Alamo.

Voice of the Army, Program #401. 1948, syndicated by the Army, 15 min. "Tailor Made" is a program explaining how the best-dressed man is one in uniform. Starring Connie Lemke, John Carradine and John Seymore.

Turning Points, Program #4. November 5, 1948, syndicated by United Hatters, Cap and Millinery Workers International, "Black Magic" 15 min. The commercials for the "union label" don't get in the way of this brief drama about incidents in the life of Harry Houdini.

Voice of the Army, Program #462. 1949, syndicated by the Army, 15 min. "Double Talk" is a celebration of Army intelligence work in occupied France. Starring John Carradine.

The Martin and Lewis Show. June 28, 1949, NBC, 30 min. Jerry Lewis is going to babysit John Carradine's nephew, a precocious young genius.

Guest Star, Program #218. May 27, 1951, syndicated by the Treasury Department, 15 min. "Abe Lincoln in Illinois." The show pitched savings bonds and usually offered actors in a scene from a timely movie or play.

The Lux Radio Theatre. December 21, 1953, CBS, 60 min. "Peter Pan." (The surviving Armed Forces Radio Service broadcast dispensed with the commercial word "Lux," and the show was called *The Hollywood Radio Theatre*.) With Bobby Driscoll, John Carradine, Kathryn Beaumont and announcer Ken Carpenter.

John Carradine's Tales of Terror. c. 1970. Periodically an effort was made to revive old-time radio via new productions. Vincent Price hosted episodes for Sears, E.G. Marshall hosted the *CBS Mystery Theater*, and John Carradine was called into the studio for a series that didn't last very long. Each show is about 25 minutes, optimistically leaving time for commercials. The surviving episodes are: "Legacy," "The Monkey's Paw," "Winthrop Oil Painting" and "Cask of Amontillado."

Audio

Carradine recorded both commercial vinyl and cassette audio books. He narrated an audio documentary about the *Council on Foreign Relations* (FACT 17XLP), *The Child Seducers* (American United 14 XLP), a collection of Ambrose Bierce (Pelican 147), *Gift of the Magi* (GFM 62), *Walden* by Henry David Thoreau (Blackstone Audiobooks, originally 16rpm and re-issued on cassette), *If I'm Elected* (Audio Archives 1201), and joined Jonathan Winters and Claudine Longet on the children's album *The Little Prince* (Pip 6813).

By far the most popular of his recordings is *Poe with Pipes*, which was originally on vinyl from Electric Lemon, and re-issued on CD from Orchard (the CD version includes another album of non–Carradine horror sound effects and is officially titled *Halloween Spooktacular/Poe with Pipes*).

Poe with Pipes offers six tracks of Carradine reading Poe: "Conqueror Worm," "Ulalume," "Annabel Lee" (here spelled "Annabelle Lee"), "The Sleeper," "The Raven" and "Dream Within a Dream." All feature musical composer/producer Verne Langdon on "the Haunted Palace Theatre Organ."

Famous Monsters of Filmland editor Forrest J Ackerman's album notes are as ripe as the premise, praising "The Masked Organist—Ah yes, He Who Wears the Mask of the Red Death.

Whose gimlet eyes burn bright with the insane glee of demons set free as his fertile fingers fondle and caress the organ's trembling keys and squeeze from the moaning instrument's ivory fingers frenetic notes of anguish, terror, pity, horror, wonder, fear..." The narrator himself escapes with just minor blather: "Carradine came upon this Earth endowed with a voice that gave no other choice: he must hold captive in hypnotic thrall each individual, all auditors, who lend an ear to his charismatic and commanding tongue."

In 1975, Carradine recorded a three-minute track for Langdon that was eventually released, thirty years later, as the CD single "Hollywood on Parade" (Orchard DJV-00602). As written by Langdon, with the composer's sentimental piano tinkling in the background, Carradine describes leafing through movie books while clichéd imaginings of Clark Gable, Laurel and Hardy, Gary Cooper and *The Wizard of Oz* characters come to him via catch-phrases. John signs off with: "Good night, and God keep you wherever you are."

Born in the Greenwich Village area (12th Street), and certainly a bohemian all his life, Carradine was very much at home on *Poetry and Jazz* (World Pacific WP 1409), a 1958 collection mating William Carlos Williams, Dylan Thomas, Lawrence Ferlinghetti and other poems to hip music from the Ralph Pena Quartet, Bob Dorough Quintet and Chico Hamilton Quintet.

Carradine can also be heard on a radio-style version of *White Cargo*, (Audio Masterpiece LPA 1215) with Sonia Sorel as Tondeleyo; the Broadway original cast album for *A Funny Thing Happened on the Way to the Forum* (Capitol SW 1717); and on the dais for the "Executive Reception and Dinner" held at the Hotel Pierre in Christmas of 1952, issued as a red vinyl souvenir by the Arthur Tickle Engineering Works.

The radio show "Thirsty Death" (*Mystery Playhouse*) was released on the three-lp set *Great Radio Horror Shows* (Murray Hill 93397), along with non–Carradine shows such as the Mercury Theatre production of "Dracula," and episodes of *Weird Circle* and *Inner Sanctum*.

Selected Readings of John Carradine (Heritage LP PD 100) is a ten-inch album that offers five speeches from Shakespeare ("Seven Ages of Man," "Queen Mab's Speech," "Gloucester's Speech," "Cassius' Speech" and "Instructions to the Players"), two segments from Charles Baudelaire's "Flowers of Evil," and four passages from Rupert Brooke: "The Soldier," "The Voice," "Jealousy" and "Helen and Menelaus." The album notes assert:

> As a person, John Carradine is warm and friendly. He has delighted his friends for years with his impromptu reminiscences of such notables as the Duke of Windsor, Ezio Pinza, John Barrymore and Feodor Chaliapin. He has also kept them enthralled for hours at a time with his delightful readings from Shakespeare, Shaw, Wilde, Beaudelaire, Brooke and others. These are touched with an expressive mobility which we have tried to capture in this recording.... This is John Carradine's first commercial recording, and Audio Archives proudly presents it to the public. We hope that your enjoyment will match our enthusiasm.

Basil Rathbone

Basil Rathbone found one major difference between working in films and working on radio: ads. In his autobiography he took a moment to expound: "In newspapers and magazines you may choose to look at the ads if you so wish, but with radio ... they are rammed down your throat whether you like it or not; and more often than not when perhaps you might be enjoying the development of a well-written and well-acted play."

His ire included television, too, and he wrote:

> For the most part both radio and television are merciless mediums for any artist, creative or interpretive, and have been more responsible for the growth of mass mediocrity in our culture than anything else I can think of. Baseball sends our youngsters out with a desire to play baseball and one day perhaps to play in the major leagues. Did you ever hear of a youngster having seen or listened to *David Copperfield* or *Gone with the Wind* or *Hamlet* and wanting to *read* Dickens or Shakespeare or Margaret Mitchell?

Radio is unquestionably a superior medium to television because it makes us use our imaginations. I have been told by literally hundreds of people that when we were doing the Sherlock Holmes series they would turn out the lights or if they had a fire sit around it and let their imaginations go fancy free. Many have told me that the hound in *The Baskervilles* was far more frightening to them on radio than it could ever be on the screen or their television sets.

People also told Rathbone more than he wanted to hear about Holmes—which led him to abandon the tweeds of hero and more often assume the black cloak of villain. For horror audio fans, this not only included radio, but his pioneering Poe series for Caedmon records. As befitting a grand ham actor, his last screen appearances with Vincent Price, Peter Lorre and other aging horror greats offered a mixture of terror and pretention-puncturing sight gags.

Rathbone (June 13, 1892–July 21, 1967) was born in Johannesburg, South Africa, thanks to the "diamond boom" there, which was similar to California's Gold Rush. The romantic notion was that diamonds were there for the taking, but in reality, lives were there for the taking, and as the Boer War approached, Rathbone's civil engineer father was accused of being a British spy.

The family (including Basil and a younger brother and sister) had to make a perilous escape to safety in England. In 1911, Rathbone's cousin, manager of a Shakespeare company, allowed him to join and learn the profession. He progressed from small roles to better assignments, and then rose from private to 2nd lieutenant during his military service (1915–1919), which concluded with his receiving the Military Cross of England. As he briskly told interviewer Terry Thomas (on the *Voices from the Hollywood Past* interview album), "The only reason I got an MC was because I did the job I was told to do and I did it efficiently."

By 1921 he was appearing in silent movies and working on the London stage. In 1929 he came to Broadway in the show *Judas*, which he co-wrote. He was nominated for Academy Awards as a supporting actor in *Romeo and Juliet* (1936) and *If I Were King* (1938), and his real swordsmanship was on display in *The Adventures of Robin Hood* (1938) and *The Mark of Zorro* (1940).

Radio listeners were soon captivated by Rathbone's unique voice, which had a crisp precision to it, and, unlike with some other British actors, was easy for American audiences to understand: "I was told when I went into the English theater that I had what was then known as a 'colonial' accent. Now this interests me very much indeed, because I had to correct my speech."

He mentioned in his recorded interview for *Voices from the Hollywood Past* that ideally an actor in

Elegant as always, a latter-day portrait of urbane Basil Rathbone.

Shakespeare and classical theater should have a clear speaking voice devoid of regionalism:

> I don't want necessarily to say that you must have a British accent, or a typically English accent, but I think there ought to be some universal English which is acceptable on both sides of the water but which has no accent of any particular kind.... I maintain that there is no such thing as an English accent, and there is no such thing as an American accent. There are inflections used by speakers in both countries which differentiate—I think you might say it would be interesting to hear Mr. Eden speaking to Mr. Roosevelt, and I don't think any of us could say which spoke the better English.

During the Roosevelt era, which Rathbone felt was his happiest time in Hollywood, the actor was something of a British ambassador. At government request, he and his wife opened their house to parties for everyone from visiting dignitaries to Admiral Halsey. His name was known among Hollywood's elite, and at a party someone suggested to producer Darryl F. Zanuck that the Sherlock Holmes stories might make for an interesting picture. Zanuck agreed, and a moment later someone suggested that Basil Rathbone would be perfect for the role. "It was as simple as that," Rathbone recalled.

The thriller *Hound of the Baskervilles* (1939), with Rathbone as Sherlock Holmes and Nigel Bruce as Dr. Watson, led to a film series and an even longer radio run. He wrote in his autobiography:

> I have experienced nothing but embarrassment in the familiar streetcorner greeting of recognition, which is inevitably followed by horrendous imitations of my speech, loud laughter, and

A bunch of bones: Basil Rathbone poses with his dogs, his wife and his son Rodion.

ridiculing quotes of famous lines such as "Quick, Watson, the needle" or "Elementary, my dear Watson," followed by more laughter at my obvious discomfiture. Quite frankly and realistically, over the years I have been forced to accept the fact that my impersonation of one of the most famous fictional characters in all literature has not received that respectful recognition to which I feel Sir Arthur Conan Doyle's masterpieces entitle him. Has it been my fault? I do not think so. And certainly it is not the fault of those who were responsible for producing sixteen pictures and some two hundred weekly radio broadcasts between 1939 and 1946. Professionally it has always been conceded that both pictures and broadcasts were of an exceptionally high quality.

If the best remedy for a situation is to grin and bear it, Rathbone swallowed the medication, and his pride, and regularly burlesqued the Holmes character and his identification with it.

In 1944, Philip Rapp (writer of *The Bickersons* comedy series) created a short-lived novelty show about psychiatry. The pilot episode of the *Three of a Kind* radio series featured Rathbone seeking help for his bizarre problem:

"I'm an actor and I use the stage name of Basil Rathbone."
"Are you the same Rathbone who plays Sherlock Holmes on the radio?"
"Plays Sherlock Holmes? My dear sir, I am Sherlock Holmes!"

His delusion has nothing to do with mysteries. His quirk is that he prefers to carry his money with him rather than put it in a bank. He claims to have $10,000 "glued to my undershirt." That leads the psychiatrist to plot ways of getting Rathbone's clothes off, and the story gets more and more ludicrous.

The psychiatrist and his assistant ask Rathbone to recall his childhood, which immediately provokes wisecracks.

"I was left an orphan at the age of nine," Rathbone tells the shrink.
"What did he do with it?" asks the shrink's assistant.
"He turned it over to the orphan's home, of course!" quips the shrink. "Continue, Mr. Rathbone."
"I was raised by my grandmother whose sole means of support was hem stitching. She was too feeble to do her sewing in town, so she just worked on the outskirts."

On Perry Como's show, a chipper, quipping Rathbone arrives to solve a mystery involving the show's orchestra leader, Lloyd Shafer:

COMO: Why, Basil Rathbone!
RATHBONE: Not Basil Rathbone, Como, but Sherlock Holmes. Now to get on with the investigation of the crime...
COMO: What makes you think there's been a crime?
RATHBONE: Elementary, my dear Como—the corpus delecti.
COMO: A body? Where?
RATHBONE: Right there! Never in all my years as a detective have I seen anything so ghastly.
COMO: Ah, that's Lloyd Shafer, he always looks like that.
RATHBONE: Good heavens! Never have I seen a rigor so mortis. I'll track down his murderer if it's the last thing I do.
SHAFER: There must be some mistake. I'm not dead.
RATHBONE: You stay out of this. Como, I was wrong about this man. He's too stupid to be dead.

With so many fans coming up to him with a Holmes reference, it was only natural for simpering Jack Benny to slap a line at him, too. The mock-furious actor is in a scuffle over a lost dog:

BASIL: You tipped over my doghouse. I want that dog back. Where is he?
BENNY: Well *he* had pups today. You're a fine Sherlock Holmes!

Basil Rathbone pipes up to Nigel Bruce in the first of his Holmes film mysteries, *The Adventures of Sherlock Holmes* (1939).

As radio's most famous detective, Rathbone was handed a seven year contract to continue the series. This was an astonishing offer for any radio performer, and a guarantee of wealth and security, but Rathbone felt it was time to move on. He knew that author Conan Doyle had grown so tired of the character that he tried to kill off Holmes in a short story. "I could not kill Mr. Holmes," Rathbone recalled, "So I decided to run away from him." The decision alarmed fans, and most definitely the co-star playing Dr. Watson. Rathbone admitted, "For a while my long-time friendship with Nigel Bruce suffered severe and recurring shocks."

Rathbone couldn't find stage work in New York,

> So during the season of 1946–47 I did nothing but guest spots on radio, not one of them worth mentioning except an appearance with Fred Allen and a couple with the Theatre Guild of the Air. Fred Allen was one of the most generous stars I have ever worked with in any medium. Added to this he had a brilliant mind and a caustic humor. Most of his programs were contemporary satires. He had contempt for radio as a medium and his loathing of television was unsparingly expressed in a piece he wrote, I think it was for *Life* magazine. I think he enjoyed having me on his program as a guest star because he always wrote for me most amusing and intelligent "spots." I say "wrote" because, although he had writers, he was the originator of a great deal of his material, and most of the best ideas in his scripts emanated from him. He was a devout Catholic and never missed Mass on a Sunday if he could possibly help it. He was also extremely charitable. There were old friends of his that he literally "kept," and if he left town for any time his secretary was instructed that remittances were to be sent out regularly every week.

One of Allen's programs gave Rathbone a rare chance to sing a comic song. He'd done it memorably in the *Adventures of Sherlock Holmes*, his detective appearing undercover as a British Music Hall singer, performing the mildly tongue-twisting "(I Do Like to Be) Beside the Sea," which had been popularized by English vaudevillian Mark Sheridan.

On Allen's April 11, 1948, show, Rathbone sang a mock-commercial jingle for Fagel's Frozen Watermelon: "When you're buying frozen fruit, what's the fruit that's sure to suit? It's a frosted goodie, the fastest selling: Fagel's Frozen Watermelon!"

Fred Allen often enjoyed writing sketches for his ludicrous Chinese detective character, One Long Pan. Earlier, Pan had dueled with Peter Lorre's Mr. Moto; but for Rathbone, Fred didn't take the obvious path and create a battle with Sherlock Holmes. On the 1948 show, Rathbone is a suspect, not a detective, in the death of Lady Bensonhurst at her posh party:

> FRED: Who are you, Mr. Long Nose?
> BASIL: I am Norbert Nottingham, Lady Bensonhurst's solicitor.
> FRED: Mr. Nottingham need money. Empire Sun Glass Limited go bankrupt last week. You, Mr. Nottingham, principal stockholder.
> BASIL: Yes, yes, I know. I was a fool. I bought two million pairs of sunglasses to sell in England and the sun hasn't been out in England for three years.
> FRED: On back Lady Bensonhurst's head. See? Four lumps!
> BASIL: Tea anyone?

Rathbone's only comedy-radio appearance that would rival the Allen show was the time the actor appeared on Eddie Cantor's program and, to the surprise of the studio audience, rendered a manic and pretty accurate imitation of gravel-voiced singer Jimmy Durante:

"Congratulate me, Eddie, I became the father of a bouncing baby!"

"Boy or a girl?"

"I don't know, it hasn't stopped bouncing!"

Rathbone finally landed a Broadway role in an adaptation of the Henry James tale *The Heiress* in 1947, a return to "serious" acting. It didn't lead to much, and so, reluctantly, he returned to the mystery genre. His wife Ouida wrote a Holmes play—which was savaged by the critics and lasted only a few performances on Broadway. In his autobiography he admitted, "The Wednesday morning reviews dug a deep grave for us. The afternoon papers shoveled us in, and in due course the magazines covered us up."

Rathbone received some solace from an unexpected source. After the show closed, his daughter Cynthia offered him a letter that read:

> Despair is dangerous for men. Despair means that a man has given up hope. A man without hope has nothing to live for, nothing to seek, nothing to gain. He can neither respect himself, nor others, nor love God. Since he no longer trusts the divine power, he has no means by which to advance to God, and the mercy God will give him to draw him from despair.

A very religious person, Rathbone took the words seriously: "I have carried this little piece of paper with me everywhere, all over the world. I am never without it."

Radio was still a good source of income for Rathbone, especially commercials:

> Cigarettes, liquor, a new accident policy ... a diet food.... For one product I was contracted to do six one-minute radio "spots." It took a whole afternoon.... We sat around and read the spots, everyone tense and apprehensive lest one little word might detract from the saleability of the product. Then a "spot" would be rehearsed, after which they would all go into a huddle and in due course they would come up either with a deletion or one line somewhere (we were three seconds over!) or a word change.

"Try 'delectable' instead of 'delicious' please, Mr. Rathbone? All right, let's have another try. Keep it bright and interesting!"

Again—and again—and again.... One learns to be very patient under such conditions. But the knowledge that I was allowing the monster Mediocrity to still further encroach upon "my summer dream beneath the tamarind tree" disturbed me considerably.

A lack of checks would've been more disturbing, so Rathbone agreed to try a radio series again, a weekly crime show sponsored by Fatima cigarettes. He hosted the show and voiced Fatima's commercials, too. He had a chance to gently burlesque his embarrassment via an appearance on Fred Allen's show. Fred wrote some lines filled with colorful comic imagery:

FRED: Well, Basil, now that you finished your road tour I suppose you're relaxing?
BASIL: No, Fred, I'm busy with my radio program for Fatimas.... I smoke nothing but Fatimas, they're the new long Fatimas.
FRED: Oh, you smoke Fatimas because they're longer.
BASIL: Yes, I have rather a lengthy nose.
FRED: I noticed, yes.
BASIL: You know, when I try to light an ordinary sized cigarette I exhale through my nostrils and blow out the match.
FRED: Oh, I see.
BASIL: Now with the new long Fatima, I can rest my nose on the cigarette while I'm lighting it.

The Fatima mystery show didn't last long. Radio had exhausted its writers, and by the late '40s few weekly scripts had real twists or novelty. The shows were now character-driven, and Rathbone wasn't well suited to the "hard-boiled" genre. Typical of the dialogue for Rathbone is this scene from "A Time to Kill" where he's awakened from a sound sleep. The dour and tired wisecracks wouldn't have gotten much of a laugh if uttered by Vincent Price as "the Saint," or even Eve Arden:

"I'm sorry to have to call you this early in the morning."
"Early? It's the crack of dawn."
"Well, not really."
"Yes really. I just heard it crack."

A few lines later came another not-too-witty exchange:

"He looked dangerous. I thought you might like to investigate."
"I never like to investigate men who look dangerous. But I think I'd better. I'll be right over."

Aside from the sponsor's name being in the show's title, "Fatima" herself interrupted the proceedings, giving mystical advice that would've annoyed Charlie Chan. One script offered the mysterious warning: "Time is of the essence, a fact misplaced in time conceals the truth." Sometimes Rathbone's commercials contained similar pearls, including this portent of nicotine doom: "In the words of Fatima, habit is law. We are, all of us, slaves to a habit."

It was during the run of the Fatima show that Rathbone paid a visit to Spike Jones. With Rathbone introduced as "the distinguished actor of stage and screen," most of the jokes are about the affectations of the British. Spike tries to make Basil feel at home by putting on an accent and exclaiming, "It's good to see you Basil, old bean! Pip pip, cheerio, egad and all that sort of rot." Basil replies in perfect Brooklynese, "Hiya Schmoe, waddya know?"

Rathbone had narrated a record of *Peter and the Wolf* with Stokowski, so rather than a Holmes parody, Spike takes this opportunity to musically destroy Prokofiev with a script re-written as "Portia and the Hollywood Wolf." It would be Rathbone's last memorable comic appearance on radio, a medium dying of stale scripts and Fatima cigarettes.

As his credits grew in films and television, Rathbone did not neglect audio. In his autobiography he recalled "very pleasant interludes of recording for Caedmon Records, Inc." He wrote:

> They are concerned first, last, and always with quality in every department of their product. Recordings are carefully rehearsed for days by Mr. Howard Sackler, a young man of considerable talent and knowledge of all that is best in the field of letters. Mr. Sackler also directs the recording sessions and assembles and edits the tapes. The sound engineer is Mr. Bartok, son of the eminent composer, a most sensitive artist. Mr. Sackler and I worked many hours on Poe's "Raven" alone, and my recordings of Poe works, Oscar Wilde's fairy tales and two of Nathaniel Hawthorne's New England tales have had considerable success not only in the United States but abroad.

Rathbone even read some of Conan Doyle's Sherlock Holmes tales, recording four short stories between 1963 and 1967, but the Caedmon sales for the Poe records were more impressive, and Caedmon continued the series after Rathbone's death with Vincent Price at the microphone.

Rathbone's affinity for Poe seems to come from "Sonnet—To Science." While a number of poems affected Rathbone early in life, this one resonated throughout his career. "My professional and artistic life in recent years has had its ups and downs," he noted in the early '60s, "but this is normal for an actor, or anyone who pursues the arts for his livelihood, or anyone who devotes a good proportion of his time to the life of the imagination." He then quoted the Poe sonnet in its entirety, as being "terrifyingly apropos."

He might have also quoted "A Dream Within a Dream," for after praising "Sonnet—To Science" he asked,

> What is this dream which the heart pursues so relentlessly? All my life, I have had one dream or another constantly before me. If one has withered another has sprung up in its place—this dream world within and beyond a world of reality; a dream world that can be at times more real than reality itself for all those who with their hearts and from childhood have believed that one can "dream true."

Basil Rathbone's film career, like that of Karloff, Lorre and Price, ended with horror stereotyping in low-budget movies. An early entry, *Tales of Terror*, offered a few genuine chills, but soon he was playing it for laughs, and in *Comedy of Terrors* his raspy voice betrayed his ill health.

One of his last hurrahs was a one-man show. He would perform Poe and Shakespeare, and recall the highlights of his film career. One thing he stressed was his swordsmanship and athletic ability: "I could have taken Errol Flynn any time I wanted to."

Of his radio work, he knew the Holmes material would always have an audience. He took the most pride in some of his guest-star roles. He once wrote:

> In the days of radio *The Theatre Guild of the Air* ... was ever striving for quality, intelligence, and good taste.... Every time I was invited it was a worthwhile experience.
> There was a radio show I did one Christmas morning during the war. The entire live audience in the studio was in uniform. It was *A Christmas Carol* by Charles Dickens, and was performed in the NBC Studios in Hollywood for the benefit of the men and women of the Armed Forces only. The format was charming. In a room, supposedly my home, I was sitting reading the Dickens story to my daughter Cynthia. There was a knock at the door and a friend dropped in to say "Happy Christmas." He apologized for interrupting, but was persuaded to stay and hear this Christmas story. I started reading again and we imperceptibly drifted into

Basil Rathbone (front, center) takes a coffin break with his *Comedy of Terrors* (1964) co-stars Boris Karloff (left), Peter Lorre and Vincent Price.

the acting version with myself as Mr. Scrooge. When the play was finished I closed the book and we all wished each other and our listening audience a very happy Christmas, and my friend left. When we went off the air there was a rush for my autograph. I signed and signed and signed for quite some while, until I became conscious there was someone else's name on each piece of paper. In firm round copybook writing there it was, CYNTHIA RATHBONE! I looked up, and there *she* was in her little starched white Christmas frock signing away as if she had been my co-star, which indeed she had certainly proved to be.

Radio

Hollywood Hotel. November 22, 1935. Basil Rathbone appears in a production of "Captain Blood."

Shell Chateau. June 1936, NBC, 30 min. Rathbone guests with Edward G. Robinson and Alice Faye.

The Lux Radio Theatre. February 22, 1937, CBS, 60 min. "Captain Blood." Radio's version with Errol Flynn, Olivia De Havilland, Basil Rathbone and Donald Crisp.

Hollywood Hotel. July 30, 1937. Basil Rathbone joins Bobby Breen in a version of "Make a Wish."

Your Hollywood Parade. December 8, 1937, NBC, 30 min. Rathbone is one of the guests.

Lux Radio Theatre. January 10, 1938, CBS, 30 min. "Enter Madame," the drama of an opera star's romances, features Grace Moore and William Frawley, with a singing performance by Moore's eleven-year-old protégé, Jean Ellis.

On the Way to Yorktown. February 22, 1938, NBC, 30 min. A special show, sans commercials, from the Conference of Jews and Christians. Starring Basil Rathbone, Conrad Nagel, Edward Arnold and George Jessel.

The Adventures of Robin Hood. May 1938, NBC, 30 min. A special featuring the film music by Erich Korngold (conducting the Vitaphone Orchestra), with the story narrated by Basil Rathbone.

Warner Brothers Academy Theatre. May 8, 1938, syndicated by the TransAmerican Broadcasting System, 30 min. "That Certain Woman" starred Rosella Towne and Jeffrey Lynn. After the drama, special guest (not heard in the production itself) Basil Rathbone is interviewed about his new *Robin Hood* film and takes part in a short sketch.

Chase and Sanborn Hour (*The Edgar Bergen Charlie McCarthy Show*). July 10, 1938, NBC, 60 min. Basil Rathbone is a guest, along with Edward Arnold.

Information Please. September 27, 1938, Blue Network, 30 min. Clifton Fadiman hosts the panel: John Kieran, Franklin P. Adams, Sigmund Spaeth, Basil Rathbone and Milton Cross. Rathbone's specialty, naturally, involves questions about Shakespeare.

The Lux Radio Theatre. October 31, 1938, CBS, 60 min. "That Certain Woman" stars Carole Lombard, Basil Rathbone, Jeffrey Lynn, Elizabeth Wilbur and Lurene Tuttle.

The Gulf Screen Guild Theatre. January 22, 1939, CBS, 30 min. "Can We Forget." Bette Davis tries to forget her first husband. Featuring Robert Montgomery and Basil Rathbone.

Radio Tribute to the King and Queen. June 11, 1939, NBC, 60 min. The Royal visit to America sparks this one-hour special hosted by George Sanders and featuring Anna Neagle, Nigel Bruce, Brian Aherne, C. Aubrey Smith, Cedric Hardwicke, David Niven, Edna Best, Freddie Bartholomew, Gertrude Lawrence, Greer Garson, Herbert Marshall, Judith Anderson, Laurence Olivier, Leslie Howard, Madeleine Carroll, Reginald Gardiner, Roland Young, and Ronald Colman. Vivien Leigh and Basil Rathbone perform the love poems of Robert and Elizabeth Barrett Browning, including "How Do I Love Thee."

The Circle. July 9, 1939–January 15, 1940, NBC, 60 min. This talk show featured a revolving group of stars, including Cary Grant, Carole Lombard and Groucho Marx. Basil Rathbone joined the show after Ronald Colman abruptly departed after five weeks. The program was an ambitious variety-interview show that turned into a legendary fiasco. *Variety* columnist Carroll Carroll noted it "might have worked if actors weren't all children.... Each week they'd all phone each other and ask, 'Are you going to be on next Sunday? Oh no? Well then, I don't think I will either.'" With the actors receiving a reported $2,000 a week, Carroll said the stars were more concerned over who was getting the most air time and fretting about which ones were not coming across well.

The Adventures of Sherlock Holmes. October 2, 1939, NBC, 30 min. Holmes on radio was popularized back in 1932–33 via the Blue network, with Richard Gordon as Holmes and Leigh Lovel as Watson. Luis Hector took over the role in 1934 for two seasons on the Blue network,

and a final season, 1936, for Mutual. The first season (October–March 1940) of radio adaptations featuring Basil Rathbone and Nigel Bruce begins with "The Sussex Vampire." Episodes:
Oct. 2—"The Sussex Vampire"
Oct. 9—"Silver Blaze"
Oct. 16—"The Speckled Band"
Oct. 23—"The Man with the Twisted Lip"
Oct. 30—"The Devil's Foot"
Nov. 6—"The Bruce Partington Plans"
Nov. 13—"The Lion's Mane"
Nov. 20—"The Dying Detective"
Nov. 27—"The Creeping Man"
Dec. 4—"Charles Augustus Milverton"
Dec. 11—"The Musgrave Ritual"
Dec. 18—"The Wisteria Lodge"
Dec. 25—"The Three Garridebs"
Jan. 1—"The Blue Carbuncle"
Jan. 8—"The Priory School"
Jan. 15—"The Greek Interpreter"
Jan. 22—"The Cardboard Box"
Jan. 29—"The Second Stain"
Feb. 5—"Abbey Grange"
Feb. 12—"Shoscombe Old Place"
Feb. 19—"The Blanched Soldier"
Feb. 26—"The Reigate Squires"
March 4—"The Beryl Coronet"
March 11—"The Retired Colourman"

The Gulf Screen Guild Theatre. December 17, 1939, CBS, 30 min. "Smilin' Through." A soap opera starring Norma Shearer, Basil Rathbone and Louis Hayward.

The Adventures of Sherlock Holmes. September 29, 1940, NBC, 30 min. The 1940 season (September 29–March 9) opens with "The Empty House." Episodes:
Sept. 29—"The Empty House"
Oct. 6—"The Copper Beeches"
Oct. 13—"The Noble Bachelor"
Oct. 20—"The Engineer's Thumb"
Oct. 27—"The Red-Headed League"
Nov. 3—"Thor Bridge"
Nov. 10—"The Crooked Man"
Nov. 17—"The Norwood Hills Mystery"
Nov. 24—"The Three Students"
Dec. 1—"The Dancing Men"
Dec. 8—"Black Peter"
Dec. 15—"The Lost Naval Treaty"
Dec. 22—"The Boscombe Valley Mystery"
Dec. 29—"The Missing Three-Quarter"
Jan. 5—"The Mazarin Stone"
Jan. 12–Feb. 16—"The Hound of the Baskervilles" (a six-part adventure)
Feb. 23—"The Resident Patient: Chess Club Murders"
March 2—"The Speckled Band"
March 9—"Shoscombe Old Place"

The Gulf Screen Guild Theatre. October 20, 1940, CBS, 30 min. The episode titled "Variety" stars Jack Benny, Claudette Colbert, Edward Arnold and Basil Rathbone.

The Lux Radio Theatre. November 4, 1940, CBS, 60 min. "Wuthering Heights," the venerable Bronte drama that *Lux* presented a year earlier (September 18, 1939), gets a fresh treatment starring Ida Lupino and Basil Rathbone.

The Pepsodent Show with Bob Hope. January 28, 1941, NBC, 30 min. Basil Rathbone, star of a new film called *The Mad Doctor*, turns up in a jungle sketch about the search for "Yehudi," the character that Hope's sidekick Jerry Colonna had turned into an answer-less catchphrase: "Who's Yehudi?"

The Adventures of Sherlock Holmes. October 5, 1941, NBC, 30 min. The new season of Holmes dramas airs from October 5, 1941, to March 1, 1942, Sunday nights at 10:30 P.M. Episodes:
- Oct. 5—"The Illustrious Client"
- Oct. 12—"The Six Napoleons"
- Oct. 19—"The Devil's Foot"
- Oct. 26—"The Solitary Cyclist"
- Nov. 2—"The Walking Corpse"
- Nov. 9—"The Stockbroker's Clerk"
- Nov. 16—"The Missing Papers"
- Nov. 23—"The Magician"
- Nov. 30—"A Case of Identity"
- Dec. 7—"Mrs. Warren's Key"
- Dec. 14—"The Dark Gentleman"
- Dec. 21—"Donald's Death"
- Dec. 28—"The Gloria Scott"
- Jan. 4—"The Second Stain"
- Jan. 11—"The Haunted Bagpipes"
- Jan. 18—"The Three Gables"
- Jan. 25—"The Lion's Mane"
- Feb. 1—"The Five Orange Pips"
- Feb. 8—"The Voodoo Curse"
- Feb. 15—"The Dark Tragedy of the Circus"
- Feb. 22—"The Sussex Vampire"
- March 1—"The Giant Rat of Sumatra"

Gulf Screen Guild Theatre. October 26, 1941, 30 min. "Goodbye Mister Chips" stars Basil Rathbone and Greer Garson. Rathbone would perform this once again, a year later, with Merle Oberon as co-star.

The Jell-O Program Starring Jack Benny. November 2, 1941, Red Network, 30 min. Jack has a tough Halloween after throwing a rock through Basil Rathbone's window. Basil is also angry about a lost dog, and finally catches up to Benny when the comedian hides in the bushes.

Elza Schallert Reviews. NBC, c. 1942. The mother of actor William Schallert, Eliza, had an influential radio interview program in the late '30s and early '40s. Rathbone appeared on one broadcast, along with Max Reinhardt, Thornton Wilder, Richard Hageman and Don E. Gilman.

The Burns and Allen Show. January 6, 1942, NBC, 30 min. No copies of this Basil Rathbone guest appearance survive.

The Cavalcade of America. April 13, 1942, Red, 30 min. "A Continental Uniform" is the story of Benedict Arnold, featuring Basil Rathbone, Gale Gordon, Rosemary De Camp, Gerald Mohr and Hans Conried.

Ceiling Unlimited. November 1942–June 1943, CBS, 15 min. Basil Rathbone made several appearances on this patriotic program.

Gulf Screen Guild Theatre. November 16, 1942, 30 min. "Goodbye Mister Chips," performed by Basil Rathbone and Merle Oberon.

The Adventures of Sherlock Holmes. May 7, 1943, Mutual, 30 min. The great detective switches to the MBS (Mutual Broadcasting System) for Friday nights (8:30 P.M.), with a debut broadcast on May 7. Now Holmes is called upon every week, all year long! Episodes:
- May 7—"The Copper Beeches"
- May 14—"The Man with the Twisted Lip"

May 21—"The Devil's Foot"
May 28—"The Red-Headed League"
June 4—"The Engineer's Thumb"
June 11—"Silver Blaze"
June 18—"The Dying Detective"
June 25—"Wisteria Lodge"
July 2—"The Priory School"
July 9—"The Creeping Man"
July 16—"The Musgrave Ritual"
July 23—"The Greek Interpreter"
July 30—"Murder in the Waxworks"
Aug. 6—"The Missing Leonardo da Vinci"
Aug. 13—"The Syrian Mummy"
Aug. 20—"The Missing Dancer"
Aug. 27—"The Cardboard Box"
Sept. 3—"The Retired Colourman"
Sept. 10—"The Bruce-Partington Plans"
Sept. 17—"The Dying Rosebush"
Sept. 24—"The Missing Black Bag"
Oct. 1—"The Speckled Band"
Oct. 8—"The Dundas Separation Case"
Oct. 15—"The Old Russian Woman"
Oct. 25—"Ricoletti of the Club Foot" (Mutual moves the series to a new time slot, Mondays at 8:30 P.M.)
Nov. 1—"The Brother's Footsteps"
Nov. 8—"The Shocking Affair of the S.S. Friesland"
Nov. 15—"The Apparition at Sadler's Wells"
Nov. 22—"Murder at the Park"
Nov. 29—"Mrs Farintosh's Opal Tiara"
Dec. 6—"The Camberwell Poisoning Case"
Dec. 13—"The Jumping Jack"
Dec. 20—"The Missing Black Dog"
Dec. 27—"The Tired Captain"

The Adventures of Sherlock Holmes. Jan 3, 1944, Mutual, 30 min. Continuing without a break, Rathbone and Bruce begin the new year (rather than a new season) on January 3 with "The Incredible Mystery of Mr. James Philmore." Episodes:
Jan. 3 1944—"The Incredible Mystery of Mr. James Philmore"
Jan. 10—"The Unlucky White Horse"
Jan. 17—"The Departed Banker"
Jan. 24—"The Amateur Mendicant Society"
Jan. 31—"The Dog That Howled in the Night"
Feb. 7—"Death at Cornwall"
Feb. 14—"The Red Leeches"
Feb. 21—"Dr. Moore Agar"
Feb. 28—"The Missing Bullion"
March 6—"Death on the Scottish Express"
March 13—"The Peculiar Persecution of John Vincent Hardin"
March 20—"The Man Who Drowned in Paddington Station"
March 27—"The Haunted Bagpipes"
Apr. 3—"The Fingerprints That Couldn't Lie"
Apr. 10—"The Man Who Was Hanged"
Apr. 17—"The Singular Contents of the Ancient British Barrow"
Apr. 24—"The Dentist Who Used Wolfbane"
May 1—"Holmes and the HalfMan"

May 8—"The Phantom Iceberg"
May 15—"The Missing Bloodstains"
May 22—"The Superfluous Pearl"
May 29—"Skull and Bones"
June 5—"The Corpse in a Trunk"
June 12—"The Monster of Gyre"
June 19—"The Man with the Twisted Lip"
June 26—"The Dissimilar Body"
July 3—"The Amateur Mendicant Society"
July 10—"The Devil's Foot"
July 17—"The Bruce-Partington Plans"
July 24—"The Strange Case of the Aluminum Crutch"
July 31—"The Giant Rat of Sumatra"
Aug. 7—"The Lighthouse, the Frightened Politician and the Trained Cormorant"
Aug. 14—"Murder by Remote Control"
Aug. 21—"The Missing Corpse"
Aug. 28—"The African Leopard Man"
Sept. 4—"Dimitrios, the Divine"
Sept. 11—"Guardian of the Dead"
Sept. 18—"The Invisible Necklace"
Sept. 25—"The Vampire of Cadiz"
Oct. 2—"200 Year-Old Murderer"
Oct. 9—"The Third Hunchback"
Oct. 16—"The Missing Treaty"
Oct. 23—"League of Unhappy Orphans"
Oct. 30—"The Haunted Chateau"
Nov. 6—"Murder Under the Big Top"
Nov. 13—"The Strange Case of the Veiled Horseman"
Nov. 20—"The Secret of Glaive"
Nov. 27—"The Steamship Friesland"
Dec. 4—"The Telltale Bruises"
Dec. 11—"The Island of Uffa"
Dec. 18—"The Wandering Miser"
Dec 25—"The Blue Carbuncle

The Screen Guild Theater. January 4, 1943, CBS, 30 min. *Suspicion,* the Hitchcock classic, gets squeezed into a half hour, starring Joan Fontaine, Basil Rathbone and Nigel Bruce. Sponsored by Lady Esther, the show was sometimes called *Lady Esther Screen Guild Theater.*

The Screen Guild Theater. August 9, 1943, CBS, 30 min. "Spitfire" starred Basil Rathbone, Heather Angel and Reginald Gardner.

The Lux Radio Theatre. September 13, 1943, CBS, 60 min. "The Phantom of the Opera" is a radio adaptation of the then-current Claude Rains film version, which was a musical. Radio listeners get more music (via Nelson Eddy and Susanna Foster) but also the drama of Basil Rathbone.

The Cavalcade of America. September 27, 1943, Red Network, 30 min. "The Hated Hero of 1776" stars Basil Rathbone in the story of Thomas Paine. Featuring Ruth Warrick, William Johnstone and Elliott Reid.

A Christmas Carol. December 24, 1943, CBS. Special broadcast to the Armed Forces stationed overseas.

The Adventures of Sherlock Holmes. January 3, 1944, Mutual, 30 min. The new season for Holmes and Watson begins with the January 3 episode "The Incredible Mystery of Mr. James Philmore."

Yarns for Yanks, Program #67. 1944, AFRS, 15 min. "The Canterville Ghost." Basil Rathbone tells the Oscar Wilde story.

The Silver Theater. January 23, 1944, CBS, 30 min. "Quite an Order" features, along with Basil Rathbone, Conrad Nagel and John Loder.

The Lady Esther Screen Guild Theatre. March 27, 1944, CBS, 30 min. "Ham for Sale." The show noted for melodrama takes itself less seriously when Jack Benny attempts to become a serious actor opposite Barbara Stanwyck and Basil Rathbone. Sometimes called "Why Jack Is Not Going to Appear on the Show."

The Jack Benny Program. April 9, 1944. Jack Benny and Rochester start repair work on the cement sidewalk in front of Jack's house.

Three of a Kind. April 13, 1944, CBS, 30 min. Philip Rapp (who wrote *The Bickersons*) tries to get a new series off the ground. Hanley Stafford (in hiding from his role as father to Baby Snooks) and Bert Lahr scheme to steal the cash off eccentric Basil Rathbone, who claims he needs psychiatric care and is too suspicious of banks to trust them with the $10,000 he has glued to his undershirt. Ilka Chase plays Stafford's receptionist.

Duffy's Tavern. June 6, 1944, Blue Network. Each week a special guest seemed to visit the well-known saloon. Basil Rathbone turned up a week after Ozzie and Harriet, and a week before Joan Bennett.

Screen Guild Theater. August 21, 1944, CBS, 30 min. "The Ghost Goes West," an adaptation of the film, features Marsha Hunt, Basil Rathbone, Eugene Palette and Charles Irwin.

Which Is Which? October 25, 1944, CBS, 30 min. Part of the fun on this short-lived show was trying to identify a voice that could be a famous star or just an impersonator. Basil Rathbone and Frank Morgan are the real thing on the October 25 program, and a girl named Judie Manners manages to fool everyone with her impression of Kate Smith.

The Adventures of Sherlock Holmes. January 1, 1945, Mutual. Rathbone and Bruce begin the new year with one of many broadcasts that are now evidently lost. In fact, none of the January or February broadcasts for 1945 seem to have survived. Episodes:
Jan. 1—"Should Auld Acquaintance Be Forgot?"
Jan. 8—"The Play's the Thing"
Jan. 15—"Dr. Anselmo"
Jan. 22—"The Elusive Umbrella"
Jan. 29—"The Werewolf of Vair"
Feb. 5—"The Dead Adventuress"
Feb. 12—"The Newmarket Killers"
Feb. 19—"The Surrey Inn"
Feb. 26—"Lady Frances Carfax"
March 5—"The Doomed Sextet"
March 12—"The Erratic Windmill"
March 19—"The Secret of Stonehenge"
March 26—"The Book of Tobit"
Apr. 2—"The Amateur Mendicant Society"
Apr. 9—"The Viennese Strangler"
Apr. 16—"The Remarkable Worm"
Apr. 23—"The Notorious Canary Trainer"
Apr. 30—"The Unfortunate Tobacconist"
May 7—"The Purloined Ruby"
May 14—"In Flanders Field"
May 21—"The Paradol Chamber"
May 28—"Dance of Death"

Command Performance. March 1, 1945, AFRS, 30 min. Helen Forrest hosts the Armed Forces broadcast to soldiers overseas. The variety show features Roy Rogers, songs, and a comic sketch involving Jack Carson and Basil Rathbone.

The Andrews Sisters Show. May 13, 1945, 30 min. Rathbone was a guest, but no transcript seems to have survived.

The Adventures of Sherlock Holmes. September 5, 1945, Mutual, 30 min. After taking the spring and summer off, a new series of adventures begins, starting with the case of "The Limping Ghost." Episodes:
Sept. 3—"The Limping Ghost"
Sept. 10—"Colonel Warburton's Madness"
Sept. 17—"The Case of the Out of Date Murder"
Sept. 24—"The Eyes of Mr. Leyton"
Oct. 1—"The Problem of Thor Bridge"
Oct. 8—"The Vanishing White Elephant"
Oct. 15—"The Manor House Case"
Oct. 22—"The Great Gandolfo"
Oct. 29—"Murder by Moonlight"
Nov. 5—"The Gunpowder Plot"
Nov. 12—"The Adventure of the Speckled Band"
Nov. 19—"The Double Zero"
Nov. 26—"The Accidental Murderess"
Dec. 3—"Murder in the Casbah"
Dec. 10—"A Scandal in Bohemia" (aka "The Woman")
Dec. 17—"The Daughter of Irene Adler" (aka "The Second Generation")
Dec. 24—"The Night Before Christmas" (aka "The Christmas Eve Show")
Dec. 31—"The Iron Box"

The Adventures of Sherlock Holmes. January 7, 1946, Mutual, 30 min. The new year brings more stories for a Monday night.
Jan. 7—"The Strange Case of the Murderer in Wax" (aka "The Hampton Heath Killer")
Jan. 14—"Murder in the Himalayas" (aka "Murder Beyond the Mountains")
Jan. 21—"The Telltale Pigeon Feathers"
Jan. 28—"Sweeney Todd, the Demon Barber"
Feb. 4—"The Indiscretion of Mr. Edwards" (aka "The Cross of Damascus")
Feb. 11—"The Guileless Gypsy"
Feb. 18—"The Camberwell Poisoning Case"
Feb. 25—"Murder at the Opera" (aka "The Terrifying Cats") (Nigel Bruce is indisposed; Eric Snowden plays Watson)
March 4—"The Submarine Caves"
March 11—"The Living Doll"
March 18—"The Blarney Stone"
March 25—"The Girl with the Gazelle"
Apr. 1—"The April Fool's Adventure"
Apr. 8—"The Vanishing Scientists"
Apr. 15—"The Headless Monk"
Apr. 22—"The Tankerville Club"
Apr. 29—"The Waltz of Death"
May 6—"The Man with the Twisted Lip"
May 13—"The Uneasy Easy Chair"
May 20—"The Haunting of Sherlock Holmes" (Nigel Bruce can't make the show; Ben Wright substitutes)
May 27—"The Singular Affair of the Baconian Cipher"

Basil Rathbone departed the series after the May 27, 1946, broadcast. ABC picked up the show for a new season beginning October 12, 1946, offering Tom Conway as Holmes, Nigel Bruce remaining as Watson, and ex–Holmes Luis Hector as the troublesome Professor Moriarty. *Sherlock Holmes* returned to the Mutual network in September 1947 with John Stanley and Alfred Shirley as Holmes and Watson. Ian Martin became Dr. Watson for the season beginning in September 1948, and George Shelton portrayed Holmes starting in January 1949. In September 1949 the combination of Ben Wright as Holmes and Eric Snowden as Watson ended the long series' run. After five years, in January 1955, radio's last memorable team, John Gielgud and Sir Ralph Richardson, played Holmes and Watson for a few seasons.

Request Performance. November 4, 1945, CBS, 30 min. "Sherlock Holmes." No copies of the program exist. The show was a combination of songs and sketch material; other guests for the evening were Dick Powell and June Allyson.

Voice of the Army. October 15, 1946, syndicated, 15 min. "Reunion." The headmaster of a British boy's school recalls the recent war and the American soldiers who helped England. Basil Rathbone stars, with Larry Robinson, Henry Norrell and Paula Victor.

Theater Guild U.S. Steel Hour. October 27, 1946, 60 min. "Accent on Youth." No copies seem to exist of this drama co-starring Basil Rathbone and Jane Wyatt.

The Cass Daley Show. January 20, 1946, NBC, 30 min. Basil Rathbone must solve the case and find the singer-comedienne's missing earring. The program was in the time slot usually reserved for the *Fitch Bandwagon*.

Truth or Consequences. March 23, 1946, NBC, 30 min. For the sixth anniversary broadcast, host Ralph Edwards combines with Eddie Cantor, Basil Rathbone, Dinah Shore, Robert Montgomery, Phil Harris, Rudy Vallee, and Jack Benny and Rochester. It's kind of a chore to listen to, both for the singing and the poor quality of the surviving recording, but Rathbone is one of four celebs (along with William Bendix, Charlie Cantor [of *Duffy's Tavern*], and baritone John Charles Thomas) performing a raucous attempt at "Rigoletto."

Three Hundred Party. April 27, 1946, Mutual, 120 min. Mutual greets its 300th affiliate (WKRZ, Oil City, Pennsylvania) by presenting a variety show featuring the network's favorites. Elsa Maxwell, Xavier Cugat, Bert Lahr, Randolph Scott, Donald Crisp, Dick Powell, Basil Rathbone, Nigel Bruce and Parker Fennelly drop by.

The Danny Kaye Show. May 10, 1946, CBS, 30 min. Basil Rathbone and Butterfly McQueen are on the show, and the highlight is a musical version of *Julius Caesar*.

The Eddie Cantor Show. May 22, 1946, NBC, 30 min. The highlight of the show is Basil Rathbone's impersonation of Jimmy Durante.

Perry Como's Supper Club. May 28, 1946. Basil Rathbone does a send-up of his Sherlock Holmes character.

The Fred Allen Show. October 20, 1946, NBC, 30 min. This guest spot with Basil Rathbone is lost.

Theater Guild on the Air. October 27, 1946. "Accent on Youth," co-stars Basil Rathbone and Jane Wyatt.

Guest Star, Program #18. 1947, Treasury Department syndication, 15 min. Basil Rathbone stars in a sleuthing spoof, with Kenny Delmar serving as the great detective's assistant

The Radio Reader's Digest. January 9, 1947, CBS. "Doctor Donald" is the story of a British doctor working in a Chinese hospital during World War II. The show is hosted by Richard Kollmar, and stars Basil Rathbone and Al Hodge.

Scotland Yard's Inspector Burke (aka *Scotland Yard*). January 21–December 29, 1947, Mutual, 30 min. Basil Rathbone stars as Inspector Burke, with Alfred Shirley as Sergeant Abernathy. No shows have survived. The program premiered Tuesday nights at 8:30 P.M., and then on April 7 moved to Monday nights for the remainder of its run.

The Theatre Guild on the Air (aka *United States Steel Hour*). January 19, 1947, ABC, 60 min. "A Doll's House." The Ibsen play is performed by Dorothy McGuire, Basil Rathbone and Roland Winters, with a musical interlude from the Homestead Steel Works Male Chorus.

WOR Twenty-Fifth Anniversary Broadcast. February 22, 1947, WOR. Basil Rathbone was in New York, along with other Broadway actors and local celebrities, to salute the local radio station. Featuring Tommy Dorsey, Dana Andrews, Frances Langford, Shirley Ross, Dennis Day, Billie Burke, the Pied Pipers, Bob Burns, Basil Rathbone, Babe Ruth, Ella Fitzgerald, the Mills Brothers and Vic Damone.

Hollywood's Open House, Program #53. June 29, 1947, syndicated, 30 min. The variety show's highlight is a scene from *The Master Builder*, by Henrik Ibsen. Also on the show is a comedy routine from Henny Youngman. Jim Ameche is the host, with Basil Rathbone as guest star.

The Fred Allen Show. February 16, 1947, NBC, 30 min. This guest appearance by Basil Rathbone is lost.

Cavalcade of America. April 21, 1947, NBC. This series offered heroic war stories, presented by DuPont Chemical Co., to support the country. "The President and the Doctor" stars Basil Rathbone and Thomas Mitchell.

Theatre Guild on the Air. June 8, 1947. "A Church Mouse" is another lost episode of the show, with co-star Pamela Brown.

Theater Guild U.S. Steel Hour. October 5, 1947, 60 min. "The Admirable Crichton" stars Basil Rathbone and Ruth Duprez in a "lost episode" of the series.

The Cavalcade of America. March 22, 1948, NBC, 30 min. "The President and the Doctor" has George Washington helped through an illness by Dr. Samuel Bard. Starring Basil Rathbone and Thomas Mitchell, with Raymond Edward Johnson, Anne Seymour, Joseph Bell and Ted Osborne.

The Tony Awards. March 28, 1948, Mutual, 60 min. Highlights from the second annual Antoinette Perry Awards for Broadway's best were broadcast live from the Grand Ballroom of the Hotel Waldorf Astoria. A variety of presenters and happy winners were present, including Jimmy Stewart, Brock Pemberton, Judith Anderson, Jessica Tandy, Paul Kelly, Basil Rathbone, Henry Fonda and Vera-Ellen.

The Fred Allen Show. April 11, 1948, NBC, 30 min. Fred revives his Oriental detective character One Long Pan in a tale of a murdered bird watcher.

The Cavalcade of America. June 28, 1948, NBC, 30 min. "The Common Glory" is a story about the courage of Thomas Jefferson at the start of the Revolutionary War. Featuring Gale Gordon, Basil Rathbone, Margaret Draper, Cathleen Cordell and Horace Braham.

The Electric Theater. October 3, 1948–May 29, 1949, CBS, 30 min. Helen Hayes hosted the show, which adapted classic stories to radio. When she was in London working on *The Glass Menagerie*, substitute hosts were used, including Henry Fonda, Basil Rathbone and Margaret Sullivan. Rathbone was featured in "The Amazing Dr. Clitterhouse," broadcast on October 10, 1948.

Great Scenes from Great Plays. October 15, 1948, Mutual, 60 min. "The Barrets of Wimpole Street" is performed, with Basil Rathbone and Beatrice Straight.

Tales of Fatima. January 8, 1949–October 1, 1949. Basil Rathbone played himself, an actor "nosy by nature" who likes to explore crime, assisted by his wardrobe lady (Agnes Young as Lavender), and with help from the mysterious Fatima, who appears to give ghostly clues. Francis DeSales had a recurring role as Lt. Dennis Farrell. The series was sponsored by Fatima cigarettes, and aired Saturdays at 9:30 P.M. Only two episodes of the show, "Time to Kill," and "A Much Expected Murder" appear to have survived. The last episodes featured tantalizing guest stars such as Bela Lugosi ("Men in the Shadows"), Lilli Palmer ("The Bend Sinister") and Rex Harrison ("The Most Dangerous Game"). Episodes:

Jan. 8—"The Strange Mr. Smith"
Jan. 15—"Mystery at Mirador"
Jan. 22—"The Fires at Schuyler Square"
Jan. 29—"The Frozen Forest"
Feb. 5—"The Cairo Curse"
Feb. 12—"The Twisted Talisman"
Feb. 19—"The Jilted Juvenile"
Feb. 26—"The Invisible Caballero"
March 5—"The Cry for a Cat"
March 12—"The Tower of Ice"
March 19—"Design for Death"
March 26—"Murder on Stage"
April 2—"The Biggest Game"
April 9—"Murder at the Circus"

April 16—"Duet and Death"
April 23—"Country Killing"
April 30—"The Cautious Corpse"
May 7—"Murder at the Ball Game"
May 14—"Over My Dead Body"
May 21—"A Much Expected Murder"
May 28—"Time to Kill"
June 4—"One Foot in the Grave"
June 11—"Murder in Pig Latin"
June 18—"Death Sits with the Baby"
June 25—"Dead or Alive"
July 2—"The Dark Secret"
July 9—"The Sleeping Dog"
July 16—"Cargo of Death"
July 23—"Memory of Murder"
July 30—"Next of Kin"
Aug. 6—"Portrait of Death"
Aug. 13—"Dead and Buried"
Aug. 20—"Prescription for Death"
Aug. 27—"Intent to Kill"
Sept. 3—"A Dose of Death"
Sept. 10—"The Men in the Shadows"
Sept. 17—"The Bend Sinister"
Sept. 24—"The Most Dangerous Game"
Oct. 1—"Study in Suspicion"

The Spike Jones Show. January 30, 1949, 30 min. Spike enlists Basil Rathbone to parody "Peter and the Wolf," which Basil had performed on record with Leopold Stokowski.

The Fred Allen Show. April 24, 1949, NBC, 30 min. After Fred asks his alley denizens, "Do you think the techniques of teaching has improved?" Basil Rathbone arrives to discuss his new series for Fatima cigarettes, and then stars as "The Mad Doctor of Downing Street," with Fred on his trail as Oriental detective One Long Pan ("Greeting and Sholom Aleichem, kiddies ... holy smoke, you some doctor! Long Pan stick with Dr. Pepper!").

The Chesterfield Supper Club. June 23, 1949, NBC, 15 min. Basil Rathbone guests to promote Fatima cigarettes. Kay Starr and Bill Lawrence are regulars on the show, with Bob Hope promoting the Chesterfield brand.

The Chesterfield Supper Club. June 30, 1949, NBC, 15 min. starring Bill Lawrence and Kay Starr. Cesar Romero represents Chesterfield and Basil Rathbone plugs Fatima.

The Jack Benny Show. October 16, 1949, CBS, 30 min. Recovering from a cold, Basil seems like "Nasal Rathbone."

Duffy's Tavern. December 1, 1949, NBC, 30 min.

Theater Guild on the Air. December 4, 1949. "The Amazing Dr. Clitterhouse." Basil Rathbone co-stars with Madeleine Carroll.

MGM Theatre of the Air. February 17, 1950, 30 min. "Queen Christina." Basil Rathbone co-stars with Lilli Palmer.

The Cavalcade of America. May 23, 1950, NBC, 30 min. "A Portrait of the Author" covers the life of Thomas Jefferson, and features Basil Rathbone, Ginger Jones, Ronald Long, Virginia Dwyer and Denise Alexander.

The Bill Stern Colgate Sports Newsreel. July 14, 1950, NBC, 15 min. Basil Rathbone is a substitute host for the vacationing sportscaster, and manages to combine sports and melodrama by grandly reciting the story of a top boxer who later changes his name and becomes an actor—Maurice Barrymore.

The Cavalcade of America. August 29, 1950, NBC, 30 min. "John Yankee." John Adams defends eight British soldiers on a murder charge. Starring Basil Rathbone, John Griggs, Peter Capell, Ronald Long and Cathleen Cordell.

The Cavalcade of America. May 29, 1951, NBC, 30 min. "The Torchbearer" is the story of Nathaniel Bacon, and stars Basil Rathbone, Richard Green, Cynthia Stone, Mercer McLeod, Gilbert Mack and Ronald Long.

The Cavalcade of America. September 4, 1951, NBC, 30 min. "Towards a New World" is the story of Dr. Joseph Priestly, starring Alice Frost, Basil Rathbone, Mercer McLeod, Eda Heineman, Malcolm Keen, Ronald Long and Ross Martin.

Theatre Guild on the Air. September 9, 1951, 60 min. "The Heiress" stars Basil Rathbone with Cornell Wilde and Betty Field. Like most episodes of the series, this is evidently lost.

Dream World. October 19, 1951, 60 min. In this special salute to the United Nations, broadcast from the New England Mutual Hall in Boston, Basil Rathbone, his daughter Cynthia, Louise Rainer, Leonard Lyons and Mrs. Franklin D. Roosevelt all take part.

Theatre Guild on the Air. February 24, 1952. "Oliver Twist" is one of the most tantalizing lost episodes of the legendary radio series, as it features Basil Rathbone co-starring with Boris Karloff.

Favorites of the Famous. May 19, 1952. Host Wayne Howell asks celebrities about their favorite classical pieces. Basil Rathbone was a guest, probably on May 19 (but the date may be a week later).

Theatre Guild on the Air. November 2, 1952. "Lo and Behold" has Basil Rathbone co-starring with Ann Blyth and Jeffrey Lynn in another lost episode of the show.

Theatre Guild on the Air. November 23, 1952. In "That Winslow Boy" Basil Rathbone co-stars with Alan Webb and Margaret Philips. This is one of the few *Theatre Guild* shows that has survived and is available via collectors.

Skippy Hollywood Theatre, Program #380. Syndicated, 30 min. "The Man From Jamestown." Starring Basil Rathbone.

Heritage. May 28, 1953, ABC, 30 min. "The History of the Coronation."

Theater Guild on the Air. June 7, 1953. "Julius Caesar." Basil Rathbone co-stars with Maurice Evans in the last show of the series—one that is lost for the ages.

National Blood, Program #2. June 1953. Rathbone takes part in this special broadcast, along with Phil Rizzuto, John Lund and Cornelia Otis Skinner.

Sounds of Freedom, Programs #3, #7 and #10. Air Force Reserve syndication (sponsored by Air Force Reserve recruiting), 15 min. Songs and patriotic narration from Eli Wallach, Basil Rathbone and Oscar Brand. Probably from the late 1950s.

Gunsmoke. November 17, 1957, CBS, 30 min. Basil Rathbone is not in the drama itself, but performs a commercial for Four-Way Cold Tablets. This is typical of his commercial work at the time.

Helen Hayes Story Circle. September 1957.

Basil Rathbone: Word Detective. Syndicated, 2 min. This was a brief series both in timing (two minutes) and duration (it ran from October 1959 to February 1960). The idea was to provide radio stations with some filler to use on their local variety or news programs.

Basil Rathbone Presents. 15 min. Details about this program are sketchy. Evidently circa 1955–56 Rathbone recorded four fifteen-minute episodes, which may also have been titled *Basil Rathbone Presents Great American Women*. The first episode covered Emily Dickenson, Fanny Farmer, Lydia Pinkham and Dorothea Dix. The second, Helen Keller, Annie Oakley, Elizabeth Blackwell and Amelia Earheart; the third, Eleanor Roosevelt, Marian Anderson, Dolly Madison and Carrie Jacobs Bond; and the fourth, Jane Addams, Hetty Green, Sarah Hale and Mary Ann Bickerdyke.

Tales from the Reader's Digest. Basil Rathbone was a guest host for Boris Karloff and narrated five 5-minute episodes during the weeks of April 29, 1963; May 6, 1963; May 13, 1963; May 20, 1963; May 27, 1963; June 13, 1963; and February 3, 1964.

Monitor. NBC. Basil Rathbone was known to have been a frequent invited guest, and often read poetry. Most likely his appearances were in the late '50s or early '60s. In 1966 he appeared on the program to read "Beyond the Green Door," a short story by Robert Scheckley.

Flair. ABC. Similar to *Monitor*, but lasting only a year, this daytime program was hosted by Dick Van Dyke. The show, aimed at housewives, featured regular audio columnists such as Bess Myserson and Margaret Truman, recorded numbers from Peggy Lee and Patti Page (among others), and some guest advice from major stars. How many times Rathbone appeared is not known, but Show #607 survives with a comic look at "Etiquette" from Charlie Weaver, and an essay on "Pet Care" from Rathbone. Boris Karloff also was called on for short informational (if not eccentric) essays on the program.

For episode #611 the topic was hens!

> This is Basil Rathbone for Flair. If you're thinking of having hens for pets, my advice is go ahead. A hen requires but little living space and a comparatively little amount of food and care. Not only that, but where else can you get a pet that provides food for you? As a rule, you don't find many people having hens as pets. One reason for this is the common belief that hens are stupid and incapable of entering into social relationships. But recently scientists have found this is not the case.... There's a definite social structure in hen society in which genealogy rights are respected. It was found during a biological experiment that when a new bird is added to the flock, it usually got the bird! What I mean is, it was automatically placed at the bottom of the pecking order. In other words, it was pecked at by other birds in the flock.
>
> "In this experiment, when a new bird was added, the longest resident was removed. As time passed, and its superiors were removed every two days the newcomer rose in the ranks, usually achieving top rank by its last days. Of course, there were some hens who got to the top in only a few days, and one who never got off the bottom level at all. So you see, perhaps we can learn something from hens. What can we learn? Well, perhaps this: if you want to get ahead in life, don't chicken out!

Audio

- 78 RPM RECORDINGS AND RECORDINGS FOR CHILDREN

Rathbone's 78 rpm work began circa 1939 with *The Night Before Christmas* and prospered mostly between 1946 and 1949.

The Night Before Christmas & Little Jesus (Columbia Masterworks 7407-M). This offered one side for each narration.

Robin Hood (3 disc set, Columbia MM 583). This was re-issued on a full-length album (as Columbia ML 2063) and later re-issued on more modern microgroove (Columbia Harmony HL-9558), with Erroll Flynn's *The Three Musketeers* on the other side.

A Christmas Carol (Columbia M 521). This 3-disc set features Rathbone as Scrooge, Harlow Wilcox narrating, Jay Novello as Bob Cratchit, Francis X. Bushman as the Ghost of Christmas Past, Stuart Robertson as the Ghost of Christmas Present, Raymond Lawrence as Marley's Ghost, Lurene Tuttle as Martha Cratchit, and Tommy Cook as Tiny Tim. It was issued on long-play via Harmony Columbia HL9523, with added Christmas carols.

Oliver Twist and Fagin (Columbia MM700). This 3-record set was re-issued with *Oliver Twist* on one side and Erroll Flynn's *Three Musketeers* on the other as (Columbia CL674).

Peter and the Wolf (Columbia MM-477-5). This features Rathbone's narration backed by Leopold Stokowski and the All-American Orchestra. It was re-issued on long-play, along with *Treasure Island* as Columbia ML-4038, and Columbia P 14204, and re-issued with *Tubby the Tuba* (by Victor Jory) as Columbia CL 671.

Hansel & Gretel (Columbia ML2055, also issued as Columbia MM 632). This 4-disc set has Basil Rathbone narrating and playing the witch, with Jane Powell as Gretel, Ted Donaldson as Hansel, and Lurene Tuttle as their mother.

Sinbad the Sailor (Columbia MM-767). It's 3-record set features music from "Scheherazade," by Rimsky-Korsakov.

5. The Horror Hams—Basil Rathbone

Treasure Island (Columbia MM-553). This 3-record set was re-issued on long-play as *Basil Rathbone Narrates Treasure Island and Robin Hood* (Columbia LP 13895).

Walt Disney's "Mr. Toad" Narrated by Basil Rathbone (Capitol Records EAS 3048).

Great Themes in Poetry (Columbia 36481-36486). This is a six-record set with contributions from Rathbone.

The Murder of Lidice (Columbia Masterworks M-536). It's a three-record set on the dramatic work of Edna St. Vincent Millay, narrated by Basil Rathbone, and with Blanche Yurka and the Czech and Slovak chorus.

- 33⅓ RECORDINGS

Edgar Allan Poe, Poems and Tales, Vol. 1 (Caedmon TC 1028). Rathbone reads "The Raven," "Annabel Lee," "Eldorado," "To——," "The Masque of the Red Death," "Alone," "The City in the Sea," and "The Black Cat."

Volume Two: Basil Rathbone reads Edgar Allan Poe.

Edgar Allan Poe, Vol. 2 (Caedmon TC 1115). Rathbone reads "The Cask of Amontillado," "The Facts in the Case of M. Valdemar," and "The Pit and the Pendulum."

Edgar Allan Poe, Vol. 3 (Caedmon TC 1195). Here the actor reads "The Telltale Heart," "The Fall of the House of Usher," "The Bells," and "The Haunted Palace."

Edgar Allan Poe Soundbook (Caedmon Soundbook SBC 106). This includes the Rathbone recordings, plus Vincent Price reading "The Gold Bug," issued as a "soundbook" on cassette, vinyl, and ultimately on CD (the latter re-titled *The Edgar Allan Poe Audio Collection*).

The Happy Prince and Other Oscar Wilde Fairy Tales, Read by Basil Rathbone (Caedmon TC 1044). "The Happy Prince," "The Selfish Giant," and "The Nightingale and the Rose."

Idylls of the King, by Alfred Lord Tennyson (Caedmon TC 2022). 2 LPs.

Silas Marner (Caedmon TC 2024). The George Eliot novel, as a two-disc set, is read by Judith Anderson, with Basil Rathbone as Jeff, George Rose as Silas, and Cathleen Nesbitt as Dolly.

Basil Rathbone resuscitated Sherlock Holmes ... reading several short stories for Caedmon.

Classics of American Poetry (Caedmon 2041). This compilation included some of Rathbone's work.

Tales of Hawthorne, Vol. 1 (Caedmon TC 1120). This first volume has Rathbone reading "The Minister's Black Veil" and "Young Goodman Brown."

Tales of Hawthorne, Vol. 2 (Caedmon TC 1197). Volume 2 features "The Great Stone Face" and "The Secret Letter."

Stories of Sherlock Holmes, Vol. 1 (Caedmon TC 1172). Rathbone reads "The Speckled Band" and "The Final Problem."

Stories of Sherlock Holmes, Vol. 2 (Caedmon TC 1208). Rathbone reads "The Redheaded League."

Stories of Sherlock Holmes, Vol. 3 (Caedmon TC 1220). Rathbone reads "A Scandal in Bohemia."

Stories of Sherlock Holmes, Vol. 4 (Caedmon TC 1240). Rathbone reads "Silver Blaze."

The Adventures of Sherlock Holmes. In 1958, pre–Caedmon, Rathbone issued a set of stories in the 16 rpm "talking book" format for Audio Books (GL 611). The titles are: "A Scandal in Bohemia," "The Red-Headed League," "The Adventure of the Speckled Band," and "The Adventure of the Blue Carbuncle."

Rudyard Kipling: Selections from The Jungle Book (Decca DL-9109). This 1962 recording for Decca was, unlike Caedmon's output, widely available in record stores, rather than libraries.

Dinosaurs! Sir Arthur Conan Doyle's "The Lost World." Basil Rathbone played Professor Challenger on this album for MGM's children's line, Leo the Lion Records (CH-1016).

- SOUNDTRACKS AND RADIO RE-ISSUES

Rathbone's Sherlock Holmes radio episodes have been issued many times in both vinyl and CD format. In pre–VHS days, even the "voicetracks" to the Universal movie versions were available. Much of the radio and "voicetrack" material was released as multi-album sets from Murray Hill Records. These include *Sherlock Holmes* (Murray Hill 894424) and *Tales from Baker Street* (Murray Hill 894564).

Other radio shows available on record include *The Fred Allen Show* (Radiola 1146) and *Adventures of Sherlock Holmes* (Radola 1014).

The Stingiest Man in Town is a 1956 TV musical version of *A Christmas Carol*. Soundtrack from Columbia (CL 950), with Patrice Munsel, Vic Damone, the Four Lads and Johnny Desmond.

Aladdin (Columbia CL 1117). Rathbone was in the 1958 Cole Porter TV musical but is not on the soundtrack recording. It was not uncommon in the '50s to have a separate "cast recording" done in a studio weeks before or after a popular broadcast, rather than release the actual audio soundtrack. Rathbone only had one singing number, and on the record it's handled by George Hall.

- INTERVIEWS AND EPHEMERA

Basil Rathbone Reading in the Coolidge Auditorium. Released in 1961, this March 23, 1952, performance from Rathbone is typical of his one-man shows, as he reads the poetry of Rupert Brooke, John Keats, Percy Bysshe Shelley, A.E. Housman, Elizabeth Barrett Browning, Robert Browning, and Stephen Vincent Benet, as well as offering selections from Shakespeare and the Bible.

Elizabethan Poetry and Music in the Coolidge Auditorium, Nov. 29–30, 1962 (LWO 3891). This obscure souvenir issue has Basil Rathbone reading poems, then giving way to soprano Helen Boatwright, tenor Robert White, and the Consort Players.

The Christmas Story in Carols (Westminster WP-6034). This 1956 recording features Scripture read by Basil Rathbone.

Co-Star: The Record Acting Game. You Act Scenes Opposite Basil Rathbone (Co-Star CS 107). The ambitious Co-Star label (a division of Roulette) released a set of 15 albums featuring such stars as George Raft, Tallulah Bankhead, Don Ameche, Vincent Price and Paulette Goddard. Each record included a script of eight dialogue scenes. The main challenge, then and now, is to time the pauses left by the star so that "your" dialogue blends in. The choice for Rathbone was eight dramatized scenes from *The Brothers Karamazov*.

Guided Tours of the World/Guided Tours of the World's Great Museums. In 1961 and 1962 the Columbia Record Club issued a combo set of color slides, hard cover travel book and seven-inch record for various cities and tourist attractions. Rathbone narrates the guided tour of Hong Kong, a tour of India, as well as the "Tour of the Metropolitan Museum of Art" and "Tour of the Accademia Gallery, Venice." The idea was not too successful, not helped by the slide format (which didn't use the standard single-color chrome format but one that could only work with special projectors).

King David. Arthur Honegger's oratorio and symphonic psalm, with orchestra and solo performers, is narrated by Basil Rathbone. Gama Records, on two LPs.

Poe: Celebrated Poems (APPLAUSE cm1377). This indie album was released on the Applause label.

Voices from Hollywood's Past (Delos 25412). Interviews conducted by Tony Thomas in the late '50s and early '60s: Edward G. Robinson, Basil Rathbone, Walt Disney, Buster Keaton, Harold Lloyd and Stan Laurel. For about nine minutes Rathbone discusses English and American accents, his war years in Hollywood, and concludes that the key to the Holmes stories was not the mysteries but the character: "Holmes is a much more important man than just a detective ... he was a very remarkable man.... I said to my wife once, the one thing I should dread more than anything in the world, would be to find myself at a dinner party seated next to Sherlock Holmes, because he'd frighten the daylights out of me!"

6

Professors of Pain: Lionel Atwill, George Zucco and Henry Daniell

Lionel Atwill, Henry Daniell and George Zucco were all sinister, and each played the fiendish genius Prof. Moriarty in a Basil Rathbone/Sherlock Holmes film. While these professors of pain usually played diabolical devils or mad doctors, rather than actual monsters, their suave villainy wins them a place in any grand guignol hall of fame.

All three lent their grim demeanors to florid excesses such as *Mystery of the Wax Museum* (Atwill), *The Four Skulls of Jonathan Drake* (Daniell) and *Voodoo Man* (Zucco). Their distinctive voices have livened up some obscure and otherwise deadly dull radio shows, many collectible only for their star presence.

Lionel Atwill

Lionel Atwill (March 1, 1885–April 22, 1946) was the most successful of the lot, rising highest in stardom and deliberately choosing to move from leading man to arch villain. With a strong resonance and a crisply severe cadence, his voice was a sharp whip to the ears of movie audiences just beginning to experience the miracle of "talkies." He starred in several of the sound era's first horror movies, at a time when studios were in great need of stage-trained performers who could project their lines.

Raised in Croydon, England, Lionel Atwill was wealthy and well-educated, and dabbled in varied subjects from architecture to cricket. He spent five years in small touring companies, earning little but learning a lot about the acting profession. At the age of 27 he finally reached London's West End with a hit show, *Milestones*. At 30 he came to America, touring with the legendary Lily Langtry in *Mrs. Thompson and Ashes*. He had established himself as a handsome leading man, and soon married. The future looked very positive; a *New York Times* review was not.

When 32-year-old Atwill played Jack the Ripper in a 1917 production of *The Lodger*, the *Times* declared the show "well enough played except by one Lionel Atwill and one Phyllis Relph." Phyllis Relph was his wife.

The following year Atwill starred in *The Wild Duck*. Back then, any minor stage incident might be breathlessly reported to the public, the same way a radio blooper or TV talk show incident is today. The *New York Sun* headlined an article in the March 16, 1918, issue, "A Disturbing Interruption":

> The danger to a performance of a drama from rude and mal apropos laughter was strikingly illustrated last night at the Plymouth Theatre during the last act of Ibsen's *The Wild Duck*. Hjalmar Ekdal (Lionel Atwill) had just told his wife Gina (Amy Vaness) that he was going to leave home. "I am going out to beg from door to door for shelter for my poor father."
> "But you haven't any hat," objected Gina.
> At that point a man in the audience gave a loud and raucous laugh that could be heard all over the theatre. Laughter is infectious and nearly every one joined in, including the two players on the stage. The situation was critical, for in a minute or two young Hedvig was to shoot herself off stage and neither audience nor players were in the proper mood for tragedy. Mr. Atwill and Miss Vaness deserve much credit for recovering their self-possession quickly and thus saving the denouement of the play from turning into burlesque.

Navigating through the petty and the painful (he and his "bad actress" wife Phyllis Relph divorced in 1919), Atwill learned to handle any situation and all the finest leading ladies of the day, including Alla Nazimova (for a season of Ibsen), Billie Burke (the stage and silent film versions of *Eve's Daughter*), and Katharine Cornell (*The Outsider*, 1924).

Atwill toured vaudeville on the B.J. Keith circuit, doing a scene from *The White Faced Fool*. In the January 7, 1924, issue of B.J. Keith's *Theatre News* he described his enthusiasm for his live vaudeville audiences:

> There are no audiences in the world so genuinely responsive and sincere as the vaudeville audiences. They're a cagey crowd and won't applaud you out of politeness, but once you've won them, they're yours till the end of time. And they're not niggardly either, with their approval. If they do like you there's no mistaking their attitude.

Atwill was important enough to headline a film short, *Lionel Atwill in the Actor's Advice to his Son*, in 1928. He added more shows (*A Kiss of Importance* in 1930 co-starred Basil Rathbone) and more wives (number three was Henrietta Cromwell MacArthur, recently parted from not-yet-famous first husband Douglas MacArthur).

In the early days of recordings, very few stars recorded a poetry reading, recitation of a famous speech, or a Shakespeare soliloquy. Atwill, however, lent his talents to a worthy cause, *The Spoken Word Course*, by Windsor P. Daggett.

William Shaman, 78 rpm authority and author of several bibliographies on the subject, offers this report:

> Daggett's *The Spoken Word Course* was a phonetics course: there were at least four copyrighted editions, with different accompanying records: 1924, 1928, 1934, and 1936. There were two different sets of records: phonetic sounds spoken by Daggett himself and a companion set of theatrical recordings by many famous actors, included to illustrate correct or dialect pronunciations.

According to Shaman, it would be a difficult search to find the recordings, and

Vintage portrait of Lionel Atwill.

Atwill fans must be sure to get an early edition: "Atwill's was the only record in the theatrical series deleted from the package by 1936."

Atwill's quotes were from the French play *Deburau*, written by Sacha Guitry. In the accompanying workbook, students are urged to study "Mr. Atwill's pronunciation of the *Deburau* scene carefully."

Atwill's foray into talking pictures a few years later was big news. His vow to abandon the stage made for a two-part article in two weeks of the *New York Sunday Times*. His film career took off as the sound era began. He starred as *Doctor X* in 1932, gleefully joining Karloff and Lugosi in exploring the hot new field of monster movies. He and Fay Wray starred in *The Vampire Bat* (1933), and the pair won even better notices for that same year's *Mystery of the Wax Museum*. Atwill's make-up in the latter was hidden from Fay Wray until filming began; her screams in unmasking him were genuine.

Atwill lent his distinctive voice to eight sound films in 1933, and in *Motion Picture* magazine he legitimized monster film roles for skeptical readers:

> Do you realize that the two characters of drama that have survived and made the most money for producers and actors have been Richard the Third and Hamlet? Richard, that deformed man, with his horrible attitude towards women, his lust for killing and then more killing—and Hamlet, with his pitiful diseased mind ... these are the two characters that men and women have never tired of.... There is something about horror that is horribly compelling. Is it because we see our possible selves in these dark mirrors?

Unlike Karloff, who sought to assure fans that he was a gentle soul, Atwill chilled his fans when he darkly admitted that his hobby was attending murder trials. The busy actor capped the decade with nine films in 1939, including his scene-stealing role as Inspector Krogh in *Son of Frankenstein*. He balanced the visual eccentricity of his one-armed character with the impeccably severe enunciation of his most memorable line: "One does not easily forget, Herr Baron, an arm torn out by the roots." He spoke the line to Basil Rathbone, as Baron Wolf Frankenstein.

A few years later he dueled with Rathbone again, playing a particularly fiendish version of Prof. Moriarty. He voiced one of the series' few lines of dark humor when he began to siphon Holmes' blood supply. He delighted in giving Holmes "the needle to the end," an allusion to the detective's drug addiction. In terms of strong-willed, sharply-enunciated vocals, dialogue between Rathbone and Atwill was very much a verbal swordfight.

As one of the Hollywood actors who tended to appear on radio only in promotion of film work, or in an adaptation of a film, Atwill's late '30s broadcasts were few. For *Gulf Screen Guild Theatre* he starred in "Bridge of Mercy." It was a drama on one of the more taboo topics of the era, euthanasia. For *Lux Radio Theater* he appeared in productions of "Under Two Flags" and "Song of Songs."

In introducing Atwill in "Under Two Flags," host Cecil B. DeMille notes how busy the star is with movies: "Lionel Atwill is home from picture-making in England. He just finished *The Road Back* for Universal and *Last Train from Madrid* for Paramount. We meet him tonight as Major Doyle ... up with the curtain..."

Fans will find him in fine form, giving his characteristic stiff-upper-lip clipped delivery, with a gruff sense of humor. Lady Venetia inspects the barracks:

"I do hope the men don't mind."
"Mind? Why, they're honored. Well?"
"Oh, the men must be tortured with the flies. Shouldn't they have screens in their quarters?"
"Ha ha ha ha! Screens! It's said in the legion that when a fly bites a legionairre, the fly dies! Isn't that right, corporal?"
"Quite right, sir."

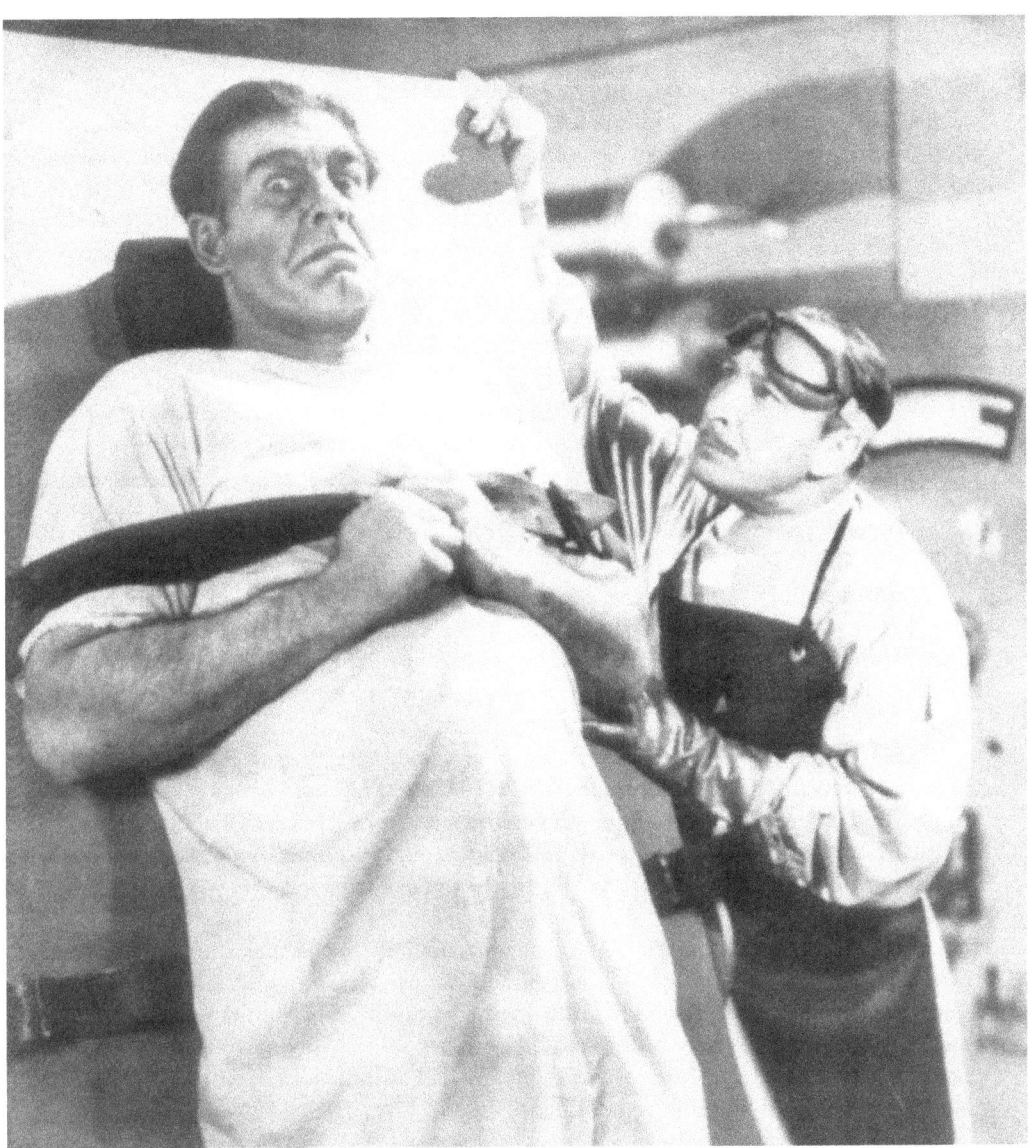

Lionel Atwill (right) goggles at Lon Chaney, Jr., the disgusted *Man-Made Monster* (1941).

"Corporal Victor, one of my best men. English, of course. Got a fine record, in the legion, I mean. Nothing to be ashamed of there at any rate, ha ha ha…"

Atwill played a mad doctor in *Man Made Monster*, opposite Lon Chaney, Jr., in 1941, but it was a year filled with the real horrors of world war. Newspapers reported on the actor's grief when he received a telegram from the British Air Ministry: "We deeply regret to inform you that your son, Flying Officer John Anthony Atwill, is reported to have lost

Opposite: **Poster Boy Lionel Atwill. X marks an early triumph.** Author John Baxter (in *Hollywood in the Thirties*) called *Doctor X* (1932) "one of the greatest of the classic horror films, incorporating … necrophilia, dismemberment and rape."

his life as the result of enemy action on April 26, 1941. The Air Council express their profound sympathy."

Separated from his socially prominent wife, Atwill became notorious for throwing parties that began with stag films and degenerated into orgies. The smut hit the fanzines after a woman's past sexual activity was exposed during a trial, and she admitted to attending one of Atwill's sex parties.

Fay Wray, interviewed decades later for *Scarlet Street* magazine, said, "I never heard of any wild parties, but how would I know? If there were any, I certainly wasn't invited to them." To Wray,

> He was a profile. He knew just how to position his head to get the right angles. He was very conscious of his contour. And that was the most significant thing about Lionel Atwill, I thought. I don't mean to put him down, but it seemed to be what he had and what he used.

When the actor was called to testify about the orgy, he simply denied everything. Most believed the rumors of a kinky side. In *Motion Picture* he had said:

> All women love the men they fear. All women kiss the hand that rules them.... I do not treat women in such soft fashion. Women are cat creatures. Their preference is for a soft fireside cushion, for delicate bowls of cream, for perfumed leisure and for a master—which is where and how they belong.

Movie fans in 1942 saw him as a mad doctor (*Ghost of Frankenstein*) and an evil professor (*Sherlock Holmes and the Secret Weapon*), and authorities suspected him of evil off-screen. Eventually, enough evidence was mounted against him to prompt a confession. Like the broken villain in the last reel of a bad movie, the contrite Atwill delivered one final line: "I lied like a gentleman to protect friends."

The Hays office (regulating movie censorship and morals) was a powerful force, and few studios were interested in hiring the disgraced actor. The court was much more lenient. He had been found guilty of perjury but sentenced to five years probation. The judge eventually agreed to revoke the guilty plea, and he addressed the anxious actor directly: "You are now in the position, Mr. Atwill, where you can truthfully say you have not been convicted of a felony."

Despite that clean legal brief, Atwill's reputation remained stained. In another court, a divorce was granted to what was now just another ex–Mrs. Atwill. Via his fourth wife, radio writer Paula Pruter, Atwill became a father again in 1945, but he wasn't producing much onscreen. Studios were hesitant to hire him for their A-list movies. Even worse for the aging actor, the interest in gruesome B-movies had dwindled. In the mid–1940s, Karloff and Lugosi weren't doing that well, either.

Atwill managed brief roles in *House of Frankenstein* (1944) and *House of Dracula* (1945), and the struggling star tried to find work at poverty-row studios such as PRC, and in such dismal second-bill items as *Lady in the Death House* (1944) and *Fog Island* (1945), co-starring George Zucco.

Lionel Atwill died of pneumonia the following year. He was 61. *Variety* thoughtfully acknowledged his lengthy stage career, "where he achieved notable success over a long period best being remembered for his portrayal of Ibsen roles," and his later days, "recognized as one of America's leading film villains."

Radio

Lux Radio Theater. May 24, 1937, CBS, 60 min. "Under Two Flags" is a story about the French Foreign Legion, starring Herbert Marshall, Olivia De Havilland, Lupe Velez, Cecil B. DeMille, James Eagles, Kenneth Hunter, Lionel Atwill, Lionel Pape and Lou Merrill.

Lux Radio Theater. December 20, 1937, CBS, 60 min. "The Song of Songs." Marlene Dietrich and Douglas Fairbanks head the cast, which includes Lionel Atwill and Pedro DeCordoba.

The Gulf Screen Guild Theatre. March 5, 1939, CBS, 30 min. "Bridge of Mercy" stars Paul Muni, Josephine Hutchinson, Lionel Atwill and Luis Alberni.

The Gulf Screen Guild Theatre. November 10, 1940, CBS, 30 min. "History Is Made at Night" offers un-romantic nights in Rio, with Greer Garson looking past her husband and toward a waiter. Starring Greer Garson, Charles Boyer and Lionel Atwill.

Audio

The Spoken Word Course (Dagget Studios, circa 1926).

George Zucco

On the bland surface, there is nothing remarkable about the face of bald, middle-aged George Zucco (January 11, 1886–May 28, 1960). This is probably his most nefarious trait; he often played model citizens who turned out to be luridly malicious.

Once discovered to be dangerous, devious and downright dirty, Zucco's dark eyes would glisten and an amused sneer would play onto his lips; and that cultured voice would begin to calmly declare an unrepentant intent to be as evil as the final reel would allow.

Fortunately, that voice was recognized by radio producer William Spier and used several times during the early days of the *Suspense* series. For a few brief years, Zucco's radio and film roles conspired to make audiences uneasy on several warm, clammy evenings in the summer of 1943 and in the chilling dead of winter in 1944.

The Englishman provides counterpoint to Peter Lorre in the *Suspense* episode "The Moment of Darkness." It's a muddled tale, with Zucco playing an officiously scoffing lawyer who doesn't believe in mystics or séances:

> You wouldn't like to think you've been deliberately tricked and imposed on, now, would you?... If I prove to you that these so-called miracles are really tricks that I can do myself ... would that shake your faith a little?"
> "How did you become so clever all of a sudden?"
> "How did you become so gullible all of a sudden?"

Zucco's assured British accent and insinuating tone bring a bit more to the script than it deserves.

Born in Manchester, England, Zucco was very young when his father (also named George) died. He was raised by his mother, Marian Rintoul Zucco, who ran a dress-making business from a modest shop. The boy majored in math, enjoyed sports (especially cricket) and ended up farming for a living in Manitoba, Canada.

He became interested in amateur theater and in 1908 turned professional, appearing as the Bishop in *What Happened to Jones* in Regina, Saskatchewan. With his wife, the former Frances Hawke, he worked up a short two-character play, *The Sufragette*, that brought them to the United States, touring in vaudeville coast to coast.

At the outbreak of World War I the couple emigrated to England. Lieutenant Zucco was wounded in France, and surgery was only partially successful. His right arm was never the same, and he lost sensation and movement in two fingers. This lends irony to his role, twenty years later, as high priest in *The Mummy's Tomb*. After having been shot and supposedly killed in the previous film, *The Mummy's Hand*, he explains: "The bullets he fired into me only crushed my arm."

In the early '30s Zucco taught at the Royal Academy of Dramatic Arts when he wasn't busy with London productions (notably in over 500 performances of *Journey's End*). In 1935 he was booked for Broadway. Publicist Helen Deutsch sent out a notice for him:

> George Zucco, well-known London actor, will play the part of Disraeli in Gilbert Miller's forthcoming production of *Victoria Regina*, starring Helen Hayes; he will arrive on the S.S. *Britannic* on November 14th. He is best known in the English theatre for his performances as Nevin Blodgett in the London production of *Lightnin'* and as the beloved Lieutenant Osborne in *Journey's End*. *Victoria Regina* will open in Washington on December 16th and in New York on December 26th at a theatre not yet selected.

Zucco's big Broadway chance was met with enthusiasm from Percy Hammond, the influential critic from the *New York Herald Tribune*: "I think you will particularly enjoy Mr. George Zucco's vivid study of Disraeli, a triumph of florid reticence." But rival critic Robert Garland in the *New York World Telegram* complained, "George Zucco puts you in mind of Dracula pretending to be George Arliss."

Film fan Doug McClelland managed to track down Helen Hayes late in life and get her to talk about her obscure co-star. She recalled, "He had a hellish Hellenic temper," but was "inspiring and exhilarating to work with."

Aging into a lurid, if not creepy character actor, Zucco turned up as "The Stinger" in *Arrest Bulldog Drummond* (1939), using a lethally poisonous cane, and Prof. Moriarty in *The Adventures of Sherlock Holmes* (1939).

Film historian William K. Everson commented on the vocal battle between the two men:

> Zucco ... had the ability to suggest intellectual superiority ... with satanic glee at his own perfidy. Obviously his Moriarty enjoyed villainy for its own sake as well as for the rewards it brought. Moreover, being British himself, and possessed of clear diction that had the kind of built-in smugness and suavity that also characterized Rathbone's speech, he made a perfect vocal as well as physical foil for Rathbone.

In November 1939 Zucco took a detour into radio, appearing in the tense episode "Bathysphere" of *Arch Oboler's Plays*. An undersea vessel is about to end up in a special type of Oboler hell, and Zucco's smug and cultured delivery leads listeners to root for the worst:

> "The sea is very quiet."
> "Yes, your excellency."
> "So it'll all be very amusing ... my dear young friend, one of the great joys of an experience is to savor it before it happens.... How far under will we have to go to break the record?"
> "Over half a mile."
> "Deeper than any man's ever gone.... Very amusing. My thoughts

"Knife to meet you, Mr. Zucco." George in a typically lurid publicity still.

tell me that this little excursion under the sea will be quite precarious; on the other hand, my emotions tell me it will be most interesting and amusing.... The press has only known me as a record breaker in the world of what they so quaintly term "power politics." By nightfall they'll herald me as a record breaker in the world of science."

"If all goes well, your excellency—no one can predict the ways of the sea..."

As a program first broadcast while Hitler's and Mussolini's tyranny were making headlines, Oboler makes sure to take a political detour into the predictable fate of the bathysphere's inhabitants:

I had a few moments of hysteria, didn't I? You liked that. You don't like this. My sitting in the dark so calmly. No don't talk, listen to me. I came into power not alone from my own strength but because the conditions of our country were such that other men sitting on their wealth came to a decision that I alone could keep them there. When an ancient rule of privilege is threatened it seeks to live no matter what the cost. The cost to them was me, and they found me worth it. Fighting phrases of prejudices and hate cost the men who made me nothing but the rent of the halls.

The conditions that made me will still exist when I'm dead. What of hunger? What of ruthless exploitation? These will still be free up there to put hate and desperation into men. So the ones who gave me power will find a new leader to stop the rumblings of rebellion with all the tricks that I've taught them. With me or without me, the game will be played just as it always has been played."

As with many of his film roles, Zucco's villain has power, and in his preening and intellectualizing, he eventually gives away clues as to how to destroy him. Oboler was not quite so cynical that he couldn't give Zucco a chance to describe the ways tyrants can be thwarted by an underground movement speaking of truth and liberty.

Fans of Zucco can read the above lines and just imagine his delivery of them. In fact, they *must*—because this is, sadly, a lost episode of the program. It was rebroadcast with other actors several times, so with a little radio-imagination magic, it's possible to envision George in the role of heartless dictator. Fortunately, his episodes of *Suspense* are still with us.

By this time Zucco realized the handwriting and the bloody fingerprints were on the wall. The same *New York World Telegram* that complained he was more in line with Lugosi and "Dracula" than Arliss and "Disraeli" ran a photo of him in their February 13, 1940, issue, and announced that he was resigned to his fate:

Above is George Zucco as the arch-villain Professor Moriarty. Mr. Zucco left New York for Hollywood today, complaining about the fact that he is always the bad man in pictures, describing himself as Hollywood's unhappiest actor because he is always cast as "a blood-letting, law-breaking evil old man."

Evil old George was probably best known in the '40s for his Mummy movies. As the fanatic Anhodeb, high priest of Karnak (*The Mummy's Hand*, 1940), he was the warped brain behind the revival of a creature dormant after Karloff wrapped the role in 1932. Zucco returned for *The Mummy's Tomb* (1942) and *The Mummy's Ghost* (1944).

At the same time he played peculiar priests, he seemed to take any mad scientist role that didn't go to Karloff or Lugosi. Zucco began by simply playing an evil doctor in *Ellery Queen and the Murder Ring* (1941), then tried to stick a man's brain into a gorilla's head for *The Monster and the Girl* (1941). He committed more madness via wolf-serum in *The Mad Monster* (1942), experimented with ape-to-man antics in *Dr. Renault's Secret* (1943), and, cooking with gas, was explosive in *The Mad Ghoul* (1943).

Also in 1943, he starred in the schlock-favorite *Dead Men Walk*. He made audiences sit still for such lines as: "You'll know that I'm no intangible figment of your imagination

George Zucco (left) and Bela Lugosi hack their way through the low budget *Voodoo Man* (1944).

when you feel the weight of my hatred." And confronting his other self, he exclaims, "You can't be standing there—you're dead!"

Zucco was not a big star, so his disappearance from B-movie horror movies in the mid–40s wasn't noticed. By the time "pop culture" became a bookshelf designation, and guys like Zucco were re-discovered, their film roles somehow turned fiction into fact.

In *Hollywood Babylon II* it was asserted that he "ended his days in the lunatic asylum, after he began believing he was the crazed villains Monogram and PRC kept paying him to play. The High Priest of Mu/Egypt/Atlantis was led away by the fellas in the white coats, dressed to the nines in borrowed Monogram bogeyman finery."

The book also insisted his wife and daughter "moved into the asylum with him," and that the elderly actor died

> one midnight dreary, working himself into a paroxysm of fear and loathing, screaming he was being stalked by the Great God Cthulu! George Zucco died in the madhouse from fright. The following midnight, Mrs. Zucco and daughter, unable to live without their meal ticket, unable to face life in Tinseltown without George, joined him in death.

Never give a Zucco an even break: George Zucco (right) is a wiseguy, Johnny Weissmuller is dumbfounded, and Brenda Joyce isn't rejoicing in *Tarzan and the Mermaids* (1948).

Actually, the aging Zucco was simply getting a little too old to be chasing small paychecks. In 1947 he had a brief role in *Where There's Life*, his third co-starring film with Bob Hope (following *The Cat and the Canary* [1939] and *My Favorite Blonde* [1942]). In 1948, after a 13 year absence, he returned to Broadway as a judge in *Let's Dance* (1950). His final film assignment came in the form of an unbilled supporting role in *David and Bathsheba* (1951).

His daughter Frances (born in Hampton Court, England, on May 30, 1931) floundered in a film career that included four small film appearances in 1952.

Zucco suffered a stroke in the early '50s and lived out his final days in a nursing home. He died peacefully of pneumonia at the age of 74.

Contrary to the claims of *Hollywood Babylon II*, George's daughter Frances and widow didn't immediately drop dead. His daughter died two years later, on March 14, 1962. His wife, Stella, passed away on April 5, 1999, at the Motion Picture and Television Fund Retirement Home in Woodland Hills at the age of 99.

It's unfortunate that the actor was not popular enough to have been given a lot of interview space in film magazines, so he remains a mysterious image on the screen. To quote from Zucco's *The Monster and the Girl*, ultimately, "The world is full of questions that will never be answered; don't try too hard."

Radio

Arch Oboler's Plays. November 18, 1939. Arch Oboler's first season featured George Zucco starring in "Bathysphere," but no copies survive. The script was revived for a *Lights Out* broadcast in 1943 (in which Oboler makes reference to the first version in 1939), and in 1964 it was revived again when *Arch Oboler's Plays*, featuring all new performances of the classic scripts, went into its brief syndication.

Suspense. April 20, 1943, CBS, 30 min. "The Moment of Darkness" centers on a nefarious man with two identities and the ultimate mystery: how can a man be killed during a séance when everyone was holding hands around the table? Story by John Dickson Carr. Starring Peter Lorre, Wendy Barrie and George Zucco.

Suspense. June 22, 1943, CBS, 30 min. In "The Man Without a Body," England has another invisible man roaming the countryside. Story by John Dickson Carr. Starring John Sutton, George Zucco and Wendy Barrie.

Suspense. August 28, 1943, CBS, 30 min. "The King's Birthday" revolves around strange rituals in Nazi-occupied Denmark. Co-starring Dolores Costello. This episode also features two veterans of the Basil Rathbone *Sherlock Holmes* film series—Ian Wolfe (usually playing a sunken-cheeked old villager) and Martin Kosleck (a budget Peter Lorre who played a knife-wielding spy in *Pursuit to Algiers*).

Suspense. January 27, 1944, CBS, 30 min. In "The Locked Room," murder stalks the owner of the second largest diamond in the world. Story by John Dickson Carr; with Allyn Joslyn, Virginia Bruce, Will Wright, William Johnstone, George Zucco and Hans Conried.

Suspense. June 6, 1946, CBS, 30 min "The High Wall" showcases a Bradbury story (no, not Ray Bradbury but Bradbury Foote) trading on a grand paranoid theme: a man finding himself incarcerated in a madhouse. Starring Robert Young, Cathy Lewis, Wally Maher and George Zucco.

Encore Theatre. June 11, 1946, CBS, 30 min. "The Life of Louis Pasteur" stars Paul Lukas, George Zucco, Lurene Tuttle, Lou Merrill and Gerald Mohr.

Encore Theatre. July 16, 1946, CBS, 30 min. "Now Voyager" is the familiar soap opera involving romance on an ocean liner. Starring Maureen O'Sullivan, George Zucco, Jeanine Roos, Elliott Lewis, Jane Morgan and Cathy Lewis.

The Cavalcade of America. September 16, 1946, NBC, 30 min. "General Benjamin Franklin" stars Charles Laughton, George Zucco, Joseph Kearns, William Johnstone, Raymond Lawrence, Howard Duff, Jay Novello and Kathleen Lockhart.

The Cavalcade of America. October 21, 1946, NBC, 30 min. "Mr. Conyngham Sweeps the Seas" is a biography of Revolutionary War hero Gustavus Conyngham. With Douglas Fairbanks, Jr., George Zucco, Herbert Rawlinson and Jay Novello.

The Cavalcade of America. April 21, 1947, NBC, 30 min. In "The Doctor and the President," Dr. Benjamin Waterhouse vaccinates President Thomas Jefferson against smallpox. Starring Douglas Fairbanks, Jr., Maureen O'Sullivan, George Zucco, Henry Blair and William Johnstone.

Henry Daniell

The most distinctive voice of any Professor Moriarty belonged to Henry Daniell (May 5, 1894–October 31, 1963). Radio fans can hear him putting his world-weary, flatly nasal voice to good use in two episodes of *Suspense*.

In films, the voice was matched to a deadpan face where a dagger-like spindly nose pointed like an arrow to the reverse pendulum of a thin, dour, downturned mouth.

The stillborn voice and frozen face would not change much over the many decades of Daniell's career as a character actor. Whether he was supervising finger amputations in a '40s Holmes adventure or pondering voodoo rituals in the creepy-cheapie *Four Skulls of Jonathan Drake*, Daniell seemed typed as an upright cadaver, rarely moving his body, his sickening speeches of epicene superiority oozing from a stiff, mask-like face.

Generally ignored by fan magazines, Daniell seemed to be an interview subject only when promoting a local stage appearance. *Philadelphia Enquirer* writer Marion Kelley interviewed him when he was appearing in a 1952 production of *The Suspects*, an Agatha Christie drama. Kelley found him

> a serious-minded person who has the physical makeup required for sinister parts—deep set penetrating blue eyes, tall spare frame, and a voice that can soothe or scare with a mere flick of inflection.... He assumes an expression of fascinating villainy until he smiles, then his whole personality changes. But generally he has little opportunity to smile on stage.

Or off-stage. The acting life gave him little gratification: "No, it is a hard way to earn a living, and I never would choose it if I had to start over again."

Born in London, Daniell attended St. Paul's and Gresham's schools, and was working on stage as early as 1913. After Army service in World War I he returned to the stage in 1916 for the British productions of *The Widow's Might* and *The Bird of Paradise*.

Early in his career Daniell was up for a role in *Peter Ibbetson* at the Savoy Theatre, a play co-starring Constance Collier. He read a scene with Collier and discussed his fee, and was delighted with her response. He celebrated at a local pub where he met some of his actor friends, including Basil Rathbone.

He was surprised to see that Rathbone had a copy of the same script with him—and even more concerned when another struggling actor, George Ralph, turned up also holding a copy of the play. Ralph pointed to one of the leading roles and told his friends that it was his.

"But I'm going to do that!" said Daniell and Rathbone at the same time. Who actually got the role?

"I asked for twenty-five pounds a week," said George.

"Twenty pounds," Henry declared.

Basil Rathbone confessed: "Ten pounds."

"You bastard!" said Henry. Ultimately, price was the deciding factor, and Rathbone got the role.

Daniell came to America in 1920 for *Declasse*, with Ethel Barrymore, and appeared with her again in *The Second Mrs. Tanqueray*. His role in the 1935 production *Kind Lady* was a turning point. In a an interview with Robert Sylvester for the *Sunday News* on May 5 of that year, Daniell said,

> I never have understood why young actors so often refuse to play unsympathetic parts. I'm really not trying to be egotistical, but I understand that it's practically impossible to get a popular player to do a role which sets him up in a bad light. I was tickled to death to play Henry Abbott. Furthermore, it's the most productive part I've ever played.

Married (to Ann Knox in 1932) and eager for more steady work, Daniell found stereotype roles as an untrustworthy bounder, a sinister spy or a world-weary fop. Critics generally passed over his work to praise the flashier performers. To interviewer Irving Drutman he admitted:

> It's terribly limiting, but I'm afraid there's nothing to be done about it. It's as if a painter were to be allowed to paint only flowers or clapboard cottages or livestock. The same thing hap-

pened to me before. When I did the languid Lord Ivor Cream in *Serena Blandish*, playwrights used to come to me and say, "I have a wonderful part for you if only you had more strength." That was ironic because I had just come from London, where I had been appearing in Arnold Bennett's play *The Return Journey*. In that I played a sinister Russian gland doctor, and I lost parts then because playwrights said I had too much strength.

He told Lucius Beebe [*New York Herald Tribune*, Feb 20, 1944], "I never was a villain until Gerald du Maurier said there was something creepingly sinister about me. I was a good, clean-living boy until then!"

The actor's distinctive nasal voice was effectively used on radio on a 1945 *Suspense* episode, playing the title role in "Dealings of Mr. Markham." Mr. Markham seems to be running a grim little antiques store where hundreds of clocks are ticking in a sickening rhythm; but, he admits, "I have no bones about it, I am a blackmailer.... What is all life but blackmail? The child says, 'If you don't give me what I want I'll scream.' The grown woman says, 'If you go on behaving like this I'll leave you.'"

His female victim insists, "You hate the world. You just want to torture people." He calmly lets her know that he is an expert in his field, and there's no escape: "If you killed me, I should haunt you within half an hour, and I don't happen to be joking."

In this far-fetched but nicely twisted tale, Daniell is impressive as an evil and confident man. After the program, Daniell appears with a plea for war bonds, and the host, Joseph Kearns, promotes Henry's latest film, *The Body Snatcher*.

Henry Daniell extends a bony hand to Boris Karloff in a grave moment from *The Body Snatcher* (1945).

In introducing himself, the actor affirms for us that despite the extra "l" in his last name, it's pronounced "Daniel" (accent on the first syllable), not "Dan-yell."

Apparently, copies of Daniell's "Last Letter of Dr. Bronson" no longer exist. Most anthologies of episodes from the show only feature the 1957 version starring John Dehner.

"The Ambassadors," from *NBC University Theater*, gave Daniell a rare starring role in a period drama, playing a 55-year-old widower attracted to a woman twenty years his junior: "She formed, for me, a continuous revelation of enchantment. I remember particularly one evening in London. We were driving home from the theater in a four-wheeler...."

And so begins the dramatization, a vivid hour that is in its way as effective as most any film version of a Henry James novel.

Daniell on the large screen was able to accentuate his vocal talents with his subtle, if not moribund, set of icy glares and faint looks of grim chagrin. The actor found film work less stressful than radio or the stage:

> The theater to me is a nervous profession because there's always such a terrible lot at stake. Primarily it's a profession the members of which do their jobs at the wrong end of the day. Nature, I'm sure, intended us all to finish our work before the sun goes down. An actor's work begins when everyone else is supposed to be relaxing.
>
> As the years go by I become increasingly aware of how hard a job acting is. When an actor makes a slip on the stage I don't think it's funny. I try to do something to regain all the scene has lost by that slip.

Daniell's most famous film appearance reunited him with his old stage rival Basil Rathbone. Rathbone was glad to see him and work with him. He wrote in his autobiography that he was impressed by "Henry Daniell's masterly Moriarty. There were other Moriartys, but none so delectably dangerous as was that of Henry Daniell."

His was the only Moriarty who hinted at an indefinite sexual orientation, thanks to the actor's nasal intonations that teetered on the edge between culture and effeminacy. Zucco and Atwill were more forthright villains with strongly defined sadistic impulses. Daniell's Moriarty was much more cruel and devious. Perhaps it was Daniell's demeanor that inspired the scriptwriter to give him and Rathbone a chance to act out the most famous lines of Moriarty-Holmes dialogue.

Sir Arthur Conan Doyle, in *The Final Problem*, wrote a masterful scene as the two play deadly, intellectual games with each other:

> "All that I have to say has already crossed your mind."
> "Then possibly my answer has crossed yours."
> "You stand fast?"
> "Absolutely.... You hope to place me in the dock. I tell you that I will never stand in the dock. You hope to beat me. I tell you that you will never beat me. If you are clever enough to bring destruction upon me, rest assured that I shall do as much to you."

In *The Woman in Green*, Daniell and Rathbone speak the dialogue fairly closely. Perhaps the scriptwriter, knowing Daniell was playing the part, added the latently homosexual last lines where the two adversaries imagine themselves arm in arm at the end of the duel:

> "Everything that I have to say to you has already crossed your mind."
> "And my answer has, no doubt, crossed yours."
> "And that's final?"
> "What do you think?"
> "We've had many encounters in the past. You hope to place me on the gallows. I tell you I shall never stand upon the gallows. But, if you are instrumental in any way in bringing about my destruction, you will not be alive to enjoy your satisfaction."
> "Then we shall walk together through the gates of Eternity hand in hand."
> "What a charming picture that would make..."

Charm was rarely part of a Daniell film character. As he told newspaper reporter Lucius Beebe, "I am resolved to be a villain whenever the occasion demands, but playing nothing but scoundrelly parts is so very limiting for an actor's technique. It's not only refreshing to be billed as a non-cad once in a while, but it's professionally advantageous not to be constantly impersonating a fellow who is forever being asked to leave the better drawing rooms."

The aging Daniell appeared on television, turning up in two episodes of *Lights Out* in 1952, five different installments of Boris Karloff's *Thriller*, and in the continuing role of the sadistic and oft-humiliated Colonel Townes in the "Swamp Fox" episodes of *Walt Disney Presents*. He had small roles in four films released in 1962, and was working almost until his death of a heart attack in 1963. He can be seen briefly as an ambassador in the posthumously released *My Fair Lady*.

Radio Credits

The Fleischmann's Yeast Hour. April 6, 1933, Red Network, 60 min. Fay Bainter and Henry Daniell preview a scene from their forthcoming Broadway show *For Services Rendered*. Host Rudy Vallee and Alice Faye supply the music, and Joe Cook offers comedy routines.

Reliable Henry Daniell (left) is cool and corrupt in *The Great Dictator* (1940), with Charles Chaplin (center) and Jack Oakie.

Suspense. June 28, 1945, CBS. In "The Dealings of Mr. Markham," Henry Daniell plays the nefarious antiques dealer Charles Markham, who is more interested in blackmail than the rare daggers he owns, and quite confident that he can't be stopped. Script by John Dickson Carr. Co-starring Joan Lorring and Gavin Gordon.

Suspense. August 15, 1946, CBS. "Last Letter of Dr. Bronson." Three actors played Dr. Bronson in three different productions of this drama. The first was Laird Cregar (7/21/43), and after Henry Daniell, another version was broadcast on 11/4/54 with John Dehner in the lead. What motivates murder? What can be done to change the impulse? Here's the story of crime theorist Dr. Bronson, who wants to find five people, give them motives to commit murder, and see how they can be "checked" before the victim checks out. Co-starring Cathy Lewis and Herbert Butterfield.

The NBC University Theatre. May 29, 1949, NBC, 60 min. "The Ambassadors," based on the Henry James tale, stars Henry Daniell, Lynn Whitney, Monty Margetts and Theodore Von Eltz.

Theater Guild on the Air (aka *U.S. Steel Hour*). ABC, 60 min. With "Wings Over Europe," Henry Daniell supports Burgess Meredith in the first show of the respected series.

Theater Guild on the Air (aka *U.S. Steel Hour*). ABC, 60 min. "Libel" has Rex Harrison and June Deprez headlining a cast that also includes Henry Daniell. No copies of the show exist.

7

Peter Lorre

Peter Lorre's voice was flat and nasal, calm and creepy. The mournful tone seemed to ask for pity, but in moments of anguish it could soar tensely into a crescendo of strangled frenzy and agonized rage. His brief but indelible role as Ugarte in *Casablanca* is a mini-exhibition of the essential Peter Lorre. First, he's suavely purring, "You despise me, don't you..." Arrested a few moments later, his eyes are wide as he chokes out a grimacing cry: "You *must* help me!"

That strange combination of sullen gloom and tormented fury made Peter Lorre the perfect voice for radio horror; and via many Lorre mimics, his voice amuses a generation who have a limited knowledge of classic black and white movies or old time radio. Young TV viewers might know Lorre's voice via the impressionists behind "Booberry," a character in cereal commercials, or half of the *Ren and Stimpy* cartoon team, or even a mournful and manic maggot in the film *The Corpse Bride*.

As Lorre's popularity grew, impressionists reveled in the contrasts between the two emotions that characterized so much of his work: the cold sociopath and hot psychotic. In fact, a mimic helped Lorre perfect his craft. The same way a director or critic can help show an actor new techniques, Paul Frees' Lorre impression was a subtle lesson in how to draw out some extra strength from a soft voice (via nasality) and contrast it with a scratchier, throatier tone for the louder, more dramatic moments.

Radio's limitations would often force actors to accentuate distinctive traits. One example was the case of Abbott & Costello on radio. Costello's natural speaking voice was too close to Abbott's for radio audiences, so Bud added more aggressive gravel, while Costello pitched his voice higher—and kept it there in subsequent movies.

Way back in the '40s Paul Frees (as guest vocalist with Spike Jones) defined the barely restrained and utterly insane Lorre character in a hit parody of "My Old Flame." The 78 rpm single appeared at the same time Lorre was making personal appearances reading Edgar A. Poe's "The Tell-Tale Heart," the perfect story of controlled pathology unraveling to a final shriek.

Lorre saw the humor in "My Old Flame," and guested on the Spike Jones radio show where Frees deadpanned the song's lyrics about an old girlfriend's name and then dearly departed from them. Following the number, Lorre tells Spike Jones (whom he calls "Spook"), "I think that imitation of me was just wonderful.... You know, Spooky, we two have a lot in common. What you do to music, I do to people."

Lorre was fairly sure what he wanted to do to people not long after he was born László Löwenstein on June 26, 1904. He wanted to perform for them on stage. His father Alois Löwenstein was the son of a rabbi and a man with strong roots in both Austria and Hungary. The family moved from Hungary to Rumania and on to Vienna, due more to Balkan turmoil than any financial problems for the family. At one point Lorre's father became a farmer in Austria, but war and political turmoil led to the territory becoming Yugoslavia, and the Löwenstein family moved yet again.

Lorre's Austro-Hungarian roots can be seen in reference sources that list Lorre's birthplace as either Rozsaghegy or Rosenberg, and his first name as Ladislav or László. The actor's name is generally mispronounced to this day. He tended to refer to himself as Peter Lahree, rhyming with sorry, but most are more comfortable with Peter Lore-ree, rhyming with gory.

The young man and his family finally settled in Vienna, and he took a day job in a local bank. Night belonged to his acting career. He became a prized student of Jacob Moreno, creator of *The Theater of Spontaneity*, and it was Moreno in 1924 who thought up the new name for his young star: Peter Lorre.

Lorre's big break came with Fritz Lang's film *M* (1931). Lorre used his moon face, baby-soft lips, owlish eyes

Peter Lorre strikes a chord of despair in this vintage publicity shot.

and stoic walk to make his depiction of a calm and methodic child-stalker a truly sinister and upsetting variation on the "normal" and more obvious grand guignol madman.

Lang recalled seeing Lorre in an improvisational stage production and choosing him strictly against type. Lang told director William Friedkin, "I thought nobody would believe that a human being, looking like Peter Lorre, could commit horrible murders."

Lorre's early film work was predicated more on his face and body than his voice. Lorre's features intrigued Alfred Hitchcock, who cast the young actor in *The Man Who Knew Too Much* at a time when Lorre was still unfamiliar with the English language, and learning lines phonetically. He was imported to America for *Mad Love* (1935), where his shaved head emphasized his baby-like brand of adult mayhem. As Vincent Price once said, "His voice came out as a funny little monotone which also made him seem very innocent—until the last reel."

That inscrutable monotone helped Lorre become the effective Mr. Moto, a mysterious man who seemed to operate on both sides of the law. The same studio that had been successful with Charlie Chan had been looking around for a completely different type of Asian sleuth, and certainly found it in Lorre, a total contrast to the portly Warner Oland as Chan.

With a pair of glasses (Lorre refused eye-slanting make-up), he began a memorable series of low-budget films in the late '30s which ended when World War II began. In a guest appearance on Fred Allen's show, it was Fred's satiric Oriental detective One Long Pan jousting with Peter's Mr. Moto:

FRED: You, little man with sneaky face, who are you?
PETER: Oh so, if you are detective, you tell me who I am.
FRED: Oh ho ho, don't make monkey business. I am detective One Long Pan!
PETER: You are One Big Joke!
FRED: Long Pan may be one big joke. You one little punk—Mr. Moto oriental nudnick!

Lorre shucked his Asian make-up in 1940–1941 to return to thrillers such as *Stranger on the Third Floor* and the depressing burn-victim "monster" movie *Face Behind the Mask*, and joined Boris Karloff and Bela Lugosi for the corny Kay Kyser comedy *You'll Find Out*.

Meanwhile, the once-popular Japanese sleuth's name was now a pseudonym for the enemy. In the 1942 war drama *Somewhere I'll Find You*, Clark Gable tells battle-bound soldier Robert Sterling, "Don't let Mr. Moto think too fast out there, kid."

Lorre played a Japanese spy in *The Invisible Agent* (1942), and Jon Hall's character tells him, "I can't tell you Japs apart, but that voice of yours haunts me!"

That year, radio audiences were being regularly haunted by Peter's guest spots on the era's best horror shows. He debuted on both *Inner Sanctum* and *Suspense* in 1942.

Unfortunately there are more "lost" episodes of *Inner Sanctum* than surviving ones. Among the tantalizing Lorre titles not in any radio collector's vaults: "Murders in the Rue Morgue" and "Dig My Grave" (both from 1942), and from 1944, "One Foot in the Grave" and "The Mind Reader."

Inner Sanctum remains dear to the throbbing heart of any classic horror fan—thanks to the production values which seemed to mirror Peter Lorre's style: somber spookiness reaching up to an over-the-top frenzy. The show's organist often established a tone with low register rumblings before shocking listeners with a screaming scramble into the upper register.

"The Black Seagull" is a seasick variation on Poe's "The Raven." Lorre discovers that his love, Barbara, has gotten her skull crushed in a boating accident:

"If you die, Barbara, I don't want to live!"

"I'll always be near you. I'll come back if it's possible..."

A doctor friend soberly tells him, "No one comes back from the grave. It's dangerous to believe that. Dangerous for your sanity." Soon he's convinced she's trying to communicate with him. He hears a gull and thinks it's her. He takes some sleeping pills and hears her voice taunting his efforts to re-unite with her: "You haven't crossed over yet..."

That sets the stage for Lorre to go full-tilt crazy. He finds a cat that seems to be yowling "Richard" at him. He's convinced she's visiting him (others insist he's spilled her perfume while in

Learning English phonetically, Peter Lorre starred in Hitchcock's *The Man Who Knew Too Much* (1935).

a daze), and he turns from mournful mewling to a rage of "Let me go! Let me go!" as he rushes off to the sea.

Is Lorre really hearing things? Is somebody trying to drive him nuts? That's hardly the point, and neither is the *Inner Sanctum* pun at the end: "He was gull-crazy!"

In a horror movie, the tension is sometimes relieved by a comic moment from a supporting player, such as Una O'Connor or Mantan Moreland. With *Inner Sanctum*, the pressure was let off via half-baked puns from the host during the commercial breaks, and by the actors being coaxed into ever-mounting excess. Only the best of the horror stars could manage the trick of keeping the guignol so very grand, and being serious without taking themselves too seriously.

"Death Is a Joker" is as much fun as a misguided murder story can be. It begins with Lorre as Charles, raging to his friend Robert about the woman they both covet:

Peter Lorre shows his original widely spaced teeth in *Stranger on the 3rd Floor* (1940).

"You must not marry Julie!"
"Not marry Julie? Well, who are you to tell me what I can do?"
"I know Julie well, and I also know you! That's why you must not marry her. She's impressed by your fame but she does not love you!"
"Now look here, we may be old friends, but I've stood all I'm going to. Oh, wait a moment. I get it now. You're in love with her yourself."
"I? I in love with Julie? No, w-we-we are just friends..."
"[Laughing] Friends? You're madly in love with her. Oh ho ho ho ... friends ... ha ha ha ... you in love with a girl like Julie! Ha ha ha..."
"Why should my love make you laugh?"
"Oh, so you admit it, huh ... [laughing]"
"All right, I do. Why is it so funny?"
"You think she'd have you? You? A clown? Ugly, clumsy. Ha ha! You in love with Julie? [Laughing more hysterically]
"Why not? Why not? Stop your laughing! Stop it!"
"How can I! Look at yourself! [choking] Charles ... let go of me."
"No! A joke, huh?... Laugh, go ahead, laugh now! Laugh!" [thumping noise] Robert! Robert! I didn't mean it. Robert! What have I done?"

He's cued the organ music, for one thing. For another, he's set up the listener for another twenty minutes of typical *Inner Sanctum* insane plot twists and delirious miseries as Lorre first agonizes over his guilt ("Every pair of eyes that looked at me seemed to accuse me of my crime..."), then discovers that the woman he loves actually does love him and might even help cover up the crime. And ... suddenly there's blackmail, more murder, and a script that continues to veer between black humor and dank horror.

The *Suspense* scripts, much deeper in psychological terrors, show off a wider range of Lorre's talents. Most are still engrossing, at least until the obligatory twist endings. The journey is usually worth the trip because *Suspense* had some of radio's better writers, including John Dickson Carr and John Collier.

Among Carr's contributions assigned to Lorre is "Till Death Do Us Part." Lorre is the chucklesome, contented husband who is happy with his domestic life in the suburbs ("So snug, so cozy!"). But his wife seems to be having an affair. Does the kindly, creepy-voiced Lorre know about it? Thanks to his ability to project both innocence and evil, the listener isn't sure, so there's suspense and menace right from the start.

When there's an odd sound in the house, he reassures his wife: "It's only a rat in the cupboard." Twenty minutes of unlikely zigs and zags complicate the mental game-playing, with Lorre at his smug best. There's the inevitable, almost stereotypical breakdown, leading to a roaring and raging Lorre finale: "You! You swine! What have you done to me!"

In "Of Maestro and Men," he gives his nervous giggle a workout when he foolishly loses too much money gambling and is forced to pay up instantly. His buttery-soft voice is all vulnerability and helplessness—until he thinks about homicide. As he plots the deed, his voice flares with manic homicidal rage, and the ending is another growling, howling success for fans of flamboyant frustration.

Lorre appeared in six episodes of *Suspense* between 1942 and 1945. Probably the sickest of the lot is "Nobody Loves Me," typical of the "trying to understand the mind of a killer" genre. The police are shocked when a notorious murderer-for-hire comes to their office. He confesses to the kidnap of an heiress. But is she still alive? He ignores their questions and insists on telling his life story, saving the disappearance and possible death of the woman for the suspenseful conclusion.

Lorre alternates between sorrow and fury as he describes his scarred life:

> I think a lot of when I was born. Maybe somebody loved me then. Maybe when I sucked in my first breath of air and let out a yell, maybe my mother loved me. Maybe she wished I was dead. She didn't live long enough for me to find out.
> But after she died, it was like I was shoved clean out of the world. Shoved off to an aunt and an uncle who had the meanest, grimiest, stinkingest little souls.... Yeah, they were a pair—faces like rotting cabbages, and their mean little mouths, yapping away. Those two would have eaten the heart out of a saint.

Those lines could be read effectively by a Humphrey Bogart—which would paint the killer as a bitter man. A Richard Widmark might read the lines to portray someone viciously pathological. But with Lorre's bruised voice and uneasy cadence he gets across the emotion of both hurt and a desire to hurt.

Next he recalls befriending a stray kitten. He recalls turning on it with brutality after the animal accidentally scratches him. What makes this sequence truly bizarre is that the producers found a child actor who could, without a mimic's comic distortion, imitate Lorre quite well in this flashback.

He becomes indifferent to death, and that includes the demise, from natural causes of his Uncle Walter, who took him in but never really cared about him. After mashing toads and stoning dogs, he grows up to become a paid killer. As for his murders of humans, his Psych 101 self-analysis is "Whenever I killed ... I was killing Uncle Walter."

As for the woman he's just abducted, he's confused by new emotions, as she frankly, but tenderly, appraises him as a human being:

> "Nobody loves me. Nobody ever loved me. Maybe a cat once. Everyone hates me, Peggy."
> "But I don't hate you..."
> "That's funny. I just thought of something. This is important. Listen, it's this way. I used to read good books—Modern Library. So I read something by a man who is called Oscar Wilde, and he says each man kills the thing he loves. Maybe that's what I am doing."

"No, Joe. You don't love me."
"You don't get it. When I start to kill you, Peggy, there won't be anyone else in the world for you but me. No one else will matter! Then your eyes will get shiny, oh, so shiny, and they'll blaze. There won't be anything in them but me ... take your neck in my hands like this.... Why don't you writhe?"
"Poor Joe."
"What did you say?"
"You've been hurt. You've been terribly hurt. Poor Joe. I'm sorry."

The scripted lines would truly sound like clichés without Lorre's voice reading them. Very few actors could soften and humanize those lines enough to make the character's actions in any way understandable (beyond being just horrible and frightening).

In John Collier's "Back from Christmas," Lorre is a professor of botany enduring a fussy and bossy wife. The couple plans a trip to America, with the wife scolding him every step of the way, and making an unusual allusion to Lorre's voice:

"Bad enough you're speaking with that accent! They'll probably think we're Germans as it is."
"I should think it would be quite easy to tell them I'm Swiss."
"Now don't be argumentative—and do as I tell you!"
"Yes, Hermoine."
"And don't look so put upon, Hubert!"

Meek Hubert is building a "Devil's Garden" in the basement. And as he digs, he snarls, "Oh, 15 men on a dead man's chest! Yo ho, and a bottle of rum!" The wife scolds: "One would think you're building a grave down there!"

It's a typical *Suspense* story of crossed wires—and it's just a matter of time before the sparks fly.

Some radio producers were so skeptical of casting Lorre in non-horror dramatic roles that they went to ludicrous lengths to explain his presence to the listening audience. For the mediocre drama "Mr. God Johnson," Les Mitchell, director on the *Skippy Hollywood Theatre* (sponsored by the peanut butter company), pretended the real Lorre was homicidal:

"It's—it's a great pleasure to welcome our star this week. Peter, I can't talk with that knife against my throat!"
"Come on, come on, read the introduction the way I told you, will ya?"
"It's a great pleasure to welcome our star this week, the young, handsome, lovable leading man, Mr. Peter Lorre."
"Oh, I like that, yes. Thank you."
"Will you take the knife away now?"
"All right. But you do have a nice throat."
"[Laughing] Well, I hope our writer's satisfied, Peter. Now you can be serious. You see, friends, our writer thought you'd recognize Peter Lorre best in a menacing role. He is not playing a menacing role in this play..."

One of the most unusual radio appearances for Lorre was on *Arch Oboler's Plays* in 1945. Many times, radio listeners were put off balance by Lorre's comical tendencies in a drama, or his pathological seriousness in a comedy; but this schizoid program starts with a lampoon of old-fashioned horror and ends with stark sobriety as the actor rages passionately at the real horrors of the day.

In the beginning, Lorre cheerfully recalls the fun of listening to *Lights Out* and Oboler's classic monstrosities:

You write such nice horror plays. Remember about the wife who turned into a cat? And the body that was turned inside out and you could hear everything happening? And the Chinaman whose head was cut off, and his ghost kept asking, "Where's my head, where's my head?" And the old man in the cage who made necklaces out of the bones of young girls!

Oboler obliges Lorre by offering "An Exercise in Horror," audio examples of the current state of terror, from an example of the average horror movie soundtrack to a wicked parody of *Inner Sanctum*, complete with creaking door and overdone organ music. But ten minutes into the show, Oboler tells Lorre that "there's horror such as I could never invent," and literally without warning (or commercial interruption) there's a long, increasingly alarming set of vignettes about German soldiers and citizens indulging in unspeakable cruelties. For instance, an apparently kindly and reasonable family are so happy with a new gift book that's arrived:

"The covering of the book."
"Some kind of skin?"
"Yes. Look at these marks. Tattoos. [sighing] What is the difference!"
"Yes, what is the difference..."
"Look what a beautiful gift!"

And on it goes, Oboler offering more unsettling glimpses at people without sympathy or morality, either looking the other way at torture, or participating in it wholeheartedly. In the end, Lorre delivers one of his most passionate rages, as Oboler's script tries to drive home the depth and scope of Nazi atrocities overseas. Lorre's controlled, intense voice begins to grow wilder and wilder as he paints a visual picture and then destroys it with devastating violence:

Fill the Yankee Stadium in New York with 100,000 people. There isn't room for that many? No matter. Jam them in. Jam them in and shut the gates. Let them wait there. Go to Chicago. Take Soldier's Field. Jam another 100,000 into it. Lock the gates on them. Tell them to wait; we'll be back very quickly. Go to the Sugar Bowl down South. Another 100,00 into it. Lock the gates on them. Go to Cleveland Stadium, lock in another 100,000. San Francisco fill that up with another 100,000. And to the Coliseum in Los Angeles—another 100,000 human beings.

Look at them. 600,000 people. Have you ever seen so many? So many people? Some relatives, neighbors, friends. Most of them strangers. But people, drawing breath as you do, looking down at you, and wondering why they are there.

I'll tell you why they are there. And why you are there. Give a signal! [A whistle blows.] Yes! Give a signal. And in New York, San Francisco, and Los Angeles, all at once, turn machine guns on these people! [Machine gun noises]

You heard me! Kill them! Kill the people! Spray the bullets around the stadium! Into the faces of the girls [roaring sound effects]. The young and the old and the children and the babies. Listen to the screams! But don't stop! Blast the bullets into them—kill them, kill them, never stop until they are all dead, until their bodies cover all the seats in Soldiers Field, in Yankee Stadium, in Cleveland, in New Orleans, in San Francisco, and in Los Angeles, until not a groan is heard, not one finger moves, until the mass of flesh is silent, and the only sound you hear is the rush of their blood as it pours down the cascade of the seats and gurgles into the gutters, right to where you stand!

Oboler takes the microphone to explain that this is not exactly fiction:

It has happened already. Yes, 600,000. Not in six places, but in one; one place where all the gates were closed and they milled around and died, and blood poured in the gutters even as I told you. People who had contributed their share to culture and civilization, worked and died all together, and the world let them die. The place: the ghetto of Warsaw.

Peter Lorre's persona on radio was that of someone urbane, sophisticated and quietly unpredictable, a man capable of strengths but handicapped by weaknesses. In real life, his weakness was nicotine and drug addiction. Lorre's perpetual cigarette habit was perhaps a mild nuisance to some fellow actors, but became a vital "prop" for him in many film scenes. He would often plead with a director to allow him to light up, or have a cigarette dangling for a particular line of dialogue.

As for the more severe addiction to drugs, just as Bela Lugosi had drifted into narcotics abuse following a prescription, Lorre found himself hooked on morphine after an operation. In Stephen D. Youngkin's Lorre biography, *The Lost One*, it was sympathetically revealed that "In 1936–37, Lorre reeled between the 'on and off' prescription of Dilaudid and what he termed 'fast cures' at various sanitariums."

Sporadically, Lorre would work while dosing himself with a maintenance level of morphine. Some fellow actors were confused by the way Lorre's energy would flag; then he'd go off to his dressing room for some kind of "vitamin" shot, and return his old self again.

Director Vincent Sherman, working with Lorre on *All Through the Night* (1941), once asked the actor, "How the hell did you make all those Mr. Motos over at 20th Century–Fox?" Lorre's quick reply: "I took dope."

Lorre's sense of humor made him a favorite on radio comedy shows as well as the dramas. With Bud Abbott and Lou Costello, for example, Lorre plays the head of a sanitarium, ready to help out with a physical exercise program:

BUD: Doctor, I told you Costello was in bad shape. What he really needs is some exercise.
LORRE: Oh, splendid. Let's go out and play some golf.
LOU: Golf? At Midnight?
LORRE: Oh yes, last night I played a fine game with my friend Frankenstein. [Lorre pronounces it "Frankensteen."]
LOU: Now there's a gruesome twosome!
LORRE: Oh, it was a very interesting game. Frankenstein made a hole in one. So I buried him in it. You know I play a very hot game.
LOU: Hot game? You probably play in the lower Hades! [Repeating for the unresponsive audience not getting or wanting the pun on "eighties"] The lower Hades!

One of the weirder comedy appearances Lorre made was on Dinah Shore's program. The writers imagined the wholesome singer and little horror star playing a sketch as a deceased couple, pre–*Addams Family*:

"Dinah, my dear Dinah Zombie. Well, it's our anniversary and I have a present for you."
"You're so thoughtful, a bottle of Chanel #5 embalming fluid. I appreciate this, but honey, we'll never save anything with your extravagance. You know the old saying, a ghoul and his money are soon parted."
"What's the difference. They say you can't take it with you. But we did!"

Thanks to radio, listeners became familiar with the dual nature of Peter's horrible yet harmless personality. From a guest appearance on Bing Crosby's Philco show:

"Here he is, the Continental Mickey Rooney, Peter Lorre!"
"Continental Mickey Rooney, huh? Why you Irish Al Jolson!"
"Nice to have you here. A few weeks ago we entertained a friend of yours, Boris Karloff."
"Ohh! How *is* the monster? You know something, Bing, between you and me, I think poor Boris is becoming a little psychopathic. Last year he sent me a Valentine."
"I'll bet it was a big red heart filled with candy."
"Oh, it was nice, but the heart is still beating.... Look, Bing, I've come on very serious business, I've come to study you from a psychiatric point of view. There are only two men in radio who are still normal. You and Smilin' Ed McConnell."
"Well skip me and go tap Smilin' Ed for your research!"
"Oh, I went to Smilin' Ed's house. But he was frowning..."

Lorre was involved in killer comedy when he met up with Jack Benny for an episode about "Murder at the Racquet Club."

JACK: Mr. Lorre, what is that gun doing in your hand?
PETER: Oh, I was just going out to shoot pheasants.
JACK: I see. What's that dagger doing in your other hand?
PETER: I have to pick my teeth, don't I?
JACK: Lorre, I want the truth here. No beating around the bush! Did you kill Cary Carew?
PETER: Who? Cary Carew? I don't think so. No, I'm positive I didn't. I haven't killed anyone by that name!
JACK: Now cut that out!

One of the more bizarre horror-comedy sketches for Lorre was "I Stand Condemned," heard on Jack Benny's program in 1946. The writers seem to have been inspired by Lorre's deadpan, mournful vocal style in creating a vignette odder than the average Benny comedy sketch. Boris Karloff was given this same script in 1947. Benny is accosted by a stranger:

"I was walking along. Suddenly a figure stepped out of the shadows. He was a small man with a round face. He reminded me somewhat of Peter Lorre. And when he spoke, his voice, too, reminded me of Peter Lorre. He tapped me on the shoulder and said,
'Pardon me, sir, but may I trouble you for a match?'"
"A match? I'm sorry, I don't have one, but I'll let you use my cigarette lighter."
"Thank you, you're very kind [sound of footsteps]."
"Hey you! Come back with that lighter! Gimme that!"
"All right, all right, here's your lighter."
"I thought you just wanted to light a cigarette."
"I do, but my cigarette is home."
"Oh yeah, then why were you running toward the railroad station?"
"My home is in Pittsburgh."
"Pittsburgh?"
"Yes. I married a smudge pot."
"Smudge pot! Now wait a minute, you were trying to steal my cigarette lighter."
"No I wasn't. As a matter of fact, I'd like to buy it. I'll give you $20,000 for it."
"$20,000. I don't want to take advantage of you. I'll tell you what. I'll throw in an extra flint..."

Jack can't believe his good fortune, and soon finds himself selling off everything he has to the eccentric, rich little man, even his clothes. He continues to talk and bargain with Lorre (every line seems to produce a histrionic stab of organ music), and seems well on his way to becoming a millionaire at the expense of the little man's weird generosity.

Too bad the eccentric little man's money is counterfeit. But that part of the plot is predictable, not the odd jokes about smudge pots, or how Lorre drives the mild-mannered Jack Benny into a murderous rage that leaves him on Death Row, about to be executed—hardly the average ending for a comedy sketch.

Many comedy writers felt that all Lorre needed was a stream of ghoulish puns, with the star comic perhaps adding a put-down reference to Lorre's conspicuous lack of height. During the opening segment of a Fred Allen broadcast:

Portland: Mr. Lorre, this is Fred Allen.

LORRE: [Gives a huge scream ... audience laughs].
ALLEN: I don't know who's getting the worst of it here! What's the matter, Mr. Lorre?
LORRE: I wish you had told me, Mr. Allen. I would have worn my makeup, too.
ALLEN: I'm not wearing any makeup Mr. Lorre.
LORRE: Well, you fooled me.
ALLEN: Say, Portland, Mr. Lorre isn't anything like we expected, is he?
PORTLAND: No, he's just a little schnook!

ALLEN: Yes, you sure are a let-down, Peter. I thought you'd come creeping in here on all fours and dripping cyanide. You're supposed to be a brutal killer; you couldn't take a fly away from a baby spider.
LORRE: That's what I keep telling them down at the morgue.

A return visit to Fred Allen in June 1944 offered some recycled jokes and more references to Lorre's seemingly harmless height:

FRED: So you are Peter Lorre. Well, Portland, Mr. Lorre isn't anything like we expected, is he?
PORTLAND: No, he's smaller than Mayor LaGuardia!
FRED: Oh I don't think so. But you sure are a let-down, Peter. I thought you'd come creeping in here on all fours, drooling arsenic, with a buzzard on a leash! You're supposed to be a brutal killer. You couldn't take a kumquat away from a Chinese baby.
PETER: That's what I keep telling them down at the morgue."

Later in the show, Lorre mentions a quaint member of his family:

PETER: My uncle had three heads. One of the heads took a violent dislike to me.
FRED: The other two heads were friendly, were they?
PETER: Yes, very friendly. But one night his bad head ordered me out of the house.
FRED: How did you live?
PETER: For a while I worked for Dr. Jekyll and Mr. Hyde. When Dr. Jekyll would turn into Mr. Hyde, I had to remind him to put his money in his other pants.

Fred wonders what Lorre does for fun:

PETER: I just hang around with Boris Karloff and Bela Lugosi.
FRED: What do you boys do for excitement?
PETER: Every day we give blood to the Red Cross.
FRED: Doesn't giving blood every day weaken you?
PETER: It isn't our blood.

On Bob Hope's show there was some good banter back and forth, with Lorre having to explain his unusual voice:

BOB: Tell me, why do you always talk with that low voice that way?
PETER: Oh, I—I was born in a library. In fact, I had to stay there for six months.
BOB: How come?
PETER: My father lost his card. Really, Bob, I don't understand, why do I frighten women? I think I speak quite softly and gently.
BOB: That's just it—that voice, it's scary! Why do you always whisper like that?
PETER: I can't help it, I ... used to sell butter during the war!

On *Duffy's Tavern* Lorre tells Archie the Bartender about a new role:

"I've been offered a radio program where I can be something different—entirely different! A children's hour."
"Sounds like a natural for ya," Archie replies. "Good evening kiddies, this is your uncle Jack. The Ripper."
"I'm serious, Archie, I've always loved children. The first story is about a little boy and girl, and they are late for dinner because on the way home from school they fall into a concrete mixer."
"Where are their parents?"
"Well, their parents would've been there but they were strolling down a country lane and got their heads cut off by a windmill. So the police try to find their uncle, but he's busy in the backyard having a barbecue. And what do you think Uncle is barbecuing?"
"Auntie!"
"Oh, you ready the story..."

Peter Lorre greets fans at a film premiere.

One of the strangest comedy appearances for Peter came on the *Amos 'n' Andy* program, a show not noted for guest stars. He plays himself, making a phone call to the duo:

"My name is Peter Lorre. I would like to see Mr. Brown about a steamer trunk. One that has metal bands around it."

"He wouldn't be interested. He bought one like that this morning..."

Lorre finally meets up with the comedy team, who are a little surprised by his apartment:

"Nice decorations you got on the wall. Tell me this, Mister, is dem real guns hangin' up there?"

"They shoot bullets, if that's what you mean."

But Lorre insists his target practice is never too vicious: "I don't shoot birds. Birds have a right to live!"

"What else *is* there to shoot?"

"Oh, there are things..."

There was method to Lorre's perceived "madness," his comic-psychopathic personality. Part of his acting technique was to insert an unsettling note of humor into his dramatic parts, and a darkly sinister edge to the comic ones. He felt it kept the audience guessing and tended to make him the curious center of attention in any scene he played.

The mysterious radio voice and film personality would sometimes make personal appearances on stage. Drama would dominate, and the highlight was his mesmerizing version of Poe's "The Tell-Tale Heart." He would sometimes perform it on radio, nationally and on local broadcasts promoting his shows.

When Lorre hosted the summer series *Mystery in the Air*, the first episode was an adaptation of the Poe tale. The trade newspaper *Variety* described the fireworks: "For grisliness and gruesomeness it was a gem raw and red and a classic triumph for Lorre, a masterpiece of character etching, and a cameo of narration. Productionwise, the eerie mood was sustained with pin-point timing [and] precisioned sound effects."

Years later, when television had replaced radio, Lorre's "Tell-Tale Heart" was a rare example of something being even more gruesome seen rather than imagined. When he was scheduled to perform the story on British television, the BBC issued a warning: "Mr. Lorre will be seen contorting his face in close-ups, and we feel that the experience of children watching this performance in a darkened room would be too alarming. We urge you to send your children to bed early."

Calvin Beck, editor of the early '60s monster magazine *Castle of Frankenstein*, reported in his book *Heroes of the Horrors* that after these horror roles Lorre,

> started receiving quite a bit of unusual fan mail. People would write him, often detailing their personal masochistic and sadistic aberrations. A continual tide of correspondence from prison inmates and asylum patients filled his mailbox with troubled questions. One Lorre fan, who was a baroness, wrote, "Dear Master, I would love to be tortured by you." To which Lorre replied, "You have been tortured enough by going to see my pictures!"

On *The Big Show*, a radio series hosted by Tallulah Bankhead, Lorre explains:

> I started my career in the theater as a romantic actor, but against my will they put me in horror pictures! I always want to be the actor who got the girl, but in my pictures, by the time I get the girl, she's dead. Well, I've struggled to get away from playing with monsters, but I guess it is my fate, for here I am today with Tallulah Bankhead.

On Bankhead's show Lorre narrated an adaptation of "The Cask of Amontillado." Somehow this version involves a lost love stolen by Fortunato. As Montresor, Lorre hides and watches his ex-lover. He speaks softly so she can't hear him:

> Oh you! You at last. Oh! Oh, you're like a beautiful painting, soft, soft in candle light. But your lips, they are cold. And your face, what has happened to your face? And your eyes, your wide staring eyes, and the light that grows in them! No, no, you don't wait for *me*, you wait for *him*! I should have known, but I did not want to know. I could not believe that you would fall for that—for that too pretty face, for that pretty voice.

He grows more and more agitated, but he is soothed by the knowledge that she will wait for Fortunato—in vain. Flashback to the actual Poe tale. Somewhat. In this abbreviated version, Lorre hardly bothers to describe how he lured the pompous Fortunato to a hiding place, or the clever way he brought him further into the catacombs. Instead:

> I shoved him and he fell forward into the opening that was waiting for him, and I slammed the stone into place. I flung away the trowel and cried out to him, "Hear me Fortunato?" But he could not answer me now, for in his mouth there was stone, and in his heart there was ice.

Poe may have allowed Montresor to get away with the crime, only faintly hinting at possible pangs of conscience. In the radio version, however, Lorre ends by declaring: "And me, I'm condemned too. Forever, for my own lust."

Lorre hosted two radio shows in the 1940s.

Mystery Playhouse was a radio compilation series put together by the Armed Forces Radio Service in 1944. The AFRS couldn't broadcast every episode of *The Thin Man*, *Big Town*, *The Whistler*, etc., so a selected title each week was used for *Mystery Playhouse*. It was Lorre's job to introduce the show with a suitable warm-up:

> Good evening. This is Peter Lorre. Welcome to another performance dedicated to the shadier side of life—the mysterious, the criminal, the often-times murderous side of life. [speaking softly, sweetly] Oh, please understand, this is not "Life Can Be Beautiful" or "Love Thy Neighbor." Oh no, no. [sternly] This is the *Mystery Playhouse*!

One schizoid episode of *Mystery Playhouse* has Peter Lorre hosting an episode of *Inner Sanctum* and then introducing the show's host, Raymond, who introduces the episode ("Death Is a Joker"), which stars ... Peter Lorre!

Many episodes of the AFRS *Mystery Playhouse* were borrowed from the *Molle Mystery Theatre*, which has caused some confusion for fans trying to dig up Lorre's acting roles (as opposed to his hosting duties). Sadly, such potential gems as the Molle production of "The Cask of Amontillado" only feature an introduction from the star, with performances by an anonymous cast of lessers.

Lorre's introduction for the *Mystery Playhouse* re-broadcast of that Molle show is typically spoken with alternating fits of calm quiet and tense growls of excitement:

> A cask of [the] finest wine is in a catacomb far under the river. Bones are there, too, human bones, the burial grounds of an old family. And deep in that dark dank tunnel [rising tension] there is no one to hear a man begging for his life! [musical stab, followed by an oboe obligato] Hello, creeps. This is Peter Lorre opening the doors of the *Mystery Playhouse*. The works of Edgar Allan Poe usually start one's acquaintance with the literature of mystery. Then as the years pass by, we're apt to forget that Poe was not only the father of the horror story but truly the master of them all. And so tonight, we bring you one of the very first and very best. It's a story of revenge [rising agitation] that communicates its terror to the listener so directly [excited emphasis] that hours afterward your spine will still feel cold! [calm again] Here, then, is Edgar Allan Poe's "The Cask of Amontillado."

In less than a minute Lorre creates an enduring virtuoso reading that, like fine classical music, moves back and forth between subtle softness and raging power. At some points the listener would have to inch closer to the radio to hear the buttery syllables and make sense of them. At other points the listener would have to step back in fear, as Lorre's tense vocal cords coil higher and louder around each syllable.

As always with Lorre, some words sound murkier and eerier with his pronunciation. In pronouncing his r's, Lorre had a puh-foaming style that was truly his own. While Karloff was known as a corpse stitched up and brought back to life, and Lugosi a vampire that could change into a bat, Lorre was worse: a little guy gone monstrously batty for no apparent reason.

In 1947 Lorre starred in his own radio show, an eight-week summer replacement for Abbott and Costello.

Titled *Mystery in the Air*, the program was introduced by a pre–*Dragnet* and pre–*M*A*S*H* Harry Morgan, then using his own brand of nasality for sinister purposes. His stock opening: "Each week at this time Peter Lorre brings us the excitement of the great stories of the strange and unusual, of dark and compelling masterpieces culled from the four corners of world literature."

Morgan still remembers his fellow actor's portrayals many decades later. Lorre, he told Stephen D. Youngkin in a 1979 interview, had "terrific intensity.... The things that he went through, contortions of the face and his whole body—everybody remarked on that. And he'd be dripping with sweat after the half-hour was over because he'd not only done a great vocal performance, he'd been through a lot physically."

Another co-star on the show was Peggy Webber. She appeared in several episodes, including "Beyond Good and Evil," based on a Ben Hecht story. She remembered a time when Lorre became so overcome with the drama of the story that he sent his script flying into the air, scattering it all over the floor. Lorre had to ad-lib his lines until staffers could re-assemble the pages.

Mystery in the Air, during its brief run, yielded several classics, most notably an adaptation of "The Black Cat." Lorre seemed to "inhale" his scripts breathing them in and out

A transcript of "The Black Cat" episode of *Mystery in the Air* gets re-issued on vinyl.

with realistic additions of "ums," "uhs," "huhs," nervous giggles and a drawling, pondering "Yes..." before saying the actual printed line.

While Poe's tale *is* about a *black* cat, which traditionally means that the hero is doomed because superstition is real, and Poe *does* call the cat Pluto (the script writer carefully points out that the cat is "black as the devil"), Lorre intuitively steers the listener toward Poe's real concern: alcoholism. Poe asked "what demon" could be worse than alcohol?

With Lorre's alternating rages and moments of remorse and moody whining, the listener knows that the problems come from within. In the original, one of the cat's eyes is cut from its socket. Lorre's version has him merely kick the cat—and notice some time later that it now has a torn ear. No wonder that Lorre's script has him "blush" as he recounts his crime. In the original, the narrator not only blushes, he "burns" as he pens the "damnable atrocity."

Lorre's choices for the program included studies in psychological torment ("Crime and Punishment") as well as serio-comic exercises such as "Mask of Medusa," a variation on the usual waxworks dramas where the figures are murdered people dipped in wax. Here, the victims are still alive but in a state of suspended animation. As the owner of the waxworks describes the crimes of each figure, one of the statues, Peter Lorre, gives an irritable monologue:

"Yes, yes, there he goes, there he goes again, telling people all the bad things we did. Oh it's terrible being nothing but figures in a wax museum. People staring at us all day long and not one of 'em, not one, ever suspects that we are still alive!"

And later: "Idiots, idiots and morons! Can't they see I'm still—I suppose not. I'd like to be alive again. Oh, alive again! I'm alive right now but I'd be better off dead! I can hear, I can see, I can feel, I can think, but I cannot move! I cannot move at all! No matter how much I try!"

The 1950s was a lost decade for Lorre. His ambitious directorial debut, *The Lost One* (1951), was not a success, and years later he grabbed for a job hosting the low-budget radio series *Nightmare* on the lackluster Mutual network in 1953. The show offered generic horror and suspense tales, with an announcer covering all the bases with his introduction: "Out of the dark of night, from the shadows of the senses, comes this, the fantasy of fear—*Nightmare*, starring, as your exciting guide to terror, Peter Lorre."

Lorre's introductions are similarly soaked in an ether of reeking hyperbole. For the episode "Hollow Footsteps," Lorre says:

> Sleep is an interesting thing. Of course you are aware that the eye of the mind never closes in slumber. It never tires of seeing things, thoughts and ideas. Some of these things seen by the mind are in turn caught by the memory, and we awake with a start: did it really happen or was I dreaming? And sometimes, sometimes you're never sure...

Similarly, opening "The Leech," he tells listeners:

> Did you ever have a dream, a dream in which you were running and running, and running away from something grotesque? Horrible things that were after you, to kill you? Oh yes? And you scream and you keep running, but yet it runs too, and no matter how you run or how fast you run, it's still after you, this thing, this thing runs faster than you and you can't get away from it no matter where you turn. You can't get away from it. Ha. And you wake up and—and you know you've been dreaming but the sweat fills your body like a wet shroud, and your heart, it beats wildly, and you find that you're still screaming. That thing's still there in the room with you...

Lorre leaves others to perform the routine stories, then returns at the end of each show for a sarcastic and reassuring remark: "Well, have a good night's sleep, and remember, it's only a story. By tomorrow you will have forgotten about the whole thing." Or "Do not be afraid—these things never happen to you. Or me. I do hope you'll sleep tonight..."

The show didn't last, and film roles were sporadic. He appeared in *Beat the Devil* (1954), and *Newsweek* was blunt about it: "Peter Lorre has got fat since his sinister prime in *The Maltese Falcon*, but a fat Lorre as a goon named O'Hara is still in the comic running..." Triviots note that in 1954 he was the first actor to play a James Bond villain when he starred as Le Chiffre in "Casino Royale," which was adapted for an episode of the *Climax* TV series. Lorre returned for three more episodes of *Climax* in 1956, and also three episodes of *Playhouse 90* in 1957, while in films he managed a few brief moments of humor in *Silk Stockings* (1957).

Most Lorre fans point to his January 3, 1960, appearance on *Alfred Hitchcock Presents* as his best acting assignment for the small screen. He's the sardonic, sadistic gambler Carlos in the nail-biting, finger-chopping adaptation of the Roald Dahl story "Man from the South." He also delighted TV audiences for the Halloween 1962 episode of *Route 66*, with Boris Karloff and Lon Chaney, Jr. Only Lorre escaped without putting on monster make-up.

The TV exposure of old horror movies created a new audience for veteran monster movie stars, and Lorre won his first meaty major film role in years via *Tales of Terror*, comprised of a trio of Poe stories. Lorre's "The Black Cat" segment, co-starring Vincent Price, was played broadly, and encouraged director Roger Corman to cast Lorre in more comic

Boris Karloff, Peter Lorre and Vincent Price play it for laughs in *The Raven* (1963).

parts, allowing the veteran actor to ad-lib as he pleased. In *The Raven* (1963), Lorre hurls manic insults at both Vincent Price and Jack Nicholson. With *The Comedy of Terrors* (1964), Lorre earns additional chuckles with his deadpan running gag of mispronouncing Price's character name of "Trumble" as "Tremble":

> "Mr. Tremble."
> "That's *Trumble*."
> "I *said* Tremble."

In *Vincent Price: A Daughter's Biography*, Vincent recalled that co-starring in *The Raven* was especially fun:

> Peter loved to make jokes and ad-lib during the filming. He didn't always know all the lines, but he had a basic idea what they were. He loved to invent; improvisation was a part of his training in Germany.... In one scene we had together I said, "Shall I ever see Lenore again?" And Peter said, "How the hell should I know? What am I—a fortune teller?"

In his introduction to the book *The Films of Peter Lorre*, Vincent wrote of Lorre's unique voice and delightful blend of horror and humor:

> Towards the end of his career, his life, he became off stage very much his on-stage self—he would hold his nose and do the best imitation of his much-imitated voice. He could roll his famous heavy-lidded ping-pong eyes and make a joke that would stop the shooting, collapse the entire crew and destroy the director and his fellow actors.

Not only did Lorre's ad-libs find their way into the finished film, so did his trademark use of "huh" to give a little extra padding at the end of a pithy line. Whether "huh" was huffed or used as an accentuating question mark, it was just another part of Lorre's natural technique.

An attempt to resurrect radio in 1963 was a false start for Lorre. The Master Artists Corporation announced it would syndicate a new series of radio programs, including an easy-listening music show from Liberace, a program called *Words on Music*, hosted by Mel Torme, and *Treasury of Terror*, featuring Peter Lorre. Demo 45s were sent to radio stations, but enthusiasm was nil. Lorre's *Treasury of Terror* sample involved a tormented man who receives a package from his ex-girlfriend containing lady fingers. Not the edible kind.

Lorre, typecast in films as a supporting player for a Vincent Price or a Jerry Lewis, was dispirited emotionally; but worse, he was dissipated physically. In the midst of painful divorce proceed-

Peter Lorre raises cane: A pop-eyed moment of mirth in *The Raven* (1963).

ings from wife number three, Lorre's maid found the actor alone and unconscious on March 23, 1964, victim of a cerebral hemorrhage. Three days later Rabbi William Sanderson presided over the funeral services, which included a few words from Vincent Price.

In a touching tribute to his friend, Price said:

> Peter had no illusions about our profession. He loved to entertain, to be a "face maker," as he said often of our kind. But his was a face that registered the thoughts of an inquisitive mind and his receptive heart, and the audience, which was his world, loved him for glimpses he gave them of that heart and mind.
>
> Peter held back nothing of himself. He always seemed to be exploring you. The aura of devotion that surrounded him made all men glad to be his friend, to feed him and be fed in turn.
>
> The something sad about him and a certain necessary madness went together to capture the hearts and give his fellow players pause lest they be unprepared to match his winsomeness. This was a man to be aware of at all times, for he was well aware of all who shared the stage with him. And working with him never failed to fulfill the seventh and perhaps most sacred sense—the sense of fun.

Radio

Funkstunde Berlin. 1930–32. Lorre appeared in six episodes of this German-language radio series: "Die Seufzerbrucke" (October 5, 1930), "Blaubart" (May 25, 1931), "Fortunios Lied" (December 12, 1931), "Vert-Vert" (January 13, 1932), "Das Notwendige und das Uberflussige" (January 20, 1932), and "Die Herilege Johanna der Schlachthofe" (April 11, 1932).

The Fleischmann Yeast Hour. May 7, 1936, NBC, 60 min. Rudy Vallee stars, and Peter Lorre joins Jean Hersholt as he plays the title role in the mini-drama "The Creation of Dr. Mallaire."

Lux Radio Theater. September 21, 1936, CBS, 60 min. "Trilby" is presented, with Grace Moore in the title role and Peter Lorre as Svengali. So far no copy of this program has been found.

The Royal Gelatin Hour. November 5, 1936, NBC, 60 min. Rudy Vallee and the Swing Kids Quartet provide the music on this variety-drama hour, with the highlight being "Prelude to Murder," starring Peter Lorre and Olivia DeHavilland. A "lost" episode.

The MGM Radio Movie Club. November 20, 1936, Syndicated, 30 minutes.

Hollywood Hotel. March 5, 1937, CBS, 60 min. A variety hour featuring Frances Langford, Burns and Allen, and a dramatic highlight, "Nancy Steele Is Missing," starring Peter Lorre.

The Royal Gelatin Hour. January 29, 1938, 60 min. Another lost episode of the Rudy Vallee–hosted program. Peter Lorre starred in the one-act play "Picture Man."

Carthay Circle Theatre. July 8, 1938, NBC, 30 min. The premiere of "Marie Antoinette" is covered, and a variety of stars walk the red carpet and greet radio listeners. Peter Lorre is in good company: Fanny Brice, Basil Rathbone, James Stewart, Norma Shearer, John Barrymore, Helen Hayes, Judy Garland and Clark Gable.

Camel Caravan. October 24, 1938, CBS, 30 min. Peter Lorre's first comic radio appearance has him as Mr. Moto, working-appearing with Eddie Cantor to try and find missing guest star Martha Raye.

The Lifebuoy Program. December 27, 1938, CBS, 30 min. Host Al Jolson enjoys the company of Peter Lorre and Martha Raye, who were together last month for Eddie Cantor's show. Albert Brooks' father, Harry Einstein, performs ethnic comedy as "Parkyakarkus."

The Royal Gelatin Hour. August 10, 1939, NBC, 60 min. Rudy Vallee hosts, and Peter Lorre gets a double work-out starring in a comic sketch as Mr. Moto and playing the dramatic lead in "The Execution of Kosky." Music is provided by Carmen Miranda, with comedy from stand-up Lou Holtz.

George Jessel Show. August 16, 1939, NBC, 30 min. Once again promoting the Mr. Moto movies, Lorre appears in a brief sketch.

The Texaco Star Theatre. October 4, 1939, CBS, 60 min. From Hollywood, Peter Lorre guest-stars as Mr. Moto in a comedy sketch with Fred Allen. From New York, Fredric March and Florence Eldridge perform a scene from Phillip Barrie's stage play *Tomorrow and Tomorrow.* Frances Langford sings "Night and Day."

Kay Kyser's Kollege of Musical Knowledge. September 25, 1940, NBC, 30 min. A frustrating "lost" episode has Kay promoting his movie *You'll Find Out,* which co-stars Peter Lorre, Boris Karloff and Bela Lugosi. All three men are on the program.

The Jack Benny Show (aka *The Jell-O Program*). March 9, 1941, NBC, 30 min. The featured sketch is "Murder at the Racquet Club." Peter Lorre, Charles Butterworth and Charles Farrell are the guest stars.

Three-Ring Time. March 6, 1942, Blue Network. Milton Berle is the host, with Peter Lorre and Bela Lugosi. No copies of this have survived.

Towards the Century of the Common Man. June 14, 1942, NBC, 60 min. A special program honoring the United Nations. The "Dramatic Sermon for a Sabbath Flag Day" features a recorded message from President Roosevelt, as well as brief words from Charles Boyer, Ronald Colman, Peter Lorre, Thomas Mitchell, Alla Nazimova and Maria Ouspenskaya, among others. Words and music by Stephen Vincent Benet and Kurt Weil.

Inner Sanctum. November 29, 1942, Blue Network. "Murders in the Rue Morgue" is a "lost" episode.

The Philip Morris Playhouse. December 11, 1942, CBS, 30 min. Peter Lorre and Anne Rutherford star in an adaptation of "Crime and Punishment."

Inner Sanctum. December 13, 1942, Blue Network, 30 min. "The Man Who Returned from the Dead" is another "lost" episode.

Suspense. December 15, 1942, CBS, 30 min. "Till Death Do Us Part." John Dickson Carr's script is performed by Peter Lorre, Mercedes McCambridge and Alice Frost.

Stage Door Canteen. December 17, 1942, CBS, 30 min. This variety program features Bert Lytell, Grace Moore and Peter Lorre in a sketch called "Footnote for Tomorrow."

Al Jolson Show. December 22, 1942, CBS, 30 min. This variety show is hosted by Al Jolson, and guest-stars Peter Lorre, Monty Woolly and Carol Bruce.

Inner Sanctum. December 27, 1942, Blue Network, 30 min. "Dig My Grave." Another episode that seems to be lost.

The Texaco Star Theatre (aka *The Fred Allen Show*). January 3, 1943, CBS, 30 min. Once again, Peter Lorre's "Mr. Moto" makes an appearance. Fred Allen's "One Long Pan" is his arch rival as they race to solve the case of "The Missing Shot, or Who Killed Balsam Beemish?" Singing guest Lois "The Reveille Sweetheart" January offers her rendition of "Dearly Beloved."

The Kate Smith Show. January 8, 1943, CBS, 30 min. Balancing the guest star comedy of Henny Youngman, Peter Lorre performs his version of "The Cask of Amontillado."

Inner Sanctum. January 17, 1943, Blue Network, 30 min. "The Bell Tolls Death" is another episode from the series that hasn't survived.

Suspense. January 19, 1943, CBS, 30 min. "The Devil's Saint," from a John Dickson Carr script, centers on Peter Lorre daring his daughter's new love to stay in the Tapestry Room overnight.

Reader's Digest. January 31, 1943, CBS, 30 min. This episode features Peter Lorre in "Education for Death."

Stage Door Canteen. February 4, 1943, CBS, 30 min. This variety show offers singers Jane Froman and Beatrice Kay, along with Peter Lorre and comedian Phil Baker. A lost program.

The Abbott & Costello Show. February 11, 1943, NBC, 30 min. In this lost episode, a sketch involves Bud & Lou stuck in a noisy New York hotel—until Peter Lorre offers to put them up at his quiet (oh so quiet) home in the country.

Treasury Star Parade, Program #159. February 22, 1943, 15 minutes. "Thirty for One" is the story of a patriotic Czech citizen's fight against Nazi oppression. The show was rebroadcast (as #210) later in the series. Starring Joseph Schildkraut and Peter Lorre.

Day of Reckoning. March 6, 1943, NBC, 30 min. Starring Edmund Gwenn. A six-part special, "The People vs. Benito Mussolini," features Peter Lorre as Mephisto in this, the second episode.

Inner Sanctum. March 7, 1943, Blue Network, 30 min. In "The Black Sea Gull" a husband seems to think his wife has made good on her promise to return from the grave. Written by Sigmund Miller, hosted by Raymond Edward Johnson.

Suspense. April 20, 1943, CBS, 30 min. "The Moment of Darkness" offers a classic horror plot: At a spooky séance where those seated around the table hold hands, somehow a murder is committed in their midst. John Dickson Carr's script is performed by Peter Lorre, Wendy Barrie and George Zucco.

The Camel Comedy Caravan. April 30, 1943, CBS, 60 min. Jack Carson is host to comedian Herb Shriner and singer Connie Haynes. A highlight sketch has Carson, along with Susan Hayward, sheltering from a storm—at Peter Lorre's spooky house.

The Lady Esther Screen Guild Theatre. September 20, 1943, CBS, 30 min. In "The Maltese Falcon," the film cast returns for a thumbnail recreation of the story, focusing mainly on hitting as many of the famous catch-phrases as possible ("You're good; awful good..."). Starring Humphrey Bogart, Mary Astor, Peter Lorre and Sydney Greenstreet.

Duffy's Tavern. October 19, 1943, Blue Network. It's not exactly the most sinister mystery he's encountered, but Peter Lorre is ready to help Archie (Ed Gardner) find out who swiped a sandwich from the bar.

The Amos 'n' Andy Show. November 5, 1943, NBC, 30 min. In one of the more low-key and eerie episodes of the show, Andy buys a sealed trunk at auction—and guest star Peter Lorre wants to be the one to open it up. Starring Freeman Gosden and Charles Correll.

Suspense. December 23, 1943, CBS, 30 min. In "Back for Christmas," Lorre is the mild-mannered professor of Botany who decides to grow a "Devil's Garden," which might be the perfect place to plant his nagging wife. From a story by John Collier, the script was re-used, sans Lorre, for episodes that aired December 23, 1948, and December 23, 1956.

The Abbott and Costello Program. January 13, 1944, NBC, 30 min. Weary Costello feels he's coming down with the flu. Things gets wearier during the inevitable comedy routine declaring, "When the flu flies, we must flee!" The boys visit Peter Lorre's sanitarium for a cure. Three years later, Lorre would become Bud and Lou's summer replacement for a season of *Mystery in the Air*.

The Frank Sinatra Show. March 22, 1944, CBS, 30 min. Frank's guests include Peter Lorre and comedians Bert Wheeler and Phil Silvers.

The Kate Smith Show. June 2, 1944, CBS, 60 min. Kate hosts a varied cast, including naval officer James Crowley, Count Basie and Peter Lorre.

The Texaco Star Theatre (aka *The Fred Allen Show*). June 4, 1944, CBS, 30 min. It's not summer yet, but in Allen's Alley the question is: "What is the hottest day you ever remember?" Later, Peter Lorre is on the receiving end of a variety of insults and jokes about his film persona.

Stars for Humanity. June 8, 1944, NBC, 60 min. This variety show stars Eddie Cantor, Paul Robeson, Peter Lorre, opera star Jan Peerce and comedian Milton Berle.

You Asked for It. June 9, 1944, NBC, 30 min. Ben Grauer's quiz show features appearances by radio comedy greats Lew Lehr and Lulu Bates, announcer Clem McCarthy, baseball's Leo Durocher and Peter Lorre.

Inner Sanctum. June 10, 1944. "Death Is the Joker" is another lost episode of the program.

Stage Door Canteen. June 16, 1944, CBS, 30 min. Jane Froman and Peter Lorre are featured.

Inner Sanctum. June 17, 1944. "The Mind Reader" is yet another lost episode of the program.

Lights of New York. June 19, 1944, Mutual, 30 min. This variety show offers guests Peter Lorre, Allen Drake and Louis Sobol.

Suspense. July 20, 1944, CBS, 30 min. In "Of Maestro and Man," fiendish Peter Lorre is an odd choice for the role of fight manager, but not when it turns out that he's homicidal and figures he can use a steam room for the perfect murder. Starring Peter Lorre, Richard Conte, John McIntire and Lou Merrill.

G. I. Journal, Program #53. July 21, 1944, 30 min. Singers Bing Crosby and Jo Stafford supply the music, and Peter Lorre supplies the comedy playing a killer looking for a new victim: Private Sad Sack. Other guests include Ransom Sherman, the Music Maids, Mel Blanc and Lynn Bari.

Stage Door Canteen. August 11, 1944, CBS, 30 min. Bert Lytell plays host to Peter Lorre, Johnny Burke and Mildred Bailey.

Inner Sanctum. September 16, 1944, CBS, 30 min. "One Foot in the Grave." No transcript of the show has turned up.

Grace Notes. October 23, 1944, WAVE, 30 min. This was a local program broadcast from Louisville, Kentucky. Interviewer Natalie Potter greets special guest Peter Lorre. What he was doing in Kentucky remains an unanswered question. No copies of this show seem to have survived.

Birdseye Open House. November 23, 1944, NBC, 30 min. Dinah Shore's guests include Sydney Greenstreet and Peter Lorre. This episode has yet to emerge from the vaults of any radio show collector.

Mystery Playhouse. In 1944, Peter Lorre was the nominal host for what was really just a selection of best single episodes from various hit shows.

The Armed Forces Radio Service didn't seem to have the time to broadcast every episode of *The Thin Man, Big Town, The Whistler*, etc., so a different title each week gained a spot in the *Mystery Playhouse*, with a fresh introduction via Lorre.

Episodes of *Mystery Playhouse* include three shows borrowed from *The Molle Mystery Theatre* (titled "Criminal at Large," "A Crime to Fit the Punishment" and "The Man in the Velvet Hat," an episode of "The Adventures of Sherlock Holmes" titled "The Superfluous Pearl") and the *Inner Sanctum* show "Elixer Number Four: The Color-Blind Formula."

The *Mystery Playhouse* program for June 10, 1944, is schizoid. It's a rerun of Lorre's "Death Is a Joker" episode from *Inner Sanctum*. So Peter Lorre introduces "Raymond," who introduces Peter Lorre as star of the show.

"The Last Laugh Murder Case" was originally broadcast on *Nero Wolfe*; "Murder in the Record Shop" originally aired on *The Thin Man*; "Death Stalks the Hunter" was originally broadcast on *Big Town*; "Nightmare" was an episode of *Mr. District Attorney*; and "Frizby Klizby" was from *Mr. and Mrs. North*.

The version of "The Doctor Prescribed Death" introduced by Lorre is a June 6, 1944, episode from *The Whistler*. Not too uncommon for radio, *The Whistler* recycled the script that had been used by *Suspense* the year earlier in a broadcast starring Bela Lugosi.

G.I. Journal. January 19, 1945, AFRS, 30 min. Jack Haley is the host, and visits the "rest home" run by Peter Lorre and John Carradine. More music and comedy is supplied by Mel Blanc and Connie Haines.

The Andrews Sisters Show. January 21, 1945, ABC Blue Network, 30 min. Guests Peter Lorre and Sydney Greenstreet join Gabby Hayes to literally "shoot" a western. Songs are featured in the sketch as well, and the guest list includes the Riders of the Purple Sage.

Milton Berle Show (aka *Let Yourself Go*). February 28, 1945. Milton Berle and fussy sidekick Joe Besser welcome Peter Lorre.

The Voice of Broadway. March 1, 1945, Mutual, 15 min. Newspaper columnist Dorothy Killgallen hosts an interview show with her guest Peter Lorre.

The Radio Hall of Fame. March 4, 1945, Blue Network, 60 min. Sponsored by Philco (sometimes referred to as *Philco Presents*), the variety show had varied casts and hosts. This episode is hosted by Bea Lillie, and offers Paul Whiteman and His Orchestra, Artie Shaw and the Gramercy Five, Jo Stafford and Bert Lahr. Featured dramatic moment: "The Tell-Tale Heart" performed by Peter Lorre.

Stage Door Canteen. March 9, 1945, CBS, 30 min. Peter Lorre once again returns to the show hosted by Bert Lytell. Other guests include singer Allan Jones and comic character stars Hugh Herbert and Ilka Chase.

Which Is Which? April 11, 1945, CBS, 30 min. Ken Murray is the master of ceremonies, with guests Peter Lorre, Bing Crosby and Frank McHugh.

The Lady Esther Screen Guild Theatre. April 16, 1945, CBS, 30 min. "The Mask of Demetrios" is a radio adaptation of the Eric Ambler adventure story, with Peter Lorre and Sydney Greenstreet repeating their film roles.

Command Performance, Program #171. April 19, 1945, 30 min. This variety show was aimed at servicemen overseas. Host Martha Stewart sings and introduces guests Jack Carson, Jack Oakie, Peter Lorre and Sydney Greenstreet. No copies of the show have surfaced. Some sources incorrectly list Lorre as guesting on an episode hosted by Kay Kyser, which was broadcast the week before—on April 12.

Arch Oboler's Plays. May 24, 1945, Mutual, 30 min. Peter Lorre heads the Oboler repertory company for "An Exercise in Horror," subtitled "a Peculiar Comedy." After greeting guest Peter Lorre, who cheerfully and morbidly urges Arch to write more gruesome shows, Oboler refuses by demonstrating how tired the genre has become, and satirizing the techniques of modern horror movies (as well as taking a bony poke at *Inner Sanctum*–type radio shows). Then there's a radical switch to the serious, as Oboler unleashes a suspenseful drama about German soldiers and citizens who are blithely murdering people and giving gifts of books covered in human skin. Featuring Bruce Elliott, Theodore Von Eltz, Winifred Wolfe, Lisa Goan, Victor Rodman, and Will Wright, the show survives but with occasional scuffing and static.

Suspense. August 30, 1945, CBS, 30 min. "Nobody Loves Me" showcases Peter Lorre as a neurotic hit man who now gets paid to do the thing he loves most: kill people. He holds all the cops at the local station hostage while he flashes back to the low points in his life.

Baby Snooks Show. September 23, 1945, CBS, 30 min. Peter Lorre and Sydney Greenstreet turn up on Fanny Brice's bratcom, but the main guest is satirist Robert Benchley.

Pabst Blue Ribbon Town. March 8, 1946, CBS, 30 min. Host Danny Kaye rents a house from spooky Lorre. Also in the cast is Butterfly McQueen.

The Lucky Strike Program (aka *The Jack Benny Show*). March 24, 1946, NBC, 30 min. Peter Lorre is the guest for "I Stand Condemned."

Mail Call. April 3, 1946, AFRS, 30 min. The Armed Forces Radio network offers a variety program featuring singer Lina Romay, the Bob Mitchell Choir, Mel Blanc, and a comic battle between Peter Lorre and "the Great Gildersleeve," Harold Peary.

Birds Eye Open House. May 9, 1946, NBC, 30 min. Dinah Shore is the host, singing wholesome songs and being a good sport about unwholesome Peter Lorre. Also on the program are Harry Von Zell and Frank Nelson.

The Dreme Show. June 20, 1946, NBC, 30 min. Rudy Vallee now hosts for Dreme, with his guests Pinky Lee and Peter Lorre, and support from veteran radio voices Marvin Miller and June Foray.

Chesterfield Supper Club. October 21, 1946, NBC, 15 min. Perry Como's quick-paced program of songs and comedy features a brief spot for Peter Lorre.

The Eddie Cantor Show. December 26, 1946, NBC, 30 min. Eddie Cantor decides that Peter Lorre might be the right person to become his manager.

The Kate Smith Show. February 9, 1947, CBS, 30 min. Peter Lorre supplies a dramatic break from Kate Smith's music as he appears in the one-act "The Painting."

The Campbell Room. February 23, 1947, CBS, 30 min. Hildegard is the host of the program, with Arnold Stang and Peter Lorre performing a comedy sketch (with Lorre playing a psychiatrist).

Kraft Music Hall. February 27, 1947, NBC, 30 min. Eddie Duchin and Eddie Foy appear in a familiar sketch—visiting the Peter Lorre Sanitarium.

Hollywood's Open House, Program #25. March 9, 1947, Syndicated, 30 min. Peter Lorre reads "The Tell-Tale Heart." Jim Ameche, Peter Donald, and Enric Madriguera and His Orchestra also appear.

The Pepsodent Show (aka *The Bob Hope Show*). May 13, 1947. Lorre co-starred with Bob Hope in *My Favorite Brunette*, and joins him here for an interview about his film with Bob, and then for a parody of a typical *Inner Sanctum* story about a murderous hitchhiker. Also featured are Martha Tilton, Desi Arnaz and His Orchestra, and Jerry Colonna.

The Victor Borge Show Starring Benny Goodman (aka *The Benny Goodman Victor Borge Show*), Program #47. June 2, 1947, NBC, 30 min. With Peter Lorre as the guest, Benny offers the musical novelty "Skeleton in the Closet." Topping that, Borge and Lorre team up for a musical sketch titled "Till the Shrouds Roll By," and Lorre plays the title character in another sketch, "Victor Borge's Ancestral Ghost."

Mail Call. June 25, 1947, AFRS, 30 min. Cathy downs is the host for a varied roster: opera star Rise Stevens, pop vocalists Lina Romay and Andy Russell, and Peter Lorre.

Mystery in the Air. July 3, 1947, NBC, 30 min. Peter Lorre gets his own 13-episode summer replacement show. The original *Mystery in the Air* starred Stephen Cortleigh as Detective Stonewall Scott, and appeared in the summer of 1945. Lorre's version was more of a traditional horror-suspense series.

Mystery in the Air. July 3, 1947. "The Tell-Tale Heart" starts things pumping in a premiere episode that wins raves from *Variety* and has announcer Harry Morgan shocked and awed at Lorre's histrionics in front of the microphone.

Mystery in the Air. July 10, 1947. "Leiningen vs. the Ants" is adapted for Peter Lorre and a supporting cast that includes Hans Conried and Jack Moyles.

Mystery in the Air. July 17, 1947. "The Touch of Your Hand" co-stars Hans Conried and Alan Reed.

Mystery in the Air. July 24, 1947. "The Interruption" co-stars Agnes Moorehead, Herb Vigran and Mary Lansing.

Mystery in the Air. July 31, 1947. Lorre once again performs "Nobody Loves Me," a tale better known via the *Suspense* version. Co-starring Lurene Tuttle and Conrad Binyon.

Mystery in the Air. August 7, 1947. "The Marvelous Barastro" is the Ben Hecht tale about a blind woman and the mysterious magician who exploits her; it had been a tour-de-force for Orson Welles (playing dual roles) in an early episode of *Suspense*. Starring Peter Lorre, Jane Morgan, Barbara Eiler, John Brown and Howard Culver.

Mystery in the Air. August 14, 1947, NBC, 30 min. "The Lodger" is the famous story of a landlady's encounter with Jack the Ripper. Starring Peter Lorre, Agnes Moorehead, Barbara Eiler, Eric Snowden, Rolfe Sedan and Conrad Binyon.

Mystery in the Air. August 21, 1947, NBC, 30 min. "The Horla," an adaptation of the Guy de Maupassant story, features Peter Lorre, Howard Culver, Jack Edwards, Jr., Ken Christy and Lurene Tuttle.

Mystery in the Air. August 28, 1947, NBC, 30 min. When a bank robber murders a minister and plots his latest caper, he figures he is "Beyond Good and Evil." The story is by Ben Hecht,

The early days of radio lived again in the '70s when record labels began to release one or two episodes at $5.98 per disc. Peter Lorre's *Mystery in the Air* was a favorite.

and stars Peter Lorre, Howard Culver, Howard Culver, Jack Edwards, Jr., John Brown, Michael Roy and Peggy Webber.

Mystery in the Air. September 4, 1947, NBC, 30 min. At a wax museum, murderers are frozen solid but could soon be walking—and murdering—once again. "The Mask of Medusa" stars Peter Lorre, Ben Wright, Lucille Meredith and Phyllis Christine Morris.

Mystery in the Air. September 11, 1947, NBC, 30 min. The Alexander Pushkin story "The Queen of Spades," about a greedy gambler, is re-told, starring Peter Lorre, Ben Wright, Jack Edwards, Jr., Lurene Tuttle and Peggy Webber.

Mystery in the Air. September 18, 1947, NBC, 30 min. For "The Black Cat," Peter Lorre does a memorable job in this legendary tale of gore and madness from Edgar A. Poe.

Mystery in the Air. September 25, 1947, NBC, 30 min. "Crime and Punishment." Peter Lorre's fascination with psychological terror leads to this thumbnail attempt at squeezing the essence from the Dostoyevsky novel. Co-starring Gloria Ann Simpson, Herb Butterfield, Joseph Kearns, Luis Van Rooten and Peggy Webber.

Hollywood Fights Back. October 26, 1947, ABC, 30 min. In a special sponsored by "the First Amendment Committee," over three dozen top stars dare to take on the House Un-American Activities Committee. Brief words are delivered by Charles Boyer, Judy Garland, Gene Kelly, Lauren Bacall, Joseph Cotten, Peter Lorre, June Havoc, John Huston, Danny Kaye, Marsha Hunt, Cornel Wilde, Melvyn Douglas, Richard Conte, Evelyn Keyes, Burt Lancaster, Paul Henreid, William Holden, Robert Ryan, Myrna Loy, Robert Young, Lucille Ball, Van Heflin, Henry Morgan, Keenan Wynn, Humphrey Bogart, Edward G. Robinson, Paulette Goddard, Audie Murphy, William Wyler, Fredric March, Vincent Price and John Garfield.

Hollywood Fights Back. November 2, 1947, ABC, 30 min. Once again "the First Amendment Committee" produces a special that promotes opposition to the House Un-American Activities Committee. Guest stars offering their comments include Burt Lancaster, Dana Andrews, Danny Kaye, Dorothy McGuire, Douglas Fairbanks, Jr., Fredric March, Gene Kelly, George S. Kaufman, Geraldine Brooks, Gregory Peck, Groucho Marx, Helen Gahagan Douglas, Humphrey Bogart, Hurd Hatfield, Jane Wyatt, John Huston, June Havoc, Keenan Wynn, Lauren Bacall, Marsha Hunt, Moss Hart, Myrna Loy, Paul Henreid, Peter Lorre, Richard Conte, Richard Rodgers and Rita Hayworth.

Philco Radio Time (aka *The Bing Crosby Show*). November 12, 1947, ABC, 30 min. This variety series hosted by Bing Crosby offers guests Kay Thompson, the Williams Brothers and Peter Lorre.

Camel Screen Guild Players. May 24, 1948, CBS, 30 min. "Casbah," starring Tony Martin and Yvonne DeCarlo, casts Peter Lorre as Inspector Slimane.

Command Performance. June 22, 1948. Betty Jane Rhodes, Sara Berner, Lenny Sherman, Joey Preston, Peter Lorre, Michel Perriere and the AFRS Orchestra appear. No surviving copies have surfaced.

Spotlight Revue. December 10, 1948. Spike Jones hosts Dorothy Shay and "mad doctor" Peter Lorre.

Theater USA. January 13, 1949, ABC, 30 min. This variety show features Rudy Vallee, Mary McCarthy, Peter Lorre, Andres Segovia and Roland Young.

The Henry Morgan Show. March 20, 1949, NBC, 30 min. Acerbic host Henry Morgan presides over an all-star guest cast, including Fred Allen, Victor Moore, Patsy Kelly and Peter Lorre.

We the People. March 22, 1949, CBS, 30 min. Peter Lorre is the guest star on a program featuring Dan Seymour and Spyros Skouras.

Skippy Hollywood Theatre, Program #386. April 5, 1949, Syndicated, 30 min. "Mr. God Johnson" is the story of a man they couldn't hang, starring Peter Lorre, Lurene Tuttle, Charlie Lung, Earl Lee and Herb Butterfield.

The Martin and Lewis Show. May 8, 1949, NBC, 30 min. The comedy team are looking for a sponsor, and they get the idea that moving to the "mystery" format might just do it. They look to Peter Lorre for advice—and in the highlight the trio sings "Drop Dead Little Darling."

Dokumentationsband Zeitfunk. September 18, 1951, Hessicher Rundfunk, 30 min. Peter Lorre went overseas to make his ambitious directorial debut with *Der Verlone* (*The Lost One*), and sits for an interview about it. Two days later he appeared on another German program, *Echo Des Tages*, broadcast from Cologne and hosted by Hans Jesse.

The Big Show. March 9, 1952, NBC, 90 minutes. The series was an attempt to produce a weekly all-star show to rival anything on TV. (Ironically, "the really big show" that Ed Sullivan produced on TV was much more successful than this!) Hostess Tallulah Bankhead greets Fibber McGee and Molly, as well as comedians Joe Frisco and Phil Foster. The show usually offered a dramatic highlight (often Tallulah doing a one-act play with a co-star). Here it's Peter Lorre with a dramatization of "The Cask of Amontillado."

The Philip Morris Playhouse. July 13, 1952, CBS, 30 min. "We Strangers" is a drama starring Peter Lorre and Carroll Conroy.

The Philip Morris Playhouse. August 19, 1953, CBS, 30 min. "The Night Has a Thousand Eyes" is a drama starring Peter Lorre, Everett Sloane and Ed Begley.

Nightmare. October 1, 1953–September 29, 1954, Mutual, 30 min. Lorre hosted one of radio's last gasps, a horror show from the Mutual Broadcasting System. Thirty episodes were recorded. Several survive among collectors, including "The Leech," "Hollow Footsteps," "The Hybrid," "Fear of Heights," "Coincidence," "The Purple Cloud," and "The Ghost." Other tempting but lost titles include: "The Frightened Frenchman," "Strange Voyage of Captain Mundsen," "The Softer Voice," "Quorum for Death," "The Lucky Stretch," "The Last Laugh," "The Rose Has Thorns," "Grave for Rent," "H Hour," "If I Should Die Before I Wake," "Desert in the Sky," "Dig the Grave Deep" and "The Brainwash."

Stage Struck. March 14, 1954, CBS, 60 min. Mike Wallace hosts an interview show, with segments on Kirk Douglas, Cedric Hardwicke, composer Vernon Duke, Noel Coward and Kaye Ballard. Peter Lorre is interviewed by correspondent Howard Barnes on location during the filming of his latest epic, *20,000 Leagues Under the Sea*.

House Party. December 6, 1954, CBS, 30 min. Peter Lorre guests on this amiable variety show hosted by Art Linkletter.

The Amos 'n' Andy Music Hall. December 16, 1954, CBS, 30 min. Peter Lorre guest stars.

The Dennis Day Show. February 13, 1955, 30 min. Peter Lorre visits Dennis Day, along with Carol Richards.

Easy as ABC. April 27, 1958, CBS, 30 min. "O Is for Old Wives Tales." A tantalizing lost show sponsored by UNESCO (United Nations Educational Scientific Cultural Organization) and featuring Boris Karloff, Peter Lorre and Alfred Hitchcock.

Assignment. May 29, 1962, CBC, 15 min. For this Canadian program, Elwood Glover conducts an interview with Peter Lorre. The recorded interview is broken up into three segments, with the other two airing May 30 and 31.

Sandy Lesberg's World. September 20, 1962, WOR, 30 min. Also the author of many travel guides and cookbooks, Lesberg was a well known New York interviewer for over two decades. He was able to secure Peter Lorre for this program, and a few years later (May 9, 1965) he managed a 15 minute sit-down with the Beatles. He's still active at WRRW in Williamsburg, Virginia.

Treasury of Terror. 1963, 15 minutes. This pilot for a proposed syndicated horror show to "bring back radio" stars Peter Lorre.

The Barry Gray Show. January 26, 1963, WOR, 120 min. A legendary lost program. Gray was a well known local radio personality in New York, able to secure both Peter Lorre and Boris Karloff as interview guests.

Audio

Unlike his contemporaries Boris Karloff and Vincent Price, Peter Lorre was not called upon to read classic stories for Caedmon. In fact, on the American International Pictures promotional 33⅓ record sent to radio stations to promote their film *The Raven*, Lorre doesn't join Price and Karloff at the microphone. (All three were available for the film's black and white trailer, which included a few lines of Poe's poem.)

On the promo "Listen to the Voice of Edgar Allan Poe's 'The Raven,'" mimic Paul Frees reads lines from the Poe poem as Lorre. Only Boris Karloff was available to stand behind a microphone, read a line from the poem, and do a comical tag at the end. Frees, who had the announcing chore of reading from a deadly serious "coming attractions"–styled script, probably volunteered to liven things up by "guesting" Lorre as well. So great is his deserved conceit that Frees segues directly from his announcing chores to his Lorre voice without worrying that anyone will know the difference.

Paul Frees can be heard imitating Lorre on the song "My Old Flame" (released on various Spike Jones compilation albums, including the original vinyl *Thank You Music Lovers* [RCA Victor LPM 2224], which is now on several CD compilations, including *The Spike Jones Anthology* [Rhino R271574]. The complete half-hour radio show with Peter Lorre guesting with Spike Jones (and Frees doing "My Old Flame") was released on CD by Rhino (R2 71156).

Frees would later reprise Lorre via a frenetic version of "Hey Jude" for his MGM stereo album *Paul Frees and the Poster People*. It opens with his spooky, dead-on version of Peter, and soon rises to ludicrousness and crazed ad-libs.

Another Lorre imitation can be heard on a segment of *Lights Out* (Capitol). Narrator Arch Oboler takes listeners on an audio journey through various types of horror, from suspense to pure horror (mostly via reenacted scripts from his old radio show). The Lorre impression (actor unidentified) is for a monologue on "sick, psycho-type" horror—in this case, a man who announces he is about to have his meal, and unveils the head of a "pretty young girl ... sawing through the bone is not easy!"

Other examples of people imitating Lorre's voice on novelty records include *The Monsters Go Disco*, a 33⅓ six-inch "flexi-disc" that was a premium in cereal boxes. The goal isn't digging graves but putting cavities in teeth, with Lorre (Boo Berry), Karloff (Frankenberry) and Lugosi (Count Chocula) imitators promoting brands of cereal.

During the '70s revival of interest in radio, a few episodes of *Mystery in the Air* were commercially released on vinyl. Nostalgia Lane (NLR 1020) offered a complete half-hour episode on each side: "The Black Cat" and "The Queen of Spades." The cover has an accurate, colorized pencil portrait of Lorre, with an angry black cat in the background.

Radio Archives (LP-1001) featured two different episodes, "Mask of Medusa" and "The Lodger." There are no album notes, but it offers one large picture of Peter Lorre on the front and a different one on the back. This combo was also released with indifferent packaging by Golden Age (Golden Age 5031).

Radiola has the "Cask of Amontillado" episode of *Mystery in the Air* on Radiola 1009, and Lorre's "Till Death Do Us Part" episode of *Suspense* is on Radiola 1041. The brief radio version of "Cask of Amontillado," performed by Lorre on *The Big Show* on March 9, 1952, is a bonus on Radiola #9, which offers "Three Skeleton Key" and "The Thing on the Fourble Board" episodes of *Escape* and *Quiet Please*.

Kay Thompson and Peter Lorre were guests together on an episode of Bing Crosby's show. Thompson, author of the "Eloise" children's books, was also a singer and contributed vocal arrangements to many film musicals. A bit of the Crosby show is evidently part of the vinyl compilation *Kay Thompson Reviews* on the obscure Amalgamated label (Amalgamated 179). The segment also appears on CD, on the Avid label, as *Bing Crosby and His Hollywood Guests*.

The only vinyl album with the actual Peter Lorre on it released in his lifetime was the soundtrack to *Silk Stockings*, which features a snippet of dialogue that includes Lorre, and the comic song "Siberia," which is sung by three Russians in unison, including Lorre (although it's entirely possible that Lorre's singing voice was dubbed). Original vinyl: MGM E 3542; CD version: Sony Special Products AK 46198.

8

Two-Shot Wonders: Claude Rains and Charles Laughton

Not every horror star is typecast permanently as a monster. Unlike "one-shot wonders" who have a hit record and never work again, Charles Laughton (*The Hunchback of Notre Dame* [1939] and mad Dr. Moreau in *Island of Lost Souls* [1933]) and Claude Rains (*The Invisible Man* [1933] and *Phantom of the Opera* [1943]) had successful careers before and after their horror roles.

Laughton and Rains each played two famous monster roles but escaped the designation of "bogeyman" rather than "actor." Rather than play two horror roles in a row, there was a gap of several years between assignments. All four roles were based on "classic" literature, which helped lift these movies to the loftier category of "film adaptation" rather than B-movie thriller. Both serious actors would turn up in radio comedy to surprise audiences by showing their lighter side.

Claude Rains

For Claude Rains (November 10, 1889–May 30, 1967), his film debut relied almost completely on his voice. In James Whale's version of the H.G. Wells novel *The Invisible Man*, Rains played the drug-maddened and increasingly power-crazed and violent scientist Jack Griffin. In his distinctive voice he uttered the famous line, "I meddled in things that man must leave alone," playing both God and monster.

Rains did not make a corporeal appearance until the last moments of the movie; yet there's hardly a more vivid or complex character in the entire monster genre. The Invisible One (as the end credits called him) could speak tenderly to his girlfriend Flora in an almost Tallulah Bankhead–styled drawl ("Flaw-rah, I'll come back to you, my daw-ling"), deliver alarming lines of crisply insane rage ("Even the moon's frightened of me!") and also sing giddy nursery rhymes while terrifying village peasants ("Here we go gathering nuts in May ... whoops!"). What other movie fiend had such a range of tenderness, violence and humor?

In terms of vocal flexibility, Rains' performance is probably the finest in horror film history.

One of Rains' first major radio appearances was also horror-themed. On Rudy Vallee's *Fleischmann's Yeast Hour* he performed Poe's "The Tell-Tale Heart." He later followed Boris Karloff into the *Inner Sanctum* radio series, and in 1943 dared to challenge the memory of Lon Chaney via the talkies' version of *The Phantom of the Opera*.

By then, fans had come to know a bit more about the middle-aged stage actor from England. Born William Claude Rains (and ditching the officious-sounding "William Claude" almost as quickly as "W.C." Fields did), the young man could hardly even dream of a stage career. He had a terrible stutter, an awful Cockney accent, and a speech impediment that made it difficult to pronounce the "R" in anything, even his last name.

His classmates made cruel fun of "Willie Wains." Disgraced and miserable, he quit school at the age of eleven. He worked in theaters as a call boy and prompter, and discovered, as many stutterers have, that he didn't have the problem when he was singing.

Ironically, decades later, Claude's daughter seemed to have inherited his stammer. The loving father knew the seven year old's cure would have to come from singing her sentences rather than speaking them. She recalled in her bio of her father,

> He was determined ... that I would pronounce my words "succinctly," and in that he was successful.... The cure for stuttering was to sing everything. I remember us sitting around the dining room table. The cook would enter the room with a silver dish holding the vegetables. "Here are the peas, Mr. Rains," she would sing in her gospel-singer's voice. Enjoying this therapy immensely, my father would belt out, "Pass them to Jennifer first, she must eat the peas before she eats the lamb chops...."

Later, Rains would coach his daughter the old fashioned way: "I had to pronounce in a well-articulated voice, 'How now, brown cow. G-r-razing in the g-r-reen g-r-reen g-r-ass." But it was the singing that proved to be the most effective way of breaking free of her problem.

Singing solo and in choirs gave Claude some confidence, and by the time he rose to the level of stage manager at His Majesty's Theatre in London, he was taking on small roles himself. He worked hard on his enunciation, creating a uniquely intense and measured delivery style, his voice much more of a selling point than his looks or slight physique. He conquered his regional accent and his other speech problems, and in 1911 made his official acting debut in *Gods of the Mountain*.

Cocky little Claude Rains strikes a publicity pose.

He continued to work more as a stage manager and assistant director until he joined a repertory company run by Harley Granville-Barker. They toured America in 1913. Rains' horizons broadened even more when he married the company's leading lady, Isabel Jeans, the same year. They divorced in 1915.

During World War I service, the use of chemical weapons was common, and a gas attack choked Rains, adding an edgy rasp to his voice. It also left him legally blind in his right eye, something he didn't mention to even some of his close friends. Captain Rains returned to the stage and won strong reviews as Casca in a production of *Julius Caesar* in London.

He married actress Marie Hemingway

in the winter of 1920, but it barely lasted through the year. In 1924 he married Beatrix Thomson, who had been a student in one of his acting classes at the Royal Academy of Dramatic Art. When Thomson was offered a role Stateside in *The Constant Nymph*, Rains took a smaller part in the show to stay with her. Soon he was winning important character parts. His wife's career went nowhere, and she left for England. The couple were officially divorced in 1935. By then, Rains had also given up the stage. *They Shall Not Die* (1934) featured his last role on the boards for nearly two decades.

Rains became a United States citizen in 1938 and proved his devotion via many wartime services, including lending his unique voice to patriotic radio programs, including the obscure *Lincoln Highway* series. In an episode of *This Is War*, written by Norman Corwin, he plays a government official who comes to a small town to visit an average family and show them the importance of doing their part. "You mean we could lose?" someone asks. "That's up to you, Jonesy," Claude answers.

While Rains had the minor (and unlikely, given the disparity in size and accent) role of Lon Chaney, Jr.'s father in *The Wolfman* (1941), his other film roles, often sinister, led him to appear in episodes of *Inner Sanctum* in 1942. Sadly, none of these war-time episodes still exist. Rains' next assignment would be the first sound version of *The Phantom of the Opera*. It was something he mentioned on Fred Allen's radio show.

Like so many horror stars, including Basil Rathbone, Peter Lorre and Boris Karloff, Rains appreciated not only Fred Allen's enthusiasm in booking him for comedy, but making sure to write quips that would be suitable for him and give added dimension to his personality.

"I don't know why you invited me over tonight, Fred," Rains deadpans. "I'm not particularly funny, you know.... Mind you, I could be funny if I had some jokes. I heard a good joke about a sailor. On duty he was a submarine chaser. Off duty he wasn't so particular."

Rains actually gets a good laugh from the crowd on that one. Later he's asked about his bucolic getaway in Pennsylvania (a legacy from his Broadway days):

> CLAUDE: I have a real farm. I raise corn, grain, soybeans. I have cattle, pigs and chickens. But like the rest of the farmers, what I raise I turn over to Uncle Sam.
> FRED: Why do actors always buy farms?
> RAINS: Well, you know, working in the theater the average actor gets to know a lot about vegetables...
> FRED: After Hollywood, don't you find farm life pretty quiet? Don't you get homesick for a little noise?
> RAINS: Well, when I do, I eat a radish to break the monotony.

Rains tells Fred that he's going to Hollywood to make *The Phantom of the Opera*, and

Claude Rains is the poster boy for *Phantom of the Opera*, the 1943 version where most of the chills involved listening to Nelson Eddy sing.

Fred claims he once worked for the "San Crisco Opera Company" and met the real thing! That cues a flashback to 1923, but, unfortunately, it doesn't really involve the guest star much. Ironically, Rains harkens back to his own early career, for here he plays the manager of the hall, not the Phantom.

The running gag, which begins to limp badly, is how Fred's operatic quartet slowly turns into a trio, then a duet and finally a solo as murders keep interrupting the deliberately bad singing. The Phantom, in this case, has good taste. Rains is left to mutter, "Now I know what *not* to do in the picture."

In films at the time, Rains rarely seemed to have a chance to use his sense of humor. The best known exception was when he played the dapper and corrupt Major Louis Renault opposite Humphrey Bogart in *Casablanca*. While he doesn't tell jokes, he wickedly delivers the famous phrase, "I am shocked, *shocked...*" to discover gambling at Rick's backroom casino (only to be handed his winnings a moment later). He steals many a scene with a cocked eyebrow and a raspy, ironic edge to his voice. The role brims with a sense of fun usually missing from his repertoire (after all, the same year he also played Dr. Jasquith in *Now, Voyager*).

On the film set or before the radio microphone, Claude Rains was known to be "all business," someone to be addressed as "Mr. Rains," and the kind of man prone to worry and rehearse his lines by himself rather than joke around with the cast. On the set of *Casablanca*, puckish Peter Lorre decided to have some fun with him. Lorre's elaborate practical joke was to bring Rains on the set and start acting a scene that wasn't in the script. Lorre happily recalled:

> When he came in the next day and saw us rehearsing the scene, he was frantic. He called me aside and said, "Peter, something terrible has happened to me. I can't remember a single line." We all broke up and he wasn't even mad—just relieved that his memory wasn't failing.

Rains' radio work became more frequent when he returned to the Broadway stage. In John T. Soister's book *Claude Rains: A Comprehensive Illustrated Reference*, Rains mentioned, "The NBC studios in the RCA building were convenient to the Broadway theater, where I often appeared—and I relished performing in radio dramas as a kind of 'relaxation' from the strain of the stage's continuing demands."

In the late '40s Rains was sometimes asked to appear as narrator for classical compositions that had spoken word portions. He made several records, including Richard Strauss' *Enoch Arden*, with

Rains was "Shocked, shocked," to find corruption in *Casablanca* (1942).

pianist Glenn Gould. Rains also lent his voice to Aaron Copland's *A Lincoln Portrait*, which was the hit of the Philadelphia Orchestra season when it was performed on April 19, 1949.

With his brittle demeanor and intense squint, he continued to play a variety of mean and menacing roles in suspense and mystery films, including the suspicious husband in Hitchcock's *Notorious* (1946). He was a commanding presence, even though in this film, as in so many, he was a smaller man playing opposite a well-proportioned rival.

Fay Wray, interviewed in *Scarlet Street* magazine, recalled:

> Oh, he was very focused, very focused—and he wanted to be taller! I always think of that in connection with him. I noticed that his heels were always quite a bit higher than anyone else's on the set—equal to mine, I suppose, but with more foundation than I had.... I liked working with Claude Rains; I had great admiration for him. He was a really serious actor. No fooling around and no nonsense!

Radio listeners continued to delight in hearing Rains in thrillers, especially *Suspense*, which was broadcast in New York where he so often appeared in stage productions. He both narrates and stars in "The Hands of Mr. Ottermole," about a British strangler who kills for pleasure and even murders a policeman. Rains is with the police, and Vincent Price is a reporter ("Mr. Newspaper Man," as Rains constantly calls him). The question arises as to which of them is the killer, since both are always at the scene of the crime. Rains describes a scene of carnage to Price, his taut voice adding extra tension to the telling:

> Inside the cottage, a whole family lay dead, fallen around the supper table. One look at their necks showed us the strangler's trademark again. There was nothing in that cottage except death. Once more he had killed and slipped away. Again, I looked out at the crowd now beginning to move back. Suddenly I saw in the front ranks, your face again, the newspaper man who seemed to be everywhere I turned. There was a light in your face, a light that was almost happiness. And looking at you in that brief second I was aware that there were two of us who now knew the identity of the murderer!

The story ends with Price and Rains sharing a curtain call, with one of them amused at not being the villain.

Fans who couldn't get enough of a favorite star in film appearances or radio work could have a permanent record via ... well, a permanent record—a 78 rpm disc. Claude Rains' vocal talent attracted record producers. In 1946 he made a children's recording called *The Christmas Tree* (Mercury Childcraft). Two years later he made two more recordings, *Bible Stories for Children* (Capitol DBS 94 and Capitol DBS 98), which told "The Story of Jesus," "Moses in the Bulrushes" and "Noah and the Ark."

Rains continued with a busy schedule of films, TV and radio work—and marriages. His marriage in 1935 to Francis Propper ended in 1956. He married Hungarian pianist Agi Jambor in 1959 and divorced in 1960, the year he married Rosemary Clark.

The four-time Oscar-nominated film star had just received praise for a 1959 *Playhouse 90* production of "Judgment at Nuremburg." For an interview with *Playbill*, author Abby Mann recalled that, for all the wrong reasons, a Rains line achieved great notoriety:

> The most discussed thing about the TV show was when Claude Rains said, "How can you ask me to predict the deaths of millions of people in‒‒‒‒‒‒‒‒?" "Gas ovens" got bleeped out because the show had a sponsor that was a gas company. This was the headline in the *New York Times*, not that we were the first to talk about German guilt.

After marrying Rosemary Clark, Rains abandoned New York television and stage work and moved with her (and the three children from her previous marriage) to Sandwich,

New Hampshire. She died in 1963 of pancreatic cancer. Rains suffered from liver problems, but made a last film appearance as King Herod in the 1965 production *The Greatest Story Ever Told*. He died of an intestinal hemorrhage.

Four years later, Bette Davis mourned him during an interview on *The Dick Cavett Show*. On the 1971 broadcast she was asked about *Now, Voyager* and the way the romance in the film ended:

> The man in that was never going to be right for her, he was too weak. I always felt in *Voyager* that she eventually married Dr. Jackwith, my gorgeous Claude Rains. I always felt that ... that she went and worked with him in his work.

A meditation on the emotional traits of actors soon turned back to Rains:

> I think we're very moody people, we have great ups and great downs.... I think we're terribly peculiar that way, and rather lonely people actually. Claude I could not say was a happy person; he was witty, amusing and beautiful, really beautiful, thoroughly enchanting to be with. And brilliant...

Davis ended up noting how all the great, classic stars of radio and film were dying away: "You think as these people go, these beautiful people go, it's going to be a new world, we're not going to have that same kind of person anymore. Like when Claude Rains died, you couldn't bear it ... they're all individuals."

She loved him in *Mr. Skeffington*, *Now, Voyager* and *Deception* ("He was so wonderful in that ... and the restaurant scene where he's talking about all the food..."), while another group remember him best for *The Invisible Man*, *Phantom of the Opera* and other mysterious movies. A few may have gotten their first introduction to Rains from his popular Bible recordings.

Reflecting his Biblical interests in film and in audio, Rains' headstone at the Red Hill Cemetery in Carroll County, New Hampshire, offers this message to his fans and friends:

> Claude Rains
> 1889–1967
> All things Once
> Are things forever,
> Soul, once living,
> Lives forever.

Radio

The Good Earth. September 3, 1932, NBC. This radio version features Claude Rains and Alla Nazimova.

The Fleischmann's Yeast Hour. February 2, 1933, NBC. "A Bill of Divorcement" co-stars Rains with Janet Beecher.

The Fleischmann's Yeast Hour. March 17, 1934, NBC, 60 min. Rains makes a guest appearance; the episode no longer survives.

Lux Radio Theater. January 6, 1935. Claude Rains plays the Raja of Rukh in "The Green Goddess."

The Fleischmann's Yeast Hour. April 4, 1935, NBC, 60 min. This variety show hosted by Rudy Vallee features vaudeville's Duncan Sisters, who reprise their blackface/whiteface act as "Topsy and Eva"; a "wonder bird" parrot that can imitate celebrities and whistle tunes; and Claude Rains performing Edgar Allan Poe's "The Tell-Tale Heart."

Hollywood Hotel. July 5, 1935. Claude Rains appears in "The Last Outpost," with Cary Grant and Gertrude Michael.

Hollywood Hotel. July 17 and July 24, 1936. Claude Rains stars in a two-part version of "Anthony Adverse," with Olivia De Havilland and Gale Sondergaard.

The Lux Radio Theatre. December 14, 1936, CBS, 60 min. "Madame Sans-Gene" is a story about the French Revolution featuring an all-star cast: Jean Harlow, Robert Taylor and Claude Rains as Napoleon.

The Royal Gelatin Hour. April 29, 1937. Rudy Vallee, Bergen and McCarthy, and a special production, "The Game of Chess," with Claude Rains.

Shakespeare Festival. June 26, 1937, CBS, 60 minutes. The third episode in this ambitious series (naturally a "sustaining" show with no sponsor) stars Claude Rains as Cassius in an adaptation of "Julius Caesar."

Sunday Night Party. July 18, 1937, NBC. Rains performs "The Cask of Amontillado."

Kraft Music Hall. August 12, 1937, NBC, 30 min.

The Park Avenue Penners (aka *The Joe Penner Show*). January 2, 1938, CBS, 30 min.

Kraft Music Hall. June 9, 1938, NBC.

Hollywood Hotel. June 10, 1938. Rains appears in a production of "White Banners," with Fay Bainter and Jackie Cooper.

Kraft Music Hall. November 3, 1938, NBC.

Great Plays. Nov 20, 1938, NBC. Claude rains appears once again in a production of "Julius Caesar."

Lux Radio Theater. Nov 21, 1938. Though Basil Rathbone starred in the film version of *Confession*, Claude Rains takes his role for this radio adaptation. Later the roles were reversed: Rathbone took the radio version of "Phantom of the Opera," which had been a screen hit for Rains.

Royal Gelatin Hour. January 5, 1939, NBC. Rudy Vallee is the host; Rains performs in "There's Always Joe Winters."

Royal Gelatin Hour. March 30, 1939. Rudy Vallee is the host; Claude Rains appears in "The Eigerwund," scripted by Arch Oboler.

Texaco Star Theater. October 11, 1939. "Kind Lady."

Kraft Music Hall. December 28, 1939, NBC.

The Cavalcade of America. April 2, 1940, Blue Network, 30 min. "The Story of Benedict Arnold" stars Claude Rains, Juano Hernandez, Jeanette Nolan, Ian MacAllaster, John McIntire, Alfred Shirley, Elliott Reid, Agnes Moorehead, Frank Readick, Kenny Delmar and Ray Collins.

The Lux Radio Theatre. October 14, 1940, CBS, 30 min. "The Littlest Rebel" is Shirley Temple, age twelve, in this Civil War drama of a girl whose father is going to be hanged as a spy. Claude Rains plays the role John Boles assayed on film. Preston Foster, Barbara Jean Wong, Bea Benaderet, Bernice Pilot, Dix Davis, Griff Barnett, Harriet Flowers, Jack Carr, and Edwin Max co-star.

The Cavalcade of America. January 15, 1941, Red Network, 30 min. "As a Man Thinketh" is a biography of Thomas Cooper, jailed over the Sedition Act. Starring Claude Rains, William Johnstone, Jeanette Nolan, Agnes Moorehead, John McIntire, Ray Collins, Kenny Delmar, Karl Swenson and Edwin Jerome.

Lincoln Highway. February 22, 1941, NBC, 30 min. Rains appears on this patriotic program hosted by the Shinola company. He also appeared on the July 25 episode.

Calling America. July 11 and July 25, 1941, Mutual, 30 min. Drew Pearson hosts the program, also known as *Listen America*.

Your Happy Birthday. July 12, 1941, NBC, 30 min. Rains appears on the quiz program.

Great Moments from Great Plays. August 1, 1941, NBC, 30 min. Rains stars in a production of "Blind Alley."

The Philip Morris Playhouse. September 26, 1941, CBS. Rains appears in production of "A Man to Remember."

Inner Sanctum. September 28, 1941, ABC, 30 min. "The Haunting Face" is a lost episode.

Millions for Defense. October 14, 1941, CBS, 60 min. Rains appears on this variety series.

The Cavalcade of America. October 27, 1941, Red Network, 30 min. "Captain Paul" is a biography of John Paul Jones, starring Claude Rains, Betty Garde, Frank Readick, Kenny Delmar, Horace Braham, Ann Starrett, Karl Swenson, Jeanette Nolan and John McIntire.

The Lux Radio Theatre. January 26, 1942, CBS, 60 min. "Here Comes Mr. Jordan" is an adaptation of the hit movie, starring Cary Grant, Claude Rains, Evelyn Keyes, James Gleason, Edward Marr, Howard McNear and Eugene Forsythe.

Keep 'Em Rolling. February 2, 1942. Claude Rains joins George S. Kaufman in this wartime variety program.

Philip Morris Playhouse. March 20, 1942, CBS. Rains stars in a production of "The Criminal Code," with John Garfield.

This Is War. March 21, 1942, NBC, 30 min. In "You're on Your Own," the average American matters; which is why a surprised Wilbur Jones gets a visit from the man in charge of "The Department of Public Interest." This patriotic script by Philip Wylie was directed by Norman Corwin, and starred Ezra Stone, Claude Rains and Everett Sloane.

Lincoln Highway. March 28, 1942, NBC. Claude Rains pays a return visit to the program.

The Cavalcade of America. April 20, 1942, Red Network, 30 min. "In This Crisis" is a biography of Thomas Paine starring Claude Rains, Ray Collins, Gale Gordon, Gavin Gordon, Agnes Moorehead, and Hans Conried.

Plays for Americans. June 7, 1942, NBC. Rains appears in Arch Oboler's production of "Back Where You Came From."

The Cavalcade of America. September 7, 1942, Red Network, 30 min. "Soldier of a Free Press" details the life of the nation's first war correspondent, Richard Harding Davis. Starring Claude Rains.

Philip Morris Playhouse. September 18, 1942. A production of "Underground."

Inner Sanctum. September 27, 1942. Rains starred in three now-lost productions of *Inner Sanctum*, which marked his return to horror notoriety (solidified with his film role in *Phantom of the Opera*). The first was "The Man Who Played with Death."

Inner Sanctum. October 11, 1942. "The King of Darkness."

Radio Reader's Digest. October 25, 1942, CBS. Claude Rains stars in "The Missionary and the Gangster."

Inner Sanctum. November 8, 1942. "The Laughing Murderer."

Radio Reader's Digest. January 24, 1943. "The French Underground."

The Texaco Star Theatre. February 7, 1943, CBS, 30 min. Fred Allen's show features a doleful comedy sketch: Claude Rains and Fred in "The Phantom of Carnegie Hall," a bow to Rains' recent remake of Lon Chaney's *Phantom of the Opera*. Starring Fred Allen, Portland Hoffa, Claude Rains, Minerva Pious, Alan Reed and Charlie Cantor.

The Radio Hall of Fame. March 18, 1945, ABC, 60 min. Chico Marx jokes with Paul Whiteman and plays the piano. Evelyn Knight is the featured singer, while Jay C. Flippen offers a subway parody of "The Trolley Song." Vic and Sade appear in a comedy sketch, and Claude Rains offers an adaptation of a Guy de Maupassant short story, "A Piece of String."

Stage Door Canteen. March 2, 1945, CBS. Guests on this variety program include Rains and Henny Youngman.

Theatre of Romance. March 20, 1945, CBS, 30 min. "The Citadel," based on the medical drama by A.J. Cronin, stars Claude Rains and Gertrude Warner.

Franklin D. Roosevelt Funeral. May 15, 1945, CBS. In a program of tributes called "A Legacy for America," Claude Rains reads poems by Walt Whitman.

Dr. Christian. June 6, June 13 and June 20, 1945, CBS, 30 min. Claude Rains substitutes for the show's star, Jean Hersholt, for three episodes in a row.

The Radio Reader's Digest. November 7, 1946, CBS, 30 min. "Murder in the Big Bowl" stars Claude Rains and Richard Kollmar.

The Fred Allen Show. December 8, 1946, NBC, 30 min. Claude Rains makes a return visit; the program has not survived.

Suspense. March 20, 1947, CBS, 30 min. "The Waxwork" is one of the few *Suspense* broadcasts that has apparently been lost.

Kraft Music Hall. May 8, 1947, NBC.

The Radio Reader's Digest. May 29, 1947, CBS, 30 min. In "Many Moons," a young Princess literally wants the moon, and looks to her Court Jester for help. Starring Claude Rains, Everett Sloane and Richard Kollmar.

Freedom Pledge. September 16, 1947. Claude Rains journeys to Philadelphia for a local program about patriotism. His pledge: "I am an American, a free American. Free to speak without fear. Free to worship my own God. Free to stand up for what I think. Free to oppose what I believe wrong. Free to choose those who govern my country. This heritage of freedom I pledge to uphold for myself and all mankind."

The Radio Reader's Digest. October 30, 1947, CBS, 30 min. The Guy de Maupassant story "A Piece of String" (which was also adapted for an episode of *Suspense*, starring Vincent Price) becomes a vehicle for Claude Rains, with support from Alan Hewitt, Les Tremayne and Tom Shirley.

Studio One. July 6, 1948, CBS. Rains stars in a production of "Topaze."

The Ford Theatre. October 18, 1948, CBS, 60 min. The Gustave Flaubert classic *Madame Bovary* is adapted for radio, with Claude Rains, Marlene Dietrich, Van Heflin, Ivor Francis, Mercedes McCambridge and Miriam Wolfe.

Theater Guild on the Air (aka *The U.S. Steel Hour*). November 14, 1948. "Valley Forge." This episode apparently no longer exists.

Suspense. December 2, 1948, CBS, 30 min. In "The Hands of Mr. Ottermole," a serial killer is on the loose in London, and the police have some clues as to the identity of the strangler. Claude Rains, Vincent Price and Verna Felton star.

Theater Guild on the Air (aka *The U.S. Steel Hour*). January 2, 1949. "The Game of Love and Death" co-stars Claude Rains with Paul Henreid and Katherine Hepburn. No copies seem to have survived.

The Jack Benny Program. February 27, 1949, CBS, 30 min. Claude Rains guest stars, and the gags involve his upcoming appearance in a radio version of Benny's notorious "Horn Blows at Midnight."

The Ford Theatre. March 4, 1949, CBS, 60 min. "The Horn Blows at Midnight." The stern voice of Claude Rains is used for humorous and ironic effect in this production co-starring Anne Whitfield, Byron Kane, Hans Conried, Herb Vigran, Jane Morgan, Jay Novello, Jeanette Nolan, Jerry Farber, John McGovern, Joseph Kearns, Julian Upton, Mercedes McCambridge and Miriam Wolfe.

The Philip Morris Playhouse. March 25, 1949. "Banquo's Chair."

The Goal Is Freedom. April 4, 1949, CBS, 30 min. Senator Lyndon Johnson is profiled in a show about prejudice in America. Starring Claude Rains.

Ford Theater. May 20, 1949, CBS. "Crime Without Passion" stars Claude Rains in a radio version of one of his recent films.

Ford Theater. October 8, 1949, CBS. "Madame Bovary" co-stars Marlene Dietrich and Van Heflin.

The Cavalcade of America. March 7, 1950, NBC, 30 min. In "Mr. Peale and the Dinosaur," Charles Wilson Peale works to create the Museum of Natural History in Philadelphia. Starring Claude Rains, Agnes Moorehead, Parker Fennelly and Alan Hewitt.

The Big Show. January 6, 1952, NBC. Claude Rains appears in the sketch "Midnight Blue."

The Big Show. February 10, 1952, NBC. Claude Rains appears in an adaptation of James Thurber's "The Catbird Seat."

Cavalcade of America. February 19, 1952, NBC. "Three Words: Victor or Death" is the story of the Battle of Trenton. Claude Rains stars as George Washington, with Bill Lipton and Kermit Murdock.

The Jeffersonian Heritage. 1952. Syndicated by the National Association of Educational Broadcasters, there were twelve half-hour programs devoted to the life and work of Thomas Jefferson, with episodes including, "The Living Declaration," "Divided We Stand," "Light and Liberty," "The Return of the Patriot," "The Danger of Freedom," "The Experiment of a Free Press," "The Ground of Justice," "Freeing the Land," "The University of the United States," "To Secure These Rights," "First Came the Word," and "Nature's Most Precious Gift." Starring Claude Rains and Dumont Malone.

Medicine USA. March 28, 1953, NBC. Claude Rains appears in "Our Hidden Wealth" in a program sponsored by the American Medical Association.

Kaleidoscope. July 4, 1953, NBC. "The Living Declaration."

Stagestruck. May 21, 1954, CBS, 60 min. In this, the last show of the series, there's "A Review of the 1953–54 Theatrical Season," featuring a look at Broadway's top stars: Alfred Drake, Audrey Hepburn, Basil Rathbone, Ben Gazzara, Carol Channing, Claude Rains, Danny Kaye, Eddie Cantor, Ezio Pinza, Harry Belafonte, Hermione Gingold, Katharine Cornell, Kaye Ballard, Mary Martin, Mel Ferrer, Noel Coward, Phil Silvers, Rodgers and Hammerstein, Shirley Booth, Victor Borge and Yul Brynner.

Anthology. May 26, 1955, NBC. Claude Rains joins Helen Hayes and Walter Huston for "Builders of America," a program of poetry readings. Also featured is "Cantata for Mixed Voices."

Presenting Claude Rains (aka *Claude Rains and His Stories*). July 11, 1955–December 11, 1955, NBC, 15 min. Claude Rains, similar to the Boris Karloff *Reader's Digest* series, offers stories culled from newspapers and magazines. Scripted by Liz Pearce and produced by Kenneth MacGregor, the program was syndicated to stations around the country.

The Titanic. March 28, 1956, NBC. A documentary about the tragic ocean liner.

Audio

Radiola issued the Shirley Temple *Lux Radio Theater* episode on vinyl, and many companies have issued CD-R and mp3 files of radio programs featuring Rains. Additionally, he appeared on several albums and singles.

"The Christmas Tree" (Mercury Childcraft) was Rains' first 78 rpm single, released in 1946.

Bible Stories for Children (Capitol DBS 98 and Capitol DBS 94). Recorded in 1948, the stories were "The Story of Jesus," "Moses in the Bulrushes" and "Noah and the Ark."

An Evening with William Shakespeare is a 1952 double album from Theatre Masterworks. Claude Rains is supported by Emerson, Nina Foch, Eva LeGallienne, Arnold Moss, Richard Dyer-Bennet and Wesley Addy.

Literary Readings in the Coolidge Auditorium is in the archives of the Library of Congress. It was not released commercially. At this October 12, 1953, performance, Rains reads a variety of poems (from Alfred Lord Tennyson to T.S. Eliot) and scenes from Shakespeare.

Builders of America (1959) is a cantata for Mixed Voices, with music by H. McDonald, and text by E. Shenton (Columbia Masterworks ML 2220).

Remember the Alamo (1960). Noble Records. Narration, with music by Tony Mottola.

Jefferson Heritage is a 7-album set of "a distinguished series of radio programs designed with respect for all Americans," presented by the National Association of Educational Broadcasters.

Enoch Arden (Columbia Records) features Claude Rains, with Glenn Gould piano (re-issued on CD).

Charles Laughton

Claude Rains and Charles Laughton would probably be mortified to be in the same chapter together. Their casual relationship as fellow working actors ended with four bitter words. This was a surprise to Rains, who didn't realize there was any bad blood between them. He was about to play Archdeacon Frollo in *The Hunchback of Notre Dame* (1939). He happened upon Laughton on the studio lot, gave him a crisp hello, and the portly actor replied, "Hello, you little shit."

Rains decided not to appear in Laughton's film, and the part of Frollo went to Cedric Hardwicke instead. Just how the studious, business-like Rains had managed to irk the moody, sensitive Laughton was never made clear to the little Brit. He only remarked about stepping away from Laughton's movie (on page 102 of the bio co-authored by Rains' daughter), "I didn't want to have any trouble with him."

In a final irony, after *The Hunchback of Notre Dame*, Laughton was suggested as the right man for a remake of *Phantom of the Opera*. After he played opposite Deanna Durbin in *It Started with Eve* (1941), the studio was especially keen on having Durbin play the opera singer trained by the hideous phantom. After the script was completed, neither performer was chosen, and Laughton's *Phantom* was given to Claude Rains.

Perhaps the one thing they had in common, aside from both playing a few monster roles amid their other drama films, is their mutual love of the Bible. Both of them recorded Bible stories for home listening.

Elsa Lanchester, in her autobiography, recalled a favorite moment when her husband Charles showed reporters around their opulent home. "Do you know how I got these paintings and this house and this swimming pool? By reading the fucking Bible!"

Unable to restrain his wit any more than he could restrain his homosexuality, Laughton often fretted about the repercussions of his "sins," and it was difficult for Laughton to reconcile his spiritual instincts with the ways of the flesh. His biographer, Simon Callow, wrote that Laughton in his last year, "haunted from the depth of his terrible conscience by

A grim character actor is rarely adored. Charles Laughton is about to be hauled into the hall.

the fear of divine retribution, demanded a test for rectal cancer." Spared that particular disease, but dying nevertheless, Laughton welcomed "a steady stream of priests," even if they gave him little comfort. "I wish they were more intelligent," he said.

One difference between reading an audio book, as Laughton did with selections from the Bible, and performing on radio is the frequent presence of a live audience. Radio stations liked the publicity and excitement, and the actors seemed to get a charge out of it, too, especially the applause at show's end. The only problem was that while comedians wanted laughs from the audience, producers of radio drama didn't.

An actor on a film set, or in a recording studio, could joke around, then "get serious." On a real stage, "breaking character" was almost impossible due to the flow of the script. But on radio? The actors were not technically in character or moving around, they were reading from a script and standing awkwardly at a microphone. If they didn't do this regularly, as so many of the supporting, multi-voiced and anonymous radio performers did, actors could feel awkward and start "playing" to the audience with a wink or a gesture.

Radio director Fletcher Markle used to warn the audience not to laugh if a script page fell from an actor's hand, and not to snicker if the "hoofbeats down the prairie road" were coming from a bored sound effects man smacking a pair of coconuts on a table. He also, as quoted in Leonard Maltin's *Great American Broadcast* (page 201), had to find ways of keeping his actors in line, too:

> If we had Charles Laughton in "Payment Deferred," or any of those extraordinarily suspenseful things ... Charles was often a comical figure when being his most dramatic. God knows there was never a greater professional than Charles, but I used to ask him to come out in the warm-up and get his round of applause, then say, "Please show our audience that extraordinary posture you adopt when you are about to put the knife into the man's chest," or whatever. And Charles would never fail to do this, to protect himself.

Of all the "horror stars," Laughton (July 1, 1899–December 15, 1962) was probably one of the few who had an authentic empathy for compulsive killers and deformed demons. While a Vincent Price or Bela Lugosi could look in the mirror and see a suave and handsome man, Laughton would peer at himself and declare, "I've got a face like an elephant's behind." The line, quoted in *Elsa Lanchester Herself*, was one of several self-inflicted insults she could recall.

She still felt there was a kind of charismatic attractiveness to Laughton. She wrote:

> When he did the murdering businessman in *The Big Clock*, he brought an erotic look to the character, as he did to his Captain Bligh in *Mutiny on the Bounty*—an animal magnetism. I wish Charles had not cared so much about the other kind of beauty, the beauty he sought in others—the physical beauty that gets tangled up in narcissism.

Sloppy Joe: Charles Laughton looks like a panhandler in *The Bribe* (1949).

She no doubt bought into the theory that many homosexuals are simply trying to make love to themselves—or an ideal vision of what they wish they were.

Laughton's career was so built on playing loathsome characters, whether good (Quasimodo) or not (Captain Bligh), he had little reason not to wince at his reflection, but at least in public he seemed to have a sense of humor about it. Witness an appearance on Fred Allen's program, heavy on jokes about his weight. Fred and his wife Portland meet up with Laughton, and Fred declares, "Why, you're Portland's favorite actor, you and Slim Summerville."

Before Laughton can say a word, Portland gushes, "Gosh, Mr. Laughton! You were wonderful in *The Hunchback of Notre Dame*. I see you're wearing it in front this year..."

Later, Fred suggests that Charles might try working in a radio soap opera, where method actors need to be miserable:

> FRED: We'll have to get you into the mood, Mr. Laughton. We'll have to make you suffer. Now close your eyes. Think of Victor Mature.
> LAUGHTON: Victor Mature, yes.
> FRED: Now open your eyes.
> LAUGHTON: All right.
> FRED: And look at yourself. How do you feel?
> LAUGHTON: Miserable.

Later, Laughton confesses that he's not very athletic.

"I played golf just once ... I went out to the links at the crack of dawn. I teed off. I made one hole. I made another hole. Then I covered up both holes and came home."

"You were through with golf. What do you do for excitement out in Hollywood?"

"Oh, some nights I sit around working on my taxidermy.... My hobby is stuffing field mice."

"Isn't it rather tiring?"

"It is a little bit strenuous overtaking them, old boy.... When I crave a rollicking evening I take my tiddlywinks set and go over to May Robson. I sit and tiddly, and May sits and winks."

In his private life, Laughton was very much a bewildering combination of sensitivity and abusiveness. Like Captain Bligh, he found pleasure in creating a difficult atmosphere for others. In Simon Callow's biography, friend and co-worker Paul Gregory put it simply: "No man had a right to have such a talent as Charles Laughton's. But Charlie also had to have utter chaos to make it go. If he didn't have fifty people absolutely miserable, he wasn't happy."

The Captain Bligh sadism was matched by a Quasimodo humility and masochism. For the Quasimodo role, he was forever urging the make-up assistants to make sure his feet were "twisted more," and he didn't mind that in the whipping scenes shots often strayed from the relatively padded hump he wore to his exposed shoulders and arms. According to Callow, when Laughton demanded that make-up man Perc Westmore construct a heavier hump to add to his agony, Westmore cracked, "Why don't you just act it?" Laughton, momentarily in full Captain Bligh mode, roared, "Don't ever speak to me like that again, you hired hand!"

Westmore got his revenge. As reported by Callow (*New York Times*, May 13, 1988, p. 27), the make-up man chose a day when the heat had risen to nearly a hundred degrees and Laughton was severely harnessed:

> "I'm thirsty, Perc. Give me a drink, will you?" says Laughton, right on cue. "Sure," says Perc, approaching him with a 7-Up bottle which he shakes up and down. "No, Perc, no, you

wouldn't!" cries the kneeling and trapped actor. "Oh yes I would," says Perc, and sprays the contents of the bottle over Laughton's face. Then he goes round to the other side of Laughton and kicks his arse. "That's for all the grief you've given me." Laughton said and did nothing. He took it, just took it, languishing in the limbo between his pain and humiliation and Quasimodo's.

There was humiliation early in Laughton's career, and the cause of it was his voice. Elsa Lanchester wrote:

> It is hard to believe that Charles' speaking voice was once raspy and weak ... the apartment was covered with throat sprays and other medication for his condition. His voice grew steadily worse and Charles became worried about his career. Critics remarked on the difficulty of hearing him on stage and began speculating as to how long his voice would last. Charles started dreading having to appear. Eventually a doctor pressed Charles to have his tonsils out. The prospect of the operation, the terror and the pain nearly turned Charles into a madman. But finally (especially after a critic said that he had "little hope for a brilliant future") Charles developed a little faith in a throat specialist and out came his tonsils. And good heavens, it worked! Charles' voice got better and he never looked back—vocally.

Born in the very bed-and-breakfast hotel his parents ran, Laughton was a lonely child. He was neglected while his mother and father spent most of their attention on the guests. He attended the Jesuit-run Stonyhurst College, and after being gassed and injured during World War I, he seemed resigned to entering his parents' line of work. Gradually, acting roles in amateur productions led to the Royal Academy of Dramatic Art.

In 1927 he starred in a production of *Prohack* with Elsa Lanchester. He played a villain in *A Man with Red Hair* and had a key role in Agatha Christie's *Alibi*, both in 1928. The following year, now a more prosperous actor with a rising future, he and Elsa were married. His stardom was affirmed by playing the role of a murderer in *Payment Deferred*. Of his performance, A.E. Wilson in *The Star* wrote: "Laughton was astonishing. At times I found it almost unendurable to contemplate the agonies and fears of the murderer ... the sight of the quivering, blubbering wretch aroused mingled feelings of disgust and pity."

The show was brought to Broadway in 1931. That same year his film career showed signs of promise. He appeared in *The Old Dark House* (1932), with Boris Karloff, and had a vignette in *If I Had a Million* (1932), an all-star film that included W.C. Fields. Fields and Laughton became well acquainted at the studio, enough for Laughton to confess an intimate problem that was becoming worse. A rectal fistula ultimately led Laughton to several weeks of hospitalization. He received a telegram from a concerned Mr. Fields: "Hope the Hole Thing is Better."

The face rings a bell: Laughton's got a hunch back at Notre Dame—that his Quasimodo character will become the subject of bad jokes.

Laughton's first memorable horror role was the moody and evil Dr. Moreau in *Island of Lost Souls* (1933). He got a lot of mileage from his whipcrack catch-phrase, "What is the law?" He won an Academy Award for *The Private Life of Henry VIII* (1933), and in 1935 he achieved film immortality as Captain Blight in *Mutiny on the Bounty*. With *The Hunchback of Notre Dame* he made the most of only one spoken word: "Sanctuary!"

Laughton mimics had very little to say when they did their impressions. They'd puff their cheeks and pout their lips and shout, "Sanctuary," or, as Captain Bligh, an officious, "Mistah Christyon!"

Laughton's stature as a horror star was evident in the 1936 Ritz Brothers movie *One in a Million*. The three Ritz Brothers performed a novelty song and dance number called "The Horror Boys of Hollywood," with one brother slouching with slicked-down hair as Peter Lorre, another made up as Frankenstein's monster and the third wearing the Captain Bligh uniform of Charles Laughton.

"What is the law?" This catch-phrase will catch up to Charles Laughton as the amoral Dr. Moreau on the *Island of Lost Souls* (1933).

Yes, while today's horror fans might think it more logical for the brothers to open the song singing, "I'm Lorre, I'm Karloff, I'm Lugosi," it was Laughton's Bligh who was considered even more of a scary blighter than Dracula.

On radio, Laughton found a very different kind of fame—not from appearing on a variety show or in a drama, but by reciting "The Gettysburg Address." Fans requested it time and again, so he went into a studio and recorded it as a single, "Lincoln's Gettysburg Address" (Columbia S-271-M).

On February 12, 1940, Laughton starred in a *Lux Radio Theatre* production of "The Sidewalks of London," with Elsa Lanchester co-starring. After the program, and in honor of Lincoln's birthday, Charles read "The Gettysburg Address."

Laughton's patriotic bouquet to his new homeland would also be immortalized on film (*Ruggles of Red Gap* [1935]), and his success with "The Gettysburg Address" led to his even more ambitious Bible readings.

In the liner notes for *Readings from the Bible* (Decca 78 rpm DU 15-16-17-18, Decca album DL 8031) he wrote:

> During the war I read to the wounded fellows in Birmingham Hospital. I had been reading Dickens, Thomas Wolfe, Whitman, Hans Andersen and so on. One evening I said I would like to read a piece from the Bible. There was a grumble of protest. I learned they thought the Bible dull. Then when I started to read they put on extra solemn puddingey faces, which was not my idea of how the Bible should be listened to. So I set about how not to make the Good Book sound dull and how to cajole them into enjoying it; and so here are a few Bible stories.

It is hard to read for a microphone. I like reading best in a small church of a Sunday evening, when I can see your eyes and you can see my eyes. Even television won't substitute for that. I shall be trying to look friendly but I won't be able to see you. However, for this recording there were two good eggs in the studio and we tried hard. We discussed whether their kids would understand and whether their wives would understand and whether their wives would like them and we drank a lot of coffee and here are the results, the best we know how.

In *Meet Charles Laughton*, the booklet sold at his tours, the program reported his dealings with Decca:

The company's desire to issue Laughton clashed with the actor's traditional thoroughness. He rehearsed his readings for a period of two years before he consented to enter their studios. When completed and placed on sale, the response was great and many thousands of copies have been sold all over the country.... The reaction confirmed Mr. Laughton's faith that there as a genuine hunger and a huge and receptive audience throughout America for his reading of the Bible.

Alfred Hitchcock is also quoted in the program as witnessing Laughton's perfectionism:

The ease with which Laughton seems to deliver his lines and gestures on the screen is misleading. No actor ever agonized more to get smooth results. A Laughton picture is one long battle from start to finish. Laughton versus Laughton. He frets and strains and argues continually with himself. And he is never satisfied.

Laughton reads "The Garden of Eden," "The Fiery Furnace," "Noah's Ark" and "David and Goliath." In the latter, few actors except Laughton could get as much out of David's line: "For who is this uncircumsized Philistine that he should defy the armies of the Living God?"

In 1944, when Laughton guested on the short-lived *Blue Ribbon Town* show with host Groucho Marx, his stature as a fine dramatic actor seemed to have eclipsed Captain Bligh, Quasimodo, Henry XIII and the rest of the tyrants and monsters and murderers he had played. Despite playing opposite a grouchy insult comic, Laughton doesn't suffer the usual monster, fat or ugly jokes. In the episode, Groucho needs an "influential" citizen to help him fix a driving ticket:

"Tell me, Charlie, are you good at, shall we say, adjusting things?"
"I rather think I am. Several years ago someone donated a Florida grapefruit tree to Beverly Hills, to plant it in the park. A friend of mine found one of the grapefruit on the ground and was arrested for picking it, but I got him off."
"Did you prove he didn't pick it?"
"No, I proved insanity. What Californian in his right mind would pick a Florida grapefruit?"

Ultimately, the learned actor decides he can't do much for Groucho's traffic problem: "You've not only camouflaged the details but you've withheld the pertinent facts about this accident, which is obviously entirely your fault. And if you want my opinion, Groucho Marx, you're a ba-a-a-a-d boy!"

After decades of serious roles, Laughton found radio comedy a relief—and movie comedy a delightful challenge. One of the happiest times he had on a film set was when he made *Abbott and Costello Meet Captain Kidd*. He avidly studied Bud and Lou's comic ad-libbing, enjoying the looseness of their filmmaking environment, and took lessons on how to do a double-take.

Just a few years earlier, on his 1949 appearance on Dorothy Lamour's *Sealtest* show, he discussed his interest in comedy with co-star Frank Nelson:

"I'm about to embark on a career as a comedian. I'm tired of people thinking of me as a heavy dramatic actor."

"How depressing."

"...I'd like to try out one of my amusing quips. I bought it from a writer for five dollars. Now, I say to you, 'Nelson, what is it that has eight wheels and flies,' and you say to me, 'I give up, what is it that has eight wheels and flies,' and I say, 'two garbage trucks'.... This is a joke!"

He tries the joke out on Dorothy Lamour and Eddie Bracken, with a similar lack of result:

"Tell me what has eight wheels and flies?"
"Two garbage trucks."
"Just a minute, Dotty, you know the answer to the joke.... You mean that joke is known to the general public?"
"Certainly, Charles."
"Heavens! I've been bilked!"

As Laughton became more of a celebrity, he could make fun of his officious persona and use his educated, brittle and belittling cadence to play straight for any wisecracking comic. Opposite Al Jolson, a 1948 broadcast turned into a measured battle of put-downs, with a fat-joke thrown in:

CHARLES: Mr. Jolson ... I've heard you sing and I've heard you act, and finally I decided to come over here and do something about it.
AL: Gee, Charlie ... there are only two Charles Laughtons. And you're both of 'em.
CHARLES: Mr. Jolson, I take that as a double affront.... I'll admit, Al, you've made something of a success of yourself. I remember when you came to England and played the Music Hall. I sat in the gallery, old boy, poor urchin, and when I heard you sing and watched you act I said to meself this man is a great star in America. I must go there, they take anybody.

What a blighter: Charles Laughton is cut adrift as the cruel captain suffering a *Mutiny on the Bounty* (1935).

In 1950 the Laughtons became United States citizens. That year he began appearing at colleges and in concert halls with a one-man show. He then created the First Drama Quartet—Agnes Moorehead, Charles Boyer, Sir Cedric Hardwicke, and Laughton himself—touring with *Don Juan in Hell*.

In his memoir, *A Victorian in Orbit*, Sir Cedric Hardwicke recalled the *Hell* tour with Boyer, Moorehead and Laughton:

Charles Boyer developed into a mild hypochondriac and, like Agnes, spent most of the day resting. The other Charles we saw little of; Laughton would be off reciting the Gettysburg Address to any school or college within miles at the drop of a hat.

"Where's Charlie?" was the constant question at mealtimes in an endless succession of hotel dining rooms. "Off on his Four-Score-and-Ten again" was the invariable reply.

Laughton did not forsake radio, and with his close ties to the New York stage he was often available to appear on *Suspense*. Laughton's first broadcast, in Agatha Christie's "The A.B.C. Murders," was typically a role that left the listener unsure if the timid and mild-

Vincent Price matches wits with a smokin' Charles Laughton in *The Bribe* (1949).

mannered gent was, in fact, a raging psychopath. The salesman himself has noted that the alphabet murders seem to occur in a pattern that matches his sales route:

> "To tell you the truth, I haven't been doing very well."
> "Oh, those headaches again?"
> "Yes, the headaches. And the murders. The murders have upset me something terrible."
> "Oh, why, you're shaking like a leaf, man.... You're inclined to be morbid. I remember that book you were reading the day we met. Stuff about epilepsy."
> "Well, it might be epilepsy, mightn't it. I forget what happens, hours at a time..."
> "You don't think you killed Mary Barnard, do you?"
> "I don't know, Mr. Clark. It said in that book that people who've had epileptic fits often do things and don't remember them. They even commit crimes... "

Suspense was known for adapting classic works such as Poe short stories into half-hour dramas, but there was never an attempt to cast Laughton in any of his best known horror roles. As for *The Hunchback of Notre Dame*, the best known radio version was not even done in America. It was George Edward's Australian radio series in 1934, the adventure spanning 30 episodes. Edward also was responsible for a 13-part adaptation of *Frankenstein*.

Laughton continued to tour in a one-man show. In the souvenir booklet sold at these shows, *Meet Charles Laughton*, he noted:

I may be ten minutes into the show before I can feel I know what the house wants. Sometimes they are apparently in the mood for the toughness of *Julius Caesar* or, on the other hand, the delicacy of *A Midsummer Night's Dream*. The occasion might be ripe for the lusty story of "David and Goliath" or the solemnity of "The Psalms." I might sense that one of Dickens' melodramatic passages or his Christmas stories are in order. Then, of course, there are the yarns that never fail me—the wit of James Thurber, the wisdom of old Aesop and stories and poems of romance.

In other words, there was no set program for the audience to follow.

In 1957 both Laughton and his wife Elsa Lanchester were nominated for Academy Awards for the same film, *Witness for the Prosecution*. They made an unusual pair in the film (she was the fussy nurse trying to keep her ill but still colorful and charismatic patient from dropping dead). In real life many wondered about their relationship; he the somewhat retiring homosexual and intellectual, and she the vivacious lady who loved to sing saucy parlor room songs. Regarding the latter, they collaborated on record, with Laughton drolly introducing the songs—sung with grand lilt and panache by Elsa.

They went to London to appear in Jane Arden's play *The Party*, and later took part in a Shakespeare festival. Laughton was crushed by negative press reviews of his *King Lear* and Bottom in *Midsummer Night's Dream*, and these may have aggravated his already failing health. He suffered a heart attack in 1959.

Time was running out, and Laughton had been increasingly melancholy about it for some time. In 1957 he published *Tell Me a Story, Tales to Be Read and Told, Selected by Charles Laughton*.

His respect for audio had led him to record portions of the Bible, and record producers were eager for him to add *Tales to Be Read and Told*. The project was never completed because of Laughton's ultimately fatal physical problems.

For the introduction to this McGraw-Hill compilation he wrote:

> When I go into a good bookstore or library, I often feel sad when I see the shelves of books of all kinds that I know I will never be able to enjoy. I think of all the wonderful tales I will never know and I wish I could live to be a thousand years old.

Radio

Royal Gelatin Hour (aka *The Rudy Vallee Show*). May 6, 1937. In a segment from London, Charles Laughton and Elsa Lanchester perform.

Freedom, the Living Tradition. February 12, 1939, Red Network, 30 min. This program on famous speeches includes Charles Laughton reading the Gettysburg Address.

The Lux Radio Theatre. July 10, 1939, CBS, 30 min. "Ruggles of Red Gap" casts Charles Laughton as an English butler out West.

Charles Laughton, ticked off in *The Big Clock* (1948).

The Gulf Screen Guild Theatre. November 12, 1939, CBS, 30 min. "The Beach-Comber" stars Charles Laughton, Jean Hersholt, Elsa Lanchester and Reginald Owen.

The Pursuit of Happiness. November 26, 1939, CBS, 30 min. This variety program features songs, and guests Charles Laughton and Elsa Lanchester starring in "John Brown's Body," by Stephen Vincent Benet.

The Texaco Star Theatre. December 27, 1939, CBS, 60 min. Ken Murray hosts W.C. Fields' nemesis Baby Leroy, along with Frances Langford and Kenny Baker. Charles Laughton stars with Elsa Lanchester in "The Great Adventure" as a famous artist who assumes the identity of his dead butler.

The Lux Radio Theatre. February 12, 1940, CBS, 60 min. "The Sidewalks of London" features Charles Laughton and Elsa Lanchester. In honor of Lincoln's birthday, Laughton performs "The Gettysburg Address."

The Chase and Sanborn Program (aka *Bergen and McCarthy*). April 21, 1940, NBC, 30 min. Guest Charles Laughton offers "The Little Match Girl" and gives Charlie some funny insights into Aesop's Fables.

Forecast. August 19, 1940, CBS, 30 min. The program offers two short plays: "Ever After" (about Snow White and Prince Charming, post-marriage) and "To Tim, at Twenty," a letter written by a dying soldier to his son. With Charles Laughton and Elsa Lanchester.

Cavalcade of Chicago. September 1940, Mutual, 60 min. This variety show features local WGN radio station owner Colonel Robert McCormick, along with Charles Laughton.

Three-Ring Time. 1941–1943, Mutual Broadcasting System. Laughton appeared often on this program, as did Milton Berle, but only one episode seems to have survived. The series was sponsored by Ballantine, and their symbol was three rings.

America Calling. February 8, 1941, 90 min. This is an all-star special for the war effort hosted by Jack Benny and Bob Hope, and featuring performances by Charles Laughton, Shirley Temple, Groucho Marx, Madeleine Carroll, Mary Martin, Myrna Loy, Clark Gable, Merle Oberon, Reginald Owen, and Ronald Colman.

The Treasury Hour. July 2, 1941, CBS, 60 min. This variety program features Charles Laughton reading "The Gettysburg Address," music by Barry Wood, and guest appearances from Mickey Rooney and Oscar Levant.

The Columbia Workshop. August 24, 1941, CBS, 30 min. The Bible story "Job" is dramatized, with Charles Laughton and Hans Conried.

The Rudy Vallee Sealtest Show. March 19, 1942, 30 min. In this variety program, Charles Laughton reads "The Gettysburg Address."

The Cavalcade of America. August 31, 1942, Red Network, 30 min. "Prophet Without Honor" is the story of Homer Lea, starring Charles Laughton.

The Texaco Star Theatre. October 4, 1942, CBS, 30 min. Fred Allen's guest is Charles Laughton, and the highlight is "Poor Old Charlie," a soap opera parody.

Command Performance. December 24, 1942, AFRS, 60 min. All three radio networks were broadcasting this Christmas special featuring the Andrews Sisters, Red Skelton, Spike Jones and the City Slickers, Ginny Simms, Bing Crosby, Ethel Waters, Charles Laughton, Edgar Bergen, Kay Kyser, Dinah Shore, Jack Benny and Fred Allen.

Over Here. January 2, 1943, Blue Network, 60 min. Charles Laughton makes a guest appearance.

The George Burns and Gracie Allen Show. February 9, 1943, CBS, 30 min. Guest Charles Laughton appears in "Gracie Runs for Club President."

The Lady Esther Screen Guild Theatre. March 8, 1943, CBS, 30 min. In "Stand by for Action," women and children don't get off first and are in the line of fire during a battle at sea. Starring Charles Laughton and Brian Donlevy.

Suspense. May 18, 1943, CBS, 30 min. "The A.B.C. Murders" is an adaptation of Agatha Christie's classic about a meek salesman who appears to be a homicidal maniac systematically murdering people. Elsa Lanchester and Bramwell Fletcher are in the cast.

Suspense. December 16, 1943, CBS, 30 min. "Wet Saturday" adapts the John Collier story for radio, with Charles Laughton and Hans Conried. The script was later performed with Boris Karloff in the lead, but that show has been lost.

The George Burns and Gracie Allen Show. December 21, 1943, CBS, 30 min. Gracie becomes friendly with Elsa Lanchester, and they scheme to get Charles Laughton to portray Santa Claus for a Christmas pageant.

Blue Ribbon Town. January 8, 1944. Charles Laughton guest stars with Groucho Marx.

The Abbott and Costello Show. February 10, 1944, NBC, 30 min. Charles Laughton appears in a comic version of "Robinson Crusoe."

Radio Almanac. March 15, 1944, CBS, 30 min. Orson Welles hosts this variety show, while Agnes Moorehead and Hans Conried are in the cast. Welles and Charles Laughton offer a scene from *Julius Caesar*, parody income tax preparation, and play on Laughton's Henry VIII film with a sketch called "The Private Life of Charles Laughton."

Duffy's Tavern. April 18, 1944, Blue Network, 30 min. In a script similar to the guest spot for Vincent Price, bartender Archie hopes to turn the place into an actors' club, and wants Charles Laughton to help.

The Lux Radio Theatre. April 24, 1944, CBS, 60 min. "This Land Is Mine" puts Charles Laughton in a familiar role as a mild-mannered teacher finding the courage to fight the Nazis. Co-starring Maureen O'Sullivan, Howard McNear and John McIntire.

Columbia Presents Corwin. June 6, 1944, CBS, 30 min. In "Sandburg," Charles Laughton and Hans Conried celebrate the poet and his works.

Columbia Presents Corwin. June 13, 1944, CBS, 30 min. With "Thomas Wolfe," Charles Laughton narrates the story of the novelist's life and career.

Columbia Presents Corwin. June 20, 1944, CBS, 30 min. For "Walt Whitman," Charles Laughton reads from the poet's work in this audio biography.

The Dinah Shore Program. June 29, 1944, CBS, 30 min. Guest Charles Laughton joins Janet Waldo, the woman who will host Dinah's show for the summer.

Columbia Presents Corwin. July 18, 1944, CBS, 30 min. "The Moat Farm Murder" is based on a true murder case. Charles Laughton plays the killer, with Elsa Lanchester as his victim. Music is by Bernard Herrmann.

Suspense. August 10, 1944, CBS, 30 min. In "The Man Who Knew How," by Dorothy L. Sayers, Charles Laughton is once again cast as an honorable, law-abiding citizen who becomes obsessed with the perfect crime—which involves a mysterious drug and a hot bath. Hans Conried is the co-star.

The Cavalcade of America. November 13, 1944, Red Network, 30 min. "The Laziest Man in the World" is the story of Benjamin Franklin, starring Charles Laughton.

The Dinah Shore Program. November 16, 1944, NBC, 30 min. The subject of college football is spoofed by guest Charles Laughton.

The Lux Radio Theatre. November 20, 1944, CBS, 60 min. "It Started with Eve" includes Charles Laughton, Susanna Foster and Dick Powell.

The Charlie McCarthy Show. December 31, 1944, NBC, 30 min. Guest star Charles Laughton takes Charlie on a time-travel trip to meet Christopher Columbus, Henry VIII, Napoleon and Nero.

The Cavalcade of America. March 26, 1945, Red Network, 30 min. "Grandpa and the Statue" is a story about the Statue of Liberty, starring Charles Laughton, John McIntire and Arthur Shields.

The Lux Radio Theatre. April 9, 1945, CBS, 60 min. In "The Suspect," Charles Laughton again plays an ordinary fellow with a murderous notion towards his wife. Starring Charles Laughton, Ella Raines, Rosalind Ivan, Tom Collins and Lester Matthews.

A Tribute to President Roosevelt. April 15, 1945, NBC, 120 min. This all-star salute, hosted by Bette Davis, features Bing Crosby, Bob Hope, Jack Benny, Charles Laughton, Deanna Durbin, Eddie Cantor, Edgar Bergen, Ethel Smith, Ingrid Bergman, Ronald Colman and James Cagney.

The Lux Radio Theatre. June 18, 1945, CBS, 60 min. The enduring British supernatural comedy "The Canterville Ghost" is performed by Charles Laughton and Margaret O'Brien.

Hedda Hopper's Hollywood. August 6, 1945, CBS, 15 min. Charles Laughton guest hosts for the star (who is on summer vacation). He reads the poetry of Walt Whitman and jokes about hat-mad Hedda while saluting her serviceman son William.

Columbia Presents Corwin. August 21, 1945, CBS, 30 min. "Gumpert" offers another tour-de-force for Laughton as an average man who finds that he may be the reincarnation of a string of famous people from the past.

Birds Eye Open House (aka *The Dinah Shore Show*). January 3, 1946, NBC, 30 min. Guest Charles Laughton arrives, and suddenly Dinah's cook and butler go missing.

The Alan Young Show. March 22, 1946, ABC, 30 min. In this episode of the sitcom, Charles Laughton tries to help when Alan is evicted.

The Theatre Guild on the Air (aka *The U.S. Steel Hour*). May 12, 1946, ABC, 60 min. With "Payment Deferred," Charles Laughton revisits the poisoner role that helped launch his stage career. Featuring Edward Marr, Elsa Lanchester, Franklyn Parker and Gale Gordon.

Academy Award Theatre. June 8, 1946, CBS, 30 min. "Ruggles of Red Gap" is another adaptation of the classic comedy, once again with Charles Laughton and Charlie Ruggles.

The Cavalcade of America. September 16, 1946, NBC, 30 min. "General Benjamin Franklin" stars Charles Laughton, George Zucco, Joseph Kearns and William Johnstone.

The Radio Reader's Digest. October 3, 1946, CBS, 30 min. "The Archer Shea Case" involves a thirteen-year-old British Naval Cadet accused of theft. Featuring Charles Laughton.

The Charlie McCarthy Show. November 10, 1946, NBC, 30 min. The unlikely combo of Bergen and his dummies visit New York harbor in Charles Laughton's tugboat.

Studio One. November 25, 1947, CBS, 60 min. In "Payment Deferred," Charles Laughton and Hester Sondergaard in another version of this crime-doesn't-pay story of a scheming murderer.

The Theatre Guild on the Air. November 30, 1947, ABC, 60 min. "Old English" stars Charles Laughton and Dorothy Hamilton.

The Kraft Music Hall. February 12, 1948, NBC, 30 min. In some role reversal of the worst type, Al Jolson takes on Shakespeare and Charles Laughton wants to sing "Swanee."

Studio One. April 27, 1948, CBS, 60 min. Charles Laughton, Hester Sondergaard and Everett Sloane star in "South Riding."

Suspense. August 5, 1948, CBS, 30 min. In "An Honest Man," Charles Laughton plays a 44-year-old mama's boy who has led a dominated and sheltered life. He narrates the unpleasant tale of conscience that begins, "My mother was dead—and I was glad." He suddenly finds himself free and attracted to his co-worker (Cathy Lewis). He starts pondering ways of earning enough money to win her over—including betting on the races. "Mother, help me!" Co-starring Jerry Hausner, with Paul Frees as the Announcer.

Suspense. February 10, 1949, CBS, 30 min. In "De Mortuis," by John Collier, a British doctor experiments with the art of murder—and finds it addictive. Starring Charles Laughton.

Sealtest Variety Theatre. February 17, 1949, NBC, 30 min. Dorothy Lamour hosts Charles Laughton for a sketch, as well as the hot new comedy team Dean Martin and Jerry Lewis.

The Theatre Guild on the Air (aka *The U.S. Steel Hour*). February 27, 1949, ABC, 60 min. Vice President Alben Barkley promotes the Red Cross, but after the speech, it's Charles Laughton promoting death as a means of attaining a fortune in yet another re-telling of his stage hit *Payment Deferred*.

Theater USA. May 5, 1949, ABC, 30 min. Charles Laughton is featured, along with Marilyn Maxwell, Ted Lewis and Henny Youngman.

Sealtest Variety Theatre. June 2, 1949, NBC, 30 min. Dorothy Lamour once again greets Charles Laughton.

Suspense. September 29, 1949, CBS, 30 min. In "Blind Date," Charles Laughton has a knife, and that's a suspenseful situation for his target, dancer June Havoc, alone in her dressing room.

The Cavalcade of America. January 3, 1950, NBC, 30 min. In "The Incomparable Doctor," Benjamin Franklin meets with Lord Howe. Charles Laughton co-stars with Elliott Reid, Katherine Grill and Cathleen Cordell.

United Nations Radio Broadcast. April 17, 1950, 60 min. The program, a Peabody Award–winner for writer Norman Corwin, is about an international "Bill of Rights." Van Heflin narrates, with guest appearances by Charles Laughton, Richard Basehart, Charles Boyer, Lee J. Cobb, Ronald Colman, Joan Crawford, Jose Ferrer, Reginald Gardiner, Vincent Price, Edward G. Robinson, Robert Ryan, Lena Horne, Marsha Hunt, Laurence Olivier, and Robert Young.

The Miracle of America. August 20, 1950, CBS, 60 min. This patriotic program features Frank Sinatra singing "The House I Live In," Charles Laughton proudly talking about becoming a U.S. Citizen, Dick Haymes singing "The Lord's Prayer" and more. Robert Young is the host, with Jack Benny, Ronald Colman, Dinah Shore, Bing Crosby and Gary Crosby.

United Nations Day, 1951. 15 min. For this program syndicated by the United Nations, Robert Cummings hosts and provides guest spots for Charles Boyer, Gary Cooper, Joan Crawford, Jack Dempsey, Maurice Evans, Van Heflin, Charles Laughton, Yehudi Menuhin, Laurence Olivier and Gregory Peck.

Suspense. September 17, 1951, CBS, 30 min. "Neil Cream, Doctor of Poison" stars Charles Laughton, Jeanette Nolan, Georgia Ellis and Alma Lawton.

Medicine U.S.A. March 29, 1952, NBC, 30 min. The American Medical Association sponsored the program. This week's episode is about alcoholism, via drama and speeches. Charles Laughton, Dr. W.W. Bauer and William Quinn appear.

Medicine U.S.A. April 5, 1952, NBC, 30 min. Charles Laughton guests in a show about psychiatry.

The Theatre Guild on the Air (aka *The U.S. Steel Hour*). May 25, 1952, NBC, 60 min. "The Bishop Misbehaves" casts Charles Laughton as the religious sleuth, with Vanessa Brown, Josephine Hull and Michael Evans.

Suspense. September 22, 1952, CBS, 30 min. "Jack Ketch," the story of the royal hangman, stars Charles Laughton, Joan Banks, Ramsay Hill, Doris Lloyd and Ben Wright.

Stagestruck. February 7, 1954, CBS, 60 min. Mike Wallace hosts a show about "Community Theatre," with guest Charles Laughton.

Stagestruck. April 18, 1954, CBS, 60 min. Mike Wallace, on "How the Stage Helped Make Hollywood History," hosts brief clips from a variety of stars, including Humphrey Bogart, Katharine Hepburn, Lilli Palmer, John Garfield, Greta Garbo, Lionel Barrymore, Robert Taylor, Elizabeth Taylor, Mickey Rooney, Charles Laughton, Clark Gable, Barbara Stanwyck and William Holden.

The Lux Radio Theatre. May 10, 1954, CBS, 60 min. With "Holy Matrimony," Charles Laughton re-visits the Arnold Bennett story, co-starring with Fay Bainter.

Suspense. May 17, 1954, CBS, 30 min. "The Revenge of Captain Bligh" answers what happened after the mutiny on the *Bounty*? Charles Laughton stars with Charles Davis, William Johnstone and Ben Wright.

Biography in Sound. August 23, 1955, NBC, 60 min. In "Actor and Director Charles Laughton," Laughton is the subject of an audio biography that promotes his new film *Night of the Hunter*. Narrated by Paul Gregory.

Recollections. March 6, 1957, NBC, 30 min. This collection of historic broadcasts and recordings includes Dinah Shore on *The Eddie Cantor Show*, Charles Laughton in London (November 15, 1936), a clip of Ray Heatherton on *The Rudy Vallee Show*, and songs by John Boles and Sir Harry Lauder.

The Mitch Miller Show. July 29, 1961, CBS, 45 min. Radio may have been dead, but the record-producer had a career on TV, so on this final show of his radio days he isn't morbidly nostalgic. He offers interview clips from various guests, including Alexander King, Carl Sandburg, Charles Laughton, Janet Gaynor, Joe E. Lewis, Lillian Gish, Moss Hart, Peter Ustinov and Richard Burton.

Audio

Voice of the Stars (Regal Zonophone MR 1234). Laughton is heard in a clip from the soundtrack of the film *The Private Life of Henry VIII*. The disc was released in 1934. Other 78s in this series (VS2, VS3, VS4, MR 2722) would also include Laughton audio clips via scenes from *The Barrets of Wimpole Street*, *Mutiny on the Bounty*, *I Claudius* and *Vessel of Wrath*.

Lincoln's Gettysburg Address (Columbia S-271-M). Recorded January 6, 1937.

Mr. Pickwick's Christmas (Decca DA-379). 1944, 78 rpm set, re-issued on long-play album Decca Dl-8010 and ultimately as Decca DL 734684 (with "A Christmas Carol," by Ronald Colman, on the flip side).

"The American Way Contests" (American Way 45770A) is a radio commercial, not for commercial release.

Greetings from Hollywood (AEI 2121). This compilation album includes Laughton and Elsa Lanchester's version of "Baby It's Cold Outside" from a radio broadcast.

Moby Dick (Decca DL 5146, re-issued as Decca DL 9071).

Readings from the Bible (Decca Dl 8031, reissued as Coral CP 34, and in England as Brunswick LAT 8275).

Don Juan in Hell (Columbia OSL 166) is an original cast, 2-disc set co-starring Charles Boyer, Cedric Hardwicke and Agnes Moorehead.

The Story-Teller (Capitol TBO 1650, STBO 1650) is a 2-disc set condensed to a single album for the British version (Ember LP CEL 907).

The Canterville Ghost (Pelican 114) is from the radio broadcast.

Laughton tried to be noteworthy in *Tales of Manhattan* (1942).

Calling All Stars (Star-Tone 203) is a radio compilation.

Hollywood's Heroes on the Air (Murray Hill 937239) is a radio compilation. Featured among the half-hour shows is Laughton's *Suspense* radio episode "The Man Who Knew How."

Rudy Vallee on the Air (Totem 1027).

Songs from a Smoke-Filled Room (Hi Fi 405) and *Songs for a Shuttered Parlor* (Hi Fi 406). Laughton's spoken introductions for Elsa Lanchester's novelty songs and old, risqué British Music Hall numbers was released in England as Vogue VA 160126 and Vogue VA 160139.

9

Strange Ladies: Elsa Lanchester, Una O'Connor and Maria Ouspenskaya

Women rarely got a chance to be screen monsters à la Karloff, Lugosi and Chaney. Aside from Elsa Lanchester as the monster's mate in *Bride of Frankenstein* (1935), women in '30s and '40s movies almost never intentionally scared people by putting on weird makeup. The *She-Wolf of London* (1946) turned out to be a sheepish fantasy; there was no snarling Catwoman among the *Cat People* (1942), and tame temptresses Gloria Holden (as *Dracula's Daughter* [1936]) and Carroll Borland (in *Mark of the Vampire* [1935]) didn't exactly get to bare their fangs—or anything else.

Elsa Lanchester

The showcase lady monster, Elsa Lanchester (October 28, 1902–December 26, 1986), is well represented on radio, but not in overtly horrific roles.

Elsa had a strong stage voice and could sing with panache and lilt, but in her famous monster movie role she had no speaking lines. Karloff muttered a few sentences, but Elsa communicated in a more primitive fashion. As she wrote in her autobiography:

> A word about the screams and that hissing sound I made to show my anger and terror when rebuffing my groom. Actually, I've always been fascinated by the sound that swans make. Regents Park in London has lots of them on the lake.... They're really very nasty creatures, always hissing at you. So I used the memory of that hiss. The sound men, in one or two cases, ran the hisses and screams backward to add to the strangeness. I spent so much time screaming that I lost my voice and I couldn't speak for days.

For most horror fans, Lanchester's career began with 1935's *Bride of Frankenstein*, but actually she was a well known star in England for a long time before that. Of her marriage to Charles Laughton, actor John Houseman noted, "At the time, she was better known and more successful than he was." Elsa had studied classical dance with Isadora Duncan, worked as a nude model, and for $100 would play "the other woman" in divorce cases (an important job at a time when British law demanded proof of adultery). She won raves for unusual stage roles, such as "The Shrimp Girl," writhing and dancing in a production of *Way of the World*. With her bright-eyes, dimpled chin and impish personality, it was no surprise that J.M. Barrie himself gave his consent (and it *was* needed) for her to play Peter Pan on stage in England. She also starred in several silent comedy shorts directed by Ivor Montagu. Her first hit film was *The Private Life of Henry VIII* (1933), co-starring Laughton.

Eventually one of Hollywood's best known couples, Laughton and Lanchester were often asked to work together, and Elsa's favorite venue was radio, where she and Charles worked with Norman Corwin on some cultural and experimental programs.

Lanchester recalled,

> Charles was influenced and intrigued by the possibilities of presenting literature in this form [radio] in front of a live audience. The first program Charles and I appeared on was Stephen Vincent Benet's "John Brown's Body," using music, chorus and sound effects. The other show we did with Norman was sections of Thomas Wolfe.

The show was produced in New York. Corwin remembered:

> In those days, it was still possible for actors of the stature of the Laughtons to speak words written by writers of the stature of Thomas Wolfe and Stephen Vincent Benet on a commercial network.... The experience was new for them, and they apparently enjoyed it.... In a burst of cordiality, they invited me to be their guest if I should ever go to Hollywood.

When Corwin decided to take them up on their offer, the Laughtons were delighted, and he received a telegram: "Dog House in Garden All Ready for You." When Corwin arrived, he enjoyed an opulent guest house and the Laughtons' sumptuous swimming pool. He immortalized it in a little poem that he presented to his hosts:

> In the most impeccable and proper House of Laughton
> It is considered de rigueur to swim with not a jot on.

Guests were often baffled by the odd morality of the couple, especially since it was common knowledge that Laughton was homosexual. The situation first presented itself when they were working in the show *Payment Deferred* on stage in England in 1930. During rehearsals, police caught Laughton in a homosexual pick-up. This problem, two years into the Laughton marriage, was something Elsa literally did not want to hear about: "I became deaf for about a week." The psychosomatic illness ended, but not the marriage: "Obviously he needed secret and degrading episodes ... perhaps my overtolerance in the beginning did Charles—and me—more harm than good."

The Laughtons maintained their marriage, working together and also touring separately. In the '50s Elsa enjoyed memorable successes with one-woman shows, even reaching Broadway with *Elsa Lanchester—Herself* in 1961. The album based on the show proves that the "Bride of Frankenstein" could not just speak, but sing. A highlight number was "I'm Glad to See Your Back," a song about a nude encounter with a man coming into her dressing room in which she describes both her reaction and his.

She recorded two studio albums of saucy British Music Hall numbers, with husband Charles supplying spoken word introductions. These were later re-issued without Laughton's introductions, which would've irked him greatly. By that time he was long gone—and Elsa was not about to join him. Ever. The couple do not share eternity. Lanchester requested cremation. Charles Laughton is alone in a wall crypt at the Court of Remembrance at Forest Lawn Cemetery.

Radio

The Royal Gelatin Hour. May 6, 1937. The show, hosted by Rudy Vallee, features both Elsa Lanchester and Charles Laughton from London.

The Gulf Screen Guild Theatre. November 12, 1939, CBS, 30 min. "The Beachcomber" is a drama about an epidemic outbreak on a tropic island. Elsa Lanchester and her husband Charles Laughton star, with support from Jean Hersholt and Reginald Owen.

The Pursuit of Happiness. November 26, 1939, CBS, 30 min. In this variety show, featuring songs by the Roy Mitchell Singers, Elsa Lanchester and her husband Charles Laughton star in a script by Norman Corwin.

Beverly Hills Library Radio Show. 1939, Local, 30 min. Elsa is interviewed by Albert Brush as a promotion for her book *Charles Laughton and I.*

The Texaco Star Theatre. December 27, 1939, CBS, 60 min. The highlights of this variety show are a guest-spot from six-year-old child star Baby LeRoy, and the drama "The Great Adventure," by Arnold Bennett, in which Laughton switches identities with his dead butler. Guests include Frances Langford, Kenny Baker, Elsa Lanchester and Irene Ryan.

The Columbia Workshop. January 18, 1940, 30 min. "An Event from the Life of Fanny Kimball" stars Elsa Lanchester in a biography of the legendary actress.

The Lux Radio Theatre. February 12, 1940, CBS, 60 min. "The Sidewalks of London" stars Elsa Lanchester and Charles Laughton.

Arch Oboler's Plays. February 24, 1940, NBC, 30 min. Very few episodes from this legendary Saturday night horror program have turned up via transcription disc; and, unfortunately, "The Women Stayed at Home," starring Elsa Lanchester, is not one of them. Oboler was so fond of this script that when he produced *Every Man's Theater* he re-used it, with Norma Shearer. That broadcast (December 20, 1940) still exists.

Every Man's Theater. November 15, 1940, NBC, 30 min. "The Flying Yorkshireman" stars Charles Laughton and Elsa Lanchester.

Forecast. August 19, 1940, CBS, 30 min. Lanchester and Laughton are reunited with Norman Corwin, who, along with Keith Fowler, wrote the two sketches performed here. "Ever After" is a comedy about what happens after Snow White and Prince Charming have been married three years. "To Tim, at Twenty," with Lanchester and Laughton, is a drama in which a soldier pens a document to be delivered to his son. Also in the cast are Edna Best, Roy Atwell and Mark Smith. The music is supplied by Wilbur Hatch, noted for his soundtrack work on the TV series *I Love Lucy* a decade later.

Information Please. March 28, 1941. Elsa Lanchester gets a chance to join the erudite quiz show panel and demonstrate her wit and knowledge.

Elsa Lanchester survived *Bride of Frankenstein* (1935) to appear in lethal and comical roles on TV, including this 1970 guest spot on *The Bill Cosby Show*, his first sitcom.

Columbia Workshop (aka *26 by Corwin*). August 31, 1941, CBS, 30 min. The wry "Mary and the Fairy" co-stars Elsa Lanchester and Ruth Gordon. Mary works in the perfume counter of a five-and-dime store, and her life changes when she reads, out loud, an ad stating: "How would you like five wishes granted absolutely free of charge?"

Suspense. May 18, 1943, CBS, 30 min. "The A.B.C. Murders" is an adaptation of the Agatha Christie classic about a mild-mannered fellow who just might be a killer. In addition to Elsa Lanchester and Charles Laughton, Bramwell Fletcher is in the cast, best known to horror fans as the archaeologist who goes mad in Karloff's classic film *The Mummy* (1932).

The George Burns and Gracie Allen Show. December 21, 1943, CBS, 30 min. Gracie has an idea that Charles Laughton should play Santa Claus for a local Christmas play, and tries to enlist Elsa Lanchester in the scheme.

Suspense. December 30, 1943, CBS, 30 min. "Finishing School" stars Elsa Lanchester, Margo and Janet Beecher.

Columbia Presents Corwin (aka *Columbia Workshop*). June 13, 1944, 30 min. "Thomas Wolfe: Wolfiana." In June of 1944 Corwin offered a trilogy of programs on famous writers. Laughton also starred in the June 6 show on Carl Sandberg, and the June 20 show on Walt Whitman.

Columbia Presents Corwin. July 18, 1944, CBS, 30 min. In "The Moat Farm Murder," Elsa Lanchester and Charles Laughton once again work with producer-writer-director Corwin as he dramatizes a real-life murder confession.

Columbia Presents Corwin. August 21, 1945, 30 min. "L'Affair Gumpert" (aka "The Case of Mr. Gumpert") stars Charles Laughton as a man who suddenly finds himself taken over by the spirits of famous men, from Julius Caesar to Paganini. Elsa Lanchester co-stars.

The Theatre Guild on the Air. May 12, 1946, ABC, 60 min. "Payment Deferred" is a nostalgic return to one of the early plays Lanchester and her husband Laughton appeared in together. It had been 16 years since they premiered it in England.

Hollywood Calling, Episode #12. 1950, Syndicated, 30 min. Dick Powell, Buster Crabbe and Elsa Lanchester are among George Fisher's guests.

Audio

Lanchester's albums include *Cockney London* (Verve 615015), *Elsa Herself* (Verve 6 15024), *Songs for a Shuttered Parlor* (HiFi S 406, re-issued as *More Bawdy Cockney Songs*, Tradition 2065) and *Songs for a Smoke-Filled Room* (HiFi S 405, re-issued as *Bawdy Cockney Songs*, Tradition 2065). A CD compilation of the HiFi/Tradition material was released, *Elsa Lanchester Sings Bawdy Cockney Songs*, by Legacy International (CD 363).

The original 1958 HiFi albums have spoken introductions by Charles Laughton (*Songs for a Smoke-Filled Room*, Hi Fi 405; *Songs for a Shuttered Parlor*, Hi Fi 406). The Tradition re-issues leave them out.

Lanchester also issued a pair of 78s. In 1926 she released "Please Sell No More Drink to My Father," b/w "He Didn't Oughter" (Columbia 4125). In 1930 she released "Don't Tell My Mother I'm Living in Sin" and "The Ladies Bar" (Columbia DB 81).

Una O'Connor

Elsa Lanchester was in a class by herself as a beautiful, beguiling eccentric, one who could make her role as a monster's bride into something fascinating and unforgettable.

There were two other women who were certainly eccentric, and have a cult following for their brief but memorable roles in vintage horror films. Neither was a raving beauty, although one, Una O'Connor, was an expert at raving—as well as shrieking.

Born Agnes Teresa McGlade (October 23, 1880–February 4, 1959), Una O'Conner stayed with her mother when her father moved from Ireland to Australia. When Una's mother died, she was raised by an aunt. She graduated from the South Kensington School of Arts and acted with the Abbey Players.

O'Connor's first stage success, as a maid in the London production of *Cavalcade*, was reprised for the 1936 *Lux Radio Theatre* radio production, hosted by Cecil B. DeMille. The play's author, Noel Coward, introduces the show and its players:

> I'm more honored than I can tell you.... I would like you to know how fine I think the *Lux Radio Theatre* is, and I'm particularly happy that I can salute my friends Herbert Marshall, Madeleine Carroll, and Una O'Connor, this last a very old friend to *Cavalcade*, as she created the part of Ellen in the original production.

Ellen, the maid role, isn't very quotable, but fans will instantly recognized the pinched tones and high pitch of Ms. O'Connor as she goes through her amusing range, bawling at one man ("Drunken brute ... leave us alone!") and gossiping with coy and spiteful delight when her lowly daughter has fallen in love with someone well above her station:

> "I just thought I'd call, madam ... rather important..."
> "Is anything wrong?"
> "Well, no, not exactly."
> "What is it?"
> "About her ... and uh, Joe..."
> "I don't understand, Ellen."
> "Well, they've been, uh, ahem, what you might call ... in love! Yes."
> "My Joe?"
> "Yes, *your* Joe ... well, I thought they ought to get married!"
> "Does Fanny want to marry him?"
> "Oh, I haven't talked to her about it, she doesn't know I know."
> "And how do you know?"
> "I found the letter he wrote!"
> "And you read it?"
> "Of course! I brought it with me, I knew you'd want to read it.... I didn't wish to *upset* you..."

One of Una's earliest film roles was in *The Invisible Man* (1933), one of the two horror films that have kept her forever in the hearts of cult movie fans.

James Whale used her as bawling comedy relief. As innkeeper Mrs. Hall, she breaks the tension for the audience by voicing—in extreme fashion—her fear of the invisible enemy. In one scene her innkeeper husband is thrown down the stairs by the grouchy Invisible One. As she cradles the injured man she begins to bawl—in his ear.

In 1935, the same year she made *David Copperfield* (playing Mrs. Gummidge in a film with an all-star cast that included Basil Rathbone, W.C. Fields and Elsa Lanchester), she made her second classic appearance for James Whale. She's the servant Minnie, speaking aloud what has to be on the mind of most any member of the audience watching the Frankenstein Monster stagger around: "I'd hate to find him under my bed at night!" She delivers another amusing line when Dr. Pretorius (Ernest Thesiger) asks to see her employer "on a secret matter of grave importance." She finds Dr. Frankenstein and straightfaces: "A Dr. Pretorius is here to see you on a secret grave matter."

She was typed for servant roles, admitting, "I'm a slavey whether I like it or not." Appearing on a film set in "my usual frumpy clothes and makeup," her characters were usually quirky and high spirited. She had plentiful roles in the '40s, and made her final bow with Elsa Lanchester and Charles Laughton as a fussy, half-deaf maid in *Witness for the Prosecution* (1957).

9. Strange Ladies—Una O'Connor 201

Hapless Una O'Connor has apparently gotten the bird in *The Sea Hawk* (1940).

O'Connor, who ended her days at the Mary Manning Walsh Home on 72nd Street on the East Side, did take a final radio bow on the series *Crime Does Not Pay*, which was originally produced in New York and aired over WMGM. Finally getting a chance voicing a character with a bit more depth and toughness than usual, she plays Jackie, a bookie who operates out of a luncheonette across the street from a college. She employs a pretty waitress named Josie, who wonders about Jackie's past:

"One of the new kids wanted to know if you was really a Follies girl."
"Aha! And what did you tell 'em, Josie?"
"I said how should I know, I wasn't even born then!"
"Ohhhh. Thanks for the compliment!"

Josie becomes friendly with Bob, the center on the basketball team, and she bets two bucks with her boss. When she wins, Jackie isn't too pleased paying out, especially when other students have also bet and won: "All I do is lose."

Josie has an idea: " Why don't you move the joint.... If you ran a lunch room across the street from State instead of here, you could take bets against our team! You'd never lose!"

The trouble is that Jackie can't move into another bookie's territory. Is there some other way of making a dishonest dollar? "Before I'm through I'm gonna take the chance out of basketball, and put a wad of dough where it belongs—in my bank account."

She explains to her waitress friend: "Your friend Bob Warren will be in here for his lunch on Thursday. You know anything about race horses? Sometimes a horse can be pepped up by what he eats. Or slowed down. And the same thing can be arranged for basketball players. Understand?"

Yes, she's a tough paloma here, although, as is customary with this show, at the episode's end she steps out of character to deliver a minute's lecture on morality and the fact that "crime does not pay." Unfortunately for fans of her screaming and fretting in horror films, most of her other radio appearances are mild roles in straight dramas:

Radio

The Packard Hour. September 22, 1936, Red Network, 60 min. This variety show stars Fred Astaire, who sings "A Fine Romance," "Top Hat, White Tie and Tails" and "Give Me a Swing Song and Let Me Dance." Una O'Connor and Barry Fitzgerald, of "The Abbey Players of Dublin," perform the drama "The End of the Beginning," by Sean O'Casey—heavy fare for the usually light-hearted radio show.

The Lux Radio Theatre. December 28, 1936, CBS, 60 min. For "Cavalcade," Noel Coward himself appears at intermission in this study of a British couple's life from the Boer War to the unrest in the current world. The cast features Herbert Marshall, Madeleine Carroll, David Niven, Elsa Buchanan, June Lockhart and Una O'Connor, who was in the original stage and film versions (as the maid, of course.)

Bundles for Britain. 1940, Syndicated, 15 min. A "filler" series distributed to radio stations with some time to spare, this was sponsored by the Bundles for Britain fund. The brief drama proves that even when British citizens are forced to take refuge in a bomb shelter, they can still come out on top. Frank Morgan and Una O'Connor star in the script by Vina Del Mar, which is produced and directed by R.E. Messer.

The Cavalcade of America. January 31, 1949, NBC, 30 min. "One Last Romance" details the unusual story of how Benjamin Franklin saved artist Benjamin West and his true love from

West's villainous brother. Starring Una O'Connor, Walter Hampden, Craig McDonnell and Michael Alexander.

Crime Does Not Pay. March 21, 1951, MGM syndication, 30 min. Una O'Connor plays a lunchroom lady who has a money-making scheme involving the local college basketball team; and you can bet it won't pay off in the end.

The Cavalcade of America. October 14, 1952, NBC, 30 min. "The Saga of Jerry O'Brien" takes a look at one of the first battles of the Revolutionary War. With Dennis O'Keefe, Parker Fennelly, Staats Cotsworth, James O'Neill, George Petrie and Una O'Connor.

Audio

Cavalcade: Original Drury Lane Cast Recording (AEI CD 033). The recording features Herbert Marsall, Madeliene Carroll and Una O'Connor.

Maria Ouspenskaya

Una O'Connor's low-class British accent made her a stock character in many films. Likewise, Maria Ouspenskaya's Slavic accent was her ticket to consistent character roles in various atmospheric melodramas.

Born in Russia (July 29, 1876–December 3, 1949), she studied opera but found greater success in straight stage productions. She taught classes at Konstantin Stanislavski's Moscow Art Theater and settled in America in 1924, where she became a teacher at the American Laboratory Theater in New York. She was successful and strong-willed about her methods of thesping, and opened the Maria Ouspenskaya School of Dramatic Arts in 1929, teaching and showing off her own technique in various Broadway productions. She came to Hollywood in 1936 to reprise her stage success as Baroness Von Obersdorf in *Dodsworth*, earning an Academy Award nomination.

The feisty old actress re-opened her acting school in California and enjoyed more lucrative film work—and a second Academy Award nomination for her role in *Love Affair* (1939). In 1941 she combined grandmotherly concern and stoic strength in her most famous role, Maleva, the gypsy in *The Wolfman.*

When her son Bela (a very minor and brief role for Bela Lugosi) is killed by the silver-handled cane of Larry Talbot (Lon Chaney, Jr.), she delivers the memorable eulogy:

> The way you walked was thorny
> through no fault of your own.
> But as the rain enters the soil,
> the river enters the sea,
> so tears run to a predestined end.
> Your suffering is over, Bela, my son.
> Now you will find peace.

While Ouspenskaya and company never got to *Lux Radio Theatre* with a dramatization of *The Wolfman* (monster films being considered low melodramas), her words do turn up on the Decca album *An Evening with Boris Karloff and Friends*, as narrator Boris lovingly picks through soundtrack clips from various Universal classics.

Two years later, for *Frankenstein Meets the Wolfman*, Ouspenskaya reprised her role as Maleva the old gypsy woman. Wolfman Larry Talbot is still tormented by being alive and killing. Maleva offers her insight: "He is not insane; he only wants to die."

Madame Ouspenskaya made it through many a tough day with a cigarette dangling

Maria Ouspenskaya, immortal as the soup gypsy in *The Wolfman* (1941).

from her prominent lips. One night the odds caught up with her. Smoking in bed, the elderly woman suffered a stroke and was taken to the hospital with serious burns. Some stoic gypsy might've stood over her corpse, lamenting the irony that while we only go around once in life, Ouspenskaya had two causes of death.

Ouspenskaya's brief audio forays are hard to find...

Radio

Towards the Century of the Common Man. June 14, 1942, NBC, 60 min. A special broadcast honoring the United Nations, subtitled "A Dramatic Sermon for a Sabbath Flag Day," this show includes a prayer from Franklin D. Roosevelt and a few words from a variety of celebrities (with an international flavor): Charles Boyer, Ronald Colman, Peter Lorre, Thomas Mitchell, Alla Nazimova and Maria Ouspenskaya.

Treasury Star Parade. Circa 1943. "Deliver Us from Our Enemy" features Maria Ouspenskaya in a dramatization that warns of how the Nazis use radio propaganda to spread lies and destroy morale. Only about 90 episodes from the series survive, and this does not seem to be one of them.

Audio

Ouspenskaya's sorrowful words about lycanthropy, from the soundtrack to *The Wolfman*, are featured on *An Evening with Boris Karloff and His Friends* (Decca DL 4833 and DL 74833 stereo).

10

Sinister Women: Gale Sondergaard and Agnes Moorehead

Instead of brutal lumps or scars, most evil women in mystery films and thrillers sported glamorous make-up. Rather than shrieks, their insinuating voices had the ring of culture and cunning. They projected assurance and intelligence, twin traits that could strike fear in the heart of any average Joe.

Gale Sondergaard

Only one woman had her own monster nickname, and lived up to it. "The Spider Woman" was Gale Sondergaard (born Edith Sondergaard in Minnesota on February 15, 1899; she died August 14, 1985), winner of the Academy Award for Best Supporting Actress the first time that category was added to the ceremonies. The win was for her first screen role, in *Anthony Adverse* in 1936.

With just a raised eyebrow, the veteran actress could instantly create a sense of menace and suspicion. A screenwriter didn't have to offer much dialogue for her. Her presence was instantly intimidating. A murderess? A psychic? A red herring? Mystery surrounded any role she played.

She seemed to specialize in playing the sinister housekeeper who knew far more than her master. When she played a disturbingly psychic housekeeper in Abbott and Costello's ghost comedy *The Time of Their Lives* (1946), one of the characters cracks, "Pardon me, but did I see you in *Rebecca*?" Actually, the part of the starkly dour Mrs. Danvers in the 1940 Hitchcock film was one of the few that Gale missed; it was played by Judith Anderson.

Sondergaard was originally considered for the "Wicked Witch of the West" in *The Wizard of Oz* (1939), but was rejected on the grounds that she'd make villainy seem glamorous.

Sondergaard glared her way through melodramas such as *The Cat and the Canary* (1939) and *The Black Cat* (1941) before turning up as femme fatale Adrea Spedding in *Sherlock Holmes and the Spider Woman* (1944). She reprised the role, sans Holmes, in *The Spider Woman Strikes Back* (1946), but soon faced an enemy she could not hope to tame.

The Spider Woman was no match for the web spun by the House Un-American Activities Committee (HUAC), a group that chased after Communists and most anyone who refused to sign loyalty oaths or "name names" of co-workers.

"The Hollywood Ten," including Ring Lardner, Jr., and Dalton Trumbo, pleaded the Fifth Amendment and refused to answer questions. Among the lesser known eight others was Herbert Biberman—husband of Gale Sondergaard. Two years later she was dragged in to testify. She wrote an open letter to her union, the Screen Actors Guild, which was printed in a few newspapers. She asked for support:

> Dear Board Members: I am addressing you of the Board not only as the directors of our union but also as fellow actors. I am addressing you because I have been subpoenaed, together with other members of our union before the UnAmerican Activities Committee. I will appear next Wednesday.
>
> I would be naive if I did not recognize that there is a danger that by the following day I may have arrived at the end of my career as a motion picture actress. Surely it is

This publicity shot offers the sunny side of Gale Sondergaard.

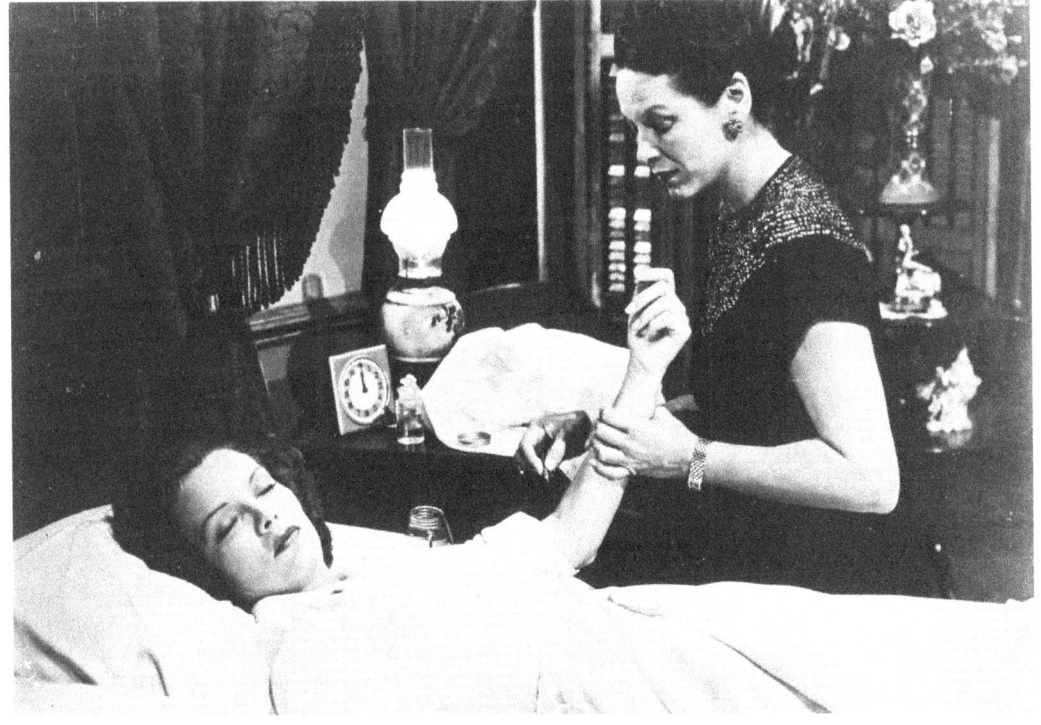

Brenda Joyce is in Gale Sondergaard's web-sight. A scene from the sleeper *The Spider Woman Strikes Back* (1946).

not necessary for me to say to this Board that I love my profession and that I have tried to bring to it honesty of feeling, clarity of thought and a real devotion. Surely it is also unnecessary for me to state that I consider myself a deeply loyal American with genuine concern for the welfare and peace of my own countrymen and all humanity...

She asked her organization to take a stand and give its members "the comfort and the dignity of belonging to a union" in the name of a "higher moral dedication."

She ended her letter:

A blacklist already exists. It may now be widened. It may ultimately be extended to include any freedom-loving nonconformist or any member of a particular race or any member of a union.... For my own security ... for the security of all our members, I ask our Board ... whether it can afford to witness its approach with passivity. I can find no reason in my conduct as an actress or as a union member why I should have to contemplate a severing of the main artery of my life: my career as a performer.

In movies, a clever Spider Woman would have concocted some kind of devious blackmail scheme to get what she wanted. But in real life, this helpless heroine only begged for mercy.

She received the following reply:

The Board of Directors of the Screen Actors Guild has received and carefully considered your letter of March 13 which you saw fit also to publish in the press. The Guild's answer should be equally available to the public and will be published. Your letter (1) attacks as an inquisition the pending hearing by the House Committee on Un-American Activities into alleged Communist Party activities by a few individuals and (2) asks that the Guild protect you against any consequences of your own personal decisions and actions.

The Communist Party press also has attacked the hearing as a "warmongering, labor and freedom-busting witch-hunt by Congressional inquisitors."

The Guild Board totally rejects this quoted typical Communist Party line. We recognize its obvious purposes of attempting to smear the hearings in advance and to create disrespect for the American form of government.

Like the overwhelming majority of the American people, we believe that a "clear and present danger" to our nation exists. The Guild Board believes that all participants in the international Communist Party conspiracy against our nation should be exposed for what they are—enemies of our country and of our form of government.

The Guild as a labor union will fight against any secret blacklist created by any group of employers. On the other hand, if any actor by his own actions outside of union activities has so offended American public opinion that he has made himself unsaleable at the box office, the Guild cannot and would not want to force any employer to hire him. That is the individual actor's personal responsibility and it cannot be shifted to his union.

Red scare victim Gale Sondergaard testified before the microphones in 1950.

Sondergaard was blacklisted for nearly two decades.

By the time she received some assignments on television, viewers only vaguely remembered her from the classic movies she made in the '40s. She guested on Rod Serling's *Night Gallery*, and played an amusingly gothic parody of her "old dark house" character in the *Get Smart* episode "Rebecca of Funny-Folk Farm." Her classic work in the '30s and '40s brings chills to this day. So does the reason behind her lack of work in the '50s and '60s.

Radio

Federal Theatre Special. June 26, 1939, NBC, 30 min. This is a kind of "propaganda" program put together by the various Hollywood unions (Writer's Guild, Screen Actor's Guild, Screen Director's Guild). The idea was to rally support for the Federal Arts Project, which in the pre-war environment was in danger of losing all funding. A light-hearted moment offers the song "Ciribiribin," sung by Donald Duck, and "The Florida Wheel," from the orchestra conducted by Gordon Jenkins, and composed by Victor Young. The celebrity list of guests: James Cagney, Henry Fonda, Hugh Herbert, Joan Blondell, Ralph Bellamy, Robert Benchley, Lionel Barrymore, Dick Powell, Al Jolson, Gale Sondergaard and Patricia Morrison.

Arch Oboler's Plays. November 11, 1939, NBC, 30 min. Very few episodes from this Saturday night horror program survive; and, unfortunately, "I'll Tell My Husband," starring Gale Sondergaard, is not one of them.

The Pursuit of Happiness. April 21, 1940, CBS, 15 min. This variety show offers folk artist Woody Guthrie and sketches written by Norman Corwin. "The Oracle of Philidelphi" features Gale Sondergaard and Burgess Meredith.

The Columbia Workshop. September 7, 1941, CBS, 30 min. "The Anatomy of Sound" is 18th in a series dubbed *26 by Corwin*. Another adventurous script by Norman Corwin, one of radio's most respected writers, has Gail Sondergaard starring in "A Treatise for Solo Voice."

Democratic National Committee Program. November 6, 1944, CBS, 60 min. A pre-election plea for Franklin D. Roosevelt features dozens of top name celebrities, including James Cagney, Groucho Marx, Claudette Colbert, Paul Muni, George Raft, Edward G. Robinson, Dorothy Parker, Humphrey Bogart, Danny Kaye, Evelyn Keyes, Gale Sondergaard, Lana Turner, Monty Woolley and Jane Wyman.

The Lux Radio Theatre. February 12, 1945, CBS, 60 min. "For Whom the Bell Tolls" was a radio adaptation for those who missed the recently released Hemingway movie. Several members of the original cast are present. Starring Gary Cooper, Ingrid Bergman, Akim Tamiroff, Gale Sondergaard, Howard McNear and Jay Novello.

Agnes Moorehead

When fans think of Agnes Moorehead (December 9, 1900–April 30, 1974), they imagine the tilt-eyed Endora of *Bewitched*, a drag queen's role model with low, menopausal deprecations, flowing gowns, that mane of red hair, and an evil use of too much mascara and paint. Arch, world-weary, causing trouble merely for her own amusement, Moorehead's Endora character drawled insults and whipped up instant magical humiliations for her son-in-law.

"I have played so many authoritative and strong characters that some people are nervous at the prospect of meeting me for the first time," she once wrote. She acknowledged that part of the intimidation was that she preferred that people keep their distance:

> There is a certain amount of aloofness on my part at times; because an actor can so easily be hurt by unfair criticism. I think an artist should be kept separated to maintain glamour and a

kind of mystery.... What the actor has to sell to the public is fantasy, a magic kind of ingredient that should not be analyzed.

Born in Clinton, Massachusetts (with *Bewitched* fans wondering how close it was to Salem), Moorehead's family moved to St. Louis before she was a year old. Her father was a minister. She earned a B.A. from Muskingum College in Ohio, then attended the University of Wisconsin and worked as a teacher. She found a job at the Dalton School in New York, and was both a teacher there and a student at the American Academy of Dramatic Arts. She married her first husband, John Lee, in 1930 (they divorced in 1952).

With radio studios all thriving in New York, Agnes found steady work between Broadway assignments. She toured vaudeville with entertainer Phil Baker, appearing on Baker's radio show in 1936.

In September of 1937 she became Margot Lane, "constant friend and companion" to Lamont Cranston, *The Shadow*. The sleuth was originally just the mysterious host of a show called *Detective Story*. When it was spun into a real series, the character of Margot Lane was invented so that the program would appeal to a broader audience.

Orson Welles was 22 and Moorehead 38 when the show began. Already an "enfante terrible," Welles refused to rehearse. "Not rehearsing," he once said, "made it much more interesting. When I was thrown down the well into some fiendish snake pit, I never knew how I'd get out."

The only humility Welles seemed to have was in allowing a recording of the original Shadow, Frank Readick, to open and close the program. It was whispered that Orson simply couldn't duplicate the sinister comic strip snickers that accompanied the familiar sneer: "Who knows what evil lurks in the hearts of men! The Shadow knows..."

In a typical episode ("The Plot Murder," February 27, 1938), it's Margot who instigates the investigation:

MARGOT: Lamont Cranston, I tell you John Wilson can't be guilty. He just can't!
LAMONT: Why not, Margot? After all, traitorous army officers are not unknown to history.
MARGOT: Yes, but the particular way John Wilson talked on the stand makes me think there's something strange about the whole thing. He acted ... well, almost like a man in a trance. Lamont, you don't suppose its possible [Professor] Arkeles has the boy under some strong mental influence?
LAMONT: It's possible.... Margot, do you honestly think this case warrants my attention as the Shadow?
MARGOT: I have a feeling John Wilson is innocent.
LAMONT: Alright Margot, if you're really serious, the Shadow will pay a call on John Wilson, in the city jail.

Later in the episode, Margot is the one who discovers a vital clue (blood on a corner of the desk). Cranston takes this information and literally runs with it: "I'm going to make one more desperate attempt to get John Wilson to talk. We've got to find out what this is all about before it's too late!"

It was never too late for Lamont Cranston. As he said at the end of each show, "Heh heh, as you sow evil, so shall you reap evil. Crime does not pay. The Shadow knows. Heh heh heh..."

By the following year, Welles had gone on to other radio assignments, and William Johnstone replaced him, followed by Bret Morrison. As for Moorehead, she held onto the Margot role until 1940. (Following Moorehead, Marjorie Anderson played the role until her death from cancer in 1944, followed by Grace Matthews, Amzie Strickland [during Matthews' maternity leave], and, ultimately, Gertrude Warner [doing 300 shows from 1949 to 1954]).

Moorehead was also the first "Dragon Lady" in the *Terry and the Pirates* radio series (replaced by Adelaide Klein and then Marion Sweet), and triviasts like to note that she played Lara on the premiere broadcast of radio's *Superman* show, the man of steel's mother on Krypton.

Moorehead was cast in *Mercury Radio Theatre* productions with Orson Welles, and finally made her film debut in Welles' *Citizen Kane* in 1941 as Kane's mother. The following year she received the first of an eventual five Best Supporting Actress Oscar nominations for the Welles drama *The Magnificent Ambersons*. That year she also joined the cast of a new Lionel Barrymore radio drama, a homey, soap opera–styled effort (sponsored by Rinso) called *The Mayor of the Town*. She played his housekeeper, Marilly.

Moorehead was also one of the regulars on the educational *Cavalcade of America* program. The show brought to life (woodenly in most cases) famous incidents and people in American history. She did the best she could with many a dubious script. Taking the lead in "Annie Oakley," she rebuffs a local suitor:

More head shots? One Agnes Moorehead classic pose will do—an enigmatic expression that's quite moan-a lethal.

"Oh Annie, don't you ever think about anything but guns and shootin'?"
"Not right now..."
"Annie, listen, I'm getting' a part interest in the general store. I was thinkin' why don't ya marry me?"
"Because. Well. We just don't think alike, Elmer. Maybe I'll never find a man who thinks the way I do. But if I do, there won't be any doubt in my mind. That'll be the man."

Still, the episode, as with most, has a moment or two of real drama. In this one, Annie gets into a train wreck. The doctor cautions her husband Frank not to react to her changed appearance:

"I guess it was a pretty bad accident, wasn't it.... Come over here, Frank, sit here beside me. That's it. Sort of slip your arm around me so I can sit up a little and get a look at myself in that mirror.... Help me, Frank. Would you hand me that comb, doctor.... Now I can see ... Frank ... Frank!"
"Aw it's nothing, honey. Your hair just turned white, that's all. You were in a terrible accident.... Maybe the color will come back again."
"Frank, I wasn't gonna let you know just yet, but they tell me I won't shoot again. I'll never walk again."
"Annie, you know I never lied to you in my life. And I know it's not true!"

Fade out to some time later, 1903: Annie and her husband are on the boardwalk in Atlantic City. As she's wheeled along, she sees a shooting gallery. And sure enough, she wheels over and gives the target practice a try. The proprietor is shocked by her sharpshooting.

"Why ma'am, you're a regular Annie Oakley, ain't ya!"
"Why yes, yes; I guess I am."

So ends an inspiring tale about a "gallant American woman ... who became part of the American folklore. So legendary were her exploits that it became a habit to call complimentary tickets, punched with holes, Annie Oakleys."

Moorehead's mark as a compelling horror actress was truly made on radio, thanks to her May 25, 1943, performance on *Suspense*. She starred in probably the most successful program ever showcasing a woman on radio: "Sorry, Wrong Number."

The script was written by Lucille Fletcher. Her husband, Bernard Herrmann, composed and conducted the sinister music for the series. Fletcher's inspiration came from a day when she hurried to a local store to get her baby some milk and was scolded by an old lady who insisted on being served first. That old nag would have to die! And in an inventive new way. Fletcher noted:

> [The] play was originally designed as an experiment in sound and not just a murder story ... something that by its very nature should, for maximum effectiveness, be heard rather than seen. However, in the hands of a fine actress like Agnes Moorehead, the script turned out to be more the character study of a woman than a technical experiment, and the plot itself, with its O. Henry twist at the end, fell into the thriller category.... It is, as I see it, a simple tale of horror.

The show became a textbook example of radio drama at its finest. The tension builds from a whisper to a scream. There's the contrast between Moorehead's agitated voice and the muted, weary and bored tones of the policeman on the other end of her frantic call. The listener's imagination is pricked by everything from the repetitive re-dialing of the phone to the roar of a passing train, making the radio version far more effective than the subsequent film version.

Moorehead, in the September 12, 1952, issue of *TV Radio Life*, agreed that "The sound man is extremely important. A mood can be projected expertly, you know, in the mere dialing of a telephone." As for the show that many rate the greatest in radio history, she was scared the moment she was handed the script: "I couldn't even finish reading it because it made me so nervous. I was afraid it was too morbid and people would turn it off."

The producers of *Suspense* received so many requests that Moorehead was asked to perform the role a half-dozen more times. These weren't re-runs. Fans of her acting can note the subtle changes in tempo or enthusiasm over the course of 15 years. There are changes in the level of sinister intent in the supporting players, and even in the show's famous last line.

No doubt many who heard it once, heard it over and over—for the virtuoso performance, the atmosphere, and perhaps because Lucille Fletcher had made the main character someone that audiences didn't feel all that sorry for. From the opening lines, and a reference to her Murray Hill phone number and Sutton Place address, they knew this was a pampered woman of privilege—something affirmed by the quick exasperation and insults she hurled at the public servants on the phone:

> Operator, I've been dialing Murray Hill 7-0093 now for the last three quarters of an hour and the line is always busy. I don't see how it *could* be busy that long.... I don't see how it could be busy all this time. It's my husband's office. He's working late tonight, and I'm all alone here in the house. My health is very poor and I've been feeling so nervous all day.

The danger arises moments later when crossed phone wires let her overhear an evil voice and a nefarious message:

> At eleven o'clock the private patrolman goes around to the bar on Second Avenue for a beer. Make sure that all the lights downstairs are out.... At eleven-fifteen a train crosses the bridge. It makes a noise, in case her window is open and she should scream.... Make it quick. As little blood as possible. Our client does not wish to make her suffer long—our client wishes it to look like simple robbery.

She contacts the operator and so begins the first of many frustrating and tense experiences, an agitated voice coming up against a stone wall of calm indifference:

> "I was cut into a wrong number and I—I-I've just heard the most dreadful thing—something about a murder and, operator, you simply have to retrace that call at once."
> "What number did you call?"
> "Oh, why are you so stupid? What time is it? Do you mean to tell me you can't find out what that number was just now.... Your finger must have slipped.... I simply fail to see why you couldn't make that same mistake again on purpose, why you couldn't try to dial Murray Hill 7-0093 in the same sort of careless way!"

The police turn out to be even less helpful:

> "A lot of murders are plotted in this city every day, ma'am. We manage to prevent most all of 'em, but a clue of this kind is so vague.... Unless, of course, you have some reason for thinking this call was phony and—that someone may be planning to murder you."
> "Oh—oh, no—no, I hardly think so. My husband, Elbert, he's crazy about me—he-he just adores me. He waits on me hand and foot. He's scarcely left my side since I took sick, well, twelve years ago.

After the May 25, 1943, broadcast, there was an almost immediate demand to hear it again. Three months later, on August 21, 1943, Moorehead went through the drama again. And again on February 24, 1944, September 6, 1945, November 18, 1948, September 15, 1952, October 20, 1957, and February 14, 1960. She also performed a monologue version on Rudy Vallee's *Philco Radio Hall of Fame* on March 24, 1946.

Not a box office draw, Moorehead lost the 1948 film version to Barbara Stanwyck, who also voiced the January 9, 1950, *Lux Radio Theatre* radio version.

Another unusual radio appearance for Moorehead was a United Jewish Appeal broadcast in 1949 in which Al Jolson presented speeches and joined Agnes in acting out scenes of the hope and frustrations of Israel's fight to exist and provide shelter for "homeless and tortured people who are at long last going home, having known only misery and oppression."

An announcer asks for donations:

> The remnants of a persecuted people are rebuilding their lives on the ancient soil of their fathers. Everyone who had a part in the past few years of the United Jewish Appeal can justly feel proud to have contributed to the survival of a people. We have actually changed the course of history. We defied hate and apathy. But survival is not enough. The United Jewish Appeal is now engaged in a vast task of reconstruction and resettlement.

A typical vignette, with Jolson as a son and Agnes as his mother waiting to emigrate, is as follows:

> AGNES: Why don't we go?
> AL: Just a little longer, just wait a little longer. There are no restrictions ... none at all, I give you my word. You have to wait.
> AGNES: We've waited two thousand years.
> AL: They take money.

AGNES: Oh, money! Isn't blood enough?
AL: I'm afraid not. You see, the world isn't run that way.

Moorehead's last foray into radio horror was a set of three appearances in 1952 on *Inner Sanctum*. Only one episode survives: "Terror by Night." She plays a businesswoman who is driving toward her vacation home, worrying about a news report about an escaped criminal: "There was a storm coming on, and I was driving into it. And the night was black, and I felt small and lonely and frightened in the car. And then..."

Well, give her five or ten minutes to build up the suspense, *and then* she'll be cowering from a knife-wielding bad man and screaming with terror. Yes, it's one last set of gasps for Agnes, who, with shows like *Inner Sanctum* dying off, would scream into a radio microphone no more.

Always seeking varied challenges, Moorehead enjoyed touring the country in recitals. In the early '50s (when she had her brief second marriage, which ended in divorce) she joined Charles Boyer and Charles Laughton in performances of *Don Juan in Hell* both in America and in England. In 1954 she created her own show, *That Fabulous Redhead*, performing short stories by James Thurber and Guy De Maupassant, readings from Proust and the Bible, poetry by Rupert Brooke, and, of course, "Sorry, Wrong Number." Over the years she added and subtracted from the show, especially once she became famous through *Bewitched*, so that fans might be surprised by something like "Household Hints Down Through the Centuries" and "Where to Bury a Dog."

In the '60s, the "fabulous redhead" was also known as "the Lavender Lady." Fan magazines had long reported on her love of the color purple, which was on the walls of her *Bewitched* dressing room, and the predominant color of both her sumptuous home and her vintage 1956 Thunderbird. An amateur tape of a 1969 concert at the University of Wisconsin was re-mastered as a private-issue CD. It's simply titled *The Lavender Lady*.

Although she had plenty of fans who adored her in *Bewitched*, and who could name a favorite movie, she always had a fondness for her radio days: "You had to work to make the audience visualize you, and that isn't easy to do." She also felt her radio work was important training for her success in other media: "Many stage actors fall by the wayside because of their inability to make an audience 'see.'"

Radio

The Adventures of Sherlock Holmes. May 3, 1933, Blue Network, 30 min. In "The Walking Corpse," Richard Gordon plays Sherlock Holmes, with Alfred Shirley and Agnes Moorehead. Edith Meiser's script is based on the Doyle short story "The Final Problem."

Way Down East. 1936, Syndicated, 15 min. This soap opera ran for several years, with Agnes Moorehead appearing in dozens of episodes during the show's run. It was based on the film.

The Phil Baker Show. January 19, 1936, CBS, 30 min. Agnes Moorehead appears in a "Cecil B. de Mealticket" sketch. Other guests include Ed Small and the Seven G's, Eddie Rickenbacker, and Skinnay Ennis.

Les Miserables. 1937, Mutual, 30 min. The seven-episode summer series was adapted from the Victor Hugo novel by Orson Welles, who also directed and starred. Shortly after, he would form the Mercury Theatre Players. The cast includes Martin Gabel, Agnes Moorehead, Ray Collins, Adelaide Klein, Virginia Wells and Everett Sloane.

The Shadow. 1937, Mutual, 30 min. The first season of this, the Orson Welles version, featured many of the Mercury Theatre Players. Agnes Moorehead was in the opening show, "The Death House Rescue," along with William Johnstone, Jeanette Nolan, Ray Collins and Everett Sloane.

The show was directed by Martin Gabel. She also was notable in many other episodes that season, including "The Temple Bells of Neban," "The Three Ghosts," "The Circle of Death" and "The Death Triangle."

The Columbia Workshop. December 23 and 30, 1937, CBS, 30 min. "Alice's Adventures Through the Looking Glass" is a two-part version of the Lewis Carroll classic featuring Helen Claire, Agnes Moorehead and Lurene Tuttle, with direction by William N. Robson.

The Shadow. 1938, Mutual, 30 min. Orson Welles is still playing Lamont Cranston this season, and once again Agnes Moorehead is a prominent co-star. Episodes include "The League of Terror," "Sabotage," "The Society of the Living Dead," "The Poison Death," "The Phantom Voice," "Hounds in the Hills," "The Plot Murder," "The Bride of Death," "The Silent Avenger," "Murder in E Flat," "Symphony of Silence," and "The White Legion."

The Mercury Theatre. July 11, 1938, CBS, 60 min. "Dracula." The cast includes Orson Welles, Martin Gabel, Agnes Moorehead, George Coulouris and Ray Collins, with atmospheric music supplied by Bernard Herrmann.

Pulitzer Prize Plays. July 14, 1938, Blue Network, 60 min. "Men in White" stars Agnes Moorehead in this version of the Pulitzer Prize–winning medical drama that had been a stage and film hit, and was even satirized by the Three Stooges via *Men in Black* (1934).

The Mercury Theatre. July 18, 1938, CBS, 60 min. "Treasure Island" is Orson Welles' version of the Robert Louis Stevenson adventure, with Ray Collins, Agnes Moorehead, Dan Seymour and George Coulouris, and music by Bernard Herrmann.

The Mercury Theatre. August 15, 1938, CBS, 60 min. "Abraham Lincoln." The drama concentrates on the Civil War years, with Orson Welles, Ray Collins, George Coulouris and Agnes Moorehead. Music by Bernard Herrmann.

The Shadow. September 25, 1938, Mutual, 30 min. William Johnstone replaces Orson Welles, with Agnes Moorehead still the action-hungry sidekick. Episodes include "The Black Abbot," "Death Stalks the Shadow," "Night Without End," "Gun Island," "The Isle of Fear," "Shyster Payoff," "Black Rock," "Death Is Blind," and "Guest of Death."

The Columbia Workshop. November 24, 1938, CBS, 30 min. "Beauty and the Beast." The experimental program commissioned this mini-opera from composer Vittorio Gianinni and librettist Robert Simon. It was sung in English but needed narration from Agnes Moorehead.

The Campbell Playhouse (aka *Mercury Theatre on the Air*). December 9, 1938, CBS, 30 min. "Rebecca." Having acquired a full-time sponsor in Campbell's Soup, *Mercury Theater* returns to the air, giving up its name to its client. Agnes Moorehead stars, with Orson Welles, Alfred Shirley, George Coulouris and Mildred Natwick. The author, Daphne du Maurier, talks to radio listeners from London.

The Shadow. January 1, 1939, Mutual, 30 min. "The Man Who Murdered Time" is the episode to mark the New Year, a tale about a time machine stuck on December 31. William Johnstone and Agnes Moorehead are featured throughout the year, with fresh episodes continuing until March. Shows include "Island of the Devil," "Ghosts Can Kill," "Valley of the Living Dead," "Prelude to Terror," "The Ghost of Captain Bayloe," "Hypnotic Death," "Friend of Darkness," "Horror in Wax," "Sabotage by Air," "Appointment with Death," and "Can the Dead Talk?"

The Cavalcade of America. January 16, 1939, CBS, 30 min. The "Stephen Foster" cast includes Agnes Moorehead, Ted Jewett, Kenny Delmar, Edwin Jerome, Elliott Reid, Dwight Weist, Ted de Corsia and Abby Lewis.

The Campbell Playhouse. January 27, 1939, CBS, 30 min. "I Lost My Girlish Laughter." Orson Welles is the host of this Mercury Theatre Players production, a change-of-pace comedy featuring Agnes Moorehead, Ray Collins, Joseph Cotten and Everett Sloane. Based on the original George S. Kaufman story.

Great Plays. April 2, 1939, Blue Network, 60 min. "The Bluebird" offers the classic children's story by Maurice Metterlinck, starring Agnes Moorehead, Barbara Weeks, Donald MacDonald, Burford Hampden, Catherine Anderson, Harry Neville, Ronald Liss and Roy Terry.

The Columbia Workshop. May 1, 1939, CBS, 30 min. "Wet Saturday" is a black comedy about a family's dull day at home—with a dead body. Agnes Moorehead stars, with music by Bernard Herrmann, and story by Lee Anderson.

The Campbell Playhouse. May 12, 1939, CBS, 60 min. "Our Town." The Mercury Theatre Players adapt the 1938 Pulitzer Prize winner for radio. Orson Welles, Ray Collins, Agnes Moorehead, Effie Palmer, Everett Sloane, John Craven and Parker Fennelly.

The Campbell Playhouse. May 26, 1939, CBS, 60 min. "The Things We Have." Orson Welles adds to his genius credits by writing this story of an immigrant discovering the wonders of his new country—and by playing nearly a half-dozen roles in his own script. The cast includes Cornelia Otis Skinner, Agnes Moorehead, Everett Sloane and Kenny Delmar.

The Campbell Playhouse. September 10, 1939, CBS, 60 min. A man sentenced to 25 years in prison still manages to find love in "Peter Ibbetson." Orson Welles hosts, Helen Hayes narrates the tale, and Everett Sloane, Agnes Moorehead and Ray Collins co-star. The music is by Bernard Herrmann.

The Campbell Playhouse. September 17, 1939, CBS, 60 min. "Ah, Wilderness!" the serio-comic Eugene O'Neill classic, features Agnes Moorehead, Arlene Francis, Everett Sloane, Orson Welles, Joseph Cotten and Ray Collins.

The Shadow. September 24, 1939, Mutual, 30 min. The new season begins with "Dead Men Talk," and once again William Johnstone and Agnes Moorehead are the stars.

The Campbell Playhouse. September 24, 1939, CBS, 60 min. "What Every Woman Knows." Orson Welles is host, with Helen Hayes narrating. The cast includes Agnes Moorehead, Alfred Shirley, Ray Collins and Everett Sloane.

The Campbell Playhouse. October 1, 1939, CBS, 60 min. "The Count of Monte Cristo" sees Orson Welles hosting the classic story, with Agnes Moorehead, Edgar Barrier, Everett Sloane, George Coulouris and Ray Collins starring.

The Campbell Playhouse. October 22, 1939, CBS, 60 min. "Liliom" is the original drama that was the basis for the musical *Carousel.* Orson Welles hosts, Helen Hayes narrates, and Agnes Moorehead, Betty Fillson, Bill Adams and Joseph Cotten star.

The Campbell Playhouse. January 7, 1940, CBS. "Vanity Fair," the William Makepeace Thackery story of an orphan who rises in British society, features host Orson Welles, narrator Helen Hayes, and players Agnes Moorehead, Betty Garde, Joseph Holland and Morgan Farley.

The Cavalcade of America. January 9, 1940, Blue Network, 30 min. Moorehead appeared in various episodes of the show: "The Raven Wins Texas" (Sam Houston in his career after the battle of the Alamo), January 30, 1940; "Thomas Jefferson," March 5; "The Stolen General" (the exploits of Colonel William Barton), March 12; "Sam Houston" (part two of the Houston saga), March 19; "Jordan's Banks" (the story of confederate spy Sam Davis), March 26; "The Story of John Fitch" (the steamboat inventor), April 2; "The Story of Benedict Arnold," April 9; "Songs of Stephen Foster, an American Legend," April 30; "The Story of Thomas Paine," May 7; "The Story of Nancy Hanks" (Abraham Lincoln's mother), June 4; "John Sutter" (and the Gold Rush), June 18; "Susan B. Anthony," June 25; "The Story of Dr. Walter Reed," October 23; "Ann Rutledge and Lincoln," October 30; "The Red Death" (about Dr. Joseph Goldberger's discovery of a cure for Pellagra), November 6; "Wild Bill Hickok: The Last of Two Gun Justice," November 13; "Doctor Franklin Goes to Court" (the story of Ben Franklin in Paris), November 20; "The Farmer Takes a Wife," November 27; "Light in the Hills" (biography of Martha Berry), December 11.

The Campbell Playhouse. February 11, 1940, CBS, 60 min. "Mr. Deeds Goes to Town," adapted from the Frank Capra movie, stars Gertrude Lawrence, Agnes Moorehead, Everett Sloane and Joseph Cotten, with host Orson Welles.

Radio Guild. April 6, 1940, Blue Network, 30 min. "The Withering Glare of Amelia Peck." An elderly woman finds that her "evil eye" has unexpected powers in this *Twilight Zone*–styled comic fantasy with Agnes Moorehead and Peter Donald.

The Columbia Workshop. May 5, 1940, CBS. "The Honest Captain" stars Parker Fennelly, Agnes Moorehead, Orth Bell, Vincent Donohue and Gene Leonard.

The Cavalcade of America. 1941. Agnes again appeared in the cast of many of the series' historical dramas. "Will Rogers," January 1; "Mightier Than the Sword" (about writer Thomas Nast battling corrupt Tammany Hall politician Boss Tweed), January 8; "As a Man Thinketh" (a biography of Thomas Cooper), January 15; "Doctor Franklin Takes It Easy" (a look at the tireless Benjamin Franklin), January 29; "Henry Clay of Kentucky," February 5; "Abraham Lincoln: The War Years," February 12; "Plain Mr. President" (the life of George Washington), February 19; "Edgar Allan Poe," February 26; "Voice in the Wilderness" (William Penn), March 5; "Black Rust" (Mark Carleton's attempt to battle a plague that was destroying America's crops), March 12; "I Sing a New World" (the story of Walt Whitman), March 19; "Down to the Sea" (Herman Melville), March 26; "Edwin Booth," March 31; "Ode to a Nightingale" (the life of John Keats), April 7; "A Passage to Georgia" (the story of James Oglethorpe), April 14; "Henry Bergh, Founder of the A.S. P.C.A.," April 21; "The Heart and the Foundation" (about foreign correspondent Margaret Fuller), April 28; "The Trials and Triumphs of Horatio Alger," May 5; "Theodosia Burr" (Aaron Burr's daughter), May 12; "David Crockett," May 19; "Johns Hopkins," May 26; "Anna Ella Carroll," June 2; "Young Andrew Jackson," June 9; "Annie Oakley," June 16; "Joel Chandler Harris" (the author of the "Uncle Remus" stories), June 23; "Jean Pierre Blanchard" June 30; "The Mystery of the Spotted Death" (the dreaded Rocky Mountain Spotted Fever epidemic), July 7; "Ann Hutchinson," July 14; "O. Henry," July 21; "Clifford Holland" (for whom the Holland Tunnel is named), July 28; "Josephine Baker" (Dr. Baker and her most famous patient, "Typhoid Mary"), August 4; "Red Lanterns on St. Michael's" (a submarine in wartime), August 11; "Eve of Conflict" (Stephen A. Douglas debates Abraham Lincoln), August 18; "Leif Ericson," September 1; "City of Illusion" (Virginia City's Comstock silver mine), September 15; "Native Land," September 29; "Waters of the Wilderness" (the story of Colonel George Rogers Clark), October 13.

The Columbia Workshop. January 26, 1941, CBS, 30 min. "This Is from David," a drama about a mother neglecting her son, stars Agnes Moorehead.

The Columbia Workshop. February 16, 1941, CBS, 30 min. "A Crop of Beans," a drama about how the Depression affected a farming couple, stars Ted de Corsia and Agnes Moorehead.

The Free Company. April 6, 1941, CBS, 30 min. "His Honor, the Mayor." Orson Welles wrote and starred in this drama, featuring Ray Collins, Agnes Moorehead and Everett Sloane.

The Columbia Workshop. July 13, 1941, CBS, 30 min. "Ann Was an Ordinary Girl," a biography of Abraham Lincoln's first love, is part of the *Twenty Six by Corwin* series, written and directed by Norman Corwin. "Ann" stars Agnes Moorehead, John McIntire and Frank Lovejoy.

The Mayor of the Town. September 6, 1942, NBC, 30 min. Lionel Barrymore is the star of this new series, which co-stars Agnes Moorehead as his housekeeper. After four shows on NBC, the program turned up on CBS, then went to ABC in 1947, with Mutual taking over in its last year, 1949. In the opening show, the mayor counsels a man who wants to join the Navy.

On September 13 the mayor's daughter is getting married. On September 20, a woman decides to volunteer for the war effort. On September 27 there's a contest to choose "Papa Dear" (and the winner is—the surprised mayor). On October 7 the mayor's heart is warmed by a young orphan. On October 21 the mayor has to deal with an abandoned baby. On November 4 the mayor counsels a doctor not to retire—and the doctor's next patient dies (guest star Sidney Blackmer). On December 2 the mayor gets involved with a pianist who wants to break up with his girlfriend. On December 9 the mayor is wary of a limping man who has made a mysterious appearance in town.

Hello Americans. November 22, 1942, CBS, 30 min. Orson Welles hosts a multi-part series about famous people and places in the Americas. For example, November 22 offered "Pizarro: El Conquistador," "Simon Bolivar: El Liberador," and Jose de San Martin. The January 10, 1943, show featured portraits of Cortez and Montezuma. The performers included Agnes Moorehead, Ray Collins, Hans Conried, Pedro De Cordoba, Edmond O'Brien and Laird Cregar.

The Cavalcade of America. Moorehead's contributions in 1942 were limited, including: "In This Crisis" (the story of Thomas Paine, starring Claude Rains), April 20; and "The Man Who Wouldn't Be President" (the story of Daniel Webster, starring Edward Arnold), December 14.

Ceiling Unlimited. December 21, 1942, CBS, 15 min. "Gremlins," about how pilots handle tricky situations in the air, is hosted by Orson Welles, and stars Joseph Cotten, Lou Merrill and Agnes Moorehead.

Words with Music, Programs #221 and #357. 1943, 15 min. Pre-dating the concept of "poetry and jazz," the program featured a variety of actors and actresses getting a chance to read poetry or dramatic dialogue, with organ music in the background. The #221 episode features the works of George Santayana.

The Mayor of the Town. 1943. Agnes Moorehead joins Mayor Lionel Barrymore in various episodes during the season. On January 6 the mayor must counsel Janie Williams, a frequently troubled citizen. On February 17, citizen Mary Meyer (Beulah Bondi) is accused of murder. On March 3 the mayor must deal with citizen Dick Miller (Richard Quine), who has developed a phobia. On March 24 the mayor discovers a shipment of cups that seem to be surprisingly valuable. On March 31 the mayor and surprise guest star Bob Hope find themselves in a haunted house. On April 14 the mayor plays host to Marlene Dietrich. On April 28 Lionel Barrymore celebrates age 65 with special guest James Cagney. On May 5 there's an amateur talent contest—and special guest Charlie Ruggles. On June 23 the mayor somehow finds himself with Charlie Ruggles again—as well as five cats. On June 30 the mayor's secretary becomes infatuated with a marine captain (and after the ensuing antics, star Lionel Barrymore is named "Favorite Radio Actor on the Air" in a ceremony conducted by *Movie-Radio Guide*).

Suspense. April 27, 1943, CBS, 30 min. "The Diary of Saphronia Winters," a classic haunted hotel yarn written by Lucille Fletcher (author of "Sorry, Wrong Number"), stars Agnes Moorehead and Ray Collins.

Suspense. May 25, 1943, CBS, 30 min. "Sorry, Wrong Number," the premiere broadcast of the most famous episode of this radio series, stars Agnes Moorehead as the frightened invalid who seems to have overheard a murder plot due to a faulty phone connection, leading to her frantic calls to get help.

The Lady Esther Screen Guild Theatre. May 31, 1943, CBS, 30 min. "Rebecca," a radio version of the classic Alfred Hitchcock film, stars Joan Fontaine, Brian Aherne and Agnes Moorehead.

Suspense. June 29, 1943, CBS, 30 min. "Uncle Henry's Rosebush" stars Agnes Moorehead, Ellen Drew and Ted Reid.

Suspense. August 21, 1943, CBS, 30 min. "Sorry, Wrong Number." This is the first reprise of the classic story which was first broadcast on May 25, 1943.

The Adventures of Leonidas Witherall. September 7, 1943, CBS, 30 min. The premiere episode of a show about a crime-solving college professor stars Walter Hampden and Agnes Moorehead.

Treasury Star Parade. September 27, 1943, Syndicated, 15 min. In "Blondie," Blondie and Dagwood do their part in buying war bonds. Starring Arthur Lake, Penny Singleton, Thelma Ritter and Agnes Moorehead.

Ceiling Unlimited. December 19, 1943, CBS, 30 min. Christmas music dominates, with Agnes Moorehead, Joseph Cotten and Hans Conried, in "Letter to an Unborn Son."

Radio Almanac. January 26, 1944, CBS, 30 min. In the premiere of a new variety series, Orson Welles and Agnes Moorehead handle the dramatic sequences, with comedy from Groucho Marx. Moorehead appeared on other programs in the series, including the February 23, March 1, March 8 (with Lucille Ball), March 15, March 22, April 5, April 12 and June 7 episodes.

Suspense. February 3, 1944, CBS, 30 min. "The Sisters" is an eerie story of twin sisters who live alone in a gloomy house. One of them decides to buy a coffin. Does the other one realize her life is in danger? Starring Ida Lupino and Agnes Moorehead.

Suspense. February 24, 1944, CBS, 30 min. "Sorry, Wrong Number," starring Agnes again, is back by popular demand.

Ceiling Unlimited. April 9, 1944, CBS, 30 min. This variety show of songs and dramatic sketches features "Hymn to a Hero" and "God's Corporals." The cast includes Joseph Cotten, Constance Moore and Agnes Moorehead.

Everything for the Boys. May 23, 1944, NBC, 30 min. "Quality Street," a dramatic James M. Barrie short story adapted by Arch Oboler, stars Ronald Colman, Agnes Moorehead and Maureen O'Sullivan.

Fifth War Loan Drive. June 12, 1944, CBS, 60 min. This patriotic special offers the Secretary of the Treasury, President Roosevelt, and guest stars Orson Welles, Walter Huston, Agnes Moorehead, Keenan Wynn, Gloria Jean and Alan Napier.

The Jack Carson Show. July 19, 1944, CBS, 30 min. This sitcom episode guest stars Agnes Moorehead, Arthur Treacher, Howard Duff and Dave Willock.

Suspense. August 17, 1944, CBS, 30 min. "The Diary of Saphronia Winters." No, *The Shining* wasn't the first horror story about a spooky, empty hotel. Written by Lucille Fletcher, and starring Ray Collins and Agnes Moorehead.

This Is My Best. September 26, 1944, CBS, 30 min. "The Leader of the People" is an episode featuring Walter Brennan and Agnes Moorehead.

Suspense. January 18, 1945, CBS, 30 min. "To Find Help," Frank Sinatra stars in a menacing tale of an old lady who is home alone—except for a killer. Co-starring Agnes Moorehead and William Johnstone.

This Is My Best. April 10, 1945, CBS, 30 min. "Master of Ballantrae" stars Orson Welles and Agnes Moorehead.

The Cavalcade of America. June 18, 1945, NBC, 30 min. "Party Line," a nostalgic look at telephone communication, stars Agnes Moorehead, Verna Felton, Norma Jean Nilsson, and Mary Jane Croft.

Guest Critic Series. September 1945, CBS, 30 min. This promotion for the CBS fall line-up focuses on *Lux Radio Theatre, Ellery Queen, Mayor of the Town* and *Thanks to the Yanks.* Jack Carson, Arthur Treacher, and Dave Willock are the stars, with Lionel Barrymore and Agnes Moorehead joining in the segments for *Your Hit Parade, The FBI in Peace and War* and *Mayor of the Town.*

Suspense. September 6, 1945, CBS, 30 min. "Sorry, Wrong Number" is another broadcast of the classic story.

The Cavalcade of America. September 17, 1945, NBC, 30 min. "Nellie Was a Lady," the story of Nellie Bly, *New York World* reporter, stars Agnes Moorehead.

This Is My Best. November 13, 1945, CBS, 30 min. "Colonel Paxton," starring Ray Collins and Agnes Moorehead, is a lost episode of the series. Her previous episodes survive.

Request Performance. 1946, CBS, 20 min. This variety show from the Masquers Club in Hollywood features drama and comedy. W.C. Fields does a slightly tipsy and tongue-tied version of "The Temperance Lecture." Also appearing on the show are Ida Lupino, Reginald Gardiner and Agnes Moorehead.

The Radio Hall of Fame. March 24, 1946, ABC, 30 min. Rudy Vallee hosts this variety show, sings, and later introduces Agnes Moorehead, who stars in an edited version of "Sorry, Wrong Number."

The Cavalcade of America. March 26, 1946, NBC, 30 min. "The General's Wife," about the bride of Zachary Taylor, stars Agnes Moorehead and William Johnstone.

The Mayor of the Town. April 1946, CBS, 30 min. Agnes Moorehead was still making appearances on the Lionel Barrymore series, and was featured in this episode, "All on an April Evening," as well as "The Rocking Chair," broadcast on July 13.

The Lady Esther Screen Guild Theatre. April 1, 1946, CBS, 30 min. "On Borrowed Time" stars Lionel Barrymore as an old man who is about to be taken off by Death himself. Co-starring Agnes Moorehead and Vincent Price.

Suspense. April 4, 1946, CBS, 30 min. "Post Mortem" features Agnes Moorehead in a drama of frustration: she has discovered that a winning sweepstakes ticket is safely tucked away in the pocket of a man—who was just buried. Co-starring Elliott Lewis, Howard Duff and Jerry Hausner.

The Mercury Summer Theatre. September 13, 1946, CBS, 30 min. Orson Welles and his players (including Agnes Moorehead, Elliott Reid, Lurene Tuttle and Edgar Barrier) offer scenes from the Shakespeare play *King Lear*.

Stars in the Afternoon. September 29, 1946, CBS, 90 min. The network offers a fall special showing off their best stars and featuring samples from new and returning shows. Ozzie and Harriet Nelson host, with Jack Carson, Arthur Treacher, Fanny Brice and Hanley Stafford (Baby Snooks and Daddy), William Demarest, Mel Blanc, Gene Autry, Herbert Marshall, Hildegarde, Agnes Moorehead and Lionel Barrymore appearing.

The Cavalcade of America. October 14, 1946, NBC, 30 min. "The Hickory Tree," about Elizabeth Jackson, the mother of Andrew "Old Hickory" Jackson, stars Agnes Moorehead, Conrad Binyon, William Johnstone and Hans Conried.

Suspense. February 13, 1947, CBS, 30 min. In "The Thirteenth Sound," a variation on Poe's "The Tell-Tale Heart," a murderess is tormented by a strange noise. Starring Agnes Moorehead, William Johnstone and John McIntire.

Betty and Bob. June 15, 1947, NBC, 15 min. Guests include Arlene Francis, Everett Sloane, Elspeth Eric, Mary Mason, Agnes Moorehead, Ray Collins, Ruth Mattison and Edmond O'Brien.

The Sunny Side of the Atom. June 30, 1947, CBS, 60 min. Or, how I stopped worrying and learned to love radiation. Agnes Moorehead plays a reporter who discovers the way doctors and atomic scientists can use potentially lethal materials for the benefit of mankind. Co-starring Al Hodge.

Mystery in the Air. August 14, 1947, NBC, 30 min. In "The Lodger," the infamous Hitchcock film about Jack the Ripper is once again adapted for radio, this time for Peter Lorre's summer series (replacing *The Abbott and Costello Show*). Co-starring Agnes Moorehead, Henry Morgan, Barbara Eiler, Eric Snowden, Rolfe Sedan, Conrad Binyon and Raymond Lawrence.

The Mayor of the Town. January 21, 1948, ABC, 30 min. The mayor wonders what good can be done with the town's old Christmas trees. Lionel Barrymore, Agnes Moorehead, Conrad Binyon and Norma Jean Nilsson star.

The Camel Screen Guild Theatre. February 9, 1948, CBS, 30 min. In "Johnny Come Lately," a reporter discovers that a small-town newspaper is having trouble dealing with political corruption. Starring James Cagney and Agnes Moorehead.

In Your Name. March 22, 1948, Syndicated. Here's a series sponsored by the Red Cross and part of their fund drive. This week's drama, "Question and Answer," co-stars Agnes Moorehead, Martha Wentworth and Peter Leeds.

Ellery Queen. March 25, 1948, ABC, 30 min. "The Farmer's Daughter" offers a terrible surprise: Cueball Mingo has broken out of prison! The cast includes Lawrence Dobkin, Herb Butterfield, Alan Reed, Jeff Chandler and Anne Morrison. Agnes Moorehead is the "Guest Armchair Detective," and her duty is to figure out whodunit.

Suspense. July 29, 1948, CBS, 30 min. Agnes Moorehead and William Johnstone co-star in "The Yellow Wallpaper."

Suspense. November 18, 1948, CBS, 30 min. In "Sorry, Wrong Number," once again listeners get to overhear Agnes Moorehead talking about overhearing a murder threat. Co-starring William Johnstone and Paul Frees.

Suspense. November 25, 1948, CBS, 30 min. "The Screaming Woman," a nightmare that could've come from Edgar A. Poe, deals with premature burial and a girl who keeps hearing the sound of "the screaming woman." Based on a story by Ray Bradbury, the episode stars Margaret O'Brien, Ted de Corsia, Lurene Tuttle and Agnes Moorehead.

One Great Hour. March 26, 1949, CBS. "World Retreat." In the aftermath of war, many in Europe are starving and need help. President Harry Truman speaks, and a variety of Hollywood stars lend their support to this special broadcast: Gregory Peck, Ida Lupino, Glenn Ford, Roddy McDowall, MacDonald Carey and Agnes Moorehead.

Operation Dawn. May 22, 1949, NBC. This United Jewish Appeal special program stars Al Jolson and Agnes Moorehead. Jolson had presented two previous appeals in two previous years, including the dire "Operation Nightmare." For this fundraiser he declares, "A cloud has lifted over the world. A new state has been born: Israel. Carved out of sand and rock by a people who would not be denied. And to millions all over the world, that state means the dawn of a new life, a new hope, a new chance at being the men and women we all have a right to be."

Suspense. June 16, 1949, CBS, 30 min. "The Trap." Is a woman losing her mind, or is it just an elaborate trap? Starring Agnes Moorehead and William Johnstone.

The Cavalcade of America. March 7, 1950, NBC, 30 min. "Mr. Peale and the Dinosaur" tells how the Museum of Natural History was established in Philadelphia. Starring Claude Rains, Agnes Moorehead and Parker Fennelly.

Suspense. April 27, 1950, CBS, 30 min. "The Chain," a variation on "Sorry, Wrong Number," sees a nasty woman convinced that sending a disturbing letter is more effective than crank phone calls. Starring Agnes Moorehead, William Conrad and Alan Reed.

Suspense. February 15, 1951, CBS, 30 min. "The Death Parade." Not long after "The Chain," and with a nod toward "Sorry, Wrong Number," Agnes Moorehead finds herself receiving a warning letter that threatens death in "The Death Parade" (story by Shirley Gordon). Co-starring Jack Kruschen, Byron Kane, Jerry Hausner, Lou Krugman, Jeanette Nolan, Jay Novello and Howard McNear.

The Hedda Hopper Show. April 1, 1951, NBC, 30 min. Hedda Hopper offers the latest gossip (including the arrival of a second child for Leo Gorcey, and Errol Flynn's back pain) and promotes Moorehead's touring in *Don Juan in Hell*. Hopper spins a recording of Agnes reading "The Harp Weaver," complete with backing string quartet.

Suspense. September 10, 1951, CBS, 30 min. In "The Evil Adelaide Winters," Adelaide is a fraud who convincingly seems to be able to "cross over" and communicate with a dead boy. Agnes Moorehead stars in this story by Arthur Ross.

Suspense. January 14, 1952, CBS, 30 min. "The Fall River Tragedy." The only person who really knew what happened to Lizzie Borden's parents in Fall River is ... Lizzie Borden. Finally, she speaks. Agnes Moorehead stars in the story by Gil Doud.

Hallmark Playhouse. January 17, 1952, CBS, 30 min. "Madame Claire," is the Susan Ertz story dramatized, with Agnes Moorehead, Lurene Tuttle, Virginia Gregg, Edgar Barrier and Ted de Corsia.

Inner Sanctum. June 29, 1952, CBS, 30 min. "Terror by Night." Agnes Moorehead turns up in this first of three summer episodes of "creaking door" murder stories.

Inner Sanctum. July 20, 1952, CBS, 30 min. "The Listener" stars Agnes Moorehead as old Mrs. Richards, who isn't too old to find ways of defending herself. Co-starring Mason Adams.

Inner Sanctum. July 27, 1952, ABC, 30 min. In "Claudia," it seems that anyone who marries Claudia ends up dead. Starring Agnes Moorehead.

Suspense. November 17, 1952, CBS, 30 min. In "Death and Miss Turner," an artist seems to enjoy painting portraits of her victim—but leaves off the face! Starring Agnes Moorehead, Jeanette Nolan and Paul Frees.

Suspense. March 23, 1953, CBS, 30 min. The classic Charles Dickens short story "The Signalman" is dramatized, starring Agnes Moorehead and Joseph Kearns.

Guest Star. August 23, 1953, Syndicated, 15 min. "Hayes versus Hayes" is a program from the Treasury Department, pushing savings bonds. The cast for this mini-play consists of Agnes Moorehead, Gerald Mohr, Betty Lou Gerson and Betty Bly.

Suspense. September 21, 1953, CBS, 30 min. "The Empty Chair." Oh, those teenagers, they simply don't know how to drive. It's a cautionary drama starring Agnes Moorehead, Herb Butterfield, Sam Edwards and Joseph Kearns.

Suspense. November 30, 1953, CBS, 30 min. "The Wreck of the Maid of Athens" is a suspense version of *Survivor* as a shipwreck leaves a few people alone on an island. Starring Agnes Moorehead, Jack Kruschen, Richard Peel and Joseph Kearns.

Stagestruck. April 4, 1954, CBS, 60 min. "The Story of Spring on Broadway." Mike Wallace is the host of this variety hour that includes Felix Adler, Agnes Moorehead, Danny Kaye and Shirley Booth.

Suspense. May 24, 1954, CBS, 30 min. In "Weekend Special: Death," Agnes Moorehead once again has to go for the telephone when she witnesses two safecrackers in action. Co-starring Joseph Kearns, Barney Phillips, Hy Averback, Whitfield Connor and Mary Jane Croft.

The Hallmark Hall of Fame. November 21, 1954, NBC, 30 min. In a salute to Lionel Barrymore, who died on November 15, Edward Arnold plays host to Helen Hayes, Gene Fowler, Jimmy Stewart and Bing Crosby, with previously recorded tributes supplied by Agnes Moorehead and Lew Ayres.

The NBC Radio Theatre. January 8, 1956, NBC, 60 min. "The Snake Pit" is a frightening look inside an insane asylum, hosted by Vincent Price, narrated by Paul Frees, and starring Agnes Moorehead, Lawrence Dobkin and Alice Reinheart.

Suspense. June 30, 1957, CBS, 30 min. "The Yellow Wallpaper." It's pretty creepy when the patterns in the wallpaper begin to move. Starring Agnes Moorehead and Joe DeSantis.

Suspense. March 9, 1958, CBS, 30 min. "The Chain" stars Agnes Moorehead, John McIntire and Jay Novello.

Suspense. August 31, 1958, CBS, 30 min. "The Whole Town's Sleeping." Once again Agnes Moorehead stars in a Ray Bradbury story. A killer is loose, and a lady is walking alone at night while, yes, the whole town's sleeping! Co-starring William Conrad, Lurene Tuttle, Barney Phillips and Charlie Lung.

Suspense. January 4, 1959, CBS, 30 min. In "Don't Call Me Mother," a son may not exactly want to call his mother—when she seems to be doing everything she can to wreck his marriage. Starring Agnes Moorehead, Cathy Lewis, James McCallion, Barney Phillips and Norman Alden.

Suspense. July 23, 1959, CBS, 30 min. "Headshrinker." Agnes Moorehead and Lawrence Dobkin star, with a script first broadcast only a year earlier (with Nina Foch and Helmut Dantine in the lead).

Suspense. February 14, 1960, CBS, 30 min. "Sorry, Wrong Number." Old-time radio had been killed by television, and now most radio stations were saying sorry, we'd rather play Top 40 hits than *Suspense*. Here's the last airing of the classic Agnes Moorehead phone drama. Co-starring Joe DeSantis, Virginia Gregg, Byron Kane, Jeanette Nolan, Ellen Morgan and Norman Alden.

The CBS Radio Mystery Theatre. January 6, 1974, CBS, 60 min. "The Old Ones Are Hard to Kill." Agnes Moorehead stars in the premiere episode of an ambitious series attempting to bring back the suspense and thrills of old-time radio. E.G. Marshall is the host, veteran *Alfred Hitchcock Presents* writer Henry Slesar provides the script, and the cast includes Leon Janney and Roger De Koven.

The CBS Radio Mystery Theatre. January 26, 1974, CBS, 60 min. "The Ring of Truth," hosted by E.G. Marshall, stars Agnes Moorehead, Ian Martin, Mandel Kramer, Santos Ortega and Dan Ocko.

Audio

Only the most affluent fans had any type of home recording device in the 1940s and '50s, so Decca Records filled the demand for "Sorry, Wrong Number" by issuing their version starring Moorehead. It was originally released as a ten-inch (Decca DL 6022), and when 12" albums became the norm, re-issued on a long-player, with James Mason reading Poe on the flip side (*Sorry, Wrong Number/Tell Tale Heart*, Decca DL 9062).

Moorehead appears on *Our Common Heritage: Great Poems Celebrating Milestones in the History of America*, a 1947 album of 78s (Decca A 536) featuring Bing Crosby, Brian Donlevy, Walter Huston and Frederic March.

Psalms of David: 2 Cycles for Violin and Speech was released via Lyric Art Recording (AMRH 003).

Lavender Lady (Quinto QR 100) is a CD of a 1969 University of Wisconsin appearance featuring nine tracks, including "Moses and the Bullrush," "Devil's Speech on Destruction," "Ballad of the Harp Weaver," "Household Hints Down Through the Centuries," "These Have I Loved," "Lavender with a Difference," "Agnes' Aunt Cam," and "The Traveling Ladies."

11

Scream Queens: Helen Chandler, Julie Bishop, Ann Doran, Louise Allbritton, Hillary Brooke, Evelyn Ankers, Jane Adams, Gloria Stuart, Elena Verdugo and Fay Wray

Some B-movie beauties are still enthralling horror film fans today via their immortal ear-splitting screams. These women provided the necessary charm and delicacy to put in motion ugly, monstrous villainy. While the heroes of classic horror films seem to be easily forgotten by the mostly male fans of the genre (the list includes genial gents Patric Knowles, David Manners and Robert Paige), the women who cried, fainted, hid, gasped or even died—live on.

Few of these actresses have extensive radio credits, since their fame was based more on distinctive beauty than a unique voice. Also, as they tended to be interested in movie careers over Broadway (where the radio stations were mainly located), they simply weren't in the right place to get in front of a microphone. In New York, radio had plenty of semi-anonymous actresses to play damsels in distress, such as Virginia Gregg, Lurene Tuttle and Cathy Lewis, and as a bonus, these women could often perform dozens of different dialects and take many roles in the same script.

Helen Chandler

Many women known for one or two appearances in horror films don't even have one or two radio appearances that have survived. For Helen Chandler, who played opposite Bela Lugosi in *Dracula* (1931), only two minor radio appearances seem to exist.

Chandler's *Dracula* co-star, David Manners, at age 97, recalled, "She died young. Did I like her? Yes, I did. Yes, she was a beautiful person. But she was sad. I had a feeling she would never grow old, never even grow up."

Radio

Lux Radio Theatre. April 19, 1937, CBS, 60 min. In "Alibi Ike," Chandler co-stars with Joe E. Brown in this adaptation of his popular movie about an unlikely baseball pitcher. During an intermission in the show, Babe Ruth and his wife Claire make a guest appearance.

The Lux Radio Theatre. May 27, 1940, CBS, 60 min. "Vigil in the Night" stars Olivia De Havilland, Herbert Marshall and Helen Chandler, with Frederic Worlock, Ethel Griffies, Martha Wentworth, Claire Verdera and Lou Merrill.

Julie Bishop

Lucille Lund (June 3, 1912– February 15, 2002), who appeared in *The Black Cat* (1934), along with David Manners, has no radio credits. Thanks to that film, she is still remembered fondly, even though she had little dialogue. She plays the dual role of a dead woman in a glass display case and the dead woman's daughter (married to Boris Karloff).

Helen Chandler's range extended from limp to glassy-eyed in her lone enduring role as the victim of Bela Lugosi in *Dracula* (1931).

At a movie convention in 1995 Lund greeted an audience with this opening salvo: "I really think that the reason you all remember me is because I went to bed with Boris Karloff."

The other female co-star of *The Black Cat* also had little radio work, but at least a much longer film career. Her name? Well, in that movie it was Jacqueline Wells. In others it was Diane Duval. Eventually she settled on Julie Bishop.

Born Jacqueline Brown (August 30, 1914–August 30, 2001), she became a child actress as Jacqueline Wells. With a voice trained at the Pasadena Playhouse, she easily won roles in sound films, co-starring with W.C. Fields (*Tillie and Gus* in 1933) and Buster Crabbe (he Tarzan, she Jane in *Tarzan the Fearless*, also in 1933). In that one she was billed as Diane Duval. The following year she starred in *The Black Cat*, once again using her original screen name.

As the '30s waned, Wells wanted a fresh start and changed her name to Julie Bishop. She signed with Warner Bros. for action films and dramas, working with Errol Flynn (*Northern Pursuit*, 1943) Humphrey Bogart (*Action in the North Atlantic*, 1943) and John Wayne (*Sands of Iwo Jima*, 1949) Julie was a licensed pilot and married Air Force General Clarence Shoop in 1944. That year she starred in *Lux Radio Theatre*'s radio production of "Action in the North Atlantic." Julie plays Pearl O'Neill, a sexy nightclub singer with a soft heart but a tart tongue. She knows how to wisecrack with a serviceman:

> "I make my living here..."
> "You want a drink?"
> "Thanks, but I don't drink."
> "Then sing."
> "Oh, a command performance, huh."
> "Yeah, I like your voice."
> "The way you were starin' at me, that's not all you like about me."
> "Hey, don't you ever smile?"
> "Once in a while. If there's a reason for it."
> "When do you knock off here?"
> "Some time after you've left."

Bishop's family life became her primary concern, although she didn't retire completely from films. Fans of Westerns remember the movies she made co-starring with Gene Autry and Roy Rogers. Her surviving radio work reflects the action and melodrama roles she was getting in her post–Universal films.

Radio

The Lux Radio Theatre. November 6, 1939, CBS, 60 min. "Only Yesterday." Barbara Stanwyck stars in a soap opera about a woman waiting for her man to come home from war. Cecil B. DeMille hosts, with George Brent, Gloria Gordon, Dorothy Peterson, Harry Walker, Jacqueline Wells and James Eagles. Based on the book by Frederick Lewis Allen.

The Lux Radio Theatre. January 15, 1940, CBS, 60 min. "Sing You Sinners." Most folks believe a race horse called "Uncle Gus" is a longshot. But could betting on him be worth the gamble? Cecil B. Demille hosts, with Ralph Bellamy, Bing Crosby, Arthur Q. Bryan and Charles Peck. Smaller roles are filled by Edward Marr, Elizabeth Patterson, Emery Parnell, Jack Carr and Jacqueline Wells.

The Lux Radio Theatre. May 15, 1944, CBS, 60 min. In "Action in the North Atlantic," a Nazi submarine battles an American cargo ship on its way to Murmansk. By this time, Wells had changed her name to Julie Bishop. She is in the cast with Raymond Massey, George Raft, Bill Martel and Edward Marr.

Your Movietown Radio Theatre. Date unknown, ZIV Syndication, 30 min. " Solo for Two" is hosted by Les Mitchell, and stars Julie Bishop, Bob Holton and Jack Petruzzi.

Ann Doran

For many film actresses, *Lux Radio Theatre* was their only radio experience. The series specialized in performers recreating their film roles for the listening audience. Ann Doran (July 28, 1911–September 19, 2000) was one of the scream queens whose only radio appearances came on that show.

Film buffs know her as James Dean's mother in *Rebel Without a Cause* (1955), but horror fans prefer her in the giant ant melodrama *Them* (1954), *It! The Terror from Beyond Space* (1958), and *The Man They Could Not Hang* (1939), with Boris Karloff.

Like all the rest of Karloff's co-stars, she recalled him as

Adorable and durable B-movie queen Anne Doran.

> the sweetest man that God ever made on this earth. He was just the gentlest, kindest man — and he did all those horrible pictures! Like he said, "It's a job and they pay me very well for it." We worked very late hours on that one, and Karloff never lost his good humor.... I don't know whether we looked on it as a horror movie. It was just a movie. It happened to be a little strange.... That was the kind of picture that Karloff made. You knew that, if you worked with Karloff, it would be strange.

As for her audio work, Ann said:

> I only did *Lux Radio Theatre*. I didn't particularly enjoy radio. I move a lot, and in radio, you had to just stand there, because you were close to the mike. You can't use your body, and I had learned, through the years, to use my body as much as I used my voice. I thought radio was confining. There were people who loved it; they had a wonderful ability to mimic other people's voices. They were great at that. I was lousy at it. I was never a parrot!

Radio

The Lux Radio Theatre. July 6, 1942, CBS, 60 min. "Love Affair." Charles Boyer, Irene Dunne, Ann Doran, Barbara Jean Wong, Bea Benaderet, Charles Peck, Ferdinand Munier, Griff Barnett and Joe Pennario.

The Lux Radio Theatre. October 12, 1942, CBS, 60 min. "Morning Glory." Starring Judy Garland, John Payne, Adolphe Menjou, Ann Doran, Bea Benaderet, Dick Ryan, Fred MacKaye and Gloria Blondell.

The Lux Radio Theatre. March 1, 1943, CBS, 60 min. "The Lady Is Willing." Starring Kay Francis, George Brent, Ann Doran, Arthur Q. Bryan, Edward Marr and Fred MacKaye.

The Lux Radio Theatre. May 10, 1943, CBS, 60 min. "Now Voyager." Starring Ida Lupino, Paul Henreid, Dame May Whitty, Albert Dekker, Ann Doran, Charles Seel, Claudia Dell, Duane Thompson and Fred MacKaye.

The Lone Ranger. December 4, 1952, ABC, 30 min. In "Treason at Dry Creek," a nefarious couple (Ann Doran and Frank Fenton) are selling information to the Indians. The Lone Ranger is played by John Hart, with Jay Silverheels as Tonto.

Louise Allbritton

Some of Universal's beauties had romantic voices, which served them well for light comedy and melodrama. One of the studio's most charming contract players was Louise Allbritton (July 3, 1920–February 16, 1979), whose last name was a typo waiting to happen.

Born in Oklahoma City, she studied at the University of Oklahoma and learned the fundamentals of acting on stage at the Pasadena Playhouse when she arrived on the coast.

Universal gave her mild and easy roles, including the tolerant radio exec who doesn't really mind when Abbott and Costello try to solve a murder in *Who Done It?* (1942). After minor and fluffy comedies, Louise asked for a better role. The headstrong actress was put in her place—assigned to *Son of Dracula* (1943) and threatened with suspension if she refused to appear in it.

Ironically, this role gave her a chance to

A slightly hard-bitten Louise Allbritton in an unusually serious publicity pose.

stretch, and as the very strange heroine who is drawn toward the concept of eternal life and vampirism, she won over horror film fans who know her for nothing else. "It was great fun making this film," she said, "but, I had to wear a black wig, and I hated it. I got constant headaches from it."

Playing pranks helped liven up the deadly seriousness on the set. She and the director

> used to play gags on each other occasionally on the set and were scolded for killing time. So, one day I played a good one on them. It was a scene where the sheriff and some men discover my body in a coffin in the tomb after I had been turned into a vampire. Well, the sheriff [Pat Moriarty] wanders into the tomb and flips open the coffin lid. The astonished look on his face and the reaction of Bob [Paige] and the others was priceless because I was stark naked! Needless to say, the front office was even more upset.

Louise found herself teamed with *Son of Dracula* co-star Robert Paige in a series of romantic comedies, including the politically incorrect *Her Primitive Man* (1944), co-starring Robert Benchley and Edward Everett Horton. In that one she played the typical rich, headstrong heroine who has to fall—against her better nature—for a boyishly charming rogue. Paige played a writer who made up a story about a headhunter and now has to paint himself up to impersonate one (a good reason this film isn't on DVD).

Louise appeared on TV's *Alfred Hitchcock Presents* but preferred her home life with broadcaster Charles Collingwood.

Louise Allbritton tugs at Robert Paige, her co-star in *Her Primitive Man* (1944), *Son of Dracula* (1943), and several more.

Radio

Screen Guild Theatre. July 19, 1943, CBS, 30 min. "Men in White." The well-known medical drama gets a new treatment from Jean Hersholt, Louise Allbritton and James Craig.

Screen Guild Theatre. August 2, 1943, CBS, 30 min. "Come Live with Me" features Louise Allbritton in a supporting role behind Hedy Lamarr, Vincent Price and John Loder.

Screen Guild Theatre. September 11, 1944, CBS, 30 min. "Phantom Lady" sees Ralph Bellamy falsely accused. Along for the mystery are Louise Allbritton and Walter Abel.

Mail Call. September 13, 1944, AFRS syndication, 30 min. This patriotic variety show centers on the comedy of Amos 'n' Andy, and a monologue by Garry Moore. Louise Allbritton and Marilyn Maxwell supply the decoration, with music from the Les Paul Trio.

This Is My Best. November 28, 1944, CBS, 30 min. "Romance of Rosie Ridge" stars Robert Cummings as a drifter who finds romance with Louise Allbritton.

Screen Guild Theater. September 11, 1944, CBS, 30 min. "Phantom Lady" stars Ralph Bellamy, Louise Allbritton, Walter Abel and David Bruce.

Screen Guild Theater. December 11, 1944, CBS, 30 min. "San Diego, I Love You" stars Jon Hall, Edward Everett Horton and Louise Allbritton.

Screen Guild Theater. January 1, 1945, CBS, 30 min. "Mr. and Mrs. Smith" stars Preston Foster, Louise Allbritton and Stuart Erwin.

Screen Guild Theater. May 28, 1945, CBS, 30 min. "The Joy of Living" stars Robert Young and Louise Allbritton.

Screen Guild Theater. November 26, 1945, CBS, 30 min. "Biography of a Bachelor Girl" stars Louise Allbritton, Joseph Cotten and Harry Von Zell.

This Is My Best. December 4, 1945, CBS, 30 min. "Happily Ever After" is a situation comedy starring Robert Young and Louise Allbritton.

The Cavalcade of America. May 27, 1952, NBC, 30 min. "The Valley of the Swans" stars Dana Andrews as Pieter Plockhoy, a settler exploring Delaware. Co-starring, Louise Allbritton, Charles Dingle and Luis Van Rooten.

Hillary Brooke

Louise Allbritton was one of Universal's classiest blondes, but she wasn't their most dangerous one. Hillary Brooke (September 8, 1914–May 25, 1999) might claim that title, having dueled Sherlock Holmes to near death in *The Woman in Green* (1945). Her educated, smooth voice has a quiet, unsettling quality, and it's unfortunate that it was not used more often on radio. Late in her career her softly sophisticated inflections served as contrast to the low comedy of Abbott and Costello. Tolerant and almost motherly, Hillary won legions of fans for the way she so gently put up with "Louis" (never "Lou") Costello on their TV series. Why she would live anywhere near a rundown rooming house filled with denizens like Joe Besser and Sid Fields was never explained.

Brooke's best surviving radio appearance is on *Suspense* in the later years of its run. It's one of those tense, disquieting tales of premonitions and madness where the ride is better than the conclusion. Brooke is the narrator and star as she describes peculiar incidents, like the time she came home to find her apartment inhabited by someone else, and the nightmare of learning her husband had died a week ago. She begins to wonder if she's the one who is dead. Dreams and reality keep swirling together in her brain:

> One thought kept repeating itself, repeating: I'm afraid of Harry. I'm afraid. My husband is going to kill me. I know, because I dreamed it last night. It was a warning! My husband is going to kill me.... I had a dream, that was all. Just a nightmare. Nothing more sinister than that. I was just another girl who'd had a bad dream. The afternoon dragged all too slowly.... I was all right now. I'd let a silly dream play tricks with me. Afraid of Harry? I almost laughed out loud, but I felt more like crying. I was on my way home to the man I loved, and this time I knew I wasn't dreaming. Home. Harry would be there...

A script like this requires a compelling and sympathetic performance, and Brooke supplies it.

Radio

Obsession. Circa 1955, MacGregor syndication, 30 min. In "The Silver Cord," Hillary Brooke plays Sarah, who lives under the thumb of her evil grandmother—and a family secret. C.P. MacGregor was a pioneer in radio, beginning with MacGregor and Ingram Co. in 1929. John

Dunning, in his book *On the Air*, wrote that MacGregor "argued that transcriptions enabled him to produce flawless shows, losing the excitement of live performance was a small price to pay." By the mid–'40s he was on his own, (C.P. MacGregor, 729 South Western Ave., Hollywood), producing singles (a variety of jazz and pop music) for radio use, as well as full-length shows, including *Proudly We Hail* (1947–54), *Salute to Reservists* (1950–1952) and the Salvation Army–sponsored *Heartbeat Theatre* (1956–65).

Suspense. January 5, 1958, CBS, 30 min. "A Week Ago Wednesday" is a script recycled from a November 29, 1945, broadcast. This one stars Hillary Brooke, D. J. Thompson, Dick Beals and John Dehner.

Evelyn Ankers

Evelyn Ankers (August 17, 1918–August 28, 1985) was Universal's favorite "Scream Queen" of the 1940s. Born in Chile and raised in England, she studied at the Royal Academy of Dramatic Arts and made her American stage debut in the Broadway hit *Ladies in Retirement* in 1940. Signed to MGM with no success, she was put to work at Universal as the pleasant heroine in Abbott and Costello's *Hold That Ghost* (1941). She was upstaged by Joan Davis, who played a fictional radio "scream queen" known for the opening shriek on the equally fictional "Tales of Terror" show.

In Universal melodramas Ankers played attractive, sensible types who could be won over by heroes displaying charm and humility. That was Lon Chaney, Jr.'s Larry Talbot in *The Wolfman* (1941), who blunders while trying to impress her, but eventually wins her sympathy. Like the more modern heroines of the '40s (compared to Helen Chandler's fragile role in *Dracula*), she can take care of herself *almost* throughout the entire film. There was a scene where she's attacked in the fog and faints:

> If I remember the sequence properly, after I am dropped into this chemical fog, I was to lie still for a few seconds until I heard "cut." I didn't hear "cut." They started to prepare for Lon to finish the fight scene with Claude Rains. Well, they forgot me in all the hustle and bustle of changing camera setups. I had been overcome by the fumes and passed out. Fortunately, someone in the crew nearly tripped over me and I was saved.

Ankers weighed in for several of Chaney Jr.'s films, including *Man Made Monster* (1941), *Ghost of Frankenstein* (1942), *Son of Dracula* (1943), and *Frozen Ghost* (1945). She faced George Zucco (*The Mad Ghoul*,

Evelyn Ankers and Lon Chaney, Jr., are scared of each other's hairstyle. A scene from *The Wolfman* (1941).

1943), and had the distinction of playing a whore with a heart of gold in the Sherlock Holmes movie *Sherlock Holmes and the Voice of Terror* (1942), and an evil mastermind pitted against Holmes in *The Pearl of Death* (1944). She was the title character of Lon Chaney, Jr.'s low-budged Inner Sanctum B-film *Weird Woman* (1944).

Although he only had minor roles in the films he made with her, Bela Lugosi was well remembered by Miss Ankers:

> Bela Lugosi was a gentleman of the "old world." I think he admired my British accent, being a famous actor from the Hungarian Theater. I didn't recognize Bela when I met him out of make-up! We had been talking about this and that for quite some time when he ended the conversation by him saying how much he enjoyed working with me on *The Ghost of Frankenstein*. It hit me right then that the snaggle-toothed horrifying character that he played in the film [Ygor] was the same man.

Bela also had a brief scene in *The Wolfman*, but in that one,

> Bela wore a bushy wig and a gypsy mustache.... But Mr. Lugosi was quite the opposite from his screen characters; he was refined, cultivated and charming. This transition is not an easy thing to do as an actor. I learned from first hand experience when I made *Weird Woman* a few years later, again with Lon Chaney, Jr. The studio made me the villain in that film! Every time I would try to work myself up to look evil, especially in the scenes with Anne Gwynne, I would scrunch my eyebrows, try for a mean look. When I turned to Anne we would both become hysterical with laughter.

With her flawless complexion and long, tousled hair, she was as winsome as she was classy, and in real life married to one of the handsome leading men of movie melodramas and sci-fi movies, Richard Denning.

She can be heard on one classic radio show, the briefly syndicated *Obsession* series. A variation on *Suspense* (complete with a clanky, off-key gong going off to indicate menace), the show made good use of sound effects and florid music. With a compelling narrator, the stories could build nicely to the twist ending. Ankers, so rarely given a complex character to play, makes the most of it in this production.

An envious sister and her boring husband pay a visit to her rich twin. Before long, the jealous woman is trying to convince her husband to help her commit fratricide: "All this is here for us.... Look what we would have! The house! The money! Freedom! All the things you wanted and I wanted. Murder? It's merely retribution — a retribution she deserves!"

Narrating the story, as well as acting in it, evil Evelyn breathes life into the scripted murder scene:

> That night we waited until well after Teresa had gone to bed. Then we slipped up to her bedroom. I knew she practically knocked herself out with sleeping pills every night. We opened the door and crept into the room. We had her gagged and her arms bound almost before she knew it. We carried her downstairs and into the sailboat. There was a good breeze. We sailed out quickly. About half a mile off shore we untied Teresa and pushed her over the side!

The story itself is overboard, but Ankers doesn't disappoint her fans in this rare radio effort that allows this damsel to commit some distress instead of suffer it.

Radio

Obsession. MacGregor syndication, 30 min. "Surrender Is Farewell" is an apparently lost episode of this obscure series.

Obsession. MacGregor syndication, 30 min. "On the Wild Sea." Syndicated, and often re-broadcast for Armed Forces Radio, it's difficult to obtain exact dates for the approximately 70 episodes of this show, produced by C.P. MacGregor. It apparently aired circa 1955. Perhaps a half dozen shows have survived. MacGregor was able to get some major talent for his obscure enterprise, including Bonita Granville for "Cousin Charley," and Barry Sullivan (for "Faith Is the Evidence"). A show titled "The Solitary Genius" explored the world of Edgar A. Poe, with Ted Osborne in the lead role.

Jane Adams

Jane Adams (August 7, 1921) doesn't dwell on her horror career, though it includes a hunchback role in Universal's *House of Dracula* (1945) and a part opposite Rondo Hatton in the notorious B-movie *The Brute Man* (1946). She probably could've been even more of a scream queen if she'd kept her original name, which would've made her seem like a distant relative to the author of *The Devil's Dictionary*: Betty Jane Bierce.

In a 1998 letter to a writer for *Videoscope* (a national magazine devoted to horror classics), she wrote:

> You are kind to propose an interview—and I am confident that the final result of your effort would reflect the highest professional standards. The foregoing notwithstanding, a review of the magazine and as you state: "its appeal to all fans of monster movies ... thrills and chills," leads to my decision to decline your thoughtful invitation. My involvement with such movies was only a limited part of my overall career and probably not of sufficient interest to justify your time and effort. Thanks again for thinking of me.

For those thinking of her still, the radio shows available on which she appears stray far from the horror genre.

Radio

The Lux Radio Theatre. May 5, 1947, CBS, "The Egg and I." The Betty MacDonald novel and film is now adapted for radio with the original stars Claudette Colbert and Fred MacMurray. Featuring Elvia Allman, Frances Robinson, William Johnstone, Janet Scott, Jeff Chandler (using his real name of "Ira Grossel"), Norman Field, Cliff Clark and Howard Jeffrey. Jane Adams is a special guest during the show's intermission. She's on hand to help promote a new movie, and the "interview," with many a plug for Lux products, hardly sounds ad-libbed. Responding to a compliment on her "lovely face" having appeared on the cover of magazines, she says, "I guess I'm not the only girl whose job as a model led to a movie career, but I think my experience as a radio actress helped a lot too."

"I'm sure it did," the announcer responds. "You know, when a producer finds dramatic talent combined with beauty, he knows he's in luck."

"I know what you mean by that when

Jane Adams wasn't scared of Glenn Strange. A publicity still for *House of Dracula* (1945), autographed to the author.

I watch Ella Raines before the camera. I used to visit the set of her new film *The Web* everyday.... Edmond O'Brien, William Bendix and Vincent Price—a wonderful cast, and they all worked hard."

"Ella Raines was married recently."

"Yes, she was a bride of only a few weeks when she was given her role in *The Web*. In spite of long hours at the studio she managed to have breakfast every day with her new husband. Only it had to be at five A.M. 'Imagine,' Ella Raines said to me, 'Having to look one's best at five in the morning'.... She always looks fresh as a flower, with that lovely smooth skin of hers. I guess it pays to be a Lux girl."

"I'd say it's a wise girl who depends on daily Lux soap care."

"And so would I. When I was a model I learned what a really effective care lather facials with Lux soap can be. Ella Raines says it's wonderful to have a care that's so easy, too. She always has Lux toilet soap in her dressing room for a quick beauty facial."

"Perhaps you'll tell us, Miss Adams, just how she uses her beauty soap."

"The same way I do. I just smooth the Lux lather well in, rinse with warm water then cold, then pat my face dry with a soft towel. The lather's so rich and fragrant. It's a joy to smooth it over your skin."

"Thank you Miss Jane Adams."

The Lux Radio Theatre. October 13, 1947, CBS. "Great Expectations" stars Ann Blyth, Howard Da Silva, Lee J. Cobb, Robert Cummings, Jeff Corey, June Whitley, Michael Ann Barrett, Colin Campbell, Norman Field, Herb Butterfield, Jimmy Ogg and Noreen Gammill. Once again Jane Adams appears for a commercial and interview during the intermission.

Gloria Stuart

One of the first horror movie queens of the sound era was Gloria Stuart (July 4, 1910). Like Jane Adams, she didn't want to stay in melodramas, and retired in the '40s when she simply wasn't getting interesting film roles. She had a very active social life through her husband (screenwriter and Groucho Marx crony Arthur Sheekman), and it included a circle of influential poets and artists. She un-retired for the film *Titanic* (1997), and was nominated for various "Best Supporting Actress" honors, winning more acting accolades than she'd received in the '30s and '40s.

Back at the turn of the 1930s, Stuart's agent received two offers for her: $150 a week from Paramount and $250 a week from Universal. Naturally, he told her to sign with Universal. She recalled in her autobiography,

> It's too bad, because I would have had, I think, a much different career at Paramount. They had Lubitsch, they had Chevalier, they had Dietrich. They had so many wonderful stars. A wonderful studio. Universal was a B studio in every department.

However, while the average moviegoer may barely know who Lubitsch is, and few could name more than one film by Dietrich or Chevalier, most everyone has seen Universal's horror classic *The Invisible Man* (1933).

Before that one, she was the blonde centerpiece (in a slinky and form-fitting white gown) in another James Whale horror film, *The Old Dark House* (1932). He told her that she was the film's "streak of white light" in an otherwise dark and stormy nightmare inhabited by hulks (Boris Karloff and Charles Laughton) and a bunch of old people in decay. She recalled:

> Boris was dear. Very soft spoken. Very laid back. He was a beautiful actor, and very private. He was the most charming, the most considerate actor you could possibly imagine, the complete antithesis of the kind of character he played in the movies. But with that makeup ... when he

made his entrance in *The Old Dark House*, it was very easy for me to act frightened, because I *was* frightened!

Laughton, on the other hand, "was very involved in his characterization," and quite serious, the same as Claude Rains, who starred in Whale's horror-comedy *The Invisible Man*, the film in which Gloria has the more traditional role of confused and hapless heroine. In one scene she tries to talk sense to the madman: "Jack, listen to me! My father knows something about monocaine even you don't know. It alters you, changes you, makes you feel ... differently."

Claude Rains in response: "Your father? He has the brain of a tapeworm, a maggot, compared to mine!"

It was a thankless role, and her costumes (including a dismal beret cemented onto her blonde hair) did not help the cause. Neither did Rains, who, despite having all the best lines, wanted to make sure the audience was always looking his way. Even though his face was completely covered in bandages during his scenes with her, he tried to block her from the camera:

> When he started to move me around during a scene so that the back of my neck was to the camera and he was full-face, I stopped him. I said to the director, "James, look what he's doing. Upstaging me." James got up from his director's chair and said, "Now, Claude, this is film. This is not stage ... and if we don't get it on the next shot, we can do it over and over again until we do.

As she wrote in her autobiography, "But he did try to do it again—the eternal ego at work.... Claude Rains was what we call 'an actor's actor'—and twenty-four hours a day, on a set, on a stage, in a bar, going to the loo, baking a cake, he was giving a performance." She did allow that although "he was very grand," he did have great acting skill and charm; "he was interesting, and beautifully educated, and for that it was a pleasure working with him."

In 1942, a long decade after her initial horror film success, she made her lone surviving radio appearance—an episode of *Suspense* entitled "The Ketler Method." She happened to be in New York at the time trying to ignite her stage career, and also happened to know the show's producer, William Spier, and his wife, children's book author Kay Thompson.

Stuart is the heroine of the piece. She and her husband arrive at a sanitarium on a dark and rainy night. Unfortunately, mad doctor Ketler has gotten loose and has taken over the asylum. At first Gloria delivers the innocent straight lines: "I don't like places like this. I suppose it's very foolish of me, but I always feel as if I'm in some sort of danger..." Later she's the damsel in distress, and if you think it's easy to con-

Gloria Stuart, in dark danger and white lingerie, about to scream in *The Old Dark House* (1932). She signed the still for the author during her *Titanic* comeback.

vey a pitiful sense of torment, try reading Gloria's lines out loud: "Please, let me go. Let me go—please! Let me go, oh, let me go—oh let me out of here!"

Roles like this, thankless though they might be, were vital to all horror and suspense shows, and it took a special kind of woman to scream and cry without becoming so shrill and tiresome that the listener—and the hero—would not want her to be saved.

Radio

The Royal Hawaiian Hotel Show. 1934, Transco syndication, 15 min. This syndicated show (air dates varied) featured the music of the Royal Hawaiian Orchestra. The hotel's guest is Gloria Stuart.

Information Please. January 2, 1940, Blue Network, 30 min. It's a gala evening as host Clifton Fadiman accepts the award from *Radio Guide Magazine* for being the "Outstanding Program of 1939." Panelists are the usual trio of Franklin P. Adams, John Kieran and Carl Van Doren, plus special guest Gloria Stuart.

Suspense. September 16, 1942, CBS, 30 min. In "The Kettler Method," a mental patient warns his doctor, "Tables turn"; and on a dark and stormy night—he's right. With Roger De Koven, John Gibson, Gloria Stuart, Martha Falkner, and Ralph Smiley.

Elena Verdugo

Elena Verdugo (April 25, 1926) is beloved by film fans for co-starring in Abbott and Costello's 1946 effort *Little Giant* (she married and later divorced the duo's comedy writer, Charles R. Marion), and for playing the sympathetic gypsy who sees the sorrow and the pity in Larry Talbot, the Wolfman (*House of Frankenstein*, 1944). She played opposite Chaney once again in *The Frozen Ghost* (1945). The multi-talented starlet also explored a career as a singer, recording "Tico Tico" with Xavier Cugat's orchestra.

A bit young for a radio career, Elena did explore the medium when she replaced Audrey Totter on the frisky sitcom *Meet Millie*. The tag line for the show was "A gay, new comedy about the life and loves of a secretary in Manhattan. It's time to Meet Millie." When radio gave way to television, she was given the starring role in the TV series, which lasted from 1954 to 1956. She would turn up in a variety of TV sitcoms (*The New Phil Silvers Show*, *Many Happy Returns* and *Mona McCluskey*) before going "straight"

Elena Verdugo is the gypsy who finds something tame about wolfman Lon Chaney, Jr., in *House of Frankenstein* (1944). She signed the photo to the author in 1996.

Who? Wray! Evil and glamorous Fay Wray in a studio pose she autographed for the author.

for her last major role, Consuelo Lopez opposite Robert Young in the ABC medical drama *Marcus Welby, M.D.* For that series she was twice nominated for an Emmy award.

Radio

One Night Stand. February 18, 1945, AFRS, 30 min. Live from the Trocadero in Hollywood, Xavier Cugat and His Orchestra perform. Their male vocalist is Luis Del Campo, and their female vocalist is Elena Verdugo.

Meet Millie. July 2, 1951–September 23, 1954, CBS, 30 min. Elena Verdugo replaced Audrey Totter in 1952. CBS was eager for the program to be augmented by a TV version, and Totter's film contract wouldn't permit it. Millie's boyfriend was played by Ross Ford, her boss was played by Roland Winters, and Marvin Kaplan supplied extra comedy as the peculiar poet Alfred Prinzmetal.

Audio

A hit 78 rpm (Columbia 36780) featured "Tico Tico" by Elena Verdugo, and on the flip side, "Linda Mujer," with a vocal by Luis Del Campo. The song became a perennial, and was released as a 45 rpm (Columbia 33317), and on many Cugat long-play albums. It is on most any Cugat re-issue CD, including *Xavier Cugat—16 Most Requested Songs* (Legacy 189441) and *South America Take It Away* (Asv Living Era).

Fay Wray

Fay Wray (September 15, 1907–August 8, 2004) is best known for screaming at King Kong, but as *Films in Review* noted in 1987, "Only five of the impressive total of 77 features she was seen in from 1925 to 1958 (67 of them as a leading lady) can be classified as horror."

But one of them was the really big one.

"They told me I was going to have the tallest, darkest leading man in Hollywood," Fay Wray liked to say. "Naturally, I thought of Clark Gable."

Born in Alberta, Canada, she came to Los Angeles and at 16 appeared in Hal Roach comedies. By the age of 19 she was a respected actress and starred in *The Wedding March* (1928) for Erich Von Stroheim. Signed to Paramount, she made a few indifferent films, including *The Four Feathers* (1929), produced and directed by Merian Cooper and Ernest B. Schoedsack.

The duo hired her for *The Most Dangerous Game* (1932), a film about a sadist playing a unique game of "Survivor" on a tropical island. She also made *Mystery of the Wax Museum* (1933)—something to scream about; but, ironically for a scream queen, on the first take she froze. Her key scene involved unmasking Lionel Atwill and seeing his scorched face:

> That was one time when my technique absolutely deserted me, I must admit. There was a wax face that he had created himself to cover his own ugliness. I was in his clutches and I had to hit him in the face. It was necessary for the audience to see this and be shocked. But when I struck him, and the moment I saw part of him, I just froze! I wanted to run; I just couldn't go on! So they had to make another mask and do it over when I recovered. It was just so real.

She recalled, "I was asked to do horror film after horror film ... and some of those were a little too gruesome. I wasn't too comfortable all the time in those. I didn't really care for them." As for Kong? "When the script came I was absolutely appalled! I thought it was a practical joke."

Once she took the assignment, she made screaming an art form.

On November 9, 1963, 30 years after *King Kong*, Fay gave an interview on *The Today Show*. One of the interviewers was Pat Fontaine.

PAT FONTAINE: What about those screams?
FAY WRAY: Well, I just imagined I was four miles from help and, well, you'd scream too if you just imagined that situation with that monster up there! And then when the picture was

finished, they took me into the sound room and then I screamed more for about five minutes—just steady screaming, and then they'd cut that in and add it.

PAT FONTAINE: Miss Wray, I wondered—I believe I heard that you had some children. Do they watch *King Kong* with you?

FAY WRAY: They didn't when they were little because I thought that they had to be of a certain age. I hoped they liked me well enough not to want to see me in that sort of a spot. So I think the youngest was seven when she saw it. And she was fascinated by it. It is a compelling, suspenseful film. When it was over she said, "Oh, I felt so sorry for him. He didn't want to hurt you. He liked you."

In a later interview for *Scarlet Street* magazine (February 1998, Vol. 7, Issue 27, conducted by Rick McKay), Fay elaborated on her exercise in screaming for the *King Kong* soundtrack:

> I went into the sound room and made an aria of horror sounds. I was in charge of it; there was no one there to listen to me. I was totally in charge of what I wanted to do.... I directed me entirely.... The producers liked me and trusted me, and more than one scene was only one take, because I'd plan ahead what I thought would be appropriate for that scene—so one take was enough.
>
> Anyone who sings knows that you don't wear it out if you're used to using it, and use it without hurting yourself. Screaming or singing will not make you hoarse if you do it correctly.

Over-the-top horror films were no longer of interest to her. She made only one more horror film, the ridiculous *The Vampire Bat* (1933), with Lionel Atwill and Dwight Frye. She went on to a wide range of melodramas, and did try a radio series in 1942 called *Rosemary*. In her autobiography, *On the Other Hand*, she briefly noted that the show was the creation of a pair of odd women:

The X-Wray: Fay Wray wasn't thrilled with Lionel Atwill as *Doctor X* (1932).

> The writers of *Rosemary*, two ladies who shared an apartment at 25 Central Park West, let me sublet their place so that I would have room enough.... They also told me about their psychiatrist, a warm and sensitive man who let me go to see him once a week for a period of six weeks for the price of five dollars per visit. (A radio series paid very little.) For the five dollars, he also offered me Russian tea, which I sometimes took and sometimes didn't.

She had every reason to seek some therapy. Her income wasn't much by 1942, and she'd gone through a harrowing divorce from her first husband, who then killed himself. This first marriage was to a bizarre alcoholic and anti–Semite named John Monk Saunders. In her autobiography (page 99) she wrote:

> Making love, he thought, was essential to him—and a danger. Drinking was essential to him—and a danger.... He thought himself as part of the Lost Generation.... Scott and Zelda Fitzgerald had visited him in his house in the

Hollywood Hills. Standing on a balcony, the three had competed to see who could urinate farther. Yes, Zelda too.

About the only time Saunders showed any great interest in her was when she was pregnant and her breasts swelled. She recalled in her book, "I was wearing a two-piece bathing suit and obliged him by removing the top and letting him take pictures of my now well-enlarged breasts. He seemed satisfied, finally, with the size and shape of them."

After their divorce, he hanged himself. She recalled how he had quoted lines from Oscar Wilde. "Each man kills the thing he loves," Wilde wrote. Fay wrote:

> He had quoted that to me, about me. But he didn't kill me. He killed *himself*!! "The thing he loves." Never, until this moment, have I had that thought. I'm either very wrong or exactly right to find that meaning now, such a long, long time after. I often thought of him as narcissistic. I think he did love his books, his clothes, the women who had judgement to love him for those things, too, for the externals. He loved his own image.

In 1942, two years after Saunders' death, she married screenwriter Robert Riskin. As Fay Wray Riskin, she dabbled in a writing career herself, and received a credit on the radio show *The Halls of Ivy* (April 18, 1951). The light-hearted show starred Ronald Colman.

After Riskin's death in 1955, she married the neurosurgeon who had treated him, Dr. Sandy Rothenberg.

She remained best known for *King Kong* to the end:

> I would have loved to have had more roles of more unusual character and depth, and I often thought that was too bad. However, it's a strange thing. I think I have at least one film that people have cared enough about to make them feel good. I think it's a strange, strange kind of magic that *King Kong* has. People who see it—their lives have changed because of it and they have so told me.

On radio, Fay Wray doesn't shriek. All that survives are some melodramas and mild publicity cameos.

Radio

Hollywood on the Air (aka *Hollywood on Parade*). November 13, 1933, NBC, 30 min. Celebrities on hand to say hello (but little more) include Fay Wray, Gene Raymond, Joel McCrea, John Boles, Johnny Mack Brown, and Sidney Blackmer.

The Lux Radio Theatre. October 25, 1937, CBS, 60 min. *Arrowsmith*, a classic Sinclair Lewis drama, is adapted from a popular film of the day. Starring Spencer Tracy, Fay Wray, Frank Reicher, Emery Parnell, John Qualen, Frank Nelson and Lou Merrill.

The Lux Radio Theatre. March 14, 1938, CBS, 60 min. "The Boss" stars Edward Arnold, Fay Wray, H.B. Warner, Frank Shannon and Howard Phillips.

The Lux Radio Theatre. May 2, 1938, CBS, 60 min. "Prisoner of Shark Island"

Somebody ripped Fay Wray's dress for a studio publicity pose, and it wasn't heavy-handed *King Kong*.

is a sympathetic drama about Dr. Samuel Mudd, arrested for having treated John Wilkes Booth as the hobbled assassin tried to make his escape from Washington, D.C., to the South. Gary Cooper, Fay Wray, John Carradine, Ted Osborne, Walter Connolly and Victor Rodman star, and during the halfway mark, there's a special appearance from one of Dr. Mudd's surviving children, Nettie Mudd Monroe.

The Lux Radio Theatre. March 13, 1939, CBS, 60 min. "So Big." The Edna Ferber story is adapted for radio, starring Otto Kruger, Barbara Stanwyck, Preston Foster, Fay Wray, Lou Merrill, Lurene Tuttle, Janet Young, Frank Nelson and Ted Osborne. The intermission guest is President Roosevelt's mother, Sarah Delano Roosevelt.

The Lux Radio Theatre. October 2, 1939, CBS, 60 min. "You Can't Take It with You" is a chance for Fay Wray to appear in a light "sitcom"-styled radio show. Based on the George S. Kaufman and Moss Hart play, it stars Edward Arnold, Walter Connolly, Fay Wray, Robert Cummings, John Fee, Lee Patrick, Sally Payne, and Lou Merrill.

Good News of 1940. November 30, 1939, NBC, 60 min. In this episode of a variety show featuring both songs and sketches, the hour is dominated by guest Fanny Brice as Baby Snooks and second banana comedian Lou Holtz. The cast includes Edward Arnold, Fay Wray and Gale Gordon, who appear in the comic farce "The Curse of the Paddingtons, or What Made the Tea Cozy?"

The Lux Radio Theatre. December 2, 1940, CBS, 60 min. "Knute Rockne, All American" is a radio version of the hit film, featuring Pat O'Brien, Ronald Reagan, Donald Crisp, Fay Wray, Arthur Q. Bryan, Celeste Rush and Forrest Taylor.

The Lux Radio Theatre. March 31, 1941, CBS, 60 min. In "Stablemates," Wallace Beery is an old horse doctor, and Mickey Rooney the young kid who yearns to ride a racehorse. Also appearing are Fay Wray, Noah Beery, Griff Barnett and Verna Felton.

The Treasury Hour. October 28, 1941, Mutual, 60 min. On this variety show offering both songs and a dramatic play, the song highlight, quite appropriate for wartime, is Dick Powell's "When This Crazy World Is Sane Again." Fay Wray and John Beal star in "The Last Boat," by D.H. Johnson.

Keeping Up with Rosemary. July 4–September 5, 1942, NBC, 30 min. In this brief Saturday evening summer venture, Fay Wray plays a magazine reporter. Cast members include Ben Lockwood, Sydney Smith, Ruth McDevitt and Henry M. Neely.

Hollywood's Open House, Program #11. 1944, NBC, 30 min. Fay Wray stars in "The March of Nothing," a drama based on *Crime and Punishment*. Other performers include Jim Ameche, Pat Harrington, Frankie Hyers, and Joseph Calleia.

Hollywood's Open House, Program #14. 1944, NBC, Fay Wray stars in "The Lord and the Lady," featuring Jim Ameche, Eddie Norris, Mabel Todd, Morey Amsterdam and Patricia Gilmore.

Any Bonds Today? Program #4. 1944, Syndicated, 15 min. This program was a production from the Treasury Department. In "The Last Boat," a soldier about to desert learns a lesson in patriotism from "Miss Liberty" herself. With Fay Wray, John Beal and Barry Wood.

Democratic National Committee Special. November 6, 1944, CBS, 60 min. For this political broadcast the night before the general elections, the idea was to find as many stars as possible willing to say a few good words for Franklin D. Roosevelt and other democratic candidates. Cameo appearances are made by James Cagney, Keenan Wynn, Groucho Marx, Lana Turner, Tallulah Bankhead, Gene Kelly, Evelyn Keyes, Paul Muni, Joan Bennett, Irving Berlin, Milton Berle, Charles Boyer, Edna Ferber, Virginia Bruce, George Jessel, Danny Kaye, George Raft, Claudette Colbert, Joseph Cotten, Susan Hayward, Rita Hayworth, Walter Huston, Rex Ingram, Edward G. Robinson, Gale Sondergaard, Monty Woolley, Jane Wyman, Constance Bennett, Fannie Hurst, Fay Wray, Eddie Dowling, Dorothy Parker, the Ink Spots, Gertrude Berg, Franchot Tone, Frank Sinatra, Judy Garland and Humphrey Bogart.

12
Radio's Own Horror Stars

Radio drew a lot of talent from the pool of actors, writers and producers already established on stage or screen, but many were "homegrown." They got their start in radio and stayed behind the microphone, believing that this was the medium best suited for their message.

The other chapters in this book have chronicled the famous screen stars who journeyed into radio, but this chapter is a salute to some of the less visible people who contributed much of their best work to radio alone.

This will be a brief chapter, as many books have ably chronicled the broadcast-based actors and actresses who made the "golden age" of radio truly shine. Radio fans not only know their names, they can even match them to the faces so infrequently seen in the pages of fan magazines or newspapers.

Included here are some of the important masters of radio horror known primarily for the chills they produced over the airwaves, rather than on film or television.

Raymond Edward Johnson

Foremost on any list of "Spook Radio" is Raymond Edward Johnson. Johnson (July 24, 1911–August 15, 2001) hosted *Inner Sanctum* for years, and was probably responsible for an entire genre of "punny," snickering horror hosts to follow, including those of the video generation (such as Zacherley, Ghoulardi, the Cryptkeeper, Vampira and Elvira).

He was one of the longest-lived of radio's horror personalities. He lived into the 21st century and had seen the revival of interest in old-time radio—which included requests for him to resurrect and perform some of "the good old" horror stories.

Born in Kenosha, Wisconsin, Johnson had a day job as a bank teller while studying at Chicago's Goodman School of Drama. In 1932 he was in the cast of *Welcome Valley*, a serial produced by Edward A. Guest. He played the Forest Ranger for *The National Farm and Home Hour*, and ultimately arrived in New York, working on *Arch Oboler's Plays* and Oboler's pioneering *Lights Out* series. Among his more infamous parts was the starring role in "The Ugliest Man in the World."

Johnson and his sister Dora were all over the radio dial in the late 1930s and '40s. She was Evey on the soap opera *Ma Perkins*; and he turned up as everything from *Don Winslow of the Navy* to *Mandrake the Magician*.

In 1941 he initiated his most famous role—"Raymond," the giddy ghoul behind the famous creaking door of the *Inner Sanctum*. The episodes didn't bother to mention its star was Raymond Edward Johnson; "Raymond" was just fine.

Although he did take stage work (he played Thomas Jefferson in the 1943 Broadway drama *The Patriots*), he made sure, even after a long week on the boards, to be as fresh as a newly-murdered body for the Sunday night broadcast. Every show was loaded with killer puns, but his audience had an even dopier sense of humor, often sending him gift packages containing oil cans "to fix that squeaky door."

Once, an overly helpful stagehand actually did fix the real squeaky and rusted hinge that soundman Terry Ross had so lovingly mounted for use on the show. Ross was shocked. As he told Leonard Maltin, quoted in *The Great American Broadcast* (published in 1997), "This was just before showtime. What do you do when the signature of the show was a squeaky door?" Answer: he moved close to the microphone and did a pretty decent vocal imitation. Then he went out to find a new hunk of rust.

According to producer Hiram Brown, as quoted in the *New York Times* (September 16, 2001), "There are only two sounds in radio that are trademarked—the creaking door and the NBC chimes."

In the fall of 1945, Paul McGrath (1904–1978) took over as the *Sanctum*'s host, with occasional subbing from House Johnson (1903–1971). Raymond Johnson moved on to other assignments. In 1953 he hosted another beloved fantasy series, *Tales of Tomorrow*.

In the 1970s Johnson was suffering from multiple sclerosis, but his voice was still strong and magnetic. Fans were delighted when he appeared in front of the Society of American Vintage Radio Enthusiasts. A small pressing of the evening's entertainment was released: *Raymond Edward Johnson Alive and Well* (on the Renaissance Radio indie label), featuring his gloriously over-dramatic versions of Arch Oboler's "Steel" and Poe's "Tell-Tale Heart," as well as an epilogue that paraphrased Shakespeare.

As late as 1997, his wheelchair replaced by a portable bed, Johnson would still make appearances in front of old-time radio societies, giving readings and saluting *Inner Sanctum*, Poe and Arch Oboler.

Arch Oboler

Arch Oboler (December 7, 1907 [some sources say 1909]–March 19, 1987) was one of radio's finest writers, but, like Rod Serling, despite a résumé including non-fantasy work, he remains best known for his stories about the eerie and the supernatural. Certainly *The Twilight Zone* owes something to Oboler's *Lights Out*.

Lights Out began its sporadic run in 1936, with Oboler demonstrating his versatility on other programs, most notoriously the 1937 broadcast of *The Chase and Sanborn Hour* where his scripted double-entendres for Mae West, opposite Edgar Bergen and his dummy

Ogle Arch Oboler in a vintage publicity shot.

Charlie McCarthy, enraged NBC censors enough to ban West from the network. That same year, Oboler's "Chicken Heart" episode of *Lights Out* chilled and amazed radio listeners (one of many memorable episodes to come).

While an ever-enlarging chicken heart is a rather ludicrous notion (it spawned a classic Bill Cosby comedy routine, available on *Wonderfulness* [WB 1634]), if it didn't make kids smear Jell-O on the floor to prevent the monster's home invasion, it certainly scared the entire household.

Oboler wrote every script for *Lights Out* in its first few years (a literary feat that would have no equal until Rod Serling's run of classic *Twilight Zone* episodes). The show thrived through the '30s, was revived for a few years in the '40s, and had a brief final run in 1947.

In 1939 he premiered *Arch Oboler's Plays* to vary his diet of horror and suspense, and

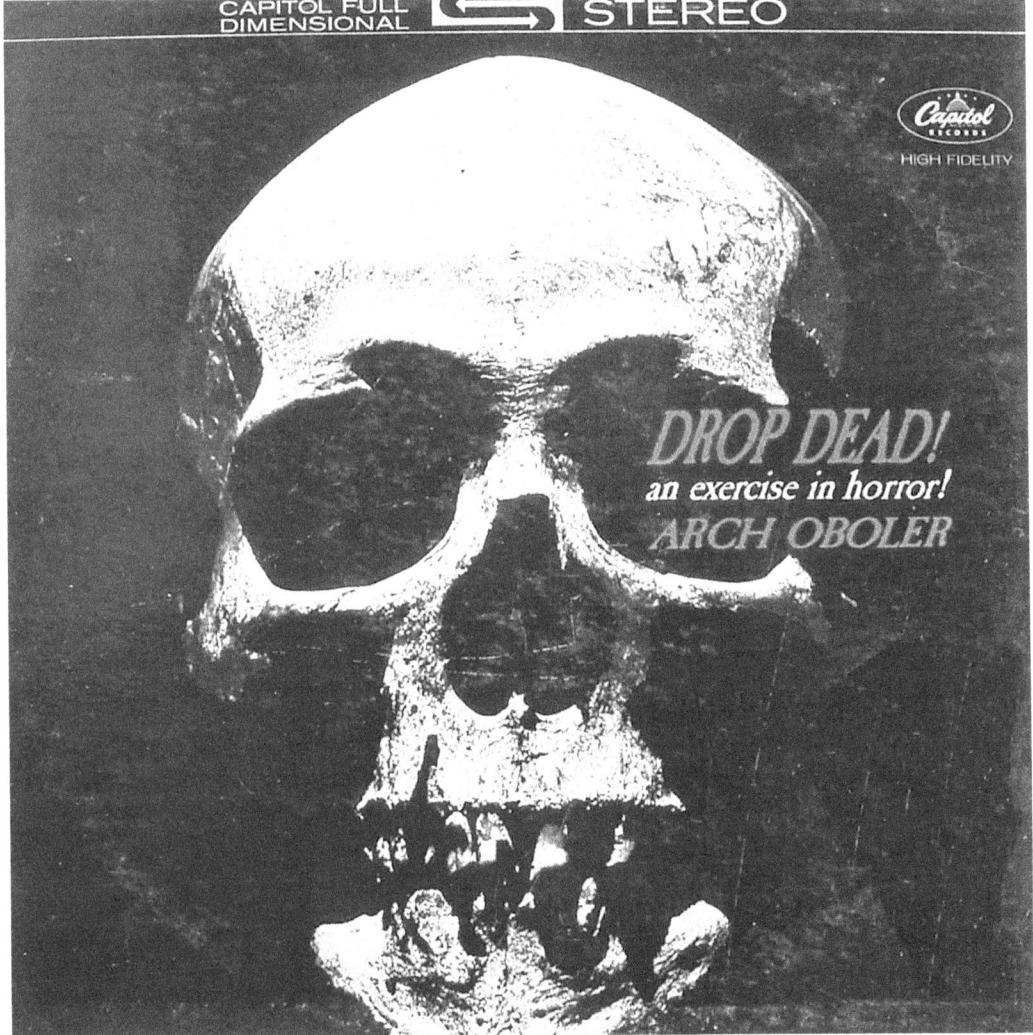

Arch Oboler was a radio pioneer with *Lights Out*, and one of the first to think of recreating his old radio show highlights for a long-play record album. In the liner notes, he joked that the front cover was an x-ray of his own skull.

the following year he scripted the film *Escape*, and went on to more film work, writing and/or directing *Five* (1951), the 3-D exploitation film *Bwana Devil* (1952), and the cult classic *The Twonky* (1953).

In 1962 Oboler was one of the first old-time radio vets to revive the genre on long-play records. At a time when radio shows were only privately circulated among collectors, and copyright issues weren't completely sorted out for vinyl, he chose to recreate some of his best-remembered horror scenes for a fresh stereo release.

His album *Lights Out* (Capitol ST 1763) featured the notorious "Chicken Heart." Other tracks explored suspense via cannibalism, a car stuck on train tracks, and a man turned inside out (sound effects courtesy of rubber gloves). Oboler narrated the album himself, while the new versions of his scripts brought back a roster of favorite radio performers, including Edgar Barrier, Lawrence Dobkin, Virginia Gregg, Jerry Hausner, Jack Johnston, Olan Soule, Hal Peary, Barney Phillips, Forrest Lewis and Ralph Moody, as well as a few who later earned some starring roles on screen or TV, such as Mercedes McCambridge and Bea Benaderet. McCambridge would later return to voice work as the devil inside Linda Blair for the film *The Exorcist* (1973).

A recreation of Oboler's notorious "Cat Wife" was released on a Longines Symphonette boxed set, *Golden Memories of Radio Narrated by Jack Benny and Frank Knight*.

While *Inner Sanctum* had a creaking door, *Lights Out* had the memorable opening lines, spoken with ominous intonation: "It is later than you think!"

This was followed by what is now considered typical horror patter, but was fresh at the time: "This is the witching hour. It is the hour when dogs howl and evil is let loose on a sleeping world. Want to hear about it? Then turn out your lights—lights out—everybody!"

The Oboler style was copied by many other radio shows. Compare his opening remarks to the opening of Raymond Morgan's *Murder at Midnight*, a show about evil doings at "the witching hour, when night is darkest, our fears the strongest, our strength at its lowest ebb. Midnight when the graves gape open and Death strikes."

Oboler valiantly kept trying to revive the audio drama format as late as the 1970s when he hosted *The Devil and Mr. O* (1970–73).

William N. Robson

Along with *Lights Out* and *Inner Sanctum*, the two most memorable horror and mystery shows on radio were *Escape* and *Suspense*, both from producer-director William N. Robson (October 8, 1906–April 10, 1995). Both used the same format: a challenging (if anonymous) host introducing a story of murder or perhaps classic horror. Robson favored adaptations of anything from Poe tales to a good yarn in the latest issue of *Esquire* magazine.

Robson's first job in radio was directing the Edward G. Robinson drama *Big Town* in 1936. A few years later he had his own hit with *Suspense*. The show lasted over twenty years and 945 programs. Robson bought literate scripts from such radio legends as Lucille Fletcher and John Dickson Carr, and he had an uncanny ability to attract big stars for guest appearances, including leading men (Cary Grant and Ronald Colman), character actors (Humphrey Bogart and Joseph Cotten), and even unlikely comedians and singers (Stan Freberg, Milton Berle, Judy Garland and Ethel Merman). The show also featured top directors, including Elliott Lewis. Lewis' wife, Cathy Lewis, was a veteran actress who was often cast in the show's supporting roles (and can be heard on many of Vincent Price's guest appearances).

Joseph Kearns

For *Suspense*, Joseph Kearns (February 12, 1907–February 17, 1962) was the original "Man in Black," later replaced by Ted Osborne. Kearns, born in Salt Lake City, Utah, worked as a silent movie theater organist and, with talkies obliterating that market, became a local staff announcer at KSL radio. He was radio's *The Whistler*, a mysterious adventure character, before he joined *Suspense* as not only the announcer, but one of the regular supporting players in the weekly dramas. He even got a chance to star in one episode, "Short Order." His other major acting assignment on radio was playing Matt Grebb on the detective show *The Lineup*. He used his voice for films once in a while, notably as Doorknob in Disney's cartoon *Alice in Wonderland*.

Kearns' forlorn and sour appearance made him a comic foil for television, and he turned up as the vault guard on Jack Benny's TV series, and as Mr. Stone on *Our Miss Brooks*, but he's best remembered as Mr. Wilson, antagonist to television's *Dennis the Menace*. Unlike Raymond of *Inner Sanctum*, Kearns' catchphrase on *Suspense* was terse. "This is the Man in Black..." was enough. No puns, no wordplay, just an introduction of the grim story of the evening.

William Conrad and Paul Frees

The two fondly remembered hosts during the run of *Escape* were William Conrad and Paul Frees. Either way, the show's opening catch-phrase was the same: "Tired of the everyday routine?"

Conrad became radio's Matt Dillon on *Gunsmoke*, and later almost burlesqued the radio style when he supplied the narration for TV's *Rocky and Bullwinkle* cartoons. He finally achieved television fame as the bulky, squinting detective *Cannon* in the hit 1971–76 series.

Paul Frees (June 22, 1920–November 2, 1986) was a legend in radio, narration, commercial voiceovers and cartoon voices. "I prefer being behind the scenes," he once told the author, although he took film work now and then, "more or less as a hobby."

Born Solomon Hersh Frees in Chicago, he did kick off his entertainment career with an impressionist act, billing himself as Buddy Young. After service, and injury, in World War II, he came home to find his multiple voices a plus for radio work.

He co-starred on *Rocky Fortune*, acted in many *Escape* programs (as well as sharing host chores with William Conrad), and in 1949 starred in the brief run of *The Green Lama*. He also starred in a gimmick program called *The Player* in which listeners were emphatically told that he voiced all the characters.

Frees' vocal timbre in narration was often compared to that of Orson Welles. In style, Frees resisted the musingly angular delivery Welles liked to use, where a sentence might be broken into a series of clustered phrases with deliberate, offbeat emphasis placed on specific words to keep the listener alert. As with Raymond Burr, the technique Welles used may have had something to do with his weight and a need to pause irregularly to catch a breath.

In the television era, Frees was the cartoon voice of Ludwig Von Drake, John Lennon and George Harrison in the original *Beatles* animated series, and Boris Badenov. He was the announcer on hundreds of commercials, and his range extended from dubbing Toshiro Mifune for the film *Midway* to the drag voice for Tony Curtis in *Some Like It Hot*. He was able to pitch his voice even higher to become the Pillsbury Doughboy.

Frees was in semi-retirement when, in 1984, he hosted one last radio series, *Bradbury 13*, a set of Ray Bradbury stories dramatized by a full cast and sound effects.

Other Horror Hosts

Radio comedians, many coming from vaudeville, were well known to their audiences thanks to stage work, personal appearances and even films. Audiences knew what Jack Benny and Fred Allen looked like, as well as Fibber McGee and Molly, the Great Gildersleeve, and Edgar Bergen and Charlie McCarthy.

Stars of adventure, action and horror shows on radio tended to be cloaked in mystery, often because their looks simply didn't match their voices. Producers may also have wanted to downplay the names of these performers so that they could always get a new Lone Ranger or Shadow when it came time for contract negotiations.

Most listeners had no idea who "the Man in Black" was, and perhaps didn't want to know who Raymond of *Inner Sanctum* was, preferring their own image. Producers didn't publicize the man behind the throaty introduction of "Murder ... at Midnight!" or the guy who hollowly beckoned listeners into *The Weird Circle*. With shows that only lasted a season or two, the names of the hosts have sometimes never been found.

Among the announcers and actors affectionately remembered by old-time radio enthusiasts are Keith Paynton (*Dark Fantasy*, 1940–42), John Kent and/or Mel Johnson (*The Hermit's Cave*, 1940–43), Maurice Tarplin (*Mysterious Traveler*, 1943–52, and *The Strange Dr. Weird*, 1944–45), Philip Clarke (*The Sealed Book*, 1945), and Ernest Chappel (*Quiet Please*, 1947–49).

The most popular horror show hosted by a woman was *Witch's Tale* (1931–1938), which thrived on the Mutual network from 1934 to 1937 and featured "Old Nancy of Salem, and Satan, the wise black cat. They're waiting for you now..."

The show's ghoulish plots and fancifully horrific twist endings inspired some writers and artists at E.C. comics to create *Tales from the Crypt*, one of the more memorable attempts at visualizing on pulp paper the kind of grim and gruesome antics that were so popular on radio.

Witch's Tale, written by Alonzo Deen Cole (who always voiced the cat and, early on, played many of the episode's lead characters), was first broadcast locally in New York over WOR. The witch host was Adelaide Fitz-Allen. When the 79-year-old actress died in 1935, fans were surprised to learn that her replacement, Miriam Wolfe, was just thirteen.

Nelson Olmsted

The last of the great radio horror performers was Nelson Olmsted. Olmsted, in typical radio fashion, was heard more than seen or written about, so his last name was often phonetically spelled Almstead, Almsted or Olmstead in radio fan club journals. Olmsted (Leroy Nelson Olmsted, Jr., January 28, 1914–April 8, 1992) was born in Minnesota but raised in Texas, where he was an announcer for local radio stations.

For the album notes on his *Sleep No More* album, he offered a bit of biography:

> By the time I moved to WBAP in Ft. Worth ... the announcer's life seemed endlessly sterile. What to do about it? Dramatic shows cost money and there were no budgets. The cheapest drama for radio I could think of was good literature, read aloud. Especially the work of that great dramatist who never wrote a play—Edgar Allan Poe. WBAP gave me some time with which to experiment. That was way back in 1939—and it worked. By 1940 the story-telling show was on NBC for a 10 year run."

Olmsted's skill at narration, and in assuming the voices of each character as he told the tale, led to a variety of programs, such as *Story for Today* and *World's Greatest Stories*. In 1956 he starred in one of the last gasps of radio horror, NBC's *Sleep No More*, a half-hour that usually featured two dramatized short stories from Olmsted, with an introduction from host Ben Grauer.

Nelson Olmsted hosted his own series, reading classic chillers, and later recorded three exceptional albums for Vangaurd, reading Poe, Bierce, Stevenson and others.

Typical gruesome twosomes were "Mr. Mergenthurker's Loblies" and "August Heat" (November 28, 1956), "Waxwork" and "The Man and the Snake" (January 9, 1957), and "To Build a Fire" and "Three Skeleton Key" (February 27, 1957). The show lasted 21 episodes in 1956–57 and was resurrected by Vanguard Records for a disc called *Sleep No More* (VRS 9008), featuring six short stories (including "What Was It," by Fitz-James O'Brien, and a memorable version of "The Body Snatcher," by Robert Louis Stevenson, complete with sound effects and Olmsted expertly playing both Donald Fettes and Wolfe MacFarlane).

Olmsted also recorded *Edgar Allan Poe: Tales of Terror* (Vanguard VRS 9007) and *Poems and Stories by Edgar Allan Poe* (Vanguard VRS 9046).

Most actors, reading a Fitz-James O'Brien line like, "I felt two sinewy hands grasp me around the throat endeavoring to choke me," would not act it out. Olmsted did, his voice tightening up as if he actually did have two hands around his throat. In this regard, he was one of the last narrators showing the influence of old-time radio. Voice-over artists who often recorded for the burgeoning spoken arts labels—performers such as Alexander Scourby, Norman Rose and Martin Donegan—did not use the technique.

THE LAST WORD

The last word?

Inner Sanctum's Raymond Johnson, after performing classic radio horror stories for old-time radio buffs, liked to end with the following, which can be heard on his lone vinyl album *Raymond Edward Johnson, Alive and Well*:

> So, with apologies to my dear old buddy Will Shakespeare, here goes. Our revels now are ended. These, my actors, as you now very well know, were all spirits, and are melted into air. Into *thin* air. And, like the baseless fabric of this; all of these visions that I've given you, the red-hot furnaces, the steel that cuts and kills, the heart that beats and beats and will not stop, this *everything*, our great world itself will dissolve.... We, you listeners and I, we are only *stuff* that dreams are made of. And our little life is ended with a sleep! Yes! A sleep. So to complete this tango, I *dare* you fellow listening lovers, I *dare* you just *try* to sleep tonight! Ha ha! Ha ha ha!

Bibliography

Ackerman, Forrest J (ed.). *The Best of Famous Monsters of Filmland*. New York: Paperback Library, 1964.

_____. *Famous Monsters of Filmland Strikes Back*. New York: Paperback Library, 1965.

Ackerman, Forrest J. *Forrest J Ackerman Presents the Frankenscience Monster: Everything You Could Possibly Wish to Know About the Late Great Boris Karloff*. New York: Ace, 1969.

Atkins, Rick, Kevin G. Shinnick, Kevin, and Richard Valley. "Keep Young and Beautiful: Gloria Stuart Interviewed," *Scarlet Street*, #28, 1998.

Bannerman, R. LeRoy. "Norman Corwin and Radio: The Golden Years." Tuscaloosa: University of Alabama Press, 1986.

Baxter, John. *Hollywood in the Thirties*. New York: Paperback Library, 1970.

Beck, Calvin Thomas. *Heroes of the Horrors*. New York: Macmillan, 1974.

Beebe, Lucious. "Henry Daniell," *New York Herald Tribune*, February 20, 1944.

Behlmer, Rudy. *America's Favorite Movies: Behind the Scenes*. New York: Frederick Ungar, 1982.

Bojarski, Richard. *The Films of Bela Lugosi*. Secaucus, NJ: Citadel, 1980.

_____, and Kenneth Beals. *The Films of Boris Karloff*. Secaucus, NJ: Citadel, 1974.

Bordman, Gerald. *The Oxford Companion to the American Theatre*. New York: Oxford University Press, 1984.

Brosnan, John. *The Horror People*. New York: New American Library, 1976.

Brunas, Michael, John Brunas, and Tom Weaver. *Universal Horrors: The Studio's Classic Films, 1931–1946*. Jefferson, NC: McFarland, 1990.

Buxton, Frank, and Bill Owen. *Radio's Golden Age: The Programs and the Personalities*. New York: Easton Valley, 1966.

Callow, Simon. *Charles Laughton: A Difficult Actor*. New York: Grove, 1988.

Cremer, Robert. *Lugosi: The Man Behind the Cape*. Chicago: Henry Regnery, 1976.

Dunning, John. *Tune in Yesterday: The Ultimate Encyclopedia of Old-Time Radio*. Englewood Cliffs, NJ: Prentice Hall, 1976.

Everson, William K. *Classics of the Horror Film*. Secaucus, NJ: Citadel, 1974.

French, Lawrence. "Interview with Vincent Price," *Famous Monsters of Filmland*, #203, 1993.

Giddens, Gary. "Fox Classics Pay Tribute to Brahm," *New York Sun*, October 9, 2007.

Gifford, Denis. *Karloff: The Man, the Monster, the Movies*. New York: Curtis, 1973.

_____. *A Pictorial History of Horror Movies*. New York: Book Sales, 1973.

Goldin, David J. *Radio Yesteryear Presents the Golden Age of Radio*. Sandy Hook, CT: Yesteryear, 1998.

Gow, Gordon. *Hollywood in the Fifties*. New York: A.S. Barnes, 1971.

Hagen, Bill. "John Carradine," *The News World* (NY), December 20, 1982.

Hamlin, Suzanne. "Vincent Price Milks His Image," *New York Daily News*, October 31, 1984.

Hanson, Patricia King (ed.). *Film Institute Catalog of Feature Films, 1931–1940*. Berkeley and Los Angeles: University of California Press, 1993.

Hardy, Phil (ed.). *The Encyclopedia of Horror Movies*. New York: Harper & Row, 1986.

Henderson, Jan A., and George E. Turner. "Bride of Frankenstein," *American Cinematographer*, January 1998.

Hendrick, Kimmis. "Henry Hull," *Christian Science Monitor*, June 3, 1965.
Higham, Charles. *Charles Laughton: An Intimate Biography*. New York: Doubleday, 1976.
_____. *Orson Welles: The Rise and Fall of an American Genius*. New York: St. Martin's, 1985.
Hogan, David. *Who's Who of the Horrors*. San Diego: Barnes, 1980.
Hull, Henry. "A Word About Audiences," *Cue*, September 11, 1937.
Josten, Henry E. "Henry Hull," *New Era* (CT), April 23, 1964.
_____. "Henry Hull," *The Pictorial*, March 22, 1977.
Karloff, Boris. *The Boris Karloff Horror Anthology*. London: Corgi, 1967.
Keylin, Arleen, and Suri Fleischer. *Hollywood Album, Lives and Deaths of Hollywood Stars from the Pages of the New York Times*. New York: Arno, 1977.
Koontz, Dean. "Why We Love Horror," *TV Guide*, October 23, 1993.
Lanchester, Elsa. *Elsa Lanchester: Herself*. New York: St. Martin's, 1983.
Laughton, Charles. *The Laughton Story*. Philadelphia: John C. Winston, 1954.
_____. *Tell Me a Story*, New York: McGraw-Hill, 1957.
Lennig, Arthur. *The Count: The Life and Films of Bela Lugosi*. New York: Putnam, 1974.
Lilley, Jessie. "Carroll Borland," *Scarlet Street*, #12, 1993.
Lindsay, Cynthia. *Dear Boris: The Life of William Henry Pratt, aka Boris Karloff*. New York: Knopf, 1975.
London, Rose. *Cinema of Mystery*. New York: Bounty Books/Crown, 1975.
Luft, Herbert G. "Peter Lorre," *Films in Review*, May 1960.
Maeder, Jay. "Vincent Price Is a Nice Guy. Except When He's a Rat," *New York Daily News*, July 2, 1986.
Maltin, Leonard. *The Great American Broadcast*. New York: Dutton, 1997.
Mank, Gregory. "Lionel Atwill," *Films in Review*, March 1977.
McKay, Rick. "A Return to Manners: David Manners' Final Interview," *Scarlet Street*, #31, 1999.
_____. "To the Manners Born: David Manners," *Scarlet Street*, #27, 1997.
Meikle, Denis. *Vincent Price: The Art of Fear*. Pennsylvania: Reynolds & Hearn, 2003.
Moss, Robert F. *Karloff and Company: The Horror Film*. New York: Pyramid, 1978.
Nolan, Jack Edmund. "Karloff on TV," *Film Fan Monthly*, December 1969.
Poe, Edgar Allan. *18 Best Stories by Edgar Allan Poe, with an Introduction by Vincent Price*. New York: Dell, 1965.
Price, Victoria. *Vincent Price: A Daughter's Biography*. New York: St. Martin's, 1999.
Price, Vincent. *I Like What I Know*. Garden City, NY: Doubleday, 1959.
_____. *Vincent Price: His Movies, His Plays, His Life*. Garden City, NY: Doubleday, 1978.
Randall, Tony, and Michael Mindlin. *Which Reminds Me*. New York: Delacorte, 1989.
Rathbone, Basil. *In and Out of Character*. New York: Doubleday, 1962.
Rhodes, Gary Don. *Lugosi: His Life in Films, on Stage, and in the Hearts of Horror Lovers*. Jefferson, NC: McFarland, 1997.
Richards, Jeffrey. "In Praise of Claude Rains," and "Claude Rains—A Career to Remember," in *Films and Filming* (London), February and March 1982.
Rigden, Walter (ed.). *The Biographical Encyclopedia and Who's Who of the American Theatre*. New York: Jame H. Heineman, 1965.
Rosenfield, Paul. "Interview with John Carradine," *Los Angeles Times*, May 3, 1983.
Scadden, Joe, Jr. "Laird Cregar," *Hollywood Studio Magazine*, September 1982.
Schaden, Chuck. *Speaking of Radio: Chuck Schaden's Conversations with the Stars of the Golden Age of Radio*. Chicago, IL: Nostalgia Digest Press, 2003.
Schulz, Clair. "Vincent Price, the Prince of Players," *Chuck Schaden's Nostalgia Digest and Radio Guide*, October-November, 1993.
Service, Faith. "Women Scream at the Sight of Him," *Motion Picture*, February 1935.
Settel, Irving. *A Pictorial History of Radio*. New York: Grossett and Dunlap, 1960.
Skal, David J., and Jessica Rains. *Claude Rains: An Actor's Voice*. Lexington: University Press of Kentucky, 2008.
Smith, Don G. *Lon Chaney, Jr.: Horror Film Star*. Jefferson, NC: McFarland, 1996.
Sneed, Michael. "John Carradine Interview," *Chicago Sun Times*, November 30, 1988.
Soister, John T., and JoAnna Wioskowski. *Claude Rains: A Comprehensive Illustrated Reference to His Work in Film, Stage, Radio, Television and Recordings*. Jefferson, NC: McFarland, 2006.

Stein, Jeanne. "Claude Rains," *Films in Review*, November 1963.
Stuart, Gloria, with Sylvia Thompson. *I Just Kept Hoping*. Boston: Little, Brown, 1999.
Sylvster, Robert. "Henry Daniell," *Sunday News*, May 3, 1935.
Tallmer, Jerry. "John Carradine Interview," *New York Post*, November 29, 1988.
Terrace, Vincent. *Complete Encyclopedia of Television Productions*. South Brunswick, NJ: A.S. Barnes, 1980.
Underwood, Peter. *Karloff: The Life of Boris Karloff*. New York: Drake, 1972.
Valley, Richard. "Ann Doran," *Scarlet Street*, #17, 1995.
Weaver, Tom. *John Carradine: The Films*. Jefferson, NC: McFarland, 1999.
Williams, Lucy Chase. *The Complete Films of Vincent Price*. Secaucus, NJ: Citadel, 1995.
Wray, Fay. *On the Other Hand: A Life Story*. New York: St. Martin's, 1989.
Wright, Gene. *Who's Who and What's What in Science Fiction Film, Television, Radio and Theater*. New York: Bonanza, 1985.
Youngkin, Stephen D. *The Lost One: A Life of Peter Lorre*. Lexington: University of Kentucky Press, 2003.
_____, James Bigwood, and Raymond Cabana. *The Films of Peter Lorre*. Secaucus, NJ: Citadel, 1982.

Index

Abbott and Costello 40–41, 44, 58, 62, 66, 101, 151, 162, 164, 186
Ackerman, Forrest J 17, 28, 44
Adams, Jane 232–233
Allbritton, Louise 227–229
Allen, Fred 4, 12, 22, 43–44, 106–108, 118–120, 145–146, 152–153, 162, 168, 173–174, 178–179, 183, 190
Amos 'n' Andy 154, 169
Ankers, Evelyn 42, 230–232
Arthur Tickle Engineering Works 97
Atwill, Lionel 127–133, 237
Avallone, Michael 15–16

Bankhead, Tallulah 66, 75, 153, 168
Baudelaire, Charles 102
Bean, Orson 81
Beck, Calvin 7, 153
Beck, Jackson 22
Beebe, Lucius 140, 142
Benny, Jack 11, 23, 105, 112–113, 116, 120, 152, 162, 165, 179, 190, 192–193
Bergen, Edgar 12, 19, 21–22, 24, 111, 192
Bible, recordings from 97, 125, 176, 180–181, 185–186, 191, 194, 214
The Black Seagull 146–147
Bloch, Robert 3
Blood Bath 70–71, 84
Borland, Carol 46–47, 56
Bowden, Dorris 93
Bracken, Eddie 187
Brooke, Hillary 229–230
Brooke, Rupert 102, 125, 214
Bruce, Nigel 106, 111–117
Burke, Billie 56, 128
Burr, Raymond 35

Caedmon Records 26–27, 73, 83, 123–125
Candid Microphone 57–58, 62
Cantor, Eddie 12, 20–21, 107, 118, 165, 180
Carr, John Dickson 36, 38, 143, 244
Carradine, John 53, 87, 92–102, 164
Cat Wife 10, 19
Cavalcade 200
Chandler, Helen 223–225
Chaney, Lon 9, 39–40
Chaney, Lon, Jr. 29, 39–45, 53, 131, 203, 230, 236
Chanukah 39
Chaplin, Charles 142
Christie, Agatha 188
Co Star, The Record Acting Game 85, 125
Como, Perry 105, 118
Conrad, William 39, 76, 221, 245
Conried, Hans 4, 75, 78–79, 81, 91–92, 138, 166, 178–179, 190–191, 219
Cooper, Gary 30
Cosby, Bill 198
Cregar, Laird 87–92

Daniell, Henry 127, 138–143
Davis, Bette 176, 192
Denning, Richard 231
Dietrich, Marlene 100
DiSantis, Joe 4
Doran, Ann 42, 226–227
Duffy's Tavern 21, 77, 120, 153, 191

Escape 69–71, 77
Everson, William 134

Fields, W.C. 184, 225
Films and Filming 17
Flanders, Michael 27

Fletcher, Lucille 212
Flynn, Errol 109, 122
Foch, Nina 180
Fonda, Henry 93
Foray, June 77
Freedom Pledge 179
Frees, Paul 78, 144, 169–170, 220, 245–246
Frye, Dwight 3, 49

Garland, Beverly 42
Garland, Robert 134
Gasoline Cocktail 59
Greenstreet, Sidney 3, 60, 89, 164

Herrmann, Bernard 35, 90, 212
Hitchcock, Alfred 25, 145–146, 186
Holloway, Sterling 56–57
Hope, Bob 56–57, 153, 166, 192
Horton, Edward Everett 51, 62, 229
House Un-American Activities Committee (HUAC) 206–208
Houseman, John 196
Hull, Henry 29–45
Hull, Josephine 34
Hungarian Council for Democracy 59
Hutchens, John K. 32

"Inner Sanctum" 11, 20–22, 24–25, 28, 40, 53, 90, 92, 146–147, 162–164, 178, 221, 241–242

Johnson, Raymond Edward 119, 241–242, 248
Jolson, Al 187
Jones, Spike 24, 108–109, 120, 144
Joyce, Brenda 137, 207

Kane, Frank 95
Kane, Joe 94
Karloff, Boris 7–28, 30, 46, 48, 50, 95, 110, 140, 159, 226, 234
Katz, Fred 96
Kearns, Joseph 245
Kelley, Marion 139
Kirk, Lisa 14

Lanchester, Elsa 181–185, 189–191, 196–199
Lang, Fritz 145
Langdon, Verne 97, 102
Laughton, Charles 171, 181–195, 197
Laurel, Stan 126
Lavender Lady 223
Lewis, Jerry 96, 101, 168, 192
Lights Out 10, 19–20, 23
Lindsay, Cynthia 10, 13, 16
Lloyd, Harold 126
Lorre, Peter 23, 110, 133, 144–170, 174, 205
Lugosi, Bela 41, 43, 46–63, 95–96, 100, 136, 225, 231
Lund, Lucille 225

Mann, Abby 175
Manners, David 49, 224
Markle, Fletcher 182
Marx, Groucho 21, 76, 111, 168, 186, 190, 233
Mary Manning Walsh Home 202
McGrath, Paul 22
The Monkey's Paw 98, 101
Monster Mash 16, 86
Moorehead, Agnes 187, 209–223
Morgan, Harry 80, 156–157, 166

Oakie, Jack 142
Oakley, Annie 211-212
Oboler, Arch 31, 82, 134–135, 149–150, 165, 177, 198, 209, 219, 241–244; see also *Lights Out*
O'Connor, Una 199–203
Olmsted, Nelson 246–248
Ouspenskaya, Maria 203–205
Ozzie and Harriet 49–50

Paige, Robert 228
Poe, Edgar A. 21, 28, 36, 48, 60–61, 69, 72–73–74, 83–84, 97, 101, 109, 123–124, 144, 153, 157–159, 171, 176, 232, 247–248
Poe, James 69–70
Price, Vincent 4–7, 16, 64–86, 91, 110, 159–161, 175, 188, 191, 193

Rains, Claude 42, 171–181, 234
Randall, Tony 4–5
Rapp, Philip 105, 116
Rathbone, Basil 87, 95, 100, 102–126, 128–129, 139–140, 177
Rathbone, Rodion 104
Roberts, Ken 4
Robson, William N. 244–245

The Saint 67–68, 76–79
Scott, Vernon 37
Serling, Rod 242–243
The Shadow 210, 214–215
Shaman, William 128
Slesar, Henry 222
Sloan, Everett 4, 169, 178–179, 214, 216–217
Soister, John T. 174
Sondergaard, Gale 206–209

Sorry, Wrong Number 212–213
Stang, Arnold 166
Stewart, Paul 4
Strange, Glenn 232
Stuart, Gloria 233–234
Suspense 38, 51, 61–63, 69–70, 75–76–77, 80–81, 91–92, 133, 135, 140, 143, 147–149, 162–165, 179, 191–194, 199, 212–213, 218–222, 235
The Swamp Fox 142

Tales from the Reader's Digest 13, 25–26, 121–122
Tales of Fatima 108, 119
Taylor, Robert 3
Terry and the Pirates 211
Three Skeleton Key 69–70
Tiny Tim 99
Tuttle, Lurene 4, 53, 66, 75, 80, 100, 138, 220–221, 224

Underwood, Peter 10, 14

Vallee, Rudy 56, 62, 161, 171, 176–177, 189, 195, 197, 213
Verdugo, Elena 235–236

The Wailing Wall 11
Weissmuller, Johnny 137
Westmore, Perc 183–184
Wilde, Oscar 29
Witch's Tale 256
Wood, Edward D., Jr. 60
Woolcott, Alexander 31
Wray, Fay 130, 132, 175, 237–240

Youngkin, Stephen D. 151, 157

Zucco, George 133–138

www.ingramcontent.com/pod-product-compliance
Ingram Content Group UK Ltd.
Pitfield, Milton Keynes, MK11 3LW, UK
UKHW050536150426
5217IPUK00026B/1957